THE FREUD SCENARIO

JEAN-PAUL SARTRE

THE FREUD SCENARIO

Edited by J.-B. Pontalis

Translated by Quintin Hoare

The University of Chicago Press

The University of Chicago Press, Chicago 60637

© 1985 by Verso and The University of Chicago
All rights reserved. Published 1986
Printed in the United States of America

95 94 93 92 91 90 89 88 87 86   5 4 3 2 1

Le Scénario Freud was first published by Editions Gallimard 1984,
    © Editions Gallimard, Paris, 1984.

Library of Congress Cataloging-in-Publication Data

Sartre, Jean Paul, 1905–80
    The Freud scenario.

    Translation of: Le scénario Freud.
    1. Freud, Sigmund, 1856–1939—Drama.   2. Moving-
picture plays.   I. Pontalis, J. B., 1924–
I. Title.
PQ2637.A82S3413   1986   842′.914   86–11243
ISBN 0–226–73513–3

Contents

Editor's Preface   vii

First Version (1959)   1
Part One   3
Part Two   107
Part Three   237

Second Version (1959-60) – Extracts   385
Part One   387
Part Two   435
Part Three   463

Appendices   503
Synopsis (1958)   505
Comparative Table of the Two Versions   540

Editor's Preface
Freud Scenario, Sartre Scenario

Circumstances

It was in 1958 that American director John Huston invited Jean-Paul Sartre to write a screenplay on Freud; or to be more precise, in keeping with a typically Hollywood tradition, on the 'heroic' period of discovery — that key moment when Freud abandoned hypnosis and gradually, painfully, invented psychoanalysis.[1] 'The basic idea of Freud as adventurer', Huston was to say later, 'came from me. I wanted to concentrate on that episode like a detective story.'[2] Sartre accepted the proposal at once: the fee offered was apparently a large one and he needed money. An occasional work then, a commissioned work, even a work written to make ends meet — but a work that he was very quick to seize upon and to which he was to devote himself for several months with equal amusement and passion.

At the end of 1958 Sartre sent Huston a synopsis entitled simply 'Freud', which came to 95 double-spaced typed sheets. This 'initial draft' dated 15 December was accepted. The following year he wrote the screenplay. Everyone knows the sequel, or at least this is how the story is generally told: the director asked Sartre for alterations and cuts; Sartre did make some concessions — pruned, modified — but then grew bored. Eventually, the screenplay had to be reduced and substantially transformed by Charles Kaufmann and Wolfgang Reinhardt, film professionals close to Huston, whereupon Sartre insisted that his name should not appear among the credits. The film was made in 1961 and released the following year with the title *Freud*, soon altered to the more alluring *Freud, the Secret Passion* (in French *Freud, Désirs inavoués*: 'Freud, Unconfessed Desires'). It met with scant success. Montgomery Clift played the role of Freud.[3] By virtue of his very physiognomy

1. According to Huston, who had already brought *Huis Clos* to the New York stage in 1946 and who had dreamed of making a film of *Le Diable et le Bon Dieu*, Sartre was the 'ideal man to write the *Freud* screenplay ... He knew Freud's works intimately and would have an objective and logical approach.' (John Huston, *An Open Book*, New York 1980, p. 294.)

2. Interview with John Huston by Robert Benayoun, *Positif*, no. 70, June 1965.

3. In his autobiography (op. cit), Huston says that he thought of signing up Marilyn Monroe for the role of Cäcilie, which was eventually played by Susannah York. [In fact, he says that the suggestion was Sartre's. *Trans.*] Anna Freud apparently opposed the plan. Montgomery Clift and Marilyn Monroe had acted together in Huston's previous film *The Misfits* (1960).

— pure, ravaged countenance; clear, almost demented eyes[4] — and through his relentlessly pathetic performance, the great actor accentuated the tormented features, the tension and the suffering of the character he was playing. In spite of — or some would say thanks to — this interpretation, many people found the film both absurd and outrageous.

The history of this screenplay reveals a typically Sartrean pattern of behaviour. At the outset, a simple commission. Then he sets to work, seizing hold of the project gaily and seized by it, but more as a game or challenge than as an artistic endeavour. No realistic concern for proportion: if the original screenplay had been accepted as it was — 'as thick as my thigh', Huston was to say — it would have resulted in a film of around seven hours ('you can get away with a four-hour film if it's *Ben Hur*, but a Texas audience wouldn't stand for four hours of complexes', Sartre was to comment[5]). In the end, deliberate renunciation of any 'paternal' rights and total disinterest in the final outcome: did Sartre ever even see the film?

In fact, as our investigation has disclosed, things happened in a rather more complicated and even more Sartrean way. After Huston had received the completed screenplay and expressed objections, about whose precise nature we cannot be sure, Sartre went back to work and started afresh. But far from producing the shorter version he had been asked for, he expanded! Admittedly he did cut numerous sequences, and even eliminated certain characters figuring prominently in the first version, notably Freud's Berlin friend Fliess. But he also added new scenes and characters, and amplified the theoretical and didactic explanations. The truth of the matter is, he wrote a *new* screenplay. Judging from the manuscripts and typed transcripts we have managed to consult — thanks to the unfailing helpfulness of Arlette El-Kaïm Sartre — it seems he did not in fact quite complete this second version. Nevertheless, it certainly reached Huston: several sequences which appear only in this version (for example, the 'mountain dream') were to be reproduced, in more or less simplified form, in the film.

What exactly did occur between Sartre and Huston? Precise information is lacking. But we do have the accounts of the two principals, which it is entertaining to compare. In October 1959, Sartre spent a few weeks in the country-house Huston owns at St Clerans in Ireland, with the aim in principle of working on the screenplay. We may refer the reader to the cheerfully savage letter he wrote from there to Simone de Beauvoir — a real gem![6] Let us content ourselves with the following quotation: 'What a business! Dear, oh! dear, what a business! Such systematic lying here. Everyone with their complexes, ranging from masochism to savagery. But don't imagine we're in Hell. More like a vast cemetery. Everybody dead, with frozen complexes. So little life — so very, very little.' And further on: 'Huston used an odd expression to describe his "unconscious", when speaking of Freud: "In mine, there's nothing." And the tone made his meaning clear: nothing *any longer*, not even any old, unmentionable desires. A big void. You can just imagine how easy it is to get him to work. He shuns thought because it makes him sad. We'll all be together in some smoking-room, we'll all be talking, and then suddenly in

---

4. According to his biographer, he was suffering at the time from a double cataract.
5. In an interview with Kenneth Tynan in *The Observer*, 18 and 25 June 1961.
6. See *Lettres au Castor*, Paris 1983, vol. 2, p. 358.

mid–discussion he'll disappear. Very lucky if he's seen again before lunch or dinner.'

Huston, for his part, retains bitterer memories of that visit: 'I've never known anyone to work with the single-mindedness of Sartre ... There was no such thing as a conversation with him ... there was no interrupting him. You'd wait for him to catch his breath, but he wouldn't. The words came out in an absolute torrent ... Sometimes, I'd leave the room in desperation, on the verge of exhaustion from trying to follow what he was saying; the drone of his voice followed me until I was out of earshot and, when I'd return, he wouldn't even have noticed that I'd been gone.'[7] In the chapter of his autobiography devoted to the Freud film, moreover, his bitterness shows through on every page and his derogatory comments spare no one, whether collaborator or actor. On one occasion during Sartre's stay at St Clerans, after the projection of a short — *Let there be Light* — that he made in 1945 on the hypnotic treatment of war invalids suffering from traumatic neuroses, Huston attempted to hypnotize Sartre! Total failure. 'Occasionally you encounter someone like that ... hypnotically impregnable', Huston concluded.[8]

Manuscripts

The editor is faced with a problem: which text to adopt? Supposing that in his lifetime Sartre had agreed to publish his screenplay, which version would he have chosen? Perhaps, who knows, he would have produced a fresh treatment, significantly different from the two preceding ones: Sartre never liked repeating himself. One piece of evidence, among so many others: when he set about reworking the criticized screenplay, he began by making use of the original manuscript, suppressing here, adding there, changing a piece of dialogue in the right-hand column, inserting comments in the left-hand one or giving more detailed directions regarding locations or actions. Very soon, however, he was no longer using the typed text, and the pages that began to pile up — on that notorious squared paper — were new ones.

One editorial solution would have been to publish everything available. In other words:

1. the synopsis (the various versions we have looked at are all much the same);
2. the screenplay handed over to Huston in 1959 (which we shall henceforth call Version I);
3. the rewritten screenplay, the available manuscript of which is defective and incomplete (Version II);
4. various fragments that have turned up elsewhere.

Such a solution would have had the advantage of making accessible to the reader all materials so far assembled. I say 'so far', because it is by no means certain that other fragments, other stages of the screenplay may not one day become available. Quite the contrary. For we know that Sartre did not give two hoots about the fate of his manu-

---

7. Despite its tone of sustained venom, the entire chapter is worth reading. It seems clear that the film's subject was not without its effect on this whole affair, and still more so during the shooting of the film, if we are to believe the detailed account given by Robert LaGuardia in his biography *Montgomery Clift*, New York 1978, chapter 9.

8. *op. cit.* p. 276.

scripts: that he distributed them liberally, or mislaid them, or allowed them to be grabbed by any Tom, Dick or Harry. Furthermore, all those who know — even from afar like myself — the world of the film industry, know that almost always, between the time it is conceived and the time it is realized, a screenplay will pass through a whole series of stages and reworkings; that it will be altered to suit the requirements of the producer, the director and even the actors — requirements to which the author will have to accede, like it or not. It is very hard in these conditions — impossible when the edition is a post-humous one — to decide what constitutes the authentic version, the original text. Besides, since we are dealing with a screenplay, in which the author's duty is to indicate movements, feelings, settings *pending the arrival of the image*, can we speak of a *text*?

We also felt that if we were to publish all the materials *in extenso*, we should simply risk discouraging well-disposed readers — on the one hand, by presenting them with an immense volume (the present one is not exactly small!), on the other, by confronting them with a series of scattered and largely repetitive documents. Finally, at the present stage reached in the editing of Sartre's works, it would have been improper in our view to claim the eminent status of a 'scholarly edition' — with critical apparatus and list of variants — for a work that its author would surely have regarded as minor.

So the reader will not find here a scholarly edition of the 'Freud Scenario'. We shall leave to Sartre specialists the task of preparing one at some later date, if they deem it necessary. For our part, we have deliberately adopted a less ambitious course of action, which we nevertheless hope is legitimate.

As our basic text, we have retained Version I. The screenplay thus has no gaps (continuous pagination, no sheets missing) and is complete (it includes the word 'End'). Without any great risk we may conjecture that, if Huston and his collaborators had presented no objections, Sartre would have stopped at this point: once his 'product' had been handed over, he would have gone on to something else.

This screenplay, published here for the first time, has been supplemented by a number of sequences from Version II.[9] Here we cannot avoid the arbitrary nature of all anthologies. The criterion for selection is as follows: elimination of those sequences which already appear, albeit in a somewhat different form, in Version I; selection of these scenes which seem to us strongest, or most indicative of the change of style that super-vened between the two versions.

So that the reader can obtain a relatively precise idea of the difference between the first and the second version, we have provided a brief comparative table in Appendix B. In Appendix A we have also included the 1958 synopsis, which makes it clear that, even though Sartre had found his guiding theme right from the outset, he never stopped modifying this as his project required.

---

9. Extensive extracts from this version were published by Michel Sicard in 1981 in *Obliques* ('Sartre et les arts', pp. 93–136).

Sources

What were Sartre's sources? Accidents of publishing were often determinant. For, precisely in 1958, there appeared in French translation the first volume of Ernest Jones's great biography of Freud; this volume deals with the period that interested Huston and Sartre, namely the period of the 'young Freud', culminating with his father's death and the publication of *The Interpretation of Dreams*.[10] Two years earlier, there had been published, under the title *La Naissance de la Psychanalyse*, Freud's recently discovered letters to Wilhelm Fliess and the manuscripts connected with their correspondence, which even for specialists were a revelation. These represented two vital documents: today, twenty-five years later, after the vast proliferation of studies and personal accounts of Freud to which we have been subjected, it is hard to appreciate properly the wealth of new information which they supplied. Until then people had been almost totally ignorant of Freud's life and personality, as he himself had very early on come to desire — wishing, he would say with a mixture of pride and irony, 'to render the task of his future biographers arduous'; wishing above all, it seems to me, to merge his destiny with that of the psychoanalytic 'cause'. The fact is he feared, probably with good reason, that the truths of the science he had founded — which he held to be at once unique and universal — might be compromised, once the personal, familial and cultural determinants that had made their discovery possible were brought to light.

Jones, however, — even if his book had something of the character of an 'official' biography, constructed by a guardian of orthodoxy and vigilant disciple (its very shadows are intended to leave the hero in a brighter light) — furnished hitherto unsuspected details concerning Freud the man.[11] And as for the correspondence with Fliess, it bears witness among other things to the intensity of the bond which tied the two together, which above all tied Freud to Fliess: without that passion, without that as yet unnamed transference, would psychoanalysis have ever seen the light of day?

There can be no doubt that these readings radically transformed Sartre's image of Freud. They showed him a contradictory, violent, repressed personality, permanently in conflict with himself and his surroundings, stubborn and tormented. They portrayed the invention of psychoanalysis as the product of a long activity carried out upon himself — and above all, which counted for much more in Sartre's eyes, *against* himself — with breakthroughs, impasses, regressions.[12] Lastly, these readings allowed Sartre to see, in the succession of hypotheses put forward and in the sometimes drastic modification of the theory (one has only to think of Freud's abandonment of the theory of seduction), something entirely different from a purely intellectual exercise or the empirical result of a minute study of facts: rather, the actual unfolding of a treatment of which Freud — just

10. Actually I am probably wrong to invoke accidents of publishing: it in fact seems likely that Jones's biography, which came out in the United States in 1953, was what gave Huston the idea of making a film about Freud.

11. Jones's at times vengeful partisanship emerges especially when, with the founding of the 'movement', the rivals appear on the scene. But we may give general credence to his first volume, tracing Freud's formative years. The 'horde' did not yet exist, there is neither primal father nor warring sons.

12. What was necessary, Sartre said in the interview with Kenneth Tynan, was to 'show Freud not when his theories had already made him famous, but at the time when, at the age of thirty or so, he was totally mistaken and his ideas had led him into a desperate impasse' (*loc. cit.*).

as much as the neurotic patients whom he treated as best he could, and only as best he could — was the object. A doctor himself ill, Freud is seen as discovering psychoanalysis — both the method and its objectives — almost against his will, in order to cure himself, to resolve his own conflicts. The Freud revealed in that year to Sartre prefigures his *Idiot de la Famille*: neurosis and creation go hand in glove — and this is the case because neurosis is already a creation, but a private one, devoid of meaning for its author because written in a language for which he has no key (and how is one to open a strong-box when the key is inside?). Neurosis and creation: a dissertation topic, so long as these are opposed entities; but a trail perpetually to be blazed anew in its 'singular universal' — one at all events blazed anew by Sartre, from Baudelaire to Flaubert, by way of *Saint Genet* and *Les Mots*.

The idea that Sartre had of Freud previously — that of a doctrinaire and somewhat limited *chef d'école*, a mediocre philosopher none of whose concepts would stand up to scrutiny (and Heaven knows Sartre's could be devastating) — this idea would no longer do. But Sartre used to take the greatest pleasure in seeing his ideas overthrown, always provided he was the one to draw the consequences. Freud's intransigence, his uncompromising nature when there was any question of yielding on the requirements of truth, his stubborn opposition to prevailing medicine and psychiatry when these were invested with nothing but their titles, the sly anti-Semitism of which he found himself the target, his solitude or rather what he had to live as solitude, his poverty too and his long disdain of honours — it is an understatement to say that these features attracted Sartre. To a certain extent, he recognized himself in them. I would even wager that he forgave Freud his exclusive passion for Martha, his sombre jealousy — he who was capable of writing that 'you cannot expect to please and love at the same time'.[13]

While he was reading Jones's book, I recall having heard him say with real delight: 'That Freud of yours, I must say, he was neurotic through and through.' At once, he was able to understand if not accept notions which previously, as a philosopher who had remained more Cartesian than he thought, he had pulled to pieces — notions such as those of unconscious thought or repression. If I can believe one witness, Sartre, speaking of Huston, used to say: 'What's irritating about him is that he doesn't believe in the unconscious.' Piquant turning of the tables or unwitting projection? Speaking as a reader of the screenplay, I incline towards the former hypothesis. For it seems to me undeniable that Sartre succeeded in making perceptible — hence first and foremost in making perceptible to himself — a certain number of phenomena which could no longer be adequately accounted for by the notion of 'bad faith' that he had long promoted to 'counter' Freud.

Something else must have helped him to modify his former views in this way: namely his interest (maintained throughout his work) in hysteria. This interest — or rather fascination — had a twofold cause, I think, in Sartre's case. If it is true that an absolute coincidence with oneself is impossible, and that we are consequently all *actors*, why is the hysterical patient more of one than other people? Furthermore, hysteria poses an irritating problem for a philosophy of freedom: how can a freedom supposed on principle to

13. *Les Mots*, Paris 1964, p. 20 (*Words*, London 1964, p. 29).

be a conquest allow itself to be captured by the imaginary to the point of losing itself within it body and soul? We can conceive that for brief moments and under particular conditions (sleep, emotion) it may, as the 'young' Sartre used to say, turn into 'imaging' or magical consciousness. But how are we to understand that an existence may be entirely animated by the imaginary, without ever being able to recover its self-control? So what is a hysterical patient, once one has set aside the hypothesis of simulation, and that of traumatic origin? In a sense, madness appeared less strange to Sartre, since he saw in it a form of sly but superior lucidity (think of the character in *La Chambre* or Franz in *Les Séquestrés d'Altona*). Whence the sally he once came out with: 'I regard mad people as liars'. But can one regard hysterical complaints as lies, especially when they affect vital functions (blindness, anorexia, paralysis, astasia-abasia, asthma) as was the case with the patients treated by Breuer and Freud? Psychoanalysts used to call the leap from the psychic to the somatic mysterious. Far more mysterious still, for philosophers, the leap from consciousness to inertia: how the devil can transparency 'choose' opacity? How can an actor/agent fall (decline) into primal passivity?[14]

It will be noted that the cases which caught Sartre's attention here were above all hysterical cases, and in particular cases of female hysteria. Granted, the period under consideration favoured this choice; but we cannot help feeling that Sartre sympathized with those women telling their 'stories' (in both senses of the word): those Viennese ladies with their nerves and their phantasies who simultaneously attract, challenge and mock the man/doctor, cramped as he is in his formal frock-coat and his would-be flawless learning. No doubt he, who never hid the fact that he preferred the company of women to that of men, would have appreciated if he had known them these words of Lacan's (I am quoting from memory): 'There's a distraught side to every woman ... and a ridiculous side to every man.' And with what consummate ease does Sartre, in this screenplay, highlight the ridiculous and odious side of the male. Only Freud escapes, no doubt because Sartre was able to discern something feminine in the man who, albeit an excellent husband and good father, first found out how to listen to young women — and not in order to seduce them, but to allow them to speak of their suffering and their pleasure. With the recognition of bisexuality, the line of division between masculine and feminine is no longer what it used to be.

But let us return to the sources: Jones, therefore, first and foremost; the letters to Fliess; the *Studies on Hysteria* and the case-history of Dora, from which to draw clinical material and extract 'composite characters'; a reading, finally, which I imagine was fairly cursory, of *The Interpretation of Dreams*, in order to glean from it some of Freud's own dreams. We may add, anecdotally, that to illuminate Freud's visit to the Salpêtrière Sartre collected some information about Charcot via a female proxy reader. Serious or peevish minds — and these are often one and the same — will conclude that his research work was neither very extensive nor very meticulous. This may be so. But in the first place Sartre's aim was not to make a film strictly adhering to factual reality; proof of that will be found on every page here, which is why we soon abandoned the absurd plan of

14. See, in *L'Idiot de la famille* (vol. 2, Paris 1971), the pages (1854–1861) devoted by Sartre to what he terms 'hysterical engagement'.

indicating by notes — in case some credulous reader might confuse this screenplay with a historical document — the modifications to which Sartre subjected that reality. Furthermore, Sartre's inventions are sometimes of such force that even someone who thinks he knows the Freudian saga like the back of his hand will start distrusting his memory and go off to consult his library, with the idea of checking some fact or picking up some distortion or pure invention — before becoming doubtless more Freudian and recognizing that, since memory and fiction are indistinguishable, the question of truth or falsehood is no longer posed! I am thinking, for example, of the scene at the barber's (Version I, Part Three, pp. 339-40) or of the astonishing portrait of Professor Meynert (Version I, Part Two, pp. 133-37). Truer than nature! Everyday speech puts it well: 'However did he get hold of that? You'd swear he'd been there.' Later, Sartre was to 'invent' in the same way the parents and childhood of Flaubert. He got his hand in, so to speak, with his *Freud*.

Finally, and here again a comparison with *L'Idiot de la famille* would be legitimate — Sartre's project was not devoid of that 'total' ambition which was destined to seek full realization in his 'Flaubert'. The grandiose and, I fear, truly insane endeavour to know and above all understand *everything* about a man — an endeavour destined to be made explicit in that 'summa' — was assuredly a longstanding wager of Sartre's (a challenge to God, whose turn it would now be to become a 'useless passion'). But I would still tend to think that the 'Freud' made the 'Flaubert' possible. With *L'Idiot de la famille*, the wager is (almost) brought off. With the screenplay, all results remain possible, precisely inasmuch as the wager is lost. For Sartre here aims to grasp several threads at once and hold tight to all of them. In reality, he would have needed thousands upon thousands of pages, in the totalizing perspective that he espoused, in order to make *intelligible* at one and the same time the Jewish Freud and the bourgeois Freud, Freud-the-son and Freud/Fliess, Freud the neurologist and Freud the 'neurotic', Freud the civilizer and Freud the driven, the Freud of fin-de-siècle Vienna and the Freud without frontiers ... Above all, how to make visible the psychic reality which is the sole object of psychoanalysis? Psychic *reality* — and not that marshmallow the 'psyche' — made up of representations organized into networks, like nerves with their synapses or rails with their points, subjected to laws, regulated by mechanisms. The trouble is that to Sartre's blunt, insistent question: 'What can we know about a man?' — to that question which is not its own— psychoanalysis can offer only a disappointing reply: not 'Nothing', but 'What that man has always known'. First and perhaps sole obstacle: amnesia. As for the lifting of amnesia, it consists less in exhuming buried memories, in the manner of the archaeologist, than in allowing memory to make its own that which previously had not been. The *event* in psychoanalysis is not remembrance of lived experience.

The Paternal Bond

Who does not recall the phrase from *Les Mots*: 'The rule is that there are no good fathers; it is not the men who are at fault, but the paternal bond which is rotten?'[15] It was around

---

15. *Les Mots*, p. 11 (*Words*, p. 15).

that bond, nevertheless, that Sartre was to order his screenplay, in accordance with a viewpoint which we find fairly classical, but which was doubtless novel for him: Freud grappling with the figure of his father, ceaselessly retraversing with his teachers — Brücke, Meynert, Breuer — that itinerary of attachment, rejection and rupture, ceaselessly rediscovering in his patients either the seducing father (Cäcilie) or the castrating father (Karl), until the final liberation which, with Jakob's death, made him the father of psychoanalysis. Probably Sartre, who wanted no father and even in his work as a writer disliked thinking of himself as the 'father of his oeuvre', found in that destiny of the young Freud the means if not to destroy at least to shake his conviction. By centring, as he does here, Freud's studies and discoveries upon his relationship with his father,[16] he simultaneously shows that this is not necessarily condemned to the exhausting alternation of submission and revolt, to the clearcut opposition between passivity and the pure act. Perhaps he even perceives that, in wishing to dispense with a father, one is in great danger of remaining throughout one's life merely a child of words ... The advantage and the misfortune of words is that they form *bonds* only among themselves. The person who refuses to receive and to transmit will always be afraid of being a faker, a verbal being, a maker of gestures.

I do not think — the reader will judge for himself — that with his screenplay Sartre is advancing a personal, original 'interpretation' of Freud. On the other hand, I should like to think that Freud — even if, as is the case here, he has been cut up wholesale (obligatory cinematic 'cutting') — *interpreted* Sartre. Was it not after frequenting Freud that Sartre embarked upon an autobiography of which for the moment we know nothing save the title: *Jean sans terre* ('John Lackland'). Or 'Jean sans père' ('fatherless Jean')? From this project, yet again left uncompleted, there would derive *Les Mots* and later, by a more indirect route, *L'Idiot de la famille*. I recall that, in order to carry through this autobiography which was turning into a 'self-analysis', Sartre decided to note down his dreams — he, such a creature of day. To undergo projective tests — he, who had theorized the 'project'. That he even envisaged (admittedly during the course of a very brief conversation) embarking on analysis. What did psychoanalysis represent for him? A useful, no doubt indispensable, instrument of knowledge; but an *instrument* that once he had set to work he would succeed in appropriating. Transference, never heard of it! Transference: in other words, the necessity, if one is to allow the unknown to enter, to address oneself to an addressee unknown at that address, definitely absent, almost impossible to find.

Without wishing to exaggerate, one may speculate that for Sartre the scenario on Freud was also a *Freud Scenario* in which he had a role of his own (he never belittles Freud, he honestly sets out his initial conceptions); that, first envisaged as a diversion with respect to the work to which he was about to commit himself body and soul — the *Critique*, *L'Idiot* — the screenplay also diverted him from his own programme. Perhaps for a time he agreed, albeit laughing up his sleeve, to see himself as one of Freud's children like the rest of us: but as an indefatigable child, determined not to carry that particular Anchises on his shoulders for too long.

16. 'The Father! Always the Father', p. 530 below.

Psychoanalysis and the Image

Once in his lifetime, Freud too might have let himself be seduced by the cinema — by the genuinely tempting project of translating psychoanalysis into images. In 1925, Karl Abraham, the *good* disciple, pushed him to accept a serious proposition: 'This type of project', he wrote, 'is typical of our times, and is sure to be carried out.' Freud was initially cautious. The traditional argument — 'if it's not done with us, it will be done without us by incompetents, which will be much worse' — cut no ice with him. Abraham insisted. Freud grew angry, claiming that he was being rushed.[17] The underlying reason for his refusal was of a theoretical nature, one of principle, related to the very essence of the subject. Freud formulated it thus: 'My chief objection is still that I do not believe that satisfactory plastic representation of our abstractions is at all possible.[18] We do not want to give our consent to anything insipid ... The small example that you mentioned, the representation of repression by means of my Worcester simile,[19] would make an absurd rather than an instructive impact.'

What precisely does Freud mean here by 'abstraction'? The great topical instances: Ego, Id, Superego? Psychic operations such as repression or projection? Assuredly, but I think that the scope of the word — and therefore of the objection — must be extended to the psychoanalytic process as a whole: no aspect of mental life can be translated into image without thereby being falsified. The blunt refusal presented by Freud to Abraham simply expressed a primordial rejection: the image does not *admit* the unconscious.

How does it come about that a dream — even though it may appear to the dreamer as a translation into images, or indeed a film that he is viewing and that is taking place on a screen[20] — yes, why does a dream once it has been transcribed in the cinema cease to be a dream, though it may happen that the entirety of a supposedly realistic film can be perceived as oneiric?

There is a paradox here. In a sense, psychoanalysis has set the world of imagination free. It has extended the domain of the visible outside the field of perception, and discerned its hold over both individual and collective life: dreams, reveries, phantasms, visual scenes, our inner theatre, the ideal cities of visionaries — all these keep us constant company. But, in another sense, it discredits that visible realm, by stripping it of the status which it claims: the unconscious, like the being of philosophers, does not allow itself to be *seen*.

Let us take an example: when Freud uncovered through analysis the various proce-

17. The film was eventually made, with the collaboration of Abraham and Sachs but without that of Freud: *Geheimnisse einer Seele* ('Secrets of a Soul'), directed by Pabst. On this episode, see the Freud-Abraham correspondence (*A Psycho-Analytic Dialogue. The Letters of Sigmund Freud and Karl Abraham*, London and New York 1965, especially pp. 382-85). See also the article 'Chambre à part' (*Nouvelle Revue de Psychanalyse*, no. 29, 1984) by Patrick Lacoste, which reminded me of the exchange of letters to which I am referring here.

18. Whatever would Freud have said to Eisenstein, who dreamed of filming *Das Kapital*?

19. The reference is to a comparison Freud made in one of his 1909 lectures at Worcester, Mass. ('Five Lectures', in *Two Short Accounts of Psycho-Analysis*, Harmondsworth 1962, p. 50), between the repressed wish struggling to return to consciousness against the patient's resistance and a heckler who has been ejected from a lecture-hall but struggles to get back inside.

20. A confusion, rather than a slip of the tongue, that is often made by a person recounting a dream: 'At that point in the film ...' See also Bertram Lewin's studies on 'the dream screen'.

dures of dreamwork — condensation, displacement, overdetermination, secondary revision — he encountered one which he named *Darstellbarkeit*: to wit, the need for the dreamer, in view of his inability while sleeping to engage in motor activity, to 'hallucin-ate' his *Wunsch*, his unconscious wish.[21] This is a constraint imposed on dreaming, nothing more, and one which is not met with in other formations of the unconscious such as the symptom or the *acte manqué*. In other words, the image is less expression than figuration: 'plastic presentation' as Freud says in the reply to Abraham which we have been quoting. Now the cinema like the dream is condemned to this form of presentation (*Darstellung*): all that the scriptwriter inscribes in words in the left-hand column of his script — gestures, movements, emotions, intonations, description of places and objects, etc. — must ideally pass into the image. Otherwise, it is pure waste. 'Plastic presentation', or figurability, ceases to be a mere condition and becomes a law. The 'non-figurative' (our 'abstractions') thus submits to the 'figurative'. Everything must be reduced imperceptibly to the image: all that constitutes the analytic investigation, in other words the tiered movement of the drive and that to which it delegates its powers — affects and signs, usually isolated, 'insignificant', out of context and outside the main text. The drive operates and, at the end of its thought operations, it *flashes through* the image; it makes a sign, it does not *make* an image. Whence a wealth of incomprehension, wherein the relative failure of the 'psychoanalytic cinema' is simply one manifestation, and a benign one at that. The misunderstanding will not disappear — should it indeed disappear? — when it has been said and demonstrated a hundred times that the Freudian sexual theory is not reducible to sex, and that it lives off that gap; that the Oedipus complex is not what binds us to mother or father; that the horror of incest is born of an unbearable represent-ation, not a social prescription.

This misunderstanding did not escape the author of the screenplay which you are about to read. It seems to me that had he been freer in relation to the 'genre' imposed on him, he would have succeeded in smuggling through *more* of the unconscious, so to speak. I feel him as oddly more of a Freudian when — with all his playwright's audacity and effectiveness — he is staging the emotional relationships between his characters, than during his enforced incursions into the phantasmagoria of Cäcilie, or into dreams whose Oedipal symbolism — but only the symbolism, never the unique trajectory of elective 'representations' — leaps to the eye.

One final remark: the reader may be surprised to see Sartre's screenplay appearing in a collection called 'Psychoanalysis through its History',[22] which has hitherto comprised original documents or detailed studies whose main concern was truth. However, this is indeed a document: an important item to add to the file on Sartre's relations with Freud.

---

21. This constraint may entail long detours via the image for the message to get through. For example, in order for the word *court* ('runs', 'chases', etc.), with its full semantic charge and all its sexual connotations, to be sure of crossing the threshold of consciousness, it will be represented visually in the form of images of a tennis *court*; of a *cour* ('courtyard, court' including that paid to a woman, etc.); of a *course* ('race, running, errand', etc.); a character will be named Monsieur *Courtat*; and so on. The emphasis here will emerge only in the *recounting* of the dream, all that is available for interpreta-tion.

22. The original French edition was included by the publisher Gallimard in the series *La Psychanalyse dans son histoire*, part of a more general collection *Connaissance de l'Inconscient* edited for them by J.-B. Pontalis.

And the long, complex history of those relations unquestionably forms part both of Sartre's own history and of that of psychoanalysis (at least in France, where almost all intellectuals have had to define themselves in relation to Freud): it belongs to the history of ideas, hence to our history.

J.-B. Pontalis

VERSION I

(1959)

PART ONE

[1]

September 1885

Seven o'clock in the morning. A hospital corridor. The lamp (Welsbach burner) goes out; a little daylight filters in through the windows. An entrance-door gives onto a ward that can be made out dimly. Nurses are bustling about at the back of the ward: it is waking-up time, they are changing bandages, tending and washing the patients (all women). The dilapidated, gaslit ward has a sinister air. Over the door, a sign: Ophthalmological Ward. Dr Heinz in charge.

Two porters appear in the corridor, carrying an old woman on a stretcher: her eyes are staring and apparently sightless. They halt in front of the door and put down the stretcher to recover their breath. Both are elderly, with grey moustaches. They mop their brows.

A nurse — forty years old, with spectacles and harsh features — appears at the door, coming from inside the ward. She surveys the old woman and the porters with a sullen, harassed look. They lower their eyes, resigned in advance.

The nurse looks at the old woman.

NURSE   What do you want?

She recognizes her.

Again! This is too much!

FIRST PORTER   What are we supposed to do with her then?

NURSE   I told you: psychiatric ward.

She taps her forehead.

That's what's wrong with her.

SECOND PORTER   They don't want her.

NURSE   The psychiatrists?

SECOND PORTER   They say there's nothing wrong with her.

NURSE   Well send her home then.

The old woman raises herself slightly. She looks distraught.

PATIENT   I'm blind.

She is addressing no one in particular.

NURSE, *with a harsh, disagreeable laugh*   I wish I could see as well as you, my good woman! (*To the porters:*) Dr Heinz examined her yesterday, the organs are perfectly sound. She's putting on an act, that's all!

5

FIRST PORTER   Putting on an act or no, she weighs a ton. You've got some free beds.

The nurses slams the door in their faces. They look at each other disconsolately.

SECOND PORTER, *to the old woman*   What an old misery! Couldn't you be really blind?

OLD WOMAN, *tonelessly*   I am blind.

The first porter looks at her, then abruptly takes upon himself to hammer at the door. It reopens and the nurse reappears in a rage.

NURSE   I told you …

Seeing how old and tired they are, she feels sorry for them.

FIRST PORTER, *piteously*   We've been carting her around for two hours.

NURSE   Go and see Dr Freud. In Professor Scholz's absence, he's the one who's handling the administration.

FIRST PORTER   Where is he?

NURSE   In his room, I imagine. Room 120, Neurology Department.

SECOND PORTER, *sadly*   That's miles!

The nurse shrugs her shoulders and shuts the door in his face for the second time. The first porter scratches his head.

FIRST PORTER, *to the old woman*   I don't suppose you could walk?

OLD WOMAN, *scared*   No!

FIRST PORTER, *disappointed*   That's right! There's her leg, into the bargain!

SECOND PORTER, *in the same tone*   Her leg, my foot!

OLD WOMAN, *shouting*   I'm paralysed!

FIRST PORTER   Yes, and I've got one leg!

They spit on their hands and pick up the stretcher again.
Another corridor. A door. A number: 120. Day is beginning to break. Thick smoke is emerging from under the door. The porters appear with their burden, quite exhausted. They put down the stretcher. The first porter mops his brow. The second begins to cough. The first porter looks at him in surprise and sniffs.

FIRST PORTER   Hey! There's a fire!

They look around them and see the smoke coming out of the room. The second porter knocks on the door. No answer. He turns to his comrade with an inquiring look.

FIRST PORTER   Knock harder.

The second porter knocks harder.

The scene moves to a room which is of considerable size but very dingy. An unmade iron bed (same type as patients' beds), water-jug and washbasin on a stand, a shelf stuffed full of medical books, a desk. An open trunk, near the bed; one closed suitcase, another open (full of clothes and linen).

In the middle of the room, a cast-iron stove with a long chimney running up through the ceiling. A man, seen from behind, is squatting in front of the stove, from which clouds of smoke are belching.

On the ground near him, bundles of papers and notebooks which he is picking up methodically and stuffing into the stove, where they catch fire. The window is tightly shut and the shutters closed; the room is lit only by the flames of the stove.

Freud finally hears the knocking, gets up and goes over to the door. We see that he is smoking a cigar.

It is Freud: twenty-nine years old, thick black beard, thick eyebrows. Fine eyes, dark and forbidding, sunk deep in their sockets. He looks as if he has just woken up. Dazed air. Face blackened by ash. Though his hands are well cared for, they too are black. He is fully dressed. Carefully, but poorly.

He goes to the door, turns the key and draws the bolt. The porters appear through the smoke; both are coughing.

They stare at Freud in amazement. Freud, now in full possession of his senses, observes them with a harsh, impassive gaze.

FIRST PORTER, *apologetically*   We thought something was on fire.
FREUD   Nothing's on fire.
SECOND PORTER   Really?
FREUD, *curt and ironical*   Really.

He moves to close the door again. The porters gesture imploringly towards the patient.

Aha! it's the hysterical patient. What's up?
FIRST PORTER   Nobody wants her.
FREUD   I can imagine not.

He throws away his cigar-butt and moves towards the hysterical patient: she stares in fascination.

OLD WOMAN   I'm blind.

He approaches her and peers into her eyes.

FREUD, *gently*   No, Madam, you don't see but you're not blind.

He pulls off the old woman's blanket. She is wearing a shift. Her left leg is paralysed; the toes are

7

clenched and as if folded into the sole of her foot. He palpates her leg without the patient seeming to notice.

He straightens himself and replaces the blanket over the patient's legs.

Take her to the Neurology Ward. There's an empty bed.

SECOND PORTER   Professor Meynert has forbidden ...

FREUD   I'll go and have a word with him in a minute. Be off with you!

He closes the door again, goes towards the stove, squats down and resumes his strange labours with a kind of unremitting fury.

The same hospital. Another corridor, equally dilapidated. The walls cracked, puffed and blistered; bits of plaster hanging from the ceiling. Not many windows; day is beginning to break.

    Students are gathered in front of a door. (Frock coats. Opera hats. Others, interns or residents, are wearing white coats. Almost all have beards. Average age: between twenty-five and thirty.)

    Hubbub of voices.

On the (closed) door, a sign: 'Neurology Ward. Professor Meynert in charge. Professor Meynert's lesson takes place on Monday, Wednesday, Thursday and Saturday, at 7.15.'

    The porters carrying the old woman suffering from hysteria appear in the corridor, staggering with exhaustion. The students squeeze back against the wall to let them pass. One of the porters knocks on the door. The porters have put the stretcher down on the ground. The students look curiously at the old woman.

A STUDENT   What's wrong with her?

The porters shrug their shoulders.

OLD WOMAN   I'm blind.

The door opens. The porters pick up the stretcher and go in.

A STUDENT, *authoritatively, to the others*   Lesion of the optic nerve. Or of the optic centres of the brain.

The door has closed again. At this moment, at the far end of the corridor, Professor Meynert appears. Around fifty.

    The students stop talking. Respectful hush.

    Very youthful figure. Very handsome, but harrowed face. Long red beard, tall graceful body, agile in spite of a very slight limp. Top hat and black gloves, frock coat, high starched collar, four-in-hand tie, fancy waistcoat. He leans lightly upon a round-headed cane.

    The students freeze into respectful poses. Those who are wearing hats remove them. Meynert, very majestic and self-assured, raises his top hat carelessly and replaces it at once. He is wearing gloves.

MEYNERT   Gentlemen …

The door has opened. The neurology ward (women's section) is visible. Nurses and orderlies stand to attention between the beds.

Let's go in.

The head nurse presents herself before him. He raises two fingers of his left hand in greeting. She will follow him, at a respectful distance.

He comes in, still wearing his hat. Long, dismal ward in semi-darkness. No artificial light. A little sunlight enters through two open windows.

The group of students — most of them poorly dressed, clumsy of bearing and lacking any particular charm — respectfully follows (like a corps de ballet) this graceful person who appears almost to dance (in spite of his limp, or perhaps thanks to it): who is more like a principal dancer than a professor of medicine.

Nurses and orderlies stand between the beds, once again almost at attention. Meynert points out patients with his cane; they watch him, sitting up in their beds (when they can do so). From time to time he lightly strikes the iron upright of one of the beds with the tip of his cane.

In front of the first two patients, he halts only very briefly. One of them — a young woman — greets him. Meynert looks at her without returning her greeting.

PATIENT   Good morning, Sir.
MEYNERT   How do you feel, my girl?
PATIENT   Still the same.

He nods his head, and proceeds on his way. The third patient is a woman of about forty. Her lower jaw is twisted to the right. She is asleep. Meynert strikes the tip of his cane against the iron upright of the bed.

MEYNERT   Double mastoiditis. Surgical intervention. In the course of trephination, the facial nerve was touched. We saw her yesterday. Massage is being used, and I envisage electrical treatment.

He proceeds on his way. The patient, awakened by the tapping of the cane, follows him with her eyes.

MEYNERT   Nothing very new, today. Except a hemiplegic . . . *(To the head nurse)* Hospitalized yesterday?

Respectful nod from the sister.

Very good. We'll examine her.

He continues on his way. A few steps further on the porters, who have finally deposited the old blind woman on a bed, are standing to attention, very stiffly, on either side of her bed. Meynert halts and looks at her.

A new admission?

The two porters look at one another in great anxiety.

FIRST ORDERLY She ... comes from the psychiatric department.

Meynert, authoritarian and disagreeable:

MEYNERT Well, then? What's she doing here?

The orderlies remain silent.

Take her away.

Tapping the bed with his cane.

How often have I told you: everyone in the proper place. We don't have enough beds ...

FIRST ORDERLY, *piteously* The thing is ...

Meynert glares at him.

MEYNERT What?
FIRST ORDERLY Dr Mannheim doesn't want her.
MEYNERT And why is that?
FIRST PORTER He says she's a hy ... a hy ...

Meynert's face alters. White with anger, his eyes sparkling.

MEYNERT A hysterical patient? We'll not have that here.
OLD WOMAN, *piteously* I'm blind.
MEYNERT Have her eyes been examined?
FIRST PORTER Yes. There's nothing wrong with them.
OLD WOMAN, *in distress* I'm blind.

(*The students murmur.*)

MEYNERT You're a liar, my fine lady. Putting on an act. You can see as well as anyone else and you're wasting my time.
OLD WOMAN I'm blind, one of my legs is paralysed ...

Freud has just come in through the open door and he hurries over to Meynert. He still has a smudge of soot on his face and his hands are still blackened. At the moment when he joins the group of students, who draw aside respectfully to make room for him, Meynert has just turned to the sister and asks her with sovereign authority and crushing scorn:

11

MEYNERT   Who is the imbecile who put her in my department?

The nurse looks at him without daring to reply, then looks at Freud who has finally reached Meynert. Freud, who is wearing a sombre expression, receives Meynert's last words full in the face. He nevertheless replies with a touch of irony and very gently:

FREUD   The imbecile is me, Sir.

Meynert looks at him, disconcerted. Suddenly, he bursts out laughing.

MEYNERT, *amiably*   I might have known it. Forgive me, Freud my words were stronger than I intended.

His anger gradually returns, but he makes a visible effort to control himself.

I shall never understand why hysterical patients interest you. (*Violently:*) You know very well they're malingerers.

Freud, mild but stubborn, with deep respect:

FREUD   I don't know, Sir. I don't know anything yet.

Meynert, peremptorily:

MEYNERT   You know it because I tell you so.

To the despairing porters:

Take her away.
FIRST PORTER   Where to?
MEYNERT   That's no concern of mine.

He turns towards the cowed students and points to a bed at the end of the ward.

MEYNERT   Let's go and see my hemiplegic.

The group begins to move forward again. Meynert has taken Freud's arm, to erase the painful impression that his violence has made upon the latter. He speaks to him in an undertone:

You're still leaving tomorrow?
FREUD   Yes, Sir.

At the same instant, piercing screams are heard. The students turn round. Meynert and Freud turn likewise. The old blind woman is struggling with the two porters. Screams, violent convulsions, she tears off her sheets and arches her back. Her legs flail convulsively. Meynert takes an abrupt decision.

MEYNERT, *authoritarian and brusque* Gentlemen, this morning I shall give you my lecture on hysteria.

He retraces his steps, followed by Freud, the head nurse and the students. He comes to a halt before the old woman's bed. To the porters:

Let her go.

Psychiatrists distinguish two types of mental illness: the psychoses and the neuroses. The former are the more serious: they are characterized by deep disturbances affecting the personality of the patients and their sense of reality; their origin is to be sought in the cerebral centres. The neuroses, for their part, affect only feelings — as with neurasthenia or anxiety neurosis — or behaviour, as with obsessional neuroses.

Pointing with the tip of his cane at the old woman, who is still thrashing about in all directions:

As for hysteria, of which you're looking at a very fine example, vain attempts have been made to introduce it into one or other of these two categories. In reality, this supposed illness does not exist: in obsessional neurosis, it is *true* that the patient is obsessed; in neurasthenia, the patient is *truly* anxious. Here, all is false; it's all a lie.

Stretching out his cane, he lightly touches both the old woman's legs.

A paralysed leg? Where is it?

Laughter from the students. The old woman continues to writhe about; her gestures all have a meaning: terror, refusal, pity, entreaty, etc.

Epileptic crisis? Epileptiform crisis? (*He laughs.*) Epileptics throw their limbs about in every direction. In epilepsy, we observe brief clonic shudders with short oscillations.

Miming with one gloved hand the clonic shudders.

Where are they, here? Where are they? You see a bad actress, all of those movements are intentional.

Very discreetly, he mimes the old woman's movements; the students watch, laughing sometimes at Meynert and sometimes at the old woman. Meynert's movements become slightly exaggerated, as if he were soon going to lose control of them. He realizes this and stops in time. To the porters:

Hold her. No, just her head.

To the students:

A match.

A student searches his pockets and, with almost servile eagerness, holds out a match to Meynert. The latter puts his cane down on the neighbouring bed. He unhurriedly removes his gloves. To the student:

How about lighting it?

The student strikes the match.

(In the tone of the teacher giving a lecture:) What do you see?

The woman's eyes: contraction of the pupils under the light.

STUDENT'S VOICE OFF   Her pupils. They've contracted.
MEYNERT   Do you think a blind person's pupils would contract if exposed to light?

Numerous students reply in chorus.

STUDENTS   No.
MEYNERT   The case rests. Enough of this, old lady: we're not swallowing it.

The old woman gradually quietens down. She stops moving, but as her left leg falls still, it resumes its appearance of paralytic contraction.

Oh, no! You can leave off now! *(Laughter.)*

Her shift, drawn up to the knee, reveals what has happened. Meynert is triumphant.

Well, Freud, do you know now what a malingerer is?

Freud hesitates. All eyes are fixed upon him. He is torn between anger and timidity. At last he says, in a still respectful tone but with a perceptible undercurrent of anger:

FREUD   If I may be so bold, Sir?

Meynert stares at him in feigned astonishment, to intimidate him. Freud remains courteous, but his stubbornness can be divined.

I examined the patient myself yesterday, in the Psychiatric Ward.

He goes up to a student wearing a gold pin in his cravat. Removing the pin with a smile:

Excuse me.

He goes over to a little table standing between the two rows of beds. On the table a lighted burner; on the burner a kettle full of water. He puts the kettle to one side and holds the end of the pin in the flame to sterilize it. Meynert and the students watch him curiously. Meynert is frowning.

Freud returns to the patient, holding the pin. Persuasively and almost in an undertone:

FREUD   Madam! Madam! You'll be staying here. I'm sure Professor Meynert will allow you to stay.

The patient relaxes somewhat. Her eyes are wide open but still staring.

Observe her face.

Freud takes the 'paralysed' leg by the foot and raises it. Her whole body is raised with it. Her face remains indifferent.

MEYNERT   One further proof: with an authentic paralysis, it wouldn't be possible to raise the body by lifting the paralysed limb.

FREUD   Of course, Sir.

He pricks the patient's calf with the student's pin. At first very lightly, then harder, until finally he sticks the pin right in and lets it go. The pin remains embedded in the leg. The patient's face remains entirely tranquil. Her body is motionless.

No reaction.

He removes the pin, replaces the patient's leg on the bed, goes to the little table and wipes the pin with a piece of cottonwool.

FREUD   She feels nothing. Anaesthesia of the limb which she claims is paralysed.

He sterilizes the pin once more, replaces the kettle on the burner and holds out the pin to the student. The latter inspects it in puzzlement and, instead of putting it back in his cravat, sticks it with a gesture of disgust into the lapel of his jacket.

All eyes are fixed on Meynert, who manages to control himself and even to smile.

MEYNERT, *a good loser*   Bravo, Freud! *(To the others:)* That experiment proves that the patient is suffering from a slight hemi-anaesthesia, most probably due to disturbances of the coronary circulation.

He goes to pick up his glove and cane from the bed where he has deposited them.

And that is the truth. The humble truth, Gentlemen. As for the rest, that old woman is neither paralytic nor blind. Her real malady is lying, as I proved to you. *(To the head nurse:)* Let her remain here, I'll examine her.

Relieved smiles from the orderlies.

Let's go and see our hemiplegic.

He moves off. Freud makes as if to follow him. Meynert checks him in friendly fashion.

MEYNERT   Be off with you, Freud, you're leaving tomorrow and you must have hundreds of things to do. *(Amiably:)* In any case, Herr Privatdozent, so far as you are concerned, I have nothing more to teach you.

Freud, suddenly moved, but controlling himself:

FREUD   I should have liked to thank you.
MEYNERT   I shall be in my laboratory in half an hour. Come if you have time; I have a proposition to put to you.

Freud bows and goes off. Meynert's face hardens slightly as he watches his assistant leave the room. Then he turns away and approaches the bed of the hemiplegic, followed by his students.
Shot of the orderlies picking up their stretcher again. The first orderly waves a hand at the patient.

FIRST ORDERLY   No hard feelings. And may God bless you.

The old woman, exhausted, her mouth twisted by a painful spasm, stares with empty eyes.

SECOND ORDERLY, *surveying the old woman resentfully*   Don't say that: she's possessed.

The second orderly makes a sign to ward off the evil eye. They move off.

[3]

A laboratory (Anatomy of the Nervous System) in the same hospital. A bright, clean room. Students and doctors (in white coats) grouped around various tables, each of which (in addition to various accessories such as instruments, glass slides, test-tubes, etc.) bears a microscope.

Freud is bending over a microscope, inspecting the preparation of two students standing behind him, who have a foreign air.

FREUD   It has got off to a good start.

He straightens up and surveys them kindly.

Good luck!

One of the students, a tall fair boy with an Irish look about him, smiling at Freud:

STUDENT   The best luck for us would be to meet up with you again soon.

FREUD   We'll be meeting at the beginning of next year: my scholarship is only for three months.

STUDENT   We'll have gone back to Boston.

FREUD   So soon?

STUDENT   Once you're not there any more, we'll be wasting our time: we might as well be home for Christmas.

SECOND STUDENT   Dr Freud, whatever may happen to me in later life, I shall always consider it an honour to have worked with you.

The janitor of the hospital has come in a moment earlier; he circles the group without daring to approach Freud.

Freud and the students shake hands, the janitor comes up.

JANITOR   Your fiancée's here and she says you're supposed to be meeting her.

FREUD   Where is she?

The janitor points to the window.

In the courtyard.

Freud goes over to the window. (The laboratory is on the second floor.) Down below in the court-yard he sees a girl with a parasol and a big straw hat; her back is turned to him.

FREUD   Ask her kindly to wait for a little while: I have an appointment with Professor Meynert.

Meynert has just come in. All heads turn towards him. He takes off his hat with a sweeping gesture.

MEYNERT   Good morning, Gentlemen.

He looks around for Freud. Freud goes over to him. Meynert takes Freud by the arm and coaxes him along.

We shall be more comfortable in my office.

At the back of the laboratory, a door: Professor Meynert's Office. Meynert pulls a key from his pocket, opens the door and ushers Freud in.

Freud enters a comfortable, well-lit room. A large table covered with books, a glass-fronted bookcase, armchairs. With the slightest touch of surprise he notices a small carafe of schnapps and a little glass on a tray. The tray is placed on the work-desk, very prominently.

Meynert, who has not noticed the tray, comes in with easy assurance and waves Freud to a chair opposite the desk. Seated opposite him, in his leather armchair, he perceives the tray and carafe. A moment of embarrassment. Meynert hesitates for a moment, then calmly pushes the tray aside. Freud begins to speak.

FREUD   Sir, I should like to thank you ...

Freud speaks in a friendly tone. Meynert remains majestic and inscrutable. A dismissive movement of the hand.

MEYNERT   Don't thank me: I didn't vote for you.

Freud wishes to speak. Majestic gesture from Meynert. At this juncture, Meynert is still master of himself, his expressions and movements are controlled.

It was thanks to Brücke that you obtained the scholarship. Yet I consider you to be my disciple, the best of my assistants, and I'm deeply convinced that you deserve this reward. I voted against because you're going to do something crazy.

His hand, as soon as he has pronounced the word 'crazy', begins to feel its way towards the carafe. He catches himself just in time and starts to grope in his beard (the gesture of Michelangelo's Moses).

There are eminent physiologists in Berlin. In London, too.

Freud has stiffened, but he remains extremely courteous. Simply, his face darkens; he has become mistrustful.

And where are you going? To Paris! To attend the lectures of a charlatan.

Meynert's hand has returned to pick up the little glass. It plays with it.
    Freud wishes to speak. The hand leaves the beard to stretch out towards him, majestically, and impose silence on him.

A charlatan! Freud! What's the choroidal?

FREUD   A little branch of the inner carotid artery.

MEYNERT   Precisely. Well, Charcot doesn't know that!

He picks up a pamphlet from the table and throws it across to Freud.

MEYNERT   Read that: you'll see for yourself that he knows nothing about it.

The hand returns to the beard and gropes in the reddish fur.

And that's your teacher-to-be!

Fresh mannerism: the hand every so often leaves the beard and the left index finger begins to tap the left side of the nose.

A charlatan who treats neuroses by hypnotism.

Freud, very politely:

FREUD   Not all, Sir: hysteria.

He stops, amazed at the unexpected result of his words. At the word 'hysteria', the left hand has abruptly quit the nose.

MEYNERT   More quackery!

With assurance, yet seemingly without Meynert's noticing, the hand picks up the carafe and firmly pours some schnapps into the little glass. It replaces the carafe and raises the glass as Meynert speaks. But all this so little affects the majesty of Meynert's countenance (he did not look at it even when it was pouring the spirit — not even in order to control the operation) that one would say the hand was totally distinct from the professor's person.
    With the greatest authority:

MEYNERT   The illness of which you speak does not exist.
    Charcot's students pick up girls from the street and send them to the Salpêtrière to perform his 'grande crise' for him. He's the laughing-stock of the medical profession.

He drains the little glass of schnapps in a single gulp.

Hypnotism! A music-hall turn.

He puts the glass down again. He taps his nose with his left index finger.

Your work last year on the anatomy of the cerebellum, in my view, advanced scientific knowledge. And now, hypnotism! What a degeneration. You no longer believe in physiology.

Freud: just a nod to indicate that he does still believe in it.

And how about that? Don't you believe in that?

Meynert points to a placard on the rear wall, printed in block capitals:
    'The living organism is part of the physical world; it is made up of systems of atoms moved by attractive and repulsive forces, following the principle of conservation of energy. Helmholtz.'
    Very sincere:

That's my Creed.

Freud replies briefly, politely and drily:

FREUD   I believe in science.

MEYNERT, *gesturing towards the placard*   That's Science.

Meynert has poured himself a little glass of schnapps. At once he pours it back into the carafe and places both hands flat on his desk-blotter. He indicates the placard with a nod of his head.

FREUD   It is experimentation and Reason.

Meynert pours himself a drink without further ado, and drinks it.

MEYNERT   Charcot may perhaps represent experimentation, but he certainly doesn't represent Reason.

He drinks and pours himself another glass.

If mental illnesses interest you, go and study psychiatry in Berlin.

Freud appears hypnotized by Meynert's hands. To break the spell he looks at his own hands, which are still black with soot.

FREUD   I should like . . .

Upset:

Oh!, forgive me. I ... I burned some papers this morning.

MEYNERT, *indifferently*   It doesn't bother me. But if it bothers you ...

He nods towards a washbasin standing against the left-hand wall. Freud gets up and goes over to wash his hands. Freud, while his back is turned and he cannot see Meynert, finds the courage to speak.

Meynert, for his part, takes advantage of the fact that Freud cannot see him to pour himself a third little glass, which he drinks furtively.

FREUD   Psychiatry is not yet out of its infancy. Perhaps one day it will be possible to cure madness by acting directly upon the cells of the brain. We're not at that point yet: there are forces within us which today cannot be reduced to physical forces.

He points at the placard:

I'm suffocating in those shackles.

With a kind of violence:

I should like ...

He is frightened by his violence, turns away from the placard and looks at his hands, which he is soaping vigorously.

I should like to wash myself.

Meynert gives a start.

MEYNERT, *astonished*   What's that?

Freud shivers very slightly, then resumes in too natural a voice:

FREUD   I said I should like to know myself.

He dries his hands on a towel.

MEYNERT   To what end? *(A pause.)* You're a doctor and you've no time to waste. Why should I know myself? I study the nervous system and not my own moods.

Numerous, rapid twitches of the left hand.

Besides, I do know myself; I'm as clear as a mountain stream.

Freud has returned to his seat. He looks at Meynert with a kind of sorrowful anger. Politely, and without the least irony:

FREUD   You're very lucky, Sir.

MEYNERT   If you don't understand yourself, do you think hysterical patients will teach you what you are?

FREUD   Why not?

MEYNERT   What relationship can there possibly be between a Privatdozent of the Faculty and an old wreck like that one this morning?

FREUD   I don't know.

Meynert puts his hands flat on the table and recovers all his authority.

MEYNERT   Enough on that subject. Here's what I propose to you: I need rest. If you give up your scholarship, I shall nominate you as my locum; from tomorrow, you'll lecture on the anatomy of the brain in my place.

Freud appears deeply moved by this proposition.

Just reflect. In ten years you'll be Professor Freud, and sitting at this desk.

Freud, with a real surge of gratitude:

FREUD   I ... I'm very grateful.

MEYNERT, *icy*   But?

FREUD, *sincerely*   I ... I don't deserve ...

Meynert brushes aside the objection with his hand.

MEYNERT, *same tone*   Go on.

FREUD, *with a kind of passion*   I need to go there ...

Meynert stands up. Very sharp:

MEYNERT   Very well. If you change your mind, let me know. And if you prefer to leave, goodbye.

He shakes Freud's hand and accompanies him to the door without limping. When Freud has left, Meynert locks the door and shoots the bolt. Then he turns round and goes to the work-desk with a heavy limp. He pours himself a glassful of schnapps and gulps it down standing. His face is crumpled, his eyes haunted.

4

Freud in the courtyard. He looks for Martha. The courtyard is empty. He grows impatient.

FREUD   Herr Muller!

The janitor opens the door of his lodge.

Where's the young lady …

The janitor points to the second floor. Freud runs back into the hospital.

The stairs. Freud is running up them.

A corridor. As Freud reaches his room he knocks against a dustbin, stops in his tracks and looks at it: it is stuffed full of charred papers and half-burned notebooks. He looks worried, takes one of the notebooks, opens it and perceives that certain words can still be read; he picks up the bin, after throwing the notebook back into it, and makes his way to his room carrying the bin with him.

Fresh surprise: the door of Room 120 is open. Inside, the daylight is streaming in through windows thrown wide open: it is a fine autumn morning.

The room — which we previously saw full of rubbish, ash and smoke — is spotlessly clean; the stove is extinguished.

Near the window, a young woman is finishing the sweeping. She has put down her straw hat and parasol on the bed and slipped on one of Freud's white coats, much too big for her. Martha is not really pretty, but very graceful: black tresses, fine eyes, a demeanour that is serious but at the same time lively and gay.

Freud looks at her with joyful surprise, then throws himself ardently upon her, lifts her off the ground, sets her down again and covers her face with kisses. She yields laughingly, but turns adroitly away when he seeks to kiss her on the lips.

He stops abruptly, looks at her somewhat mistrustfully and draws away from her.

FREUD   What are you doing here with that broom?
MARTHA   How about you, with that dustbin?
FREUD   We were supposed to meet in the courtyard.
MARTHA   Yes, but you were supposed to arrive on time.

He is brusque and touchy; she stands up to him, tenderly but with gentle mockery.

FREUD, *suspicious*   Who showed you the way? Who opened this door for you?
MARTHA   A charming man.

Freud frowns. She bursts out laughing.

The janitor!

Freud, very severely:

FREUD   Martha, you shouldn't enter a man's room. Not even if the man is your fiancé.

Abruptly, he starts laughing. A short, violent laugh, with no gaiety in it but full of irony.

FREUD   And the white coat? Was it the janitor who lent you that?

Martha removes the white coat with a coquettish expression of vexation. She now appears in a suit which is elegant and charming, albeit modest.

MARTHA   Do you prefer me like this?

He throws himself upon her anew and kisses her ardently. She pushes him away and frees herself.

Let me breathe.

She points at the dustbin.

Were you trying to set the hospital on fire?

Freud looks at the bin and grows sullen again.

FREUD   I've been burning some papers.
MARTHA   What papers?
FREUD   All of them!
MARTHA, *suddenly furious*   My letters?
FREUD, *seriously — but only to tease her*   Those first.

She does not have time to protest: he has gone over to the open suitcase and taken out a bundle of letters.

So far as your letters are concerned, I'm taking them with me.
MARTHA   Your journal?

Freud bends over the dustbin; he pulls out some notebooks burnt virtually to a cinder.

FREUD   There it is.

He stands up laughing.

Fourteen years of my diary. I used to record even my night-time dreams in it.

He drops the notebooks back into the dustbin.

No more past. Martha, you'll be marrying a man who's totally naked.

MARTHA   For shame!

FREUD   Your fiancé has no more memories than a newborn babe.

Jokingly, he strikes a flattering pose.

MARTHA   My fiancé's a blackamoor. I adore black men, but since I'm marrying a white one, I should like him to remain white.

She moistens a towel in the water-jug.

Come here.

She scrubs him energetically.

Whatever would your mother say if you came to say goodbye to her in this state?

While she is rubbing, she points with her left hand at the dustbin.

Whatever got into you?

FREUD   I'm leaving, so I'm wiping out everything: one should never leave tracks.

MARTHA   Wipe me out, then!

FREUD   No, you're my future.

He kisses her. She frees herself.

MARTHA   Don't squander your future.

She takes her hat and goes to put it on in front of the mirror, over the washbasin.
A hat-pin between her teeth:

What are you trying to wipe out? Have you killed someone? Have you had mistresses?

Removing the pin:

Answer! Have you had mistresses?

Freud, very sincere:

FREUD   You know I haven't.

MARTHA   Well, then? You've nothing to hide.

Freud jokes, but with an undertone of deep conviction.

FREUD   I want to give my future biographers a hard time. They'll shed tears of blood.

Martha looks at herself in the mirror and suddenly hears the noise of an explosion (virtually).
She turns round: Freud has abruptly poured paraffin onto the papers in the dustbin, put them into the stove and ignited the whole lot.

MARTHA, *indignantly*   What are you doing?

Freud has begun to laugh, with a slightly distraught look.

FREUD   Ashes! Ashes! They'll find only ashes.

Martha, indignantly, takes him by the arm and drags him out of the room.
He picks up his hat on the way and follows her docilely.

The Courtyard.

Martha and Freud cross it and enter the main doors of the hospital.

MARTHA, *continuing their conversation; laughing, but irritated really*   In the first place, you won't have any biographers.
FREUD   Yes, I will.
MARTHA   No, you won't.
FREUD, *with a smile which does little to conceal his deep seriousness*   Great men always have biographers.
MARTHA   You have no need to be a great man, because I love you.

Freud laughs affectionately, but not without bitterness.

In a street.

They are walking side by side, very properly, not arm in arm.
They are not speaking to one another. After a moment, Freud pulls his cigar-case from his pocket with a box of matches.
She notices and taps him on the sleeve with the knob of her parasol. He starts.

FREUD   Forgive me.

He puts the case back in his pocket.

I am ... upset.

She looks at him with a questioning expression.

Meynert blames me for leaving ...

Her face becomes expressionless again. This departure of his visibly displeases her.

MARTHA, *very drily*   I blame you too.

Freud laughs, without being willing to understand her.

FREUD   That's because you love me. *(His face clouds.)*

The street is deserted.

But in his case, I don't think he likes me any more.

A silence. Suddenly he regains his composure, smiles and signals to a passing cab.
   The driver has not noticed Freud's signal.

MARTHA   You're crazy!
FREUD   No, I'm rich.

He jingles some money in his pocket and brings out a little box of gold coins.

MARTHA   Is it the proceeds from a robbery?
FREUD   It's the money for my scholarship: I received it yesterday, 2,000 florins.

The cab draws closer.
   Freud signals to the driver:

Cabman!
MARTHA, *indignant*   Your scholarship's for Paris. You'll barely have enough to live on.
FREUD   I can still spend a kreutzer.
MARTHA   Nothing at all.

The cab has come to a halt in front of them. Martha drags Freud forward with a firm grasp.
   To the driver:

It was a mistake.

The driver shrugs his shoulders, whips up his horse and the cab moves off again. Freud watches it wistfully:

FREUD, *amused at himself*   The one occasion when I had some money.

MARTHA   Are your parents expecting us for lunch?

He nods in confirmation.

Well, we'll go by the Ring and we'll walk.

The Ring.

A building under construction. Martha looks at it admiringly. On the facade, in big letters: 'SKATING — Opens 10 November'.

MARTHA   What luck!

To Freud, who looks at her with a frown:

I shall be able to skate.

Freud, in a rage, pulls her by the arm. She resists.

FREUD   You shan't skate.

MARTHA   But you won't be here!

FREUD   Exactly!

MARTHA   How tiresome you are! I shall be bored to death.

FREUD   I don't want a man taking you in his arms.

MARTHA, *spiritedly*   All you have to do is not go.

FREUD, *in very bad faith*   If you asked it of me, I shouldn't go. Do you ask it of me?

She does not reply. But we can sense that she is somewhat resentful.

You see, I could sacrifice my whole career for you and you wouldn't even sacrifice the most commonplace pleasure for me. Swear to me you won't go skating.

MARTHA   I won't swear anything at all.

She turns her back on him. They sulk and walk in silence amid the passers-by. The latter become more and more numerous.

A crowd in front of a street-vendor. On the pavement, two tiny little cardboard wrestlers dance about; they are joined at the wrists and seem to move spontaneously.

Martha stops and looks at them with amusement. We can vaguely hear some more distant voices.

VOICES OFF, *quite indistinct*   Ask for the Protocols of the Elders of Zion, the Thousand and One Jewish stories.

Buy the story of the Jew and the Pig.

Freud does not hear these voices: he is watching the two wrestlers, with so gloomy an expression that it makes him almost comical.

He is annoyed by the interest which Martha is taking in these little cardboard figures. At the same time, he wants to make up with her.

He touches her arm clumsily, tries to take her hand. But Martha remains unmoved.

At last, he explains in a conciliatory tone of voice:

FREUD   There's a trick. The pedlar holds them by one end of a thread and the other end is held by a confederate.

He succeeds only in irritating her further.

MARTHA   Oh, do be quiet; we'd be able to see it.

Freud seems to believe that he has been forgiven. But he cannot deceive his fiancée, who discerns beneath his voluble explanations the desire he has — out of jealousy — to break the spell of the spectacle.

FREUD   It must be no thicker than a hair. Wait: I'll try and find the confederate. It should be possible to recognize him by his expression. He'll look as if he's hiding something.

He scrutinizes the faces of the passers-by; their features are ordinary, but the open expressions of some make them look more 'relaxed', while the serious expressions of others make them look less so.

FREUD, *discouraged*   They all look as if they're hiding something.

He suddenly catches sight of a face which holds his attention. Someone to his left looks as if he is acting the innocent onlooker.

There he is. Over on the left. He has put his hands in his pockets so that nobody will see them moving.

MARTHA, *furious*   Leave me alone.

He looks at her in surprise.

You always spoil everything.

He makes his crime worse by insisting:

FREUD   But just look at him.
MARTHA   Explanations! Explanations! You want to find the reason for everything.

But I'm just amusing myself; so leave me in peace.

The spell has in fact been broken for her, but sulkiness causes her to pretend to immerse herself ecstatically anew in contemplation of the little cardboard men.

Freud, disconcerted and at a loose end, moves away slightly from the crowd; some newcomers push him aside and he suddenly finds himself in the midst of another crowd. A vendor is selling lampoons and songs.

VENDOR   Buy the Protocols of the Elders of Zion. How the Jews aim to control the universe.

Lament of the child eaten by a rabbi.

Ask for the story of the Jew and the Pig.

He is totally unconcerned with what he is doing. He thinks only of selling them and does not even understand what he is saying.

Freud surveys the onlookers: same assortment of curious and impassive faces as in the other group. Yet Freud has turned white with anger. His eyes sparkle, he has clenched his fists.

At this very moment a jolly, fat man pushes past him in order to make his way to the vendor. He is holding a coin in his hand.

FAT MAN   Give me the Story of the Jew and the Pig.

The vendor gives him one of the little lampoons he is holding in his hand. The fat man gives him the coin he is holding in his hand.

Freud, sickened, turns his back on the bystanders. He has left the crowd and stops to look for Martha. But the fat man leaves the crowd in his turn.

He has opened the little booklet and — laughing in anticipation — is reading the Story of the Jew and the Pig, as a result of which he bumps into Freud for the second time. Freud starts and looks at him. He recognizes him and sees what he is reading.

His eyes sparkle. He seizes the lampoon from him and tears it into tiny pieces.

The fat man cannot understand what is happening to him; he stares at Freud with a bewildered look.

Freud towers over him. He says to him with crushing scorn:

FREUD   Imbecile!

The bystanders begin to turn and stare.

A hand is laid on his arm. Martha drags him back vigorously. He turns round in a fury, recognizes her and yields.

She pushes him along and before he knows it he finds himself seated in a cab, which sets off at once.

MARTHA   66 Sturmgasse.

The curious have almost all turned away. The cab leaves.

FREUD, *ironically*   How's this, Martha, are you the one who's squandering my poor money now?

MARTHA   You're overwrought this morning. I prefer to lock you up.
     I hate scenes!

The cab (an open barouche) bowls gently along the Ring.

FREUD, *sincerely*   So do I!
MARTHA   Perhaps so. But you're always provoking them.

She looks at him. Very tenderly and with only a hint of teasing:

You're as crazy as your patients.

He does indeed look crazy: he sits there stiff and gloomy, bristling, his hair all dishevelled.

That poor man didn't really look all that nasty.
FREUD   You think he's nice because he's fat. Do you know what he'd bought?

Martha shrugs her shoulders.

MARTHA   He just happened to be passing by. He wanted to see for himself ... It had no importance.

Freud speaks with great force and authority. We realize that he has reflected at length upon all that he says:

FREUD   Everything is important. And nothing just happens by chance.

The Ring.

The young couple, as they talk, can see cafés, buildings and above all people flit by. Officers, fine ladies — and fine gentlemen in frock coats.

FREUD   Look.

With authority:

The enemy.

Martha starts and looks at all those elegant personages parading by in procession, who do not seem fierce at all.

FREUD   When the time comes, they'll hunt us down mercilessly and cut our throats. If we allow them to do so.

Martha is annoyed and worried; but when he speaks with such authority she is accustomed to yield to him.

MARTHA   Who do you mean, we? You and I?
FREUD   You and I and all the others. We Jews.

The crowd seen from the cab.
  We can hear Freud's voice.

FREUD'S VOICE OFF   Leave nothing behind you. Anything the goys discover about our lives, they'll use against us.

Martha returns to her favourite theme.

MARTHA   If you believe that, don't put yourself forward; just be an ordinary doctor, don't try to make a name for yourself.
FREUD, *gloomily*   A Jew cannot allow himself to be just ordinary.
MARTHA   Why not?
FREUD   Because ordinary means the goys. If Jews don't prove they're among the best, people will say they're the worst.

The carriage has entered a street that is quite poor and very crowded.
  Kids are playing in the street and they look at the cab in astonishment.

FREUD, *with relief*   Are we home?

One of them runs after the carriage and tries to cling on to it. Martha smilingly raises a threatening finger.
  This poor neighbourhood is a kind of ghetto.
  Numerous Jews in front of Jewish shops (inscriptions in Yiddish).

When I was that kid's age, I used to call the goys Romans; we, the Jews, were Carthaginians. There was a picture in a prize-book. I tore it out of the book and kept it. Hamilcar, the great man of Carthage, was making his son Hannibal swear to wreak vengeance upon Rome.
  Hannibal was me.
MARTHA, *ironically*   And your father was Hamilcar?

Freud twists his features into a stubborn grimace.

FREUD, *with more force than conviction*   Yes.

MARTHA, *still teasing*   The most gentle of men! He made you swear to avenge him?

Freud's countenance grows even darker. The more conscious he is of lying, the more firm and stubborn he appears.

Despite the authority of his voice, his words sound false.

FREUD   To avenge *us*. Yes. By becoming the best doctor in Vienna.

She looks at him dumbfounded.

MARTHA   You never told me that.

FREUD   You know very well how hard I find it to talk about myself.

5

The cab stops in front of a large, dingy edifice. An apartment-house, it looks more like a barracks. Sheets hanging from the windows to dry. Before the entrance, a pack of squealing urchins.

Freud raises his head mechanically. A woman of about fifty, tall and still very beautiful, is leaning out of a first-floor window. She waves to him with charm and a certain coquetry.

She has thrown a shawl over her beautiful, bare arms. Freud's face becomes transformed: it expresses a deep, restrained passion.

Mother and son exchange a long, silent smile. For the first time we have the impression that Freud finds himself at ease in the time and place where he actually is.

He even forgets to pay the cabman, who looks at him in surprise. Martha notices this and takes advantage of it to pay the cabman herself, slipping a kreutzer into his hand.

Then she tugs at Freud's arm to rouse him.

MARTHA   Come on!

The first-floor landing.

Several doors, fairly mean. A dirty kid covered in scabs is sitting on the stairs. A woman is doing her household washing at a tap which is apparently shared by the whole floor.

But one of the doors has been opened and Freud's mother, radiant with joy, is waiting for her son and his fiancée.

Freud and Martha almost run up the last few steps. Martha avoids the child sitting on the stairs and kisses her future mother-in-law affectionately.

Freud follows her. He does not kiss his mother: he takes her hand and kisses it. Then he raises his head and smiles at her.

FREUD   Mama ...

His attitude is utterly different from that which he adopted with Martha (ardour, jealousy, violence). He looks more like a suitor than a son. But a discreet, ceremonious suitor.

Between the two of them we sense a deep, intimate accord which is never expressed in words, barely by gestures.

His mother's smile is serious and concerned.

What's the matter? Is my father unwell?

MOTHER   No. Come in, Martha.

She steps aside. They enter a tiny hallway. She closes the door. They are all three in semi-darkness.

Sigmund, I'm telling you because Father won't do so: we're in a desperate plight.
    That cloth business ...

Freud's countenance hardens.

FREUD   **What about it?**

MOTHER   Your father finally decided to go into partnership with Gerstem.

FREUD   I've told him a hundred times ...

MOTHER, *with authority*   He had his reasons. Remember, Sigmund! *(As if reciting a proverb:)* What Father does is always well done.

A pause.

The wool industry is in crisis. They've filed their petition for bankruptcy.

FREUD   When?

His mother speaks with true nobility. She does not for one instant give the impression that she is trying to make excuses for his father. Authoritarian and firm, she seems on the contrary to think that a father never has any need of excuses in his children's eyes.

MOTHER   Last month.

FREUD   Why wasn't I told?

MOTHER   We knew you were about to go away.

Freud is subdued.

FREUD   I understand. Father has never had any luck.

MOTHER   We have to meet our obligations now. We haven't found any money.

Freud takes his mother's hand and squeezes it.

FREUD, *warmly*   Don't be afraid, Mama. I'll do what's right.

(She is about to speak, he lays a finger on her lips.)

It's my father who should tell me the rest of it.

He goes almost roughly into the neighbouring room, where Jakob Freud (a man in his seventies, who appears still older; very gentle, his mental faculties somewhat enfeebled) ...
    (There would be some advantage in having his role played by the same actor, in order to bring out not the similarities but the differences.)
    He is sitting in an armchair.

JAKOB   My son!

He wants to get up, genuinely delighted to see his son. His son rushes to prevent him.

Kiss me!

Freud kisses him, awkward and constrained. The old man is as tender as a woman:

Hello, Martha. Hello, lucky Martha!

Martha comes to kiss him, smiling tenderly at him.

MARTHA   Why so lucky, would you say?

JAKOB   Because you'll have the best of husbands: Herr Privatdozent Freud. His poor father used to sell wool, but he's a man of learning.

Freud listens, stiff and gloomy. The old man babbles on; what is striking is his extreme gentleness, combined with an old man's deep sadness. Sigmund and Martha sit down beside him. Freud's mother remains standing.

Sit down, both of you.

Freud is stiff and silent. Very respectful. But patently his father's quite sincere admiration does not please him.

Listen to this, Martha.
     When my Sigmund was eight years old, I once came upon the Menuhin boy arguing with his father.

FREUD   You've told her the story already, Papa.

JAKOB   I've told you both the story. So you know what I said to him: 'There's more intelligence in one of my Sigmund's big toes than in my whole body, and yet he respects me as much as if I were the chief rabbi ...'

Freud waits for the end of the story, then asks gravely:

FREUD   Father ...

His mother halts at the back of the room and watches them, worriedly.

You're in trouble?

Jakob, to his wife, reproachfully:

JAKOB   He should have been allowed to leave in peace.

MOTHER   No. He's my son. If he doesn't share my worries, who will do so?

Beneath the demands of Freud's mother, we must sense a far stronger passion even than that which inspires his father's fond babbling.

FREUD   You have a settlement date.

His father is overcome, and does not reply. His mother replies in the clear, uncompromising tone of voice she has used since the outset.

MOTHER Monday.
FREUD How much?
MOTHER Two thousand guilders.

Freud pulls the little boxes of gold coins from his pocket.

MARTHA, *worried* But Sigmund, that's …
FATHER What is it?

Freud gives Martha a meaning look.

FREUD Nothing, Father. Nothing.

Martha turns to his mother.

MOTHER Martha? *(A pause.)* Is it what he's been given to live on in Paris?

Nod from Martha. Freud's father shrinks back in his chair, his face distraught.

Give us half what you've got. We'll get by.

FREUD I'll give you all of it. All of it.

He takes little stacks of gold coins from the boxes and places them on the table. Counting:

Five hundred. One thousand. Two thousand.
MARTHA But if they say …
MOTHER Let him do it. If he didn't give it all, he'd never forgive himself.
MARTHA, *in despair* It's the money for his journey.

Freud's mother makes no reply. Freud is piling up the gold coins on the table with a fanatical expression. Suddenly, his father bursts out sobbing.

JAKOB I'm worthless! Worthless! I couldn't earn my children's keep, and now my children are supporting me.

Protracted, senile sobbing. Freud is unwilling to look at his father, he remains glued to his chair (which he has turned to one side, in order to pile up the gold coins on the table), stiff and pale. He begins to speak, abruptly, improvising as he goes along, with a painfully false gaiety.

FREUD   But that doesn't bother me. That doesn't bother me at all.

He turns round slightly, as he speaks.

I shall give lessons in Paris. I've been assured of that: I shall have twice as much money as I need.

His father is still weeping. Freud stretches out his hand to lay it on his head (as one would with a weeping child), then withdraws it in sudden horror.
   A long silence. He has stiffened again. A hand is laid on his shoulder; he raises his head and sees his mother standing beside him, and smiling at him. A beautiful smile of calm and grateful love. He grows somewhat calmer and returns her smile. His father has calmed down. Martha bends over him.

MARTHA   Time for lunch, father.

She helps him up. Jakob gets us with difficulty. As he makes his way to the table, he asks his son, who steps out of his path;

JAKOB, *almost humbly*   You'll still be leaving tomorrow?
FREUD, *gaily*   Of course. Tomorrow morning at five past eight.

6

Same afternoon. Freud and Martha leave his parents' house. They walk along in silence. Freud has an irritable, tense expression. The street leads to a little, deserted square. They enter it. Martha, equally sombre, watches Freud with a worried expression.

FREUD, *in a sudden outburst*   You've won. I won't go.

Astonishment and anger on Martha's part.

MARTHA, *in a flat tone*   Who has won?
FREUD   The whole lot of you! You wanted me to stay here yourself, didn't you.

Martha does not reply, but we can sense that she is deeply wounded.

Very well, be happy: Meynert has asked me to take over his lectures. I'll accept. What do you say to that?

MARTHA, *very coldly*   Do as you please.

He takes another few steps, with difficulty, then slumps onto a bench. He is pale and breathing painfully. Martha joins him unhurriedly, torn between her own irritation and the anxiety which her fiancé's state inspires in her.

FREUD   It's the decree of Heaven. Finish. No tampering with the Tree of Knowl-
edge.
   Fine. I won't tamper with it. I'll be just anybody, like a goy. No biographers.
Not a single one. That's one advantage at least.

Suddenly worried:

I'll have to return the money to the University. Meynert will intercede for me. They'll give me extra time.

He catches hold of her wrist violently.

We'll have children, Martha, lots of children. But I'll never weep in front of them. Don't think I will. A father is the Law, he's Moses. *(Laughing.)* And if Moses weeps!

He pulls himself together.
   Cold and polite, he speaks confidently but does not believe in what he is saying.

You must excuse my father, Martha. He used to be strong and stern. This is what the Romans have made of him.

MARTHA, *outraged*   You've no need to excuse your father to me. He's a good man, I respect him and I shall be very lucky if you're like him.

Freud rises abruptly to his feet:

FREUD, *violently*   I shall never be like him, never! So much the worse for you, if it's him you prefer. (*He takes a fresh grip on himself.*) It's not my fault: I've had no youth. At the age of twenty-nine, I work twelve hours a day, I ought to be supporting my family and I pile up debts in order to live.

A pause.

You don't understand anything, you see: I *needed* to go there.

Martha, pale with anger, stands up in turn.

MARTHA, *angrily*   Well go then! Just go! You've got your ticket.
FREUD   Yes. I'm going to return it.
MARTHA, *still angry*   Why?
FREUD   How shall I keep alive? I don't have a penny left.
MARTHA   By hook or by crook.

Freud reflects for a moment, then makes his decision.

FREUD   You're right. I'll become a servant. Did you know that my sister used to be a general maid? Yes, Rosa. For two years. She used to send her wages to the family. The brother of a maid can be a footman.

He calms down somewhat. He draws closer to Martha as if to take her in his arms.

Martha, my love ...

Martha steps back, her eyes shine with anger.

MARTHA   Leave me alone! (*Laughing:*) And don't ever again come telling me how you prefer my little finger to the whole of Science.

He looks at her, sullen and greatly put out. She has regained her self-control.

(*Coldly:*) I have to go home. Don't come with me.

FREUD   Will you come to the station?

MARTHA   I don't know. I shall see.

She goes off without his attempting to detain her.

He remains alone, lost in his thoughts, then mechanically pulls a cigar-case from his pocket, takes out a cigar and lights it. From the first puff he is coughing.

He continues to smoke and cough, but pressing his left hand to his heart slumps onto the bench they have just left; he appears to be unwell, but smokes away furiously.

The entrance of a handsome apartment on the second floor of a rich-looking house.
Martha rings. A footman opens the door.

MARTHA   I should like to speak to Frau Breuer.

FOOTMAN   Good afternoon, Fräulein Bernays. I'm very sorry, Madam has gone out.

A silence.

MARTHA   Then please ask Dr Breuer if he can see me for five minutes.

FOOTMAN   The Doctor has gone out with Madam. They'll return this evening, after dinner.

Martha seems very put out by this contretemps.

MARTHA   After dinner! *(A pause.)* Very well. Please tell Frau Breuer that I'll call by during the evening.

Something is struggling to get out of the bin. Though we cannot distinguish what it is, we can divine a certain disturbing and repulsive swarming.

On the back seat, a stone tablet (like the tablet of the Law) is balanced. It slams suddenly down upon the lid of the dustbin and closes it again. Everything disappears. Darkness.

Abruptly, the room is lit up. Freud is lying on his bed, in a frock-coat. He gets up, picks up his top-hat, puts a flower in his button-hole and takes his cane.

In this garb, he resembles the elegant Professor Meynert. But although he is suddenly affected by the same limp, there is no doubt that it is Freud in person.

He crosses the room, opens the door which leads directly onto the Ring and goes out. The Ring is totally deserted, under a harsh, frozen light. A dustbin at every door. When Freud passes in front of one of these, the lid is raised very slightly then falls back with a muffled sound. In one, a rat shows its snout.

On the Ring, a man is walking alone, in military dress, he is coming towards Freud, their paths are about to cross.

Crowd noises off.

STENTORIAN VOICE, *drowning the others*   Here comes the Emperor. Father of the Fatherland.

Our Eternal Father.

VOICES, *more numerous, but confused and not so loud*   The Eternal feminine.

The Eternal couple.

Freud turns round abruptly.

FREUD, *shouting*   No!

A Carthaginian soldier who looks like Hannibal (as we saw him in the engraving) is taking careful aim at the Emperor with his crossbow. He looks brutal and cruel.

The arrow is loosed.

(More loudly:) No!

Everything is plunged into darkness.

Freud lights his candle. He is in his nightshirt, and has a worried expression. He gets out of bed, rummages in his suitcase, takes out a white notebook and a pencil, looks at his watch and begins to write:

'Night of 15/16 September 85.

Dream about the Emperor Franz-Josef.'

Six o'clock in the morning. Still dark. The platform of a large railway-station, empty.

In the distance, on another platform, passengers are waiting for a train. It arrives, all lit up; they climb into the carriages; a whistle blows, the train shudders and moves away.

In the meantime, on the first platform, a railwayman goes by pushing a trolley. He comes upon a pale, tense man. It is Freud, sitting on a bench between two bulging suitcases. Freud is smoking a cigar and coughing.

RAILWAYMAN   What are you doing here?
FREUD   I'm waiting for the train.

The railwayman points at the empty tracks and the station clock, which shows six o'clock.

RAILWAYMAN   I'd advise you to stretch out. You've got quite a wait.

Freud coughs.

Aha! the morning cigar? That can kill a man.
FREUD, *ironical and sombre*   Of course! That's what makes it taste so good.

The railwayman goes off. Freud remains alone. He seems unwell. He pulls out his watch, lays it on his knees and takes his pulse. He replaces it in his waistcoat pocket and is about to put his cigar to his lips. A hand is laid on his sleeve, he turns round with a start; it is Martha.

He stands up, throws away his cigar and kisses his fiancée ardently.

FREUD   Martha!

She struggles laughingly.

What a bit of luck!
MARTHA   I don't want to! You smell of cigars.
FREUD   Who gave you this wonderful idea?
MARTHA   What idea?
FREUD   Of coming so early.
MARTHA   You did. The longer the journey, the earlier you arrive for it.
FREUD   What are you complaining for? Before, when I went away anywhere I used to be afraid of dying; now I'm afraid of missing the train. That's progress of a kind.

He sits down again abruptly, very pale. He tries to laugh.

MARTHA, *very worried*   What's the matter with you?

44

FREUD, *laughing painfully*   Well, I still am just a tiny bit afraid of dying.

Martha has sat down beside him. She looks at him.

MARTHA   You were taking your pulse just now.

He starts to deny it.

I saw you. Why?

Freud does not answer. He looks oppressed; we sense that he cannot speak.

Is it your heart?

He nods: yes, it is his heart.
  She stands up. He restrains her with his hand.

FREUD, *painfully*   Where are you going?
MARTHA   There must be a doctor on duty in the station.

He still restrains her.

You're not leaving unless you see a doctor.
FREUD, *harshly*   Martha, don't torture me!

She looks at him in surprise.

The doctors can't do anything to help.

She tries to speak.

Hush!
  My heart is sound. The trouble lies elsewhere.
MARTHA, *furious*   Yes. There!

She touches Freud's forehead with her finger. He smiles, somewhat relieved.

FREUD, *smiling*   Precisely. There.

He obliges her to sit down beside him again and puts his arm round her.

Wait.
  Let me hold you close.
  You're good for me, Martha.
  So good.

There's no one but you who can cure me.

Like a promise:

You will cure me!

A moment later. Dawn has broken. A suburban train has just come in on another line. The passengers alight, in bustling haste. The clock stands at seven.
    Freud seems less oppressed. He is still holding Martha in his embrace. Not far away, a cleaner is filling a dustbin of the same kind as the one in the dream.

FREUD   About yesterday ... I was wanting to say ... forgive me.
MARTHA, *tenderly*   I forgave you ages ago.

He kisses her.

FREUD   Listen to me. I'm not crazy. I feel ... out of the ordinary.

The cleaner puts the lid back on the dustbin and carries it off. Freud points at himself.

A lid. And beneath it, Heaven knows ...
MARTHA, *teasingly*   Demons.
FREUD   Perhaps. Forces, in any case. If the lid were raised ... Yesterday, I was no longer in control of myself: I'd have blown up the whole world, you and me included.
MARTHA, *growing serious and worried afresh*   Why are you like that?
FREUD   I don't know. Poverty, perhaps.

He caresses her cheek tenderly. With a touch of irony.

Or an excessively long engagement. When I return, we'll be married and everything will change.

She looks as if she hopes for such a change, but does not much believe in it. Freud, forcefully:

I swear to you everything will change.

A little later.
    The train is made up as they watch. He climbs with her into a third-class carriage, carrying his heavy suitcases, and places one on the luggage-rack, the other on his seat.

FREUD   Are you angry with me for leaving?
MARTHA   No, not if you love me.
FREUD   I love you more than anything.

Seven forty-five.

She takes him by the hand and obliges him to get down.

What are you doing? We have another twenty minutes.

She looks at the people arriving and beginning to fill the carriages. Turns towards the platform barrier.

I tell you I love you and you look at people's faces.

She still looks. He clasps her to him, but she turns her head to search the crowd.

MARTHA   I'm meeting someone.
FREUD   Martha!
MARTHA   Why not? You're leaving me all alone.
FREUD   You mustn't joke …

She frees herself and signals to a tall man, very discreetly elegant, fortyish — chestnut hair and beard, with a shrewd, sceptical and above all very kindly expression — who is searching each carriage in turn.

Breuer!

He runs to Breuer with evident joy. But, as ever, he stiffens when he arrives near him. He says, as if in spite of himself:

FREUD   You took the trouble to come and bid me farewell!

At the sight of Freud, Breuer's expression lightens; he squeezes his hand really effusively. Then, with amiable but genuine authority:

BREUER   Firstly for this.

He is holding a packet and presents it to him.

And also for …

Freud steps back and his face darkens.

FREUD, *with a kind of fear*   No!
BREUER   Listen to me, Freud: I know you're leaving without a penny. You're young and you'll easily find some job, but if you have to work ten hours a day to earn your living, you'll lose the whole advantage of the scholarship and Charcot's lectures.
FREUD   I already owe you a great deal.

BREUER, *smiling*   You'll owe me 2,000 guilders more, then.

Freud hesitates.

Freud, you're leaving for Paris on an official mission. It's your duty to accept this money. Accept it as if it came from an elder brother or a father. You'll give it back to me when you can.

At the words 'as if it came from a father', Freud's face brightens. He relaxes.

FREUD   I accept.

He looks at Breuer in silence, but with deep affection. Abruptly, he laughs.

Do you know that I'm leaving under Meynert's curse?
    The prodigal son! The accursed child!

Squeezing Breuer's hand:

Well, the son is changing fathers.

With suppressed emotion:

Thank you.

BREUER, *embarrassed, very quickly*   I must leave you. Martha, Mathilde would love to see you. Come whenever you like.

Freud follows him with his eyes as he moves away. With a kind of calm, respectful tenderness. Then he turns back to rejoin Martha.

FREUD   How did he know?

Martha smiles.

You told him?

She laughs in his face. For a moment he seems on the point of growing angry, but then he smiles.

So much the better. You really don't like the idea of this trip, yet it's you who's enabling me to take it. I love you.

He casts one last glance after Breuer and his face darkens slightly.

All the same, I should have been happier if he'd come just to shake my hand.

Whistle.

VOICE OFF   Munich, Basle, Paris, all aboard.

Freud turns towards Martha.

FREUD   You will think of me.
MARTHA   All the time. And you?
FREUD   All the time.
MARTHA   During Charcot's lectures? Liar!
FREUD   Even during Charcot's lectures. You won't go skating?
MARTHA, *slightly annoyed*   Of course not.
FREUD   Do you swear?
MARTHA   You're being a bore.

Fresh whistle-blasts.

VOICE OFF   All aboard! All aboard!

The train begins to move.

FREUD   If you don't swear, the train will leave without me.
MARTHA, *seeing the train moving*   Run! Run! Of course I'll swear. Go on, you're going to miss it.

Freud runs alongside the train, which is picking up speed, and climbs into a compartment at the rear.

10

Paris – January 1886.

A dingy room in a hotel. Freud, ready to go out, puts a manuscript back inside one of his suitcases and locks both suitcases with two little keys from a bunch which he then puts back into his pocket. He pulls a cigar from his case, cuts it with his teeth, lights it, goes out and locks the door of his room with a key which he slips into his pocket.

A landlady at the hotel reception desk. She looks at Freud with disfavour. An attendant close by her, sweeping.

LANDLADY   Monsieur Freud!

Freud, who has taken a few steps towards the door, turns round.

Would you be so kind as to leave your key on the board when you go out.

Freud hesitates.

This is at least the tenth time I've had to ask you.

Freud reluctantly extracts the key from his pocket and reluctantly hangs it on the board. He goes out. The landlady follows him with her eyes.
To the attendant:

LANDLADY   What is there in his suitcases?
ATTENDANT, *in disgust*   I've no idea: he padlocks them.

The landlady looks with revulsion at Freud's back as he leaves the hotel.

LANDLADY   Not got a penny, yet he's as suspicious as if he had a fortune.

A Paris street. In the background, the hospital. We can read from afar, in big golden letters: Hôpital de la Salpêtrière.
Young men, students and doctors, are hurrying through the snow. On several houses — to left and right — we can read the word 'Hotel'. The hotels are seedy.
At the entrance of each, standing back somewhat to shelter from the snow, there are women, poorly dressed but in the classic, garish style of prostitutes. Prematurely aged faces, for the most part fairly ugly, but outrageously painted. They smile at the students and signal to them, they call out to them.
The latter, who do not appear in the least put out, joke with them as they pass and laughingly clasp them round the waist, but without stopping. One of them, however, does allow himself to be

enticed: approached by a girl somewhat less ugly than the others, he hesitates then goes into the hotel with her.

Freud appears, an unlit cigar between his lips. He looks particularly chilly under his light over-coat. Instead of taking the direct route — the street we have just seen — he sets off down the next street, which visibly leads in a quite different direction.

No sooner has he taken a few steps down this street (a street of apartment-houses and shops, without a single one of those dubious hotels) than a young Englishman, warmly and comfortably dressed, emerges suddenly from a porch beneath which he has been sheltering and lays a hand on Freud's shoulder.

Freud starts, as if thinking himself the object of a prostitute's advances. He smiles when he recognizes the Englishman, who offers him his hand with an expansive gesture.

WILKIE   Dr Freud, good morning. I was waiting for you. Allow me to assure you of my esteem.

FREUD   Good morning, Mr Wilkie.

They continue on their way. Freud replies to Wilkie's remarks ironically. It is obvious that he finds him ridiculous, but bears him no ill will. However, he remains distant and impassive.

FREUD   I am happy to have your esteem, but I'm not sure that I deserve it.

WILKIE   You deserve it, Dr Freud, because you're the only one who makes the same detour I do.

You don't like prostitutes, Doctor?

FREUD, *distant but sincere*   Not especially.

WILKIE   My father always told me: lust is Hell. Do you agree?

FREUD, *smiling*   Yes, if you place Hell in this world.

WILKIE   In this world and in the next. Heaven is our destination.

They walk in silence for a moment. Freud is cold; he shivers. Wilkie notices it.

WILKIE   Dr Freud, you're cold.

Freud starts and looks distantly at Wilkie.

FREUD   No, Sir.

Wilkie indicates their surroundings with an expansive gesture.

WILKIE, *reprovingly*   It's snowing.

Freud remains impassive and almost imperceptibly ironical.

FREUD   Yes.

WILKIE, *confidingly*   I hate Paris.

FREUD   Oh!

More marked irony.

After a moment (they are walking side by side), Wilkie pulls his gloved hands from the pockets of his fur-lined pelisse and claps them together in annoyance. Freud looks at him out of the corner of his eye.

FREUD, *imitating Wilkie's tone*   Mr Wilkie, you're angry.
WILKIE   Yes, Sir.
    I'm angry because I shall be wasting my time.
    This morning, Professor Charcot is going to hypnotize some hysterical patients.
    Well, I don't believe in either hysteria or hypnotism.
FREUD   In that case, why attend his lectures?
WILKIE   Dr Freud, that's what I'm wondering.

They have crossed the hospital courtyard. They enter a large building. The hallway — dark and gloomy.

I'm the son of a clergyman and I want to heal men for the love of God.

Groups of students. Freud and Wilkie stop to stamp their feet and shake out their coats.

WILKIE, *after a silence, abruptly*   I've seen hypnotists in Manchester: it was all faked.

Freud takes the unlit cigar from his lips and throws it away.

FREUD   Everything is always faked, Mr Wilkie.

Wilkie looks at him in turn with an expression of mistrust. A friend of Wilkie's tugs at his arm. He turns round.

WILKIE, *to his friend*   Daugin!

Freud takes the opportunity to slip away. He wears an ironical, satisfied and almost gay expression. Mechanically he follows a corridor and, his thoughts visibly elsewhere, pulls a cigar from his case and lights it pensively. At once he begins to cough. The more he puffs at his cigar, the more he coughs and grows red in the face.

A little tubby, balding man comes out of a room leading off the corridor (a sign: Dr Charcot's Office), studies him amusedly and gives him a little tap on the sleeve.

CHARCOT   There's no smoking here, Sir.

Freud starts as he recognizes Charcot.

FREUD, *coughing*   Oh! I beg your pardon.

Charcot looks at him with a smile.

CHARCOT   You cough like a soul in damnation! How many cigars a day?

Freud is open and confiding.

FREUD   I ... *(Embarrassed:)* Twenty-five.

He does not know what to do with his cigar.

CHARCOT   Wretched man! *(A pause.)* Why?
FREUD   I don't know. It's an urge that grabs me.
CHARCOT   That grabs you by the throat. Was it you who wrote asking me for an interview?
FREUD   Yes, it was.

Stiff. Clicking his heels.

Dr Sigmund Freud.

Pointing to the office he has just left:

CHARCOT   Come and see me at the end of my lesson.

He moves away. Freud sees him enter a lecture-room which leads off the same corridor a little further along.

Freud looks at his cigar with an undecided expression. He makes a move to throw it away, then changes his mind, stubs it out against a wall and puts it back into his cigar-case.

He in turn enters the lecture-room (which is exactly like the one in the famous painting 'Charcot at the Salpêtrière').

11

Everyone is standing.

Large number of students. Charcot is standing too. A table carrying two bottles. Two chairs and a trestle bed against the big rear windows.

Freud positions himself in the first row of onlookers. Wilkie and his companion Daugin enter in turn and take their places beside him.

Charcot walks around the hall as he speaks. Very sure of himself, very much at his ease and very much the showman.

CHARCOT   Last Tuesday I talked to you about the classic symptoms of hysteria: paralyses or, to use a word I prefer, contractures, hemi-anaesthesias, minor and major attacks, etc. etc. We can go no further in this domain without having recourse to an investigative procedure which, though very ancient, has only recently begun to be used in the positive sciences. I am speaking of hypnosis. Experiment shows, in fact, that hysterical patients are particularly vulnerable to suggestion and that we can easily put them into a hypnotic trance.

Interns and orderlies bring in two patients.

One is a young woman suffering from a contracture of the right arm (twisted up tightly against her chest), the other, an old woman resembling the old blind woman in Vienna, walks painfully supporting herself on crutches (hysterical paralysis of the left leg).

Both seem intimidated and wretched. He points to them with a grand gesture (throughout the scene which follows, he resembles a conjurer) as they approach him.

CHARCOT   Here we have two splendid cases.
Jeanne and Paulette.

He smiles at the two women.
An ogre's smile.

Lie down, Jeanne.

Two of his assistants help the old woman to lie down on the trestle bed.

Sit down, Paulette.

The young woman sits down on one of the two chairs, which an assistant has just shifted to the middle of the room.

Charcot first goes over to Paulette.

CHARCOT, *mock paternal*   Well, Paulette, what's the trouble?

PAULETTE   It's my arm.

She displays it.

CHARCOT   Close your eyes.

*She closes them. He gives a conspiratorial wink to his audience and violently pinches the contract-
ured arm.*

What did I do to you?
PAULETTE, *her eyes closed*   Nothing.

Charcot: fresh wink.

CHARCOT   Contracture of the right arm with hemi-anaesthesia.
        Classic. Classic.

He goes over to Jeanne.

How about you, old lady?

He bends over the trestle bed.

JEANNE, *somewhat tearfully*   With me, it's my leg.
CHARCOT   Since when?
JEANNE   1880.
CHARCOT, *busy indifference*   Six years. Fine! Fine!
        Well, we'll take a look at that.

*He tucks up the patient's shift to mid-thigh. Jeanne's legs are bare. Her left leg is like that of the old
hysterical woman in Vienna.*
        Charcot palpates it and gives his lesson.

Strong contracture of the adductor muscles of the thigh.
        Rigid joints. The lower limb resembles an inflexible bar.

He raises the left leg by the foot. The pelvis is raised along with it.

Look.

He lowers the leg again.

CHARCOT   A hysterical symptom almost never encountered in organic paralyses.

He sharply straightens the toes of the left foot. The whole left leg begins to vibrate. He lets go of Jeanne's foot. The vibration continues long after the limbs have resumed their former position.

(Laughing:) Classic! Classic!

He looks at the audience. Freud is fascinated. The Englishman wears an expression of deep disgust. Daugin is entertained: he thinks himself at the theatre. The onlookers, in one way or another, all react in a lively manner.

My collaborators are going to place these two women in a hypnotic trance.

Two doctors move towards Jeanne, two others towards Paulette. In each group, one of the assistants holds behind his back a lighted paraffin lamp, resembling a lantern. But the front face of these lanterns is entirely opaque, except for a tiny round hole which allows the light to filter through.

A DOCTOR, *to Jeanne*   Look. It's shining. Look closely.

The doctor bends over Jeanne.
   A doctor, in front of Paulette, discloses the lantern.

OTHER DOCTOR   Paulette, keep your eyes on the shining dot.

Paulette gives a start.

Come along!

Paulette looks at it docilely.
   Charcot walks up and down, his hands behind his back.

You're going to sleep!

Charcot installs himself in front of the tall Englishman (Wilkie) and looks him up and down.
   Wilkie, looking him up and down in disenchanted response, wears an expression of disgust.

Sleep! Sleep!

Paulette, docile, her eyes wide open, stiffening slightly, falls asleep.

VOICE OFF OF THE DOCTOR *who is speaking to Jeanne*   You're sleeping, Jeanne. You're sleeping.

Freud observes the two patients intently. His eyes travel from one to the other, as if he were watching a game of tennis.
   Charcot turns his back on Wilkie, goes over to Paulette and peers closely into her eyes.

CHARCOT   This one is asleep.
   (*To the assistants surrounding the other patient:*) How about the other one?

A moment's pause. Then the assistants bending over Jeanne straighten up.

AN ASSISTANT   That's it.

Charcot resumes his progress.

CHARCOT, *professorial tone, as if he were speaking from a rostrum*
   The state in which our two patients now find themselves could be defined as induced somnambulism.
   They are vulnerable to every kind of suggestion.
   Watch carefully!

He smilingly goes up to Paulette, very much the 'illusionist'. He positions himself behind her and calls out:

Paulette! Paulette!

She shivers.

PAULETTE   Eh?
CHARCOT   It's cured. It's cured, Paulette.
   (*Very much the showman. Feigning amazement:*)
   Your right arm! ... It's moving! ... Try to move it.

Paulette moves her left arm.

Not that one. The other one.

Paulette looks at her left hand which is moving. Gradually her right arm relaxes: she observes the movements of her left hand and imitates them with her right hand.
   (*During this scene:*)

VOICES OFF OF THE ASSISTANTS *taking care of Jeanne*   Jeanne!
   Jeanne! You're cured ...
   You're cured.
   You're cured.

Gradually the movements of the right hand becomes more supple.
   At last both arms are moving simultaneously.
   Charcot leaves Paulette and goes over to see Jeanne, still stretched out on her bed.

CHARCOT, *masterful, his play-acting making him almost comical*   Stand up and walk.

Jeanne sits up in bed with an effort, then helped by the assistants stands and holds herself upright without crutches.

Walk! Walk!

Jeanne totters towards the empty chair next to Paulette, and collapses into it rather than sits down.
    Paulette continues, with both hands, to make strange movements resembling magical conjurations.

First effect of suggestion: suppression of the hysterical symptoms. It goes without saying that hypnotism is inoperative in cases of organic paralysis.

Pointing at the two patients:

Second effect: through suggestion, we induce the patients to reproduce their *grande crise.*

He goes over to Jeanne.

Jeanne! ... Jeanne!

Shot of Jeanne, who seems to listen without seeing.

ASSISTANT'S VOICE OFF   Paulette! ... Paulette!

Charcot bends over Jeanne and whispers into her ear.

CHARCOT	Poor Jeanne! You're going to have your attack.
VOICE OFF	Your fit, Paulette, your fit.
CHARCOT	Jeanne! Watch out! Take care, your fit's coming. Take care!

Jeanne stands up and begins to walk. With clumsy violence she mimes dread, refusal, anger.

| *(With a touch of cynicism:)*   That makes one. |
| VOICE OFF, *in a murmur*   Paulette! Poor Paulette! |

Charcot follows old Jeanne, who is turning round and round; very much the showman, he imitates exaggeratedly her most meaningful attitudes.

This one won't say much.
    Emotive mimicry — fear — irritation — refusal.

Imitation.

(Laughter off from Paulette.)

At this moment, a burst of female laughter is heard.
This laughter, initially short and jerky, swells and becomes uncontrollable and almost painful.
Charcot's face lights up.

And that makes two!

Crossing the room, he abandons Jeanne who is beginning to stamp her feet and wave her arms about and returns to Paulette.

PAULETTE, *laughing as if being tickled*   Oh, no, Monsieur Paul. No, no! Don't do that!
Ha! Ha! I'm very ticklish.

She twists about as if being tickled.

No, Robert! You shan't leave me alone with your friend again.

Charcot seems indifferent and annoyed.

CHARCOT   The content of the delirium is of no importance.

Freud — who has been listening raptly — starts at these words and frowns.
Charcot, attentive to his audience, does not fail to notice this resistance.
It is to Freud that he declares:

The proof is that the course of her thoughts can be altered at will.

He goes over to the table, takes a bottle of Eau de Cologne, uncorks it, inhales the fragrance with satisfaction.
Rapturously:

Eau de Cologne.

With a rapid, graceful gesture he sprinkles a few drops upon Wilkie, who sniffs it with an expression of disgust. then pirouettes over to Paulette who is doubled up with laughter, just avoiding the old woman who is still revolving within the circle of onlookers and waving her arms about, miming a kind of dance.
He holds the uncorked bottle beneath the patient's nose. Paulette stops laughing and begins to simper:

PAULETTE   You've got a garden filled with fragrance. Every morning, riding in the park. My father on his mare, I on my pony. The wisteria was delightful.

As she speaks, Charcot has given a signal.
An assistant brings him the other bottle and uncorks it.
Charcot smells it.

CHARCOT   Carbon Disulphide.

Amused wink to the audience.
He abruptly switches bottles and holds the second one beneath Paulette's nostrils, handing the flask of Eau de Cologne to his assistant who takes it away.

PAULETTE, *in disgust*   Revolting! I tell you they're rotten. Like everything Madame touches. They're dead rats. I've promised my father not to kill myself.

Charcot gives a signal. An assistant takes some red spectacles from a case, shows them to the on-lookers and places them on Paulette's nose. She starts to yell.

PAULETTE   My father isn't red! The child couldn't live. He bled, he's bleeding, he's bleeding. My hands corrupted him.

The assistant deftly removes the spectacles and Charcot withdraws the bottle of carbon disulphide, then goes and puts it down on the table.
But Paulette is already twisting about on her chair, with spasmodic movements of her arms and hands to ward off some vision.
Charcot watches her, leaning on the table.
Jeanne passes in front of him, turning circles but calm.
Charcot pays her no attention: he watches Paulette, as coldly intent as a scientist in a laboratory.

CHARCOT   Jeanne is reacting badly this morning. But look at Paulette, Gentlemen. We shall have our *grande crise*.

Paulette collapses onto the floor.
She begins to scream, flailing her arms and legs in every direction.
She knocks over two chairs. Two assistants are about to rush forward to prevent her from hurting herself.
Charcot checks them with a gesture.

CHARCOT   Let her be. (*To the onlookers:*) She won't hurt herself. Hysterical patients very rarely hurt themselves during their attacks; that is what allows us to distinguish the hysterical attack at a glance from an epileptic fit.

He goes up to Paulette and presses his hands to her forehead.

(*Persuasive voice:*) The attack's over, Paulette. Over. Over.

Paulette gradually calms down.

(Same voice:) Stand up!
   Pick up the chairs!

Paulette obeys.

Sit down.

She sits.
   Charcot catches Jeanne as she passes and leads her to the empty chair.

Jeanne! Sit down. Come along! Sit down.

Jeanne sits.
   The two patients are side by side, as at the start of the scene. Eyes open and staring. They look exhausted.
   Charcot comes back towards the audience.

Monsieur Daugin! In a first phase, hypnotic suggestion has caused the hysterical contractures to disappear. What was wrong with Paulette?

DAUGIN   Her right arm.

Daugin twists up his arm to mime the contracture.

CHARCOT   How about Jeanne?
DAUGIN   Her left leg.

He points at his own leg with the index finger of his left hand.

CHARCOT   Watch carefully.

He taps Jeanne lightly on the right shoulder. She quivers; her right arm twists back and contracts.

That slight traumatism is enough, with a nervous subject specially predisposed, to produce throughout the whole limb a feeling of numbness and the first signs of paralysis.

He goes over to Paulette and taps her on the thigh and on the calf.

Through the mechanism of auto-suggestion, this embryonic paralysis has become a real paralysis.
   The phenomenon occurs in the site of psychic operations, in the cerebral cortex.

The idea of movement is already movement on the way to being carried out; the idea of absence of movement, if it is powerful, is already effective motor paralysis.

You may call this paralysis ideal, or psychic: whatever you will, but not imaginary.

With the air of a satisfied conjurer:

Paulette and Jeanne have exchanged their contractures.

Daugin, who for some time has been following the experiment open-mouthed, rapt as a spectator in a music-hall, involuntarily claps his hands.

He realizes that he is applauding, blushes, thrusts his hands into his pockets. But Charcot has already glared at him.

CHARCOT, *with haughty conviction — very noble*   Where do you think you are, Sir? This is a place of learning.

To his assistants:

Take the patients away.

Jeanne stands up without difficulty; crutches are brought for Paulette. She is helped up and walks supported on them.

As the two patients cross the room:

The production of psychic paralyses through hypnotism is the result of a dream that we have provoked. An intense dream, which in a sense is realized.

That which the hypnotist has done, he can undo. My assistants are going to wake our two friends up. They will thus free them from the ailments that I have inflicted upon them. Unfortunately, they will rediscover those with which they afflict themselves: Paulette will lose the use of her right arm at the very moment when she recovers the use of her left leg. For Jeanne, the reverse will be true.

Hypnotism can reproduce symptoms but not cure them.

To the audience:

CHARCOT   The lesson is over. Any questions?

Gazes round.

Freud appears enthusiastic — like most of those present; the Englishman Wilkie retains his expression of disgust. Piqued, Charcot goes up to him.

... You appear nauseated, Sir.

Wilkie assumes a stubborn air.

WILKIE   They are liars.

Gradually he works himself up.

… Shammers!
… Actresses!
… It's all fake.

Charcot: he points to one of the empty chairs.

CHARCOT   Would you like a control experiment? . . . Dr Freud, will you be so kind as to sit down on one of these chairs?

Freud, in spite of his respect, recoils fiercely.

FREUD, *forcefully*   No.

Charcot comes up to Freud and looks him straight in the eyes.

CHARCOT   Very well. *(A pause.)* Anyway it probably wouldn't be possible to put you to sleep. *(To everybody:)* You mustn't think that everyone is vulnerable to suggestion. *(Abruptly, descending upon Wilkie like a thunderbolt:)* You, Sir, you're suggestible.

WILKIE, *with an odd weakness*   No.
CHARCOT   Go and sit down.

Wilkie appears terrified and fascinated.
Charcot takes him by the hand, seats him on a chair and moves away from him.

Berryer!

One of his assistants goes over to Wilkie; he carries a lighted lantern (front side opaque, shining dot).

BERRYER, *to Wilkie*   Look at the shining dot.
WILKIE   No.

He immediately looks at it.

BERRYER, *in a monotone*   Sleep. You are sleeping.

Berryer, astonished, to Charcot.

He's out! Before he knew what hit him! Like a lamb!

A tense silence in the audience. Freud is so absorbed that he has mechanically taken out his cigar-case.

Charcot hands the Eau de Cologne to Berryer, who holds the flask beneath the Englishman's nostrils.

WILKIE   Mama!

Berryer removes the flask.
Everybody bursts out laughing, even Charcot. All except Freud. Charcot goes up to Wilkie.

CHARCOT, *pretending to reflect*   How are we to convince him? *(Pretending to discover what he was looking for:)* I shall give him an order that he'll have to obey once he wakes up.

He goes up to Wilkie.

Do you smoke?

Wilkie answers without seeing him.

WILKIE   Never.
CHARCOT   Why?
WILKIE, *almost mechanically*   Tobacco is a foul plant and the smoke makes me cough.
CHARCOT   When you have woken up, you'll go straight to Dr Freud, ask him for a cigar and light up. Berryer!

He moves away and goes over to Freud while Berryer is rousing Wilkie. Charcot laughs in Freud's face, the latter returns an embarrassed smile.

(To Freud:) One cigar less! At least that's one advantage for your bronchial tubes.

Wilkie, awake again, alone, seated on the chair, looks at the audience in amazement.
He stands up and looks round for Freud, then makes his way towards him without hesitation.

WILKIE   Dr Freud.

He is wearing an expression of surprise. He wipes his forehead with his hand, looking distraught.

I should like a cigar.
FREUD   Would you smoke here? In front of Professor Charcot?

Wilkie turns round in astonishment, looks at Charcot, then turns back to Freud.

WILKIE, *with an expression of simultaneous astonishment and obstinacy*   Yes.

Charcot gives a nod of acquiescence.

CHARCOT, *gaily*   I give you leave, Sir.

In astonishment the Englishman takes the cigar which Freud offers him. He is on the point of putting the wrong end of it to his lips. Freud takes it back from him, lights it and hands it to him. The Englishman smokes and coughs, like Freud a moment earlier. Charcot comes up.

CHARCOT   You're smoking? But it makes you cough. Unhappy wretch. (*In a very kindly manner, as to Freud a while before:*) Why are you smoking?
WILKIE   I don't know. It was an urge that grabbed me.
CHARCOT, *as to Freud*   Which grabbed you by the throat?

The Englishman coughs.
Charcot looks smilingly at Freud.
He turns towards Wilkie.

(*To Wilkie:*) Throw that cigar away.
WILKIE   It's beyond my power.
CHARCOT   Throw that cigar away, Sir. You were put to sleep and I ordered you to smoke.

Wilkie throws the cigar away, horrified and angry.
The whole audience bursts out laughing as he grinds it underfoot.

WILKIE   Ugh!

Charcot laughs in turn.
Expansive conjurer's gesture presenting Wilkie to the company.

CHARCOT   And there you are!

12

A corridor.

Freud is pacing up and down, in front of the closed door of Charcot's study.
  Students pass in front of him, laughing.
  Wilkie passes by, then turns back.
  He proffers his hand, waits solemnly.

WILKIE, *solemn and determined*   Dr Freud, farewell!

Freud, lost in his thoughts, listens to him absent-mindedly and gives him a rapid handshake.

FREUD   See you tomorrow.
WILKIE   No, I'm bidding you farewell! I'm going home to Manchester.

As before without raising his head:

FREUD, *with sudden interest*   Why?
WILKIE   I'm a clergyman's son and I want to look after people.
FREUD   And so?
WILKIE   If hypnotism's a sham, I'm losing time. If it's the devil's work, I'm losing my soul.

He seeks to draw Freud outside.

Are you staying here? Come along!
FREUD   I'm waiting for Professor Charcot.
WILKIE   Watch out for the Devil!

He goes off with an expression of indignation that masks his terror.
  Freud watches him thoughtfully; absent-mindedly he takes his cigar-case from his pocket.
  Finally he opens it and pulls out a cigar.
  He is just putting it to his lips when an orderly passing by taps him on the sleeve (as Charcot did).

ORDERLY, *on his way past*   No smoking!

Freud starts.

FREUD   Oh! I'm sorry.

He looks at the cigar in surprise, almost with stupefaction.

Then his eyes crinkle and a faint smile begins to curl his lips, as if the sight of the cigar between his fingers suggested something to him.

Charcot has meanwhile opened the door of his study and is watching him.

In Charcot's Study.

The latter is seated in a comfortable armchair.

He is listening to Freud, enthusiastic yet always restrained in expression — and somewhat stiff — who has sat down without taking off his overcoat, bolt upright on his chair.

FREUD   I had the greatest hopes of you, Sir, and I've not been disappointed. You have revealed a whole world to me.

    I ... I could work, now.

Freud looks confident and far younger than in the preceding scenes.

Charcot listens to him with a smile, flattered but sceptical.

CHARCOT   A world! Which world!

FREUD   Wilkie thought he had an urge to smoke. Yet that wasn't true: he took a cigar because you commanded him to. And how about me? Do I know why I smoke? I think I have an urge to do so. But what lies hidden behind that urge? ... What secret motive? What command? What lies behind *all* urges and *all* fears? An invisible world. Forces.

Charcot, initially benevolent and protective, gradually takes alarm.

CHARCOT, *alarmed*   Not so fast, Sir, not so fast.

FREUD   But it's obvious, Sir, it's obvious. You had the brilliant idea — if I may make so bold — of reproducing the symptoms of hysteria through suggestion. That proves that patients produce them by auto-suggestion, under the sway of memories, ideas and feelings that they've forgotten or of which they've never been aware.

CHARCOT   I know nothing about all that. No experiment allows us to make such an assertion.

For once Freud gives way to his enthusiasm, he stands and paces up and down.

Charcot watches him in astonishment and with some annoyance.

FREUD   Yes we do, Sir. Your experiment this morning.

    Our conscious motives are not the true ones. I arrive at the station two hours early. I claim that I'm afraid of missing the train, but that's false. There's something else. A deeper fear, which I cannot identify. Or that I don't want to identify ...

Abruptly he becomes aware of his agitation, looks hesitantly at Charcot. He is afraid. His face loses all expression; he resumes his hard, sombre air.
    A silence.

Forgive me.

He goes and sits on his chair, facing the astounded Charcot.
    Very polite, but wholly immured in himself, having lost all contact with Charcot.
FREUD   I'd come to ask your permission to translate your works into the German language.

[13]

Vienna – October 1886.

At the Freuds' home. *A few days after the wedding. There is still daylight, but evening is coming on.*

Quite a large dining-room. Two windows. A few modest pieces of furniture that seem somewhat lost in the huge room.

On the table, silver and glassware: Martha is counting the items (knives, forks, plates, glasses: wedding-presents mostly) and then putting them away in the drawers of a sideboard or in cupboards.

(Hammer-blows off.)

Freud's voice off seems to come from the heavens.

FREUD'S VOICE OFF   I don't believe he understood the meaning of his experiment himself. Since Wilkie obeyed him *after* waking up, it must be possible to cure by hypnotism.

This follows on quite naturally from the interview which took place a few months earlier and which concludes the preceding scene.

Martha, unconvinced and very busy, is transporting a pile of plates.

FREUD   Do you hear me?
MARTHA   Yes.
FREUD, *imperiously*   Martha!

She raises her eyes and Freud comes into her view, standing on a stepladder, a picture in one hand, a hammer and nails in the other. He is getting ready to hang a glass-mounted print on the wall: it is the one representing Hannibal's Oath. He looks young and gay, full of life and strength. Martha teases him. She has blossomed; happiness suits her.

(Smilingly reproachful:) Did you take an apartment to put your husband in, or a husband to put in your apartment? Listen to me!

He drops the hammer on the wooden floor.

MARTHA, *starting*   I can hear!

Freud slowly descends the ladder to pick up the hammer. Then he positions himself in front of Martha (who still has the pile of plates in her arms) and prevents her from advancing towards the cupboard.

FREUD, *playfully assuming a terrifying expression*   People can be cured by hypnotism.
MARTHA, *laughing*   By commanding the patients to recover their health?
FREUD   Precisely.
MARTHA   That's what you're going to tell them at your lecture this evening?
FREUD   Yes.

She attempts to pass; he playfully prevents her.

MARTHA, *very sceptical and teasing*   And that's going to bring you in clients?
FREUD   It will bring them in droves.
MARTHA   Let me pass! You're wasting my time.
FREUD   I'll make you a wager.

He goes and puts the hammer down on the table. She tries to seize the opportunity to pass, but he turns round, catches her by the shoulders and returns to his position in front of her, his hands now free.

(*With feigned solemnity:*) Do you know Dr Sigmund Freud, specialist in nervous disorders and mental illness?
MARTHA, *entering into the game*   I know him only too well: he's my husband.
FREUD   Today is the fifteenth of October 1886. How many patients does Dr Freud have?
MARTHA   Not one.
FREUD   A year from now, on the fifteenth of October 1887, he'll have fifty.
MARTHA   Per day?
FREUD, *reflecting*   That's a bit much. Let's say, per week.
    Do you take the bet? If I lose, I'll give you a gold necklace.
MARTHA   If you lose, you won't have a penny to buy it with.
FREUD   I shall win. Listen carefully.
MARTHA   Let me pass.

Martha has begun to show signs of fatigue. Her arms can hardly support the pile of plates.

Let me pass or I'll drop the plates.

Freud takes them, imperturbably, and puts them back on the table.

FREUD   Martha, Dr Freud is going ...

(*He takes his watch from his pocket and consults it.*)

... to deliver a communication to the Medical Society in one hour's time, in front of the most eminent doctors. He'll talk about male hysterical patients and will propose a new therapy.

In two hours' time he'll take his bow, amid general acclamation — do you hear? I say acc-la-ma-tion. By tomorrow the story of his triumph will be all over town. By the day after tomorrow, patients will be stampeding into his consulting-room.

MARTHA, *ironical*   And the next day all the newspapers report on their front pages that Dr Freud has used hypnotism to cure twelve broken legs and three fractured pelvises.

She is teasing him, but it is clear that she knows perfectly well what he means.

FREUD, *still joking*   You haven't understood a thing.

He pretends to give up the struggle, climbs back up the stepladder and strikes one of the nails.

It's neuroses that are treated by hypnotism. There are patients who have bouts of distress without any apparent reason. This is because they're worked on by psychic forces of which they're unaware; what is necessary is to produce in them, by means of suggestion, equally unconscious contrary forces to neutralize the former.

Martha stamps her foot in annoyance. Freud stops, turns round and looks at her from the top of the ladder.

MARTHA, *genuinely annoyed*   I might have expected it! You can speak of nothing else but that word!

FREUD   What word?

MARTHA, *half-ironical, half-disagreeable*   In any case, I warn you, if ever I fall ill, don't try to cure me by means of suggestion.
    I'm a decent woman, I am, and I haven't got an unconscious.

Freud comes down the ladder. He has hung the picture, and pretends to look at it, very calmly, to see whether it is hanging straight. He whistles, with an indifferent, amused expression.
    Martha is furious, but remains very gay.

Do you hear me?

Freud answers her without taking his eyes off the picture.

FREUD, *with ironical calm; carelessly*   If you had one, you wouldn't be conscious of it.

Mechanically he takes his cigar-case from his pocket. Martha raps his fingers.

MARTHA   Again! If you want to smoke, go into your study.

Freud suddenly notices that he is holding the case. He hastily puts it back into his pocket.

You see. It's you who's unconscious. You didn't even know you wanted to smoke. What pleasure do you get from it? It's revolting, it smells nasty, it burns everything.

In a playfully inquisitorial tone of voice:

What's hidden under that?

FREUD   I don't know.

MARTHA, *joking*   You see. I always know what I'm doing.

FREUD, *joking*   Always?

MARTHA, *joking*   Always.

FREUD, *joking*   How about your loathing for tobacco? I wonder if that isn't a neurosis.

MARTHA, *joking*   Really? What about my taste for you?

Freud is still joking. But beneath the play-acting we sense a deep conviction.

FREUD, *joking*   Oh, that's the most serious neurosis of all: you must be crazy to love me!

Martha plants herself in front of him, very determined, and looks at him challengingly. Beneath her words, we sense a kind of sexual challenge. But we remain in the realm of play.

MARTHA   All right, cure me! Cure me then! Have a little try at hypnotizing me.

They stare into each others' eyes. Freud is the first to turn away; he is genuinely embarrassed.

FREUD, *with a trace of sharpness that should appear inexplicable*   One does not hypnotize one's wife. It's a treatment, not a parlour game.

MARTHA, *provocatively*   So one doesn't hypnotize her? Really? What does one do with her, then?

Freud is aroused: Martha is against him; she waits.

FREUD   Do you want to know? Do you want to know?

He clasps her in his arms. For the first time we feel that he desires her. His passion — before the journey to Paris — appeared more violent, more imperious, than strictly sexual.
The bell rings. He moves away from her.
He goes over towards the door.

It's Breuer: he has come to fetch me.

As he goes out, gaily and in tones of sexual complicity:

You'll find out this evening what I have in mind for you.

Martha has recovered all her composure.

14

In Breuer's coupé.

Elegant carriage, liveried, top-hatted coachman. Breuer and Freud are chatting with each other.
  Breuer looks at Freud with warm friendship. Freud is animated, happy and a little anxious.
They are both smoking. Breuer has lit a Turkish cigarette. Freud takes rapid puffs at his cigar.

BREUER, *fatherly and slightly worried*   You'll have a difficult audience. Don't attack
them head on.

Breuer presses the point.

The Medical Society is pretty conservative, moreover your former teachers will be
there. If they get the idea that you're giving them a lesson ...
FREUD   I shall take care not to offend anyone.

Breuer contemplates him with smiling scepticism and a faint air of disquiet.

  (Very amiably:) That's a promise.
  (Forcefully:) But I shan't make any concessions.

Breuer shakes his head.

BREUER   That's just what worries me.
FREUD   When you're telling the truth, you must go right through with it.

Breuer shakes his head.

BREUER   The truth ...
FREUD, *with warm concern*   Breuer, haven't I convinced you?

Breuer hesitates.
  Freud, pressing him:

The only opinion that counts for me is yours.
BREUER, *evading the question*   In any case, I've no objection in principle to therapy by
means of hypnotism.
  But when it comes to Truth, you see ...

He smiles with an affectionate but disenchanted expression.

There are *multiple* truths: they run everywhere, like cracks, and I'm not so sure they agree among themselves. To catch one — just a tiny one — an entire life isn't too much.

Freud smiles at him in turn. But, manifestly, these considerations are too alien to him to convince him. Breuer in any case abandons the discussion, as much out of discretion as from any clear consciousness of his powerlessness.

(After sighing:) All right! Try to be prudent.

15

The Medical Society.

An amphitheatre. On the stage a chairman, a secretary and Freud, who is reading out his manuscript.

In the audience — which is a large one — not a single woman.

In the second row, Meynert. A little higher up, Breuer. Serious audience (average age close on fifty); cultured, gloomy faces. Lots of pince-nez. Everybody wears a beard.

Freud is standing in front of a table covered by a green baize cloth. Carafe, glass. He concludes his reading in a tone of voice whose aggressiveness is at once striking to his audience and involuntary.

In any case, the authority of so young a man must seem displeasing to all those elderly — or at all events very mature — men. There is no sympathy between the orator and his public, although the latter remains serious and profoundly attentive.

FREUD   These clinical observations, carried out by Dr Charcot himself, on a hundred male patients, allow us definitively to reject a thesis that I have too often heard defended in the medical circles of Vienna, according to which hysteria appears only in women and is the result of disturbances in the ovaries.

As Freud is speaking, Meynert listens inscrutably; his left hand never stops tugging at his beard.

Breuer casts furtive glances to right and left: he is watching the reactions of the audience. The rest of the time he listens attentively, smiling slightly to encourage Freud — who actually has no need of encouragement.

FREUD   It goes without saying that it is no longer possible, after these masterly experiments, to retain the least doubt as to the neurotic reality of hysterical behaviour. Hysteria has citizen's rights among the mental illnesses, and whatever the merits may be of certain great minds, they must respectfully be invited to bow to Experience: hysteria is not a simulated illness, nor even an illness of simulation. It is characterized, in its somatic symptoms, by a certain *connivance on the body's part*, which provides psychic conflicts with a corporeal outcome.

This suggestibility — which distinguishes hysteria from all the other psychoneuroses — has allowed me to show you the extent to which the prevailing therapeutic methods are ineffective.

With a scorn that is truly offensive:

A hysteria cannot be cured by massage, showers or electrical treatment. May I be permitted, in conclusion, to hope that recourse will finally be had to hypnotism, and that advantage will be taken of the extreme suggestibility of the patients to deliver them, by means of suggestion, from the ailments they have implanted in themselves by means of auto-suggestion.

He has reached the end. He bows. Weak applause, most of it ceasing almost immediately. Breuer alone applauds at length.

    Meynert does not applaud. He has placed his hands very prominently on the back of the empty seat in front of him.

    Freud seems ill at ease. He does not know if he should sit or remain standing. He gains time by putting his notes away in his briefcase. This operation takes place amid a deep silence. Having exhausted every expedient, he moves to sit down, but the Chairman stops him.

CHAIRMAN, *icily*   Dr Freud, I thank you for your communication. But I am sure that our colleagues have observations to make and objections to present.

    Who requests the floor?

Three doctors raise their fingers.

(Noting the names:)

Dr Rosenthal.
Dr Bomberg.
Dr Stein.

Meynert speaks without raising his finger. Manifestly, he reigns supreme over this assembly.

MEYNERT   I shall add a few words.
CHAIRMAN, *noting*   Dr Meynert.

(A pause.)

Dr Rosenthal has the floor.

Dr Rosenthal rises to his feet.

DR ROSENTHAL   I know that on these questions I share the opinion of my eminent colleague.

He points to Meynert.

I am convinced that he will express better than I could what I was intending to say.
    I surrender the floor.

Dr Stein and Dr Bomberg have risen to their feet.

STEIN AND BOMBERG   We agree with Dr Rosenthal.
CHAIRMAN   You surrender the floor to Dr Meynert?
ALL THREE DOCTORS   Yes.

They sit down again, the audience applauds. Meynert grips the back of the empty seat with both hands, but he does not stand. He speaks with authority and with caustic irony.

MEYNERT   I thank my colleagues for their trust. I shall try to make myself worthy of it. In the honour that they do me, I see one advantage in particular: we shall sooner be done. For I do not think — and I regret this — that Dr Freud's communication should hold our attention too long.

All heads turn towards Meynert. When he makes a joke, his colleagues laugh delightedly, with a kind of servility. Breuer alone seems distressed and indignant.

In this paper, I found many new ideas and many true ideas. Unfortunately, the true ideas are not new and the new ideas are not true.

Freud, standing, impassive and sombre, listens to this dressing-down without flinching.

It is true, for example, that certain patients exhibit nervous disorders similar to those which our colleague has described. But I here appeal to those of my colleagues who are of the same age as I, or a few years older: were these symptoms not known long before we first stepped across the threshold of the Faculty of Medicine?

What is new, on the other hand, is the fact that Dr Freud has forcibly grouped them together to give some content to the mythical illness which he calls hysteria.

We all know, dear colleagues, that a patient, after a violent traumatism — for example, a railway accident — may temporarily exhibit one or another of these symptoms. The emotional shock, the fear, provoke nervous lesions so exquisitely fine that they still escape our microscopes. But these disorders, which soon vanish — hemianopsy, psychic deafness, epileptiform fits, hallucinatory delirium and *even* paralyses — fall under the jurisdiction of neurology and generally appear as the effects of periods of mental confusion consequent upon the accident.

I do not think it necessary to debate further: I have never encountered male hysterical patients, Gentlemen, but I must confess to you that — if hysteria is an illness — I have not been so lucky as our young orator and I have not encountered female hysterical patients either, unless we are to call by that name the unfortunate creatures who attempt to catch the attention of doctors by lies and absurd play-acting. Hysteria *does not ex-ist.*

Applause. Breuer alone does not applaud.

One word in conclusion. I do not contest the existence of hypnotism, quite the contrary. But I consider the hypnotist and his subject as twin patients, of whom it is not the subject who is the more seriously afflicted. And I pity those colleagues who, perhaps through altruism, lower themselves to playing the role of children's nannies.

Gentlemen and dear colleagues, let us return to our profession — the finest of all professions. So long as our physiological research has not disclosed to us new properties of the nervous system, let us stick to the well-tried methods. Massage, baths, electricity: these treatments may make our young colleague smile and yet experience shows that no cure is possible outside of them. Let us be patient, and above all let us be modest: that is the first duty of doctors and men of science.

Loud applause. The Chairman turns to Freud.

CHAIRMAN   Dr Freud, do you wish to reply to Dr Meynert?

Freud has assumed once more the sombre countenance we saw him wear before his departure for Paris.

FREUD, *in a hard, assured voice*   Dr Meynert has condemned without argument. He has not even deigned to present any objections of a scientific character. Under these conditions, I see no way of replying to him. And, as his age and his great merits make it my duty to respect him, I prefer to remain silent.

He abruptly picks up his briefcase and goes off, without taking his leave, through a little door situated behind the stage and at the rear of the hall.

Confronted with this rapid departure, many faces brighten; a gentle laugh runs through the hall as the spectators rise to their feet. Some of them go over to Meynert with outstretched hands, wearing expressions of enthusiastic approval.

Around Meynert, hubbub of voices:

VOICES   — You really put him in his place.
        — Trying to teach his grandmother how to suck eggs.
        — The young puppy ... Etc. etc.

Meynert bestows handshakes, impassive, a bit condescending; he replies only with a rather careless smile.

Behind Meynert, two doctors are deep in discussion.

FIRST DOCTOR   What do you expect? He's a Jew!
SECOND DOCTOR, *pleasurably shocked*   Oh!
FIRST DOCTOR   No, I'm not anti-Semitic. I just say it takes a Jew to go to Paris to look for theories that everybody knows in Vienna and that have long ago been abandoned.
SECOND DOCTOR, *shaking his head sadly*   I know! Those people really have no country.

[16]

Night-time. A deserted street.

Freud is walking alone, eyes sparkling, intensely annoyed. He is smoking a cigar.

In the same street, a prostitute on her beat.

She approaches Freud.

Freud sees her coming; he crosses over to avoid her. No sooner has he arrived on the other pavement than a woman emerges from the shadows and takes his arm.

PROSTITUTE   Are you coming?

FREUD, *outraged*   No!

He frees himself by leaping to one side, resumes his awesome and dignified bearing, and looks straight in front of him as he hurries on.

No luck: every fifty metres, under the streetlamps, we can see prostitutes waiting for clients. A kind of (slight) panic seizes Freud. And seeing one of these women making her way towards him, he spots a cafe and turns to enter it.

As he is about to push open the glass-panelled door, the grotesquely mirthful face of a prostitute presses against the glass (from the other side of the door) and smiles at him with a vile wink. He turns sharply away, abandons his plan and continues on his way, but only to perceive that the prostitute trying to waylay him is now only ten metres away. Already she is giving him the same wink.

Freud turns back in distress. He is on the brink of taking to his heels. At the same moment, a coupé draws up against the pavement alongside Freud. And Freud starts at the sound of Breuer's voice.

BREUER'S VOICE OFF   Freud!

Breuer appears at the coupé door.

BREUER   Get in! Come on, get in! I've been searching for you for the past hour. Why did you come this way?

Freud, after a moment's hesitation, climbs into the carriage. He sits down beside Breuer. He is manifestly relieved; he seems appreciative and we can sense his gratitude. But he has recovered his sombre expression and all his inhibitions: he has trouble in communicating.

From time to time his face brightens, but when he speaks of the defeat he has suffered his face loses all expression.

In Breuer's carriage.

FREUD, *seated at Breuer's side*   I wanted to go home on foot.

A gesture in the direction of the prostitutes. Testily:

I'd forgotten that all these streets are impossible in the evening.
  My thanks to you.

A woman on the pavement signals to them. Freud raises the carriage window, with an abrupt, impulsive gesture. Then, somewhat conscience-stricken, he turns to Breuer:

Forgive me. Perhaps you wanted some fresh air?

BREUER   I'll lower the other window.

*Breuer smiles at him. Freud's cigar smoke has already filled the carriage.
  A moment's silence. Breuer turns paternally towards Freud.*

I found Meynert very unpleasant.

Freud puffs at his cigar without replying. Breuer continues, without allowing himself to be discouraged.

There were some excellent things in your presentation.

Freud exhales a jet of smoke. He drives the smoke towards the open window by waving his hand. But he looks as if he were driving away, with this gesture, the unpleasant memory of the lecture. He endeavours to smile.

FREUD, *voice controlled rather than calm*   No one is deafer than the man who doesn't want to hear.
BREUER, *gently*   I'm afraid you set them against you right from the outset.

Freud shrugs his shoulders.

I advised you to be careful.

Freud looks at him and smiles more sincerely.

FREUD   I followed your advice: I was as meek as a lamb.

He laughs.

That's not the reason for their resistance.

(A pause.)

I'm a Jew, that's all.

BREUER, *indignantly*   What on earth are you talking about? I'm Jewish too, and I've never felt any hostility from either my colleagues or my patients.

Anti-Semitism is a mark of the uneducated, the lower classes ...

Freud listens uneasily.
Breuer resumes very gently:

Don't fight me: I'm on your side.

FREUD, *with a certain resentment*   You didn't believe me. Any more than the others did.

BREUER   I *don't yet* believe in your theory. But I believe in you.

At these words, Freud relaxes somewhat. He looks at Breuer with a deep, almost feminine tenderness that contrasts strangely with his former hardness.

What's necessary is to give you the means to confirm your ideas through experiment.

There are patients whom I cannot treat: psychiatry and neurology are powerless. You shall see them, they'll be your first clients. Perhaps you'll cure them. In any case, at the stage they've reached you can't risk harming them.

He takes a notebook from his pocket, with a pencil. He scrawls an address on one of the pages, tears it out and hands it to Freud.

I gave up treating this one a few days ago. Here's his address. Go there tomorrow morning, I shall have warned his father.

Freud takes the address with manifest gratitude. He reads it attentively and puts it into his pocket. His face suddenly hardens, and he looks straight in front of him. His anger seems to have taken hold of him afresh.
Breuer studies him worriedly.

BREUER   What's the matter?

FREUD, *in a constrained voice*   Nothing. But if you'll allow it, I'll go and see him in the afternoon. Tomorrow morning, I must have things out with Meynert.

A pause. His countenance changes once more and he turns towards Breuer. He appears childlike, trusting and somewhat embarrassed.

Can you lend me five hundred guilders? Settling in has been dreadfully expensive and I don't have a single patient.

[17]

In Meynert's study (at his home) the next morning.

Big, airy room, furnished with considerable taste. Meynert is obviously very wealthy.

Behind a large and handsome desk, at which Meynert is seated, there is a scaled-down repro-duction (in white plaster) of Michelangelo's 'Moses', in a kind of niche.

Meynert, seated at the desk, drinks glasses of schnapps angrily. Freud stands facing him. He is so furious that he can hardly speak, but he has turned his head towards the window and avoids looking at his interlocutor.

FREUD, *carrying on a dialogue which seems to have been running for some while*   I have always shown you the greatest respect, Sir, and haven't deserved to be insulted by you publicly.

MEYNERT, *brutally*   I didn't say a quarter of what I thought.

Freud, visibly hurt, makes a painful effort to recover the dignity denied him.

FREUD   I'm a man of science, Sir. I shouldn't dare call myself by that name if you'd not done so yourself, in former days. I worked for ten years with Brücke and with you. You thought sufficiently highly of me, last year, to offer me your chair.

Meynert is prey to all his tics; he no longer even attempts to conceal them.

If you think that I'm mistaken, it still seems to me that I have a right to some consid-eration.

MEYNERT, *brutal*   No!

He rises to his feet and positions himself behind his armchair and in front of the statue of Moses.

Freud — avoiding Meynert's gaze — cannot take his eyes off the statue; he sees nothing but that majestic, ferocious plaster head with its empty eye-sockets, which seems to be delivering sentence.

MEYNERT'S VOICE OFF   You are a deserter!

Freud, for the first time, beside himself with anger, dares to look Meynert in the face. The latter's fine, sinuous lips are twisted into a malevolent smile.

You rejected my offer! You preferred Charcot to me. You are frightened by the poverty of true scholars: you prefer charlatanism and money.

Freud appears dumbfounded.

FREUD   Money?

Angrily:

Look at me, Sir. And look at yourself.

MEYNERT   What does that prove? I'm rich because my father was well-to-do; as a man of science, I'm poor.

You, Freud, will die a millionaire!

Scandal pays.

FREUD, *cut to the quick*   I won't allow you to say that, Sir. I won't allow you to say that. I'm an honest doctor.

MEYNERT   An honest doctor tries to cure his patients.

FREUD   I try to do nothing else.

MEYNERT   Cure them, you? By means of hypnotism?

He comes round the desk, limping heavily. He draws close to Freud, who instinctively shrinks back.

He plants himself in front of him, holding his glass of schnapps tightly in his left hand.

Imitating an officer giving orders:

Upon my command — all fall asleep! Blind people, atten ... shun! — the scales are ordered to drop from your eyes. Paralytics, turn to the right, forward march! One two! One two!

You'll be a dictator! The monarch of neurosis.

He stops laughing, drinks, then returns to Freud and jabs him in the middle of the chest with his right index finger. Abruptly:

And what if they love their afflictions?

Do you know what a neurosis is? A way of living.

You'll kill them.

Freud smiles with great bitterness.

FREUD, *harshly*   If I'm nothing but a charlatan, I won't be able to do them much harm.

MEYNERT   You're nothing but a charlatan, but you'll become a criminal.

Hypnotism is a form of rape. You'll tyrannize your patients. If I had to choose, I'd a hundred, a thousand times prefer madness to enslavement.

Tics. Blinking. Freud looks at him in surprise and mistrust, almost in horror. A silence.

MEYNERT   How you'd like me to be ill! A nice little hysteria, Charcot style! How you'd take care of this poor old teacher of yours!

(Almost painfully.)

No such luck! I'm sound as a bell.

He limps across the room.

Poor neurotics! Heaven knows what you'll fill their heads with.

FREUD   I won't fill their heads with anything. I'll remove the fancies they've filled them with themselves.

Meynert halts abruptly and observes him.

MEYNERT   How?

FREUD   People *talk* under hypnosis: I shall learn the reasons for their distress and all their afflictions ...

He stops speaking, interrupted by a burst of laughter.

MEYNERT, *laughter*   Healing by means of enlightenment! You'll bring daylight into our poor dark souls and our vampires will all fly away at cock-crow!

He goes over to a shelf in the bookcase. On this shelf are arranged some chocolate boxes, of the kind sold in confectionery shops (coloured print on the cover, pastel-coloured ribbons). There are a dozen, approximately. The shelves above and below are entirely filled with scientific works.
    Meynert takes out a box (choosing it carefully).

MEYNERT   Look!

He opens the box. Freud is astonished to see a swarm of hideous insects (myriapods; arachnids — including scorpions).

The pretty little creatures! Poor darlings, this is the sun test.

(A pause.)

Well, Freud, does the light kill vampires?

MEYNERT'S VOICE OFF   I think it actually revives them.

We see the insects, at first dazed, begin to stir; soon this will become an unbearable swarming.

MEYNERT   If the box remains open, they'll climb out and run in all directions; the room will be crawling with them.

Meynert looks at the insects indulgently. He flicks off one of them which was attempting to climb up the inner surface.

A scorpion has escaped. Meynert notices it, motionless on a neighbouring box.

With amusement:

MEYNERT   Oh, the scorpion!

He takes a pair of forceps from the same shelf and replaces the insect in the box. Closing the box:

Return to the shadows!

He turns back to Freud and perceives the astonishment he has caused him. He resumes his serious demeanour and says with harsh authority:

These creatures are useful for my experiments.

(Falsely paternal:)

Come on, Freud! Leave to the night that which belongs to the night. To probe the soul without being corrupted, one would need the purity of an angel.

His eyes are shining. He wears a spiteful expression: he knows he is going to touch Freud on a raw spot. Once more, Meynert's index finger jabs into Freud's chest.

Are you so sure your mind is sound?

Freud looks at him with deep sorrow mingled with anger, but replies sincerely:

FREUD   No.

Meynert is triumphant.

MEYNERT   There you are! You'll hunt down the monsters hidden in others, and it's your own vampires you'll uncover.

He returns to his desk and pours himself a drink. Freud watches him with hard eyes. His anger at last gives him the courage to speak. But his voice remains strangled: he is frightened by what he is going to say.

FREUD   I don't drink.

Meynert swings round in astonishment.

MEYNERT   I know that. So what?

Meynert prepares to drink.

FREUD, *same voice*   If I were to trap an alcoholic's vampires, I'm sure they wouldn't be anything like my own.

Meynert listens, grasps the allusion and hurls his glass against the wall in a gesture of fury. Then he moves back towards Freud, with awful majesty.

MEYNERT, *forcefully*   Freud, you've sought to insult me.

They are face to face.
   A silence.

I forgive you. Do you know why? Because I've been observing you for a long while now.

Freud tries to speak. He interrupts him.

For a long while! And I've become convinced that you're threatened by neurosis. You don't drink, oh, no! You'd be too scared you might let yourself go. What would you say if you got drunk? What would you let slip? I've known you for ten years, and you haven't changed: you're still gloomy, tense, ascetic and secretive. I understand why the madness of others attracts you: you think you can forget your own, but you re-discover it in them. Call a halt, if there's still time: you'll lose your reason that way.

He starts pacing once more. He is now barely limping.

What you need is just the opposite: work that's clear and precise, rigorous, objective. I'll give you a chance: publicly disavow your idiotic theories and come back to work with me: anatomy, histology, physiology, therein lies your salvation. How about it?

Freud has regained control over himself. He speaks in a respectful but icy tone of voice.

FREUD   Dr Breuer has been so kind as to entrust one of his patients to my care; I'm going to see him this very day, and I shall treat him by means of hypnosis.

Meynert has positioned himself once more behind his desk (in front of the statue of Moses).

MEYNERT   Very well.

A pause. In a cutting, icy tone of voice he stresses the 'Herr' (in order to indicate that Freud is no longer a doctor)

MEYNERT   Herr Freud, you are no longer one of our number.

Under these circumstances, I forbid you access to my laboratory or to the hospital where I teach.

Freud looks at him with a hunted expression. But he pulls himself together at once.

FREUD, *in a calm voice*   Very well. Goodbye, Professor Meynert.
MEYNERT   Farewell.

Freud bows and goes out.

18

A living-room, large, austere and virtually bare.

In an armchair, a tall old man entirely dressed in black, of ascetic mien. Beardless, white moustache; emaciated features. He has a blanket over his knees. He is pale and nervous.
 A doorbell rings. His nervousness intensifies, but his face remains impassive and chilly. A servant opens the door.

SERVANT Dr Freud.

Freud enters. The old man greets him with a nod.

OLD MAN Good morning, Doctor; forgive me for not standing. I'm glued to this chair by an attack of rheumatoid arthritis. Please be seated.

Freud bows and sits down opposite the old man.

OLD MAN You're very young.

Gesture from Freud.

Don't be angry. I simply note that my son is older than you. It's of no importance.

He looks at Freud attentively.

You have authority.

He shows him an open letter lying on a little table within his reach.

My friend Breuer writes to me that you employ a new method.
FREUD Not new. I should like to try ...
OLD MAN It doesn't matter.

He shakes his head sadly.

My son is seriously ill. Apparently he's suffering from an obsessional neurosis. Try your method.
 Personally, I don't think you'll make him well, but you can't do him much harm; he's incurable.

Freud smiles with the faintest hint of bitterness.

FREUD   How old is he?

OLD MAN   Almost forty.

FREUD   When did the first signs of trouble appear?

OLD MAN   Let's see … My wife died in 1880. The illness made its appearance six months later, in February 1881.

He hasn't left his room for the past six years.

FREUD   Does he lock himself in?

The old man takes a key from the little table and shows it to Freud.

OLD MAN   He insists that we lock him in.

Freud rises to his feet.

FREUD   I should like to see him.

The old man presses a bell.

(Ringing of a bell.)

A servant appears.

OLD MAN   Please take the Doctor up to Master Karl.

The old man holds out the key.
The servant takes it without a word; he makes his way to another door situated at the back of the room. Freud follows him.

Dr Freud, I should like to see you again for a few moments before you leave.

19

A large room that doubles as study and bedroom.

It contrasts with the one Freud has just left, by virtue of the discreet good taste which has inspired its furnishing (German rococo).

An immense glass-fronted bookcase, full of books. At the far end of the room, as far away from the window as possible, a man of about forty, dressed in black but with elegance, is huddled against the wall. He is seated on a little kitchen stool, whose rustic simplicity forms a strange contrast with the luxury of the other furnishings.

Pleasing physique. The patient's face would be almost handsome, if he were not wearing a hunted expression. He folds and unfolds his arms nervously. A very thin red thread is wound round his legs, seeming to bind them.

(A key turning. Noise off of a door opening:)

SERVANT'S VOICE OFF   Dr Freud.

The patient does not even react. Freud goes over to him, takes a chair and sits down.

SERVANT   When the Doctor wishes to leave, he has only to ring.

Freud looks at the patient silently.

(Noise off of a door closing and a key turning.)

Freud's expression is calm and kindly, open, attentive. His nervousness has disappeared. His authority (very marked in the preceding scene) is counterbalanced by a real gentleness. He is a doctor at work, a professional of great mastery.

This man, who has so much difficulty in communicating with 'normal' people, has an immediate sympathy for his patients.

Karl makes a violent effort, then nods. His hunted expression gives way to a genuine politeness, which cannot really hide his deep unhappiness.

KARL, *introducing himself*   Karl von Schroeh.
FREUD   Dr Sigmund Freud.
KARL   You must forgive my father, Doctor. He has troubled you for nothing.

Freud looks at the red threads without replying.

My father adores me, you see. He prefers to believe that I'm mad.
I'm not mad, I'm evil. Rotten to my soul's core.

Silence from Freud: he listens without a word, but with an attentive and sympathetic expression.

    Don't you believe in Evil?

FREUD   Yes, I do.

KARL   And in the Devil?

FREUD   No.

KARL   Neither do I. In principle.

His face crumples. His hunted expression returns. He folds and unfolds his arms.
Freud stands up, looks at Karl's legs and touches the thread that is wound round them.

FREUD   What is this?

Karl mutters sullenly, without looking at it:

KARL   You can see what it is: a safety thread.

A pause. He relaxes a little.

    It protects me.

FREUD   Against whom?

KARL, *without replying directly*   I *mustn't* go out.

FREUD   You *can't.* You're locked in.

KARL, *muttering*   There's the window.

Freud appears not to react. He looks at the thread.

FREUD, *after a silence*   Where are the knots?

KARL, *muttering quickly*   Behind my back.

He bends slightly forward. Freud, leaning over him, sees the knots (bows, very easily untied).

FREUD   Why?

KARL   Harder to untie.

FREUD   Who tied them?

KARL   I did.

FREUD   Who will untie them?

KARL   I will.

FREUD   When?

KARL   This evening. When the streets are deserted.

Freud undoes the knots with his fingertips. The patient does not seem to notice.

FREUD   If you weren't tied up, what would happen?

KARL   I'd go out.

FREUD   And then?

He gently slips the thread down Karl's legs.

KARL, *same mechanical muttering*   I should kill.

FREUD   Whom?

KARL   Anyone.

FREUD   When the servant brings you dinner, do you want to kill him?

KARL   No.

FREUD   Why?

KARL   Because I know him.

FREUD   It must be somebody unknown?

KARL, *mechanical tone of voice*   A passer-by. Outside. In the street.

The thread falls at Karl's feet. Freud points at the thread.

FREUD   Look.

You're free, Herr von Schroeh.

Karl looks at the thread and begins to tremble.

What are you going to do?

A silence. Karl rises. He takes a few steps towards the window. Freud has not even turned round. He waits.

    Karl's face has altered dramatically: it suddenly expresses a kind of hatred. Freud waits.

    Karl seems to be struggling with himself. Suddenly he turns on his heel, comes back towards Freud who has his back to him, goes to the stool and sits down again. He looks surprised and uneasy, but slightly more relaxed.

    Freud picks up the red thread, rolls it up and puts it into his pocket.

FREUD   Give it to me, Sir: you can see you don't need it.

I'm sorry to have to inform you that you'll never kill anybody.

Karl listens to him with polite mistrust.

KARL   I'd like to believe you, Doctor. Unfortunately, I know myself.

A pause. Grasping his neck in his left hand as if he wanted to bend it forward.

It catches me suddenly. By the neck. And I see red.

    (In an almost unintelligible mutter:)

I'm Evil.

(A brief silence.)

FREUD   Have you heard of hypnotic therapy?
KARL, *indifferently*   Yes. From Dr Breuer.

He has stopped looking at his interlocutor, and is squeezing his legs together as if they were still tied.

FREUD   Would you agree to undergo it? The main thing is not to expect a miracle cure: the treatment can last for months.
KARL   You'll put me to sleep? And while I'm asleep you'll hammer Good into my head?
      I don't believe in that. Evil will swallow up Good.

A pause.

Try, all the same. I'd like to sleep so much.

Freud takes him by the arm and leads him to the sofa-bed. He sits him down on the bed. Karl has been wearing a submissive expression since he began hoping to sleep. We can sense his deep assent in the words he murmurs.

If only I could never wake up again.

Freud has placed his right index finger along Karl's nose, between his eyes.

FREUD   Look at my finger.

Karl looks at Freud's finger. Convergent squint.

(With compelling conviction:)

You will fall asleep.
    You are going to sleep.

Karl yields trustingly.

Sleep!

Already his face expresses the most total surrender.

Sleep!

(Gently insinuating tone of voice:)

You are sleeping.
　　You are fast asleep.

Karl's eyes turn up. The whites show and he lets himself fall back. Freud supports him and helps him to stretch out on the couch. He remains stretched out, his eyes closed, his arms straight against his sides, his breathing even.

　　Freud takes a chair, carries it over to the bed and sits down on it with a smile of triumph. After a moment's silence:

Are you listening to me?

Karl answers without opening his eyes.

KARL	Yes.
FREUD	You are in the street.

Karl stiffens.

FREUD	Do you hear me? You are in the street among all the passers-by.

Intense agitation on the part of Karl, who — without opening his eyes — lifts both hands and half-makes gestures to ward off evil.

KARL	Take me back home. I implore you.
FREUD	Why?
KARL	I want to kill.
FREUD	Who?
KARL	I don't know. The people passing by.
FREUD	The men or the women?
KARL	The people.
FREUD	Why?

(Unintelligible mumbling from Karl.)

FREUD	Why?
KARL	They're outside.
FREUD	How are they dressed?
KARL	I can't see them.
FREUD	Not at all?
KARL	Not at all.
FREUD	Perhaps there isn't anybody.
KARL	There are people. I know there are. I implore you! I implore you! I want to go

back home. I tell you I'm going to kill.

FREUD   How?

Karl, bewildered and grown suddenly calm, repeats the question:

KARL   How?
FREUD   With what weapon?
KARL   I have no weapons!
FREUD   With your bare hands?
KARL   How horrible!

(Little nervous laugh.)

I couldn't. I have a woman's hands.

FREUD   You've never met your future victims. You don't know either their age or their sex; at this very moment you're walking in their midst, yet you don't manage to see them; for six years now you've been claiming you wanted to commit a crime, yet not for one instant have you asked yourself how you'd go about it.

You're in your bedroom, Herr von Schroeh. Lying on your bed. You don't want to kill, Sir.

You're afraid of wanting to.

(A very short silence.)

And you want to be afraid of it.

(With authority:) You won't be afraid any more. I forbid you. Do you hear?

KARL   Yes.
FREUD   Will you obey me?
KARL   Yes.
FREUD   Stand up.

Karl stands.
  Freud touches his eyelids lightly.

Go to the window.

Karl tenses. He tries to resist.
  Freud taps him lightly with his forefinger between the shoulder-blades.

Go on!

Karl goes over to the window.

Look at the people going by!

Karl looks at them, as if he were dreaming.

They're made of flesh and blood, they have faces. You'll never again think of killing them, I forbid it.

Karl is still looking at the passers-by; his face brightens, a faint smile appears on his lips.
  And then, all of a sudden, his features are convulsed; he makes a great, pathetic gesture and would fall if Freud were not supporting him.
  Freud holds him tightly and leads him back to his bed.
  No sooner has Karl slumped onto it than he is racked by violent convulsions.

  (Howls from Karl.)

Freud tries to calm him by pressing on his forehead. He is partially successful; the convulsive movements become less violent, but Karl seems to be in pain.
  Freud, dumbfounded, sits down on the chair at the patient's bedside.

FREUD, *between his teeth, overwhelmed and astonished*   I don't understand a thing. *(A pause.)* What's wrong? Answer!

Karl abruptly begins to speak. From time to time his voice changes to a mumble, but most of the time it retains its violence and force.
  His eyes are open and staring.

KARL   It was the lesser evil.
FREUD   What was the lesser evil?
KARL   The people outside. Every time I wanted to strangle him, I'd try very hard to think how I wanted to kill the passers-by.
  I shan't think that ever again, I've sworn it. I'll think only of him.

Freud, suddenly rapt, bends forward.

(Unintelligible mumblings.)

FREUD   Who is this 'him'? Answer! I command you.
KARL, *laughing*   Someone on the inside.

Karl seems to be dreaming.
  He raises his arms and his hands tauten, then clasp each other and squeeze together.

KARL   My hands are guiding me, they're pulling me along, I'm following them; he's in his armchair, I'm coming up behind him, my hands close and he snuffs it.
  No. I have my red thread, I slip it under his beard. He's sleeping. It's a thread for

cutting throats.

Freud has understood.
  He looks worried. He wants to place his hand on Karl's forehead, but the latter struggles and pushes him away.

FREUD   Enough for today.
KARL   Let me speak. I tell you I'm Evil.

  (In the commanding voice of someone reciting the Law:)

Parricides will have their hands severed and their heads struck off.

Freud shrinks back sharply at these words. He no longer even attempts to awaken Karl or to make him keep silent; he listens with a kind of terror.

My presence on earth is deemed suspect.
  I am the Monster.
  God forbids the son to despise his father.
  Look at his mouth beneath his white moustache.
  It's so weak.
KARL'S VOICE OFF   Again! I can see you!

  (To an interlocutor, who may be Freud:)

He's crying like a baby!

Freud has turned pale. He no longer even attempts to awaken Karl, he is stiff as a poker.

  (Addressing his father, whom he sees as if in a dream:)

You haven't the right!
  Honour thy father and mother.

Freud is perspiring. Drops of sweat are running down his forehead.

I always honoured my mother, and you made her die of shame.
  Don't cry! If God wishes me to respect you, give me the means to respect you.

  (To an invisible interlocutor:)

He's an old swine, Sir. I'm strangling him because I can't stand it any longer. Better to kill than to despise.

Karl squeezes his hands together.

Freud, very pale and very sombre, has regained control of himself. He places his right hand upon Karl's forehead with a mixture of authority and revulsion.

FREUD, *imperiously*   Hold your tongue instantly!

Karl tries to speak.

You're talking nonsense.
  Nonsense, do you hear!
  Calm yourself!
  Calm yourself!
  Forget everything.
  I command you not to think of it again.
  Not at all!
  Never again!
  Do you hear?

Karl calms down gradually.

KARL   *(Unintelligible mumblings.)*

We cannot tell whether Freud is himself convinced of what he says or whether he wants to convince his patient of it.

FREUD, *with authority*   You've never despised your father!
  You've never thought of killing him!
  There's no child anywhere on earth who's so unnatural as not to respect his parents.

Karl has relaxed. His eyes have closed, he has let his arms fall back to his sides.

His breathing becomes regular, albeit remaining rather too strong. Freud massages his forehead and neck.

Wake up.
  Wake up.

A moment of waiting.
  Karl's eyes half open.

You've woken up.

Freud moves abruptly away from Karl (as if he has struggled against his revulsion up till now and, his task once accomplished, can contain himself no longer).

As he retreats, he knocks over the chair he was previously occupying.

Karl raises himself to a sitting position and looks at him in surprise. Freud has recovered his sombre, harsh mien; he looks at the patient with hostility.

Karl looks at the room and recognizes it.

KARL, *part-assertion, part-inquiry*   You're Dr Freud?
   What have you done to me?

Freud does not reply.

   Karl becomes aware that he is sitting on his bed.

You wanted to put me to sleep. Did you ...?

Nod from Freud.

What did I say?

FREUD   Nothing.

Karl speaks gently. He would like simply to express his gratitude.

KARL   I feel better, you know.

   (A pause.)

He rises to his feet, walks over to the window. He looks at the passers-by. He comes back with an astonished smile. Freud, motionless and sombre, does not even look at him.

Am I cured?
FREUD, *brutally*   No.
KARL, *almost confidently*   I know. You told me the treatment would be lengthy.
   When will you come back, Doctor?

Freud goes over to press a bell-push situated to the right of the bed (between the bed and the door).

   (A silence.)

After a moment, we hear hurrying footsteps.

FREUD, *very sharp, very distant*   I don't know.

The servant turns the key. The door opens.

   Karl looks gaily at the servant.

KARL, *joyfully*   I'm better, Maxime.
     Till next time, Doctor.
FREUD, *formal and barely polite*   Goodbye, Sir.

They go out.

KARL, *as they are leaving*   I'm better. No need to lock me in.

In the corridor, the servant hesitates in front of the door.

FREUD, *with barely restrained violence, as if he wished to make Karl vanish for ever*   Under lock and key! Under lock and key!

The servant, dumbfounded, fits the key into the lock.
     We can still hear the noise of the key turning as we rediscover Karl's father, motionless, forbidding, who seems not to have altered his position since we left him.

MAXIME'S VOICE OFF   Dr Freud.

[20]

The old man looks at Freud with a mixture of scepticism and hope.

OLD MAN   Sit down, Doctor.

FREUD, *tense and nervous*   Thank you, Sir, it's not necessary. Unfortunately I'm in a great hurry.

OLD MAN   Well?

FREUD   Does your son love you, Sir?

OLD MAN, *astonished*   Of course.

FREUD   Does he show you proper deference?

OLD MAN, *with conviction*   He's the most respectful of my children.

FREUD   Do you see much of him since he has been ill?

OLD MAN   When my arthritis gives me some peace, I spend every afternoon with him.

As Herr von Schroeh answers his questions, Freud gradually relaxes.
By the end of this interrogation, his agitation has disappeared, but he remains sombre.

FREUD   Does he trust you? Does he tell you of his obsessions?

OLD MAN   He tells me everything.

He ends by wiping his forehead with one hand, almost dazedly.

FREUD   Your son is resistant to hypnotism, Sir.

OLD MAN   Couldn't you put him to sleep?

FREUD   Yes, but I managed only to plunge him into an absurd delirium, quite unrelated to his real worries.

The old man looks at him in surprise.

(A silence.)

Freud looks withdrawn, as if in a hypnotic trance.
He resumes in a faraway voice, as if to himself:

FREUD   What if the hypnotist's personality suddenly took possession of the patients under hypnosis?

We should endow them with our own vampires.

He comes to himself abruptly. But he remains sombre and shaken.

(In a normal voice:)

In all honesty, Sir, I can do nothing for your son.

[21]

That same day, at the Freuds' home. Night is falling. A kerosene lamp, placed on the table, illuminates the dining-room.

Martha, seated near the lamp, is sewing. She raises her head: Freud has come in. She leaves her work and runs joyfully to throw her arms round his neck.

He kisses her mechanically. She falls back in surprise, studies him attentively and sees that he is looking upset.

MARTHA   What's wrong?

He gives her a careful smile, which does little to hide the fact that his thoughts are miles away.

Is it Meynert?

She takes the quick movement of his head to be a sign of acquiescence.

I told you not to get angry, didn't I?

He does not reply. He has turned away his eyes and is contemplating the print that he hung on the wall (Hamilcar and Hannibal).

MARTHA   Did you quarrel?

(Forcefully:)

It will all work out all right! I can't believe it won't work out all right.

Freud still does not reply. He goes towards the far door, setting Martha gently aside.

You frighten me! What are you looking for?
FREUD   A stool.
MARTHA   Why?
FREUD   To give you a nice surprise.
MARTHA, *still fearful*   All right. All right. I'll go and find one myself.

She goes out swiftly. Freud, remaining alone, thrusts his hand into his jacket pocket. He takes out his cigar-case. The red thread which bound Karl's legs has caught on the case; he pulls it out of his pocket and looks at it in surprise and then almost with horror, goes over to the window, opens it and throws thread and case into the street.

He closes the window hastily when he hears Martha's footsteps, turns round and leans against the window with an air of false detachment.

An irate voice rises from the street below. We can barely hear it.

VOICE OFF   Who threw that? Can't you watch what you're doing, up there?

Martha comes in carrying the stool.

MARTHA, *in astonished indignation*   You threw something into the street. Are you crazy? What did you throw down?

FREUD, *black humour*   The murder weapon.

MARTHA   What?

Freud takes the stool from her hands and places it beneath the print.

FREUD   A thread.
  Now for the surprise, Martha! Watch carefully.

He climbs onto the stool, unhooks the print and flings it on the floor. Noise of broken glass.

MARTHA, *almost in terror*   Stop! I tell you you're frightening me.

Freud on the stool, with a deliberately comical intonation that is designed to conceal his despair.

FREUD   The Carthaginians have given up without a fight, Martha. Long live the Romans!

He climbs down from the stool and takes her in his arms.

I wasn't Hannibal, believe it or not!

A silence. Martha looks at him, lifts a hand and timidly caresses his cheek.

MARTHA, *very tenderly*   Are you sad?

FREUD, *smiling, but withdrawn*   It's my mother who will be. She was already convinced I'd end up as prime minister when I was still in my cradle.
  I'm going to make you happy, Martha: I'm giving up hypnotism.

With false gaiety:

We shall prescribe baths, massage and above all e-lec-tri-ci-ty.

MARTHA   But why?

FREUD   It's not yet perfected. I made my patient say things that were as idiotic as he is.

(With revulsion:)

He was disgusting.

With the same false gaiety, but painfully:

I give it all up; I'll treat myself to the same luxury goys enjoy and be just anybody.
    You'll be the wife of a family doctor.

Martha speaks to him with the greatest tenderness.
    But she is taken in by his playful tone, and does not realize that he really detests giving up his ambitions.

MARTHA   I shall be *your* wife whatever you become.
    And I prefer family doctors to specialists. A great man must be so lonely, Sigmund.
What would have become of me?
    Wife of the eminent Dr Freud.

    (Pretending to shiver:)

Brr … it's cold, glory is. It must kill love.

Freud hugs her. Martha, her head against Freud's shoulder, does not as he speaks see his distressed, timorous, almost demented countenance.

FREUD   Glory is stillborn.
    I've nothing any more.

He caresses her hair gently. But — more than a gesture of tenderness — it is a ruse to prevent her from raising her head.

You'll have to be my *everything.*

He is still caressing Martha's head, but he is not looking at her.
    He is stiff and tense, his gaze fixed somewhere far away.
    Gradually his expression of suffering disappears, he reassumes his sombre, harsh, impassive expression.
    Something within him has just died.
    He repeats in an altered voice, as if to himself:

Everything.

PART TWO

[1]

1892 – Six years later. Dr Freud's consulting-room.

We shall discover later on that it is furnished with a writing-table covered in papers and books, with a certain number of chairs in no particular style and with a divan-settee placed against the wall, opposite the desk.

In addition, an unfolded screen hides part of the left-hand wall opposite the window; in front of the window, a strange chair wired up with flexes and electric plugs looks more like a medieval instrument of torture than a therapeutic apparatus — it is vaguely reminiscent of the 'electric chair' used for capital punishment in the U.S.A.

For the moment we can see only Dr Freud, who is smoking a cigar with an expression of deep disgust.

He is standing over the couch, and we divine that he is carrying out some manual operation.

But he does not look at what he is doing.

His gaze is fixed upon the left-hand wall, at eye-level.

Eventually the camera reveals his arms and his hard cuffs; his hands, protruding from the cuffs, are massaging — through terry towels — the lower back, buttocks and thighs of someone lying face down on the settee.

This is a pretty young girl, with an attractive, slightly comical face.

Her body, apart from the legs — the patient has kept her stockings on — is naked beneath the towels.

Her naked arms lie by her sides on the settee.

Her face, relaxed and free from tension, seems to indicate that she does not exactly hate her massage sessions.

FREUD   One moment, please.

He goes to knock the ash from his cigar into an ashtray placed on a little pedestal table, beside the couch.

He replaces the cigar in his mouth, tries to take a puff and realizes that it has gone out. In vexation, he deposits it on the ashtray.

He was intending to continue the massage, but this slight accident is enough to make him change his mind.

FREUD   That's enough. You can get dressed again.
DORA, *with an innocent air*   The massage is getting shorter and shorter.
FREUD, *irritated*   No, it's not.

He turns his back to her and goes over towards the window.

DORA, *voice off*   It's the only thing that does me any good.

Freud is morose and grumpy.

FREUD   Don't argue.

We hear Dora getting up and going off behind the screen.
    Freud moves over to a chair and looks at it: against this chair, Dora has propped her parasol; on its seat, she has put down her handbag and a book.
    Freud looks at the title of the book and frowns.
    He turns towards the screen.

    Whatever is this book?
DORA   *Madame Bovary.*
FREUD   I can see that: but what are you doing with it?
DORA, *voice off*   What can a person do with a book? I'm reading it.
FREUD   You won't be reading it any more.
DORA   What?

Freud goes over to his desk, holding the book in one hand. Dora pokes out her head and half her body: she is wearing a combination.
    Freud does not see her: he puts the book into a drawer, which he locks.

FREUD   It's disgusting.

Dora, still in her combination, leaves her hiding-place. She stamps her foot.

DORA   You really get on my nerves.

Freud has turned round automatically; he looks at her with a frown. He is shocked, but not in the least aroused.

FREUD, *with authority*   Aren't you ashamed of yourself? You read French novels and you dare to present yourself before me dressed like that? Take care, my child: if you go on this way, you'll never be cured.

Terrified, she retreats behind the screen again.
    Freud goes over to the electric chair and switches it on.
    The chair's feet are made of glass.
    He takes a kind of round brush, at the end of a wire, and runs the current through it. It crackles. Spark. At the sound of the crackling, Dora emerges suddenly from behind the screen, this time fully dressed.

DORA   No. Not that!

Freud turns towards her with a show of indignant surprise.

FREUD   Why not?

DORA, *already defeated*   I hate your machine; I've told you so hundreds of times.

Freud goes over to fetch her and leads her to the electric chair, gently but masterfully.

FREUD, *still morose, but somewhat more gentle*   You know very well I won't hurt you.

DORA   I know you'll frighten me.

FREUD   Fear is beneficial.

He sits her down on the chair, fastens her legs with a strap, so that they are resting on an insulating step; he stretches her arms along the arms of the chair.

There.

He brings up the electric brush which begins to crackle, runs it over her face and down the back of her neck. She is frightened.
He speaks to her forcefully but gently, as to a child.

Electrotherapy is of much more use to you than massage.

She does not dare speak, but a slight movement signals that she rejects this conclusion.
Freud continues forcefully:

Your obsessions are less restricting. Some have even disappeared.

Holding herself stiffly, Dora ventures to speak: very rapid delivery.

DORA   There are others, which have returned.

FREUD   Dora, you're lying! You know very well you're getting better.

He conscientiously runs the brush over his patient's body.

And then that notorious tic of yours ...

He imitates it: a grimace which lifts the left corner of his mouth, pulls his cheek towards his ear and closes one of his eyes.

It hasn't come back for three weeks now.

She looks discontented.

You can't deny it.

DORA, *grudgingly*   No.

A pause. She has recovered some of her assurance since the brush has moved away from her face. Abruptly:

I should like to be hypnotized.

Freud's face suddenly hardens. He straightens up, holding the brush in his hand but without pointing it at Dora.

FREUD   What?

It is Dora's turn to be sulky and morose.

DORA   Apparently it cures people.
FREUD   Who has been telling you these silly stories?
DORA   Everybody's talking about it.
FREUD   And if everybody said the world was an ostrich-egg, would you believe them?

He turns off the current, switches off the machine and bends down to remove the straps that hold her prisoner.

Hypnotists are charlatans.
DORA   That's not what Dr Breuer says.

She stands up.

FREUD   Breuer?
DORA   He hypnotizes a girl-friend of my cousin's every day.

Freud begins to laugh heartily.

FREUD   Breuer! You're out of luck, Dora: Dr Breuer is my closest friend; I know his patients and I can assure you he doesn't waste his time hypnotizing them.

There is a knock at a door at the far end of the room. He answers without turning round:

Yes!

To Dora, as Martha comes in:

It's Martha, who wants to say good morning to you. I told her you were cured, but she believes only what she sees with her own eyes.

2

Martha goes over to Dora.
  They embrace.

MARTHA   How are you, Dora? *(Pointing to Freud with affectionate irony:)* Can it be true, has that man really cured you?

Dora gives a sly little glance at Freud.

DORA   Cured me entirely, Martha.

She suddenly makes the grimace that Freud was previously imitating.

  (With a blank expression:)

Well, almost entirely.

Freud is furious. He seizes Dora by the arm.

FREUD   You're doing it on purpose.

Dora repeats her 'tic'.

DORA, *dismayed*   Oh! no, Doctor, I'm not doing it on purpose at all.

Freud pushes Dora hurriedly towards the door.

FREUD, *hastily*   We'll see about that next Tuesday. I shall expect you at five o'clock.

Dora, struggling slightly, calls to Martha from the entrance:

DORA   Goodbye, Martha. Come and see me tomorrow, I never see you any more.
MARTHA, *affectionately*   Goodbye, my dear. I'll try to find time.

Freud has opened the door. He steps back to let Dora pass.

DORA   Till Tuesday …

She makes her grimace, which prevents her from speaking for a moment, then continues:

… Doctor!

Freud and Martha are left alone. Freud looks irritated and sombre. He goes over to join Martha in front of the electric chair, and on his way past gives the machine a kick.

MARTHA, *in astonishment*   What's wrong?

He grumbles, without looking at her:

FREUD   A man shouldn't treat his wife's friends, at any price.

Sullenly, he tidies the towels lying on the couch, makes them into a pile and carries it over to a chair. He stoops to collect two towels that Dora must have dropped when she stood up.

She doesn't even fold up her towels.
     The other day she stole one from me.
MARTHA, *astounded*   What?
FREUD   She stole one from me.
MARTHA   Why?
FREUD   I've no idea. A prank.

He puts the towels down on the chair and straightens up.

A classic case: obsessional neurosis. *Idées fixes.* Phobias. Impulses. She's on the way to being cured.

He looks at his watch.

We must get dressed. Otherwise we'll be late as well. *(Making his way towards the door. Martha follows him.)*

In a child's small bedroom.

Little Mathilde — five years old — is playing at the foot of her bed with a doll.
     Freud and Martha are watching her tenderly, standing with heads bent towards her.
     She lifts her eyes and smiles at them. Martha smiles at her tenderly. Freud smiles too, with great tenderness, but his eyes remain sombre. The little girl, trustful, happy to be watched, goes back to playing with the doll — she is busy undressing her, after which she will rewrap the little naked porcelain body in a splendid red cloak. Freud's smile disappears; he reassumes his sombre, prematurely aged countenance. He is obviously thinking about something quite different. Without even realizing it, he pokes his right forefinger into his right nostril.
     Martha does not notice at first. But Mathilde, who has raised her eyes, starts to laugh.

MATHILDE   Look, Papa's picking his nose!

Martha glances at Freud in annoyance. She gives him a little rap on the fore-arm. Freud looks put out, but he removes his finger from his nostril and puts his hand in his pocket.

MARTHA, *to Mathilde*   It was only to tease you. We don't put our finger into our noses. Nor into our mouths. It's forbidden.

MATHILDE   Why is it forbidden?

FREUD, *authoritarian and disagreeable*   Because it's very dirty!

A few minutes later. The Freuds' bedroom.

Martha is arranging her hair in front of a mirror.

Freud, in shirt-sleeves — shirt with starched front — is trying to fasten stiff cuffs onto the shirt by means of gold cuff-links.

He has succeeded with the right-hand cuff. But with the left-hand cuff he seems to be in some difficulty. Finally the cuff-link slips from his grasp, falls to the floor and rolls under the bed. Freud bends down, furious.

He looks under the bed and does not find it. He straightens up, intensely irritated. Martha looks at him in the mirror and sees his contorted face, but she says nothing.

We see: Martha from behind, putting pins in her hair; the looking-glass; in the glass, Martha's reflection; and behind her, the reflection of Freud.

FREUD'S VOICE OFF   You'll go to the Breuers' without me.

After this peremptory pronouncement, Martha, her eyebrows raised in surprise, her arms held motionless in mid air, looks at her husband with a worried expression, but in silence.

You'll tell them I've been summoned by a patient.

She does not reply.

Do you hear?

Martha turns round and looks at him with a calm that does not really hide her deep anxiety.

MARTHA   What's the matter? Is it your cuff-link?

He shrugs his shoulders.

She rises to her feet, goes over to him, studies the situation like a general inspecting a future battle-field, looks at the floor, stoops down, picks up the cuff-link from under the night-table and holds it out to Sigmund, who takes it without altering his furious expression.

MARTHA, *she speaks affectionately, but we can sense that it is a test — she wants to assess Sigmund's state of mind:*

Give me a kiss for my trouble.

Freud kisses her on the forehead, in a kindly manner.
It is not Martha who is the object of his anger.
He remains distracted: the kiss is somewhat mechanical.

FREUD, *rather distractedly*   Thank you, my love.

MARTHA, *aping him*   Thank you, my love, ... thank you, my love ...(*Abruptly:*) Where are you?

Abruptly roused, Freud looks at her in surprise and some confusion.

FREUD   Where am I? Where do you think I am?

He tries once more to insert the cuff-link into the button-hole of his cuff.
Just as he is about to become upset, Martha gently takes his left wrist and does the job herself.
He looks at her.

There you are! Fairy hands: just what's needed for making experiments.

She looks at him without understanding.

Yes. In a laboratory. I used to have butter-fingers.

Laughing disagreeably:

Good theoretician. Bad experimenter.
    In any case, my hands don't count any longer. It's been six years now since Meynert cut them off.

The cuff is finally fastened to the shirt.

While we're on the subject: he's a dying man.

Martha shivers and raises her head. She looks at him for the first time since the beginning of the scene without irritation, but with genuine understanding and concern.

MATHA   Meynert! What's ...

FREUD   Angina pectoris.

MARTHA   Does it upset you?

Freud releases himself and goes to fetch his jacket.

FREUD   I couldn't care less! He hates me; he's done all he could to harm me.

He looks into space, one hand resting on the collar of his jacket, which he has hung over the back of a chair.
   Abruptly:

He'll die without my seeing him again.

She looks at him, but prudently refrains from saying anything.

He was a great man, you know. Truly great.

Bitter laugh.

He must be very surprised to be dying: he took himself for God the Father!

Martha gently pushes Freud's hand out of the way in order to free the jacket, which she takes and holds out to him to put on.

FREUD   What?

He sees she is proffering him the jacket.

Not worth it. I shan't go to the Breuers for dinner.
MARTHA   You must be crazy! You adore them! It's only with them that you feel comfortable.
FREUD   When they're alone, yes. But they've invited some idiot along too.
MARTHA   Who?
FREUD   Some Dr Fliess, whom I've never met.
MARTHA   If you've never met him, how do you know he's an idiot?
FREUD   Because he has come from Berlin to attend my lectures. Can you understand that? A Berlin doctor, a man of my own age: it seems that he has been very successful there.

MARTHA   Well then?

Freud, violently:

FREUD   I shall teach him nothing! Nothing! Nothing! I'm a failure, I have nothing to teach anybody and the people who come to listen to me are cretins.

He crosses the room.
   She follows him with the jacket.

MARTHA   If he has come because of you, that's an extra reason for going to the dinner.

FREUD, *violently, but without malice*   Oh! you don't understand anything!

He turns round towards her, puts his finger into his nostril and looks at her with a vague, almost idiotic expression.

I'm at the end of my tether.
     Massage! Electrotherapy! Electrotherapy! Massage! And not a penny to my name! ... I'll give up medicine. I might just as well sell cloth.

MARTHA, *tenderly*   You promised me you'd be happy ...

FREUD, *harsh, almost insulting laugh*   Happy?

MARTHA, *sadly*   Yes, so long as we'd be living together.

Freud is touched. He puts his hands on her shoulders and looks at her with deep affection.

FREUD   My poor love, I'm spoiling your life. Oh! I should never have married you!

Martha takes a step back, deeply wounded. He advances towards her and explains:

Failures shouldn't get married.

He takes the jacket from her hands and puts it on.

Forgive me. It's because of Meynert. When I learnt he was ill, all the old memories flooded back.

She smiles at him with a touch of sadness and turns back to the mirror. Freud grows suddenly impatient.

Well? Are you ready?

Martha has picked up her hat and is fastening it on her head with pins.

Hurry up! I hate being the last to arrive.

In the child's bedroom.

Mathilde is standing, she hears a door opening and rushes out into the hall.
     Freud and Martha are about to leave. Freud is wearing black tails and striped trousers, and has a top-hat on his head. He picks Mathilde up at arm's length, then smothers her with a hug. To Martha:

FREUD, *indicating Mathilde*   The only good thing I've done in my life.

MARTHA, *irritated smile*   If that! I helped you quite a bit.

She takes the child from his hands and kisses her. She sets her down on the ground again as he opens the door. They go out.

We hear Martha's voice off as the door is closing.

MARTHA'S VOICE OFF   You haven't forgotten your keys?

Mathilde, left alone, goes down to the end of the corridor. She enters the kitchen. A young maid-servant is seated at a deal table, eating. Mathilde goes up to her.

LITTLE MATHILDE   Please, where are they going?
MAIDSERVANT   To your godmother's.

We hear the bell ring. An imperious, protracted ringing. The young maidservant looks at Mathilde with a touch of anxiety.

LITTLE MATHILDE   It's Papa who's forgotten his keys.

The maidservant rises to her feet and wipes her mouth with her apron.

MAIDSERVANT   Can't be him. It's the servants' door.

At the servants' door. The young maidservant has just opened it. A man in livery is standing on the threshold.

FOOTMAN   Is this right for Dr Freud?
MAIDSERVANT   Yes, but he's just gone out.
FOOTMAN   Dr Meynert wants to see him.
MAIDSERVANT   Is he a patient?
FOOTMAN   No, he's a doctor.

3

In an open cab.

It's a fine summer evening. The Freud couple very stiff and silent on the back seat.

Elegant streets. A two-horse cart crosses the main road in front of the cab. One horse stumbles and falls to the ground. The cab-driver pulls on his reins and stops the cab. The carter climbs down and tries to drag the horse back onto its feet.

Martha loses her balance as the cab stops. She stifles a cry and her eyes fill with tears.

Freud, who has not batted an eyelid in spite of the jolt, turns towards her and studies her anxiously. She immediately pulls herself together:

MARTHA   It was the jolt: I wasn't expecting it.

He grasps her hand, without taking his eyes off her. She forces herself to smile, but two tears hanging on her lashes now roll down her cheeks.

What can I do? I'm on edge too.

For a short while now, a tall man (perhaps thirty-four years old) — very elegant attire; handsome, satanic face (black hair and beard; large, brilliant, imperious eyes; little red mouth with scornful pout: a pout due more to the structure of the face than to any mimetic expression); gold-knobbed cane; pearl-grey suede gloves — has been wandering up and down the right-hand pavement, in search of a sign to tell him the name of the street.

His searches are fruitless. He approaches the cab, which has stopped beside the pavement, bows and removes his hat. It is Dr Fliess. He clicks his heels. The movement of his head has a certain mechanical precision; in his long, thin body, which could be graceful, there is a kind of Prussian stiffness.

FLIESS   Madam, Sir, forgive me. Could you direct me to Nathangasse?
FREUD   Which number?
FLIESS   I'm going to number 15.

Martha looks at him with a stifled air. She takes advantage of the moment when he is bowing to wipe the two tears furtively away. Freud is very amiable, showing unaccustomed helpfulness.

FREUD   Then it's to the left: the fourth street after this one.

Fliess raises his head, clicks his heels.

FLIESS   I'm infinitely grateful.

Almost military about-turn. Freud follows him with his eyes, amused and attracted.

FREUD, *to Martha*   What an extraordinary face.

MARTHA   He looks like the Devil. Anyway I hate him: he saw me crying.

FREUD, *with a certain respect*   He was a Prussian.

The carter has whipped the fallen horse to its feet. The cart lumbers away. The cab moves off.

MARTHA   He certainly was: stiff as a poker.

   (Abruptly:)

A Prussian! And he's going like us to 15 Nathangasse. I only hope he's not the Breuers' guest.

The cab overtakes Fliess just as the latter is about to cross the street. Fliess raises his hat again; Freud raises his in reply and smiles broadly. Freud turns to Martha as he replaces his hat.

FREUD   Not a chance. I shan't be that lucky.

At the Breuers' house.

A large drawing-room, opulent, comfortable but quite ugly. The window is open.
    Mathilde Breuer, rather a pretty woman of around thirty, is leaning out of the window. A chambermaid is standing waiting near the glazed door leading to the corridor.
    Mathilde turns round and goes over to her, obviously put out. Mathilde is small, plumpish and lively; she has charm and gaiety. But for the moment her face is anxious and her voice not very agreeable.

MATHILDE BREUER   There they are. Are you sure the Doctor isn't in his study?

CHAMBERMAID   I've just come from there, Madam.

MATHILDE BREUER   How about the smoking-room? Have you looked there?

Mathilde takes a fan from a pedestal table, opens it and fans herself nervously.

How annoying it is! He might have …

   (A bell rings.)

Go and let them in.

The chambermaid goes out. Mathilde fans herself, goes to the mirror, pats her hair and composes her features.

Martha and Freud come in, she smiles and kisses Martha on both cheeks.

MATHILDE   Hullo, dearest. Hullo, Sigmund.

Very quickly:

Josef's incorrigible; I told him not to be late, and of course he's not back yet.

Freud's face has brightened as soon as he came into the room. We can tell that he likes the Breuers' apartment and that he feels at home there.

FREUD, *pleasantly*   Oh! come now, Mathilde! I'm a doctor too, you know.

Mathilde is voluble out of habit and above all out of irritation. She speaks with little, charmingly affected, nervous gestures, fanning herself the while.

MATHILDE   If it were only a question of you two, I could put up with it: you're part of the family. But there's this Herr Fliess, whom I don't know. Those people from Berlin are always so touchy ...
    (Very annoyed:) He promised me he'd be on time! After all, it's his guest.
    (In the same tone:) Martha, dearest, do you want a fan! It's so hot, we're all on edge, there's a storm in the air.

(Sound off of a carriage in the street.)

There he is!

She straightens up, with a haste that Breuer's mere lateness is insufficient to justify.

(Dwindling sound of the carriage.)

No.
    It's intolerable.
FREUD, *irritably*   Come, Mathilde, he's been delayed by a patient, that happens every day.
MATHILDE   Every day, you're quite right. But in this case it's a female patient and always the same one. That Körtner girl, you know.
FREUD, *dumbfounded*   Körtner, no, I don't know.
MATHILDE   Yes you do, come on! You know all his patients. Little Cäcilie, you know. He goes there twice a day now. It seems *(terse laugh)* that she's a wonderful case.

Freud has turned pale. His face hardens.

FREUD, *very terse*   Twice a day? Cäcilie Körtner? Never heard of her.

122

A certain embarrassment and unease takes hold of the three individuals.

MATHILDE, *astounded*	Come on, he tells you everything!
FREUD, *same tone of voice*	Apparently not.
MATHILDE, *after a silence*	He hasn't spoken to you about her!

Her distress seems to exceed even her astonishment.
She closes her fan with a snap and throws it down on the pedestal table.

Well, so much the worse for both of us.

Freud does not reply. He remains in his armchair, frowning, without even attempting to hide his vexation.

(Bell peal off.)

MATHILDE   And here, of course, is the guest!

A footman opens the door.

FOOTMAN   Dr Fliess.

He steps back to let Fliess pass; the latter enters and bows, ever more satanic and Prussian.
Mathilde has risen to her feet, she offers him her hand.

MATHILDE   Good day to you, Doctor.

Fliess clicks his heels together, bows and kisses her hand.

FLIESS   My humble respects, Madam.
MATHILDE   My husband has been delayed at the bedside of one of his patients . . .

4

In the huge bedroom that serves as Cäcilie's living-room, which will be described later.

For the moment, evening is coming on and the room is almost in darkness. Breuer is seated beside Cäcilie's bed.

BREUER, *rising to his feet*   Well, Cäcilie, we've made good progress.

We can barely make out Cäcilie's head and blonde hair. Her arms are stretched out on the blanket. She has a squint (convergent strabismus).

CÄCILIE, *faint voice*   Are you leaving?

Her hands flutter from side to side, as if running across the bed in panic.

BREUER   Cäcilie! Calm yourself. I shall be here tomorrow morning.

She gives every sign of mounting agitation.

CÄCILIE   And until tomorrow there'll be nothing. *Nothing!*

She starts to cough: a dry, rasping cough.

   (Fits of coughing.)

Between spasms:

And the night to get through! Terrified of opening my eyes ... If I open them, I see the dead woman.

She fumbles awkwardly to take Breuer's hand, which rests upon hers. Breuer guesses her wish and gives her his hand. She takes it and raises it to her eyes. With a kind of passion:

Close them for me. Command me not to open them until tomorrow.

Breuer hestitates, then bends over the beautiful face disfigured by her squint. With great tenderness and authority:

BREUER   Close your eyes, Cäcilie.

He closes both her eyes with his thumbs. His other fingers gently cup Cäcilie's temples.

Don't open them until tomorrow.

CÄCILIE   It's you who'll open them for me.

(Cough.)

He does not reply; she stirs restlessly. Insisting:

Say you'll come and open them for me. Tomorrow morning, with your two thumbs. Otherwise, I won't sleep.

(Fit of coughing.)

BREUER   I'll open your eyes for you. Go to sleep, Cäcilie.

(The fit of coughing stops at once.)

In this brief scene, we must have the sensation that these two individuals — doctor and patient — form a couple more strongly united than ordinary couples of the kind, and that in a quite singular fashion it is the patient who gets her doctor to give her the orders which she wants to obey.

Breuer seems to have great authority over her, and at the same time he gives in to her with affectionate weakness.

However, Cäcilie's wish ('Close my eyes for me') is not a mere amorous fancy and must not seem solely that: it is also — and this must be evident — the sudden contrivance of a patient who is afraid of a sleepless night and who finds a way of soothing her fears.

Cäcilie has allowed herself to fall back on to the pillow, her eyes closed, her fears soothed, a faint smile on her lips.

Breuer moves away on tip-toe, picks up his top-hat from a chair, opens the French window and goes out. He finds himself in a park, where his coupé is waiting for him in front of the door; he climbs in hastily.

BREUER, *to the coachman*   Home, Karl. Hurry, hurry! I'm three quarters of an hour late.

5

In the Breuers' drawing-room.

The two women are sitting talking to one another.

VOICES OFF OF THE TWO WOMEN   Not at all, it's very cheap. A cretonne:
you can drape the walls of a room ...

We hear words from their conversation whenever there is a silence between Freud and Fliess.
Mathilde and Martha both have fans, they fan themselves as they speak.
In a window recess, Freud and Fliess are talking: Fliess only rarely turns entirely towards
Freud: one would say he was contemplating the building opposite. But when he wishes to assert or
to convince, he looks at his interlocutor — less to observe than to charm.
At such moments, the brilliance of his large eyes seems almost unbearable.
Freud is nervous, restless, still sombre; from time to time, he leans over the balcony in the hope
that Breuer's coupé has just arrived (every time a carriage passes — which is not very often in this
'residential neighbourhood'). But at the same time we sense that Fliess captivates and intimidates
him.
He addresses him with a gentleness and a desire to please that he has hitherto reserved for Breuer
and Charcot. He listens to him raptly; from time to time his nervous mannerism overtakes him
and he pokes his forefinger into his nostril.

FREUD, *desire to please that is almost servile; but the severity he demonstrates towards himself is*
utterly sincere, and has deep roots:
I cannot understand why a man of your worth, a Berlin specialist, should have
gone out of his way just to hear my lectures. You know I'm not even a Professor. A
simple lecturer, that's all.

FLIESS, *amiable but distant*   If I've come to you, it's because your reputation has come
to me.

FREUD   I teach anatomy of the brain: anyone can do that better than I can.

FLIESS   You know that's not true. The old fossils in power divide the brain up into
thousands of little compartments. Each of these corresponds to one of our gestures,
one of our sensations or one of our words. You're one of the few people in Europe to
teach that those little compartments don't exist; that everything's a matter of connec-
tions and movement.

Freud has bowed his head to conceal an almost childish smile of satisfaction.

FLIESS   I'm going to tell you a secret.

Fliess turns abruptly towards Freud and stares fixedly at him.

Breuer has told you: I'm an ear–nose-and-throat specialist. I've managed to isolate a neurosis. The nasal neurosis, if you like. There's a nervous connection between the nose and all the other organs.

Freud listens intently. He so far forgets himself as to poke his finger into his nose.

By numbing the nasal region, I've caused intestinal disturbances to disappear. Of course, they'd return as soon as the nose recovered its normal sensitivity.

A carriages goes by in the street. Freud, despite the rapt interest he is showing, cannot restrain himself from glancing down at the street. A two-horse coupé passes by and disappears.
    Fliess, annoyed by this momentary inattention, places his hand on Freud's shoulder. With great authority:

FLIESS   Listen to me, dear friend.

Freud turns towards him, captivated.

I could go further if I had a more thorough knowledge of neurology. You can help me.
FREUD   I'm not …
FLIESS, *not listening to him*   It all hangs together, Freud. The nose and the nerves in the nose are simply a relay.

Staring into Freud's eyes with his terrible gaze:

Everything's ruled by sex.
FREUD   By sex?

Freud pulls an astonished face. He hurriedly removes his finger from his nose.
    As he speaks, a carriage has drawn up beneath the window, but he is too absorbed on this occasion to pay any attention.

FLIESS   The biological development of the individual takes place under the control and direction of the sexual organs.

    (Forcefully:)

I know it but I can't prove it. You will help me.

Freud appears totally bewildered. His face, normally so hard, seems softened by a certain anxiety.

FREUD   I should like to help you …

(A pause.)

It takes so much courage to dare call into question ...

(A pause. Sombrely:) I don't have it.

The door of the drawing-room abruptly opens. Enter Breuer, hiding his confusion beneath an embarrassed joviality.

BREUER, *from the door*   Dear friends, I cast myself at your feet, I know that I'm unforgivable.

MATHILDE, *tartly*   Unforgivable indeed.

Breuer bows and kisses Martha's hand.

BREUER, *to Martha*   Unforgivable?

MARTHA, *affectionately*   Unforgivable, but you're forgiven.

Fliess and Freud have moved over towards Breuer. Fliess unconcernedly cordial, Freud irritable and sombre.

BREUER   Fliess and Freud know what professional obligations are. A patient delayed me.

FLIESS   Such are the drawbacks of our calling.

Freud remains silent: his silence, and the wooden face with which he confronts Breuer's smiles, show his deliberate intention of making his discontent clear.

MATHILDE   Well, let's go straight to table. Everything will be burnt to a cinder.

The two women rise to their feet. Mathilde is between Freud and Breuer.

(To Breuer:) How is it you've never spoken to Freud about your Cäcilie?

Breuer's face changes slightly. He looks at the still annoyed Freud with a timid expression.
  Mathilde leaves them to take Fliess's arm as the chambermaid throws wide the double doors leading to the dining-room.

In the dining-room, a few moments later.

The guests are sitting round a circular table in the following order: Mathilde; to Mathilde's right, Fliess; to Fliess's right, Martha; to Martha's right, Breuer, who thus finds himself beside Freud. Freud completes the circle: he is to Mathilde's left. A servant is handing round a turbot.

Breuer, very embarrassed despite the great ease of his manners, addresses the impassive Fliess but is really speaking for Freud's sake.

BREUER, *laughing*   As you can imagine, there's never been any question for me of hiding one of my patients from Freud: we have no secrets from each other.

He turns towards Freud, seeking his assent. Freud turns towards the servant, who is offering him the dish; by helping himself, he avoids replying.
Martha looks at Freud with irritation and embarrassment. She waits for a reply that does not come. Blushing slightly, she half turns towards Fliess and says with a smile:

MARTHA   No secrets! Never any secrets. Dr Breuer is my husband's big brother. Mathilde is my sister: I named my little daughter after her.

Mathilde listens in annoyance: she too now turns towards Fliess and says gaily:

MATHILDE   No secrets, no. Except one: the mysterious Cäcilie. Josef has been treating her for a year and a half.

A silence. Freud eats without raising his eyes. Breuer, still jovial, continues with false simplicity:

BREUER   There's nothing mysterious about Cäcilie. It's an extraordinary case, that's all.

He turns towards Freud.

So extraordinary that I didn't want to talk to you about it before the cure was complete. I was afraid I might be mistaken.

Freud, still sombre, does not answer. Breuer addresses Fliess.

What do you think of a patient who herself invents the therapy that suits her?
FLIESS   She must be unusually intelligent.
BREUER, *almost fatuously*   Unusually! Yes, unusually!

He proclaims his conviction with a mixture of admiration and naive self-satisfaction.

I've been merely her instrument. Even today, I have difficulty in believing it. Luckily, the results are there.

A pause. Glance at Freud, who has stopped eating and is looking straight in front of him.

It was a magnificent case of hysteria. The kind one finds in books. Contractures of the lower limbs, anaesthesias, pareses, visual and auditory disturbances, neuralgias, coughs, speech difficulties: she had everything.

FREUD, *amused*   A fugitive from the Salpêtrière!

BREUER, *put out*   The women in the Salpêtrière could barely read. This girl is from the best society, her culture is unrivalled and she has every talent.

FLIESS   What therapy has she invented?

Breuer has grown animated as he speaks: he has forgotten Freud; we sense that the subject enthrals him.

BREUER   She has quite simply reinvented hypnotism, adapting it to her illness.

Freud starts. He knocks his fork with his fingertips, and it chinks against his plate. For the first time, he turns towards Breuer. His eyes are bright with anger.

FREUD   Hypnotism? So it's true?

Breuer looks at him in astonishment.

I'd refused to believe it.

In response to Breuer's astonishment, he adds with deep dissatisfaction:

Little Dora Wassermann told me you were hypnotizing one of your patients. I laughed in her face.

His hands begin to tremble.

When I returned from Paris, six years ago, with my head full of all those fancies, you didn't defend me, Breuer, you let Meynert crush me like a worm — and you were quite right.

The two women listen in dismay. Breuer has turned pale. Only Fliess, discreetly amused, has lost neither his composure nor his appetite: the servant makes the rounds offering fresh helpings of turbot; everyone refuses with a curt, mechanical gesture, except Fliess who takes a discreet but copious second helping. He listens calmly, drinking white wine. None of all this denotes bad manners, simply a robust unconcern.

FREUD   I was mistaken! I was mistaken!
    And today it's you, you whom I respect like a father, it's you who's going in for all that quackery.

BREUER, *gently*   Listen to me, Freud.

Freud does not look at Breuer. His anger does not prevent him from being intimidated. By contrast Breuer, confronted with Freud's violence, has recovered all his calm and his composure. He looks at Freud affectionately and without the least irritation.

FREUD   Hypnotism doesn't cure! It's not a therapy, it's a cabaret turn! Charcot used to make contractures disappear under hypnosis. And afterwards? They'd reappear when the patient woke up.

BREUER   Doubtless you're right, Freud. Anyway, in 1887 I didn't believe in hypnotism. You know very well I believe only in experiment.

FREUD   And experiment drove you to make use of suggestion?

BREUER   Yes. But it's not a matter of treating symptoms directly. The charlatans are the ones who say: 'Stand up and walk' to a paralysed hysterical patient.

FREUD, *losing nothing of his aggressiveness*   Well then?

BREUER   When Cäcilie's under hypnosis she talks about her ailments, she recalls how the symptoms first appeared. And each time she's able to find in her memory the circumstances of their first appearance ...

FLIESS, *very interested*   They disappear?

BREUER   Yes. Today, they've almost all disappeared.

FREUD, *with a kind of frightened revulsion*   You get her to talk about herself?

Freud has become ashen; his hands tremble; he speaks without a trace of violence, but only by dint of considerable effort.

Then you're changing her neurosis into a psychosis: she'll die in a padded cell.

He addresses Fliess, speaking in a perturbed voice.

I gave up the method of induced sleep seven years ago. Do you know why? Because a maniac under hypnosis started telling me how he wanted to kill his father. A father whom he adored, of course. They say any kind of crazy thing, poor wretches! And what if all those crazy things remained stuck in their minds? If that poor imbecile raving on his couch ... if he'd convinced himself he was destined to be a parricide? Stirring up mud is useless!

A servant comes in and goes over to Breuer.

SERVANT   There's a man in the hall asking for Dr Freud. He says he has been searching for him everywhere.

Freud looks at the servant bad-temperedly.

FREUD   Can't I be left in peace? *(A pause.)* From whom?

SERVANT   I beg your pardon?

FREUD   Who has sent him?

SERVANT   Professor Meynert.

Freud rises abruptly to his feet.

FREUD, *painfully*   What does he want?
SERVANT   Professor Meynert is asking to see you. Apparently it's urgent.

All look at Freud, who is pale, with drawn features and wide eyes. For a moment he remains dumb and overwhelmed; then he regains control of himself, bows to Mathilde and forces a smile.

FREUD   Well, it comes to all of us in the end, Mathilde. (*A pause.*) I beg of you, finish the meal without waiting for me.

He goes out. The guests look at each other anxiously.
   Martha seems almost terrified. She rolls a pellet of bread between her fingers. Breuer looks at her and says to her gently:

BREUER   If Meynert's going to die, it's better they should see each other again.

Martha looks at him.

MARTHA   Better or worse, I don't know. But something's going to change, I'm sure of that.
MATHILDE   What, dearest?

She stares into space.

MARTHA   I wonder … Perhaps we'll never be happy again.

[6]

Meynert's bedroom.

Luxurious — but with a German bad taste of the period. In any case, however, the lighting is too weak for us to be able to make out the furnishings.

A kerosene lamp placed on a little round table enables us to see only a bed ready to receive the patient and, not far from the bed, a big comfortable-looking armchair in which the patient is seated.

Meynert has aged greatly: the wrinkles that ravaged his face have deepened, his beard and hair are now entirely grey. But the fact that he has grown old is less striking than his waxy pallor.

His hands themselves are white, even the fingernails. He is wearing a dressing-gown, and beneath the dressing-gown a nightshirt.

A pillow behind his head, a blanket round his knees. His feet — hidden in fact by the blanket — are propped up on a stool of which we can see the base alone.

Only Meynert's gaze has lost nothing of its hardness or force. The patient's lids were closed, but suddenly he opens his eyes and his gaze — full of intelligence, but somehow haunted — searches the shadows.

Meynert's voice is low, but this is because he is sparing it.

MEYNERT   Freud?

He does not wait for a reply.

Come over here.

Freud goes over to him.
He is almost as pale as Meynert, and his eyes are as hard. With one hand, Meynert waves him feebly to a chair.
Freud goes and sits down.

Come closer to me: I've been forbidden to speak loudly.

Freud pulls his chair up close to Meynert.

MEYNERT   Are you still searching for male hysterical patients?

At this reminder of the 1887 lecture and their quarrel, Freud frowns and shakes his head almost imperceptibly as a sign of denial. Meynert understands the sign.

Pity. I could have presented you with a fine specimen.

Freud, dumbfounded and mistrustful, guesses beforehand the reply to the question he puts.

FREUD   Who?

Meynert has recovered his bitter, ironical smile. He says with simplicity and almost with pride:

MEYNERT   Me.

Freud does not reply.
    He looks at Meynert: on his face, astonishment is mingled with a sudden, deep understanding — and, less clearly, with a certain satisfaction.
    Meynert continues, with a kind of sombre pride:

I knew the symptoms before Charcot; I learned about them the hard way — I had them all.

Still more proudly:

All. No one knew anything.

Freud speaks harshly: his resentment has not abated.

FREUD   When you threw me out of your laboratory, you already knew that?
MEYNERT   I'd known it for twenty years.
FREUD   You called me a buffoon and a charlatan.
MEYNERT   You know the story of Noah: a son mustn't see his father's nakedness.

He looks at him without tenderness and without regret. In a factual tone of voice:

You were my spiritual son.

Freud, in the same tone of voice, with an additional touch of sadness:

FREUD   Yes. And you cursed me. You ruined my life. I was a scientist, not a doctor. Medicine disgusts me: I don't like torturing people on the pretext that they're ill.

    (A pause.)

For six years I've carried out no research. I torture neurotic people I can't cure.

Meynert laughs feebly.

MEYNERT   Electrotherapy, baths and massage?
FREUD, *bitterly*   Massage, baths, electrotherapy.

134

Meynert laughs a little louder.

MEYNERT   One might just as well put a poultice on a wooden leg.

Harshly, with sparkling eyes:

It's quite useless.
FREUD   I know. And yet I prescribe nothing else.

Meynert, with a still more ironical smile:

MEYNERT   At all events, it can't do any harm.
FREUD   Not even that.

(A pause.)

Who would you call the charlatan? The young man who sincerely *believed* in the virtues of hypnotism or the man of today, who prescribes a treatment he doesn't believe in?

Meynert has closed his eyes and does not reply.
  Freud looks at him with growing anxiety.
  After a moment, he rises noiselessly to his feet and is about to go over to the patient.
  Meynert hears him and speaks without opening his eyes.

MEYNERT   Sit down. I'm not asleep, I'm gathering my thoughts. I'm very weak. I have to talk to you. Don't interrupt me.

He speaks at first with his eyes closed; in a moment, he will open them.

Sufferers from neurosis form a fraternity. They rarely know each other, yet they recognize each other. At first sight. Just one rule: silence. Normal people, that's who our enemies are.
  I've kept the secret ... All my life — even from myself; I've refused to know myself.

He opens his eyes and looks intently at Freud.

You belong to the fraternity, Freud. Or very nearly ... I hated you, because you wanted to betray ... I was wrong.

(A pause.)

My life has been nothing but play-acting. I've wasted my time hiding the truth. I was *keeping quiet.*

Result: I'm dying with pride, but in ignorance.

Bitter smile.

A disciple of knowledge must *know*, mustn't he? I don't know who I am. It's not I who has lived my life: it's an Other.

He once more closes his eyes. Freud seems overwhelmed. He leans forward and timidly lays his hand upon the sick man's pale hand, which is lying on the arm of his chair.
Meynert reopens his eyes. He looks exhausted. But for the first time since the beginning of the film, he looks at Freud almost with affection.
In a quicker, weaker voice:

Break the silence. Betray us. Find the secret. Expose it to the light of day, even if it means revealing your own.
It's necessary to dig deep down. Into the mud.

At these last words, Freud withdraws his hand and recoils somewhat.

Didn't you know that?
FREUD, *slowly*   Into the mud? Yes, I know.
MEYNERT   Does that frighten you?
FREUD   Yes. I ... I'm not an angel.
MEYNERT   So much the better. Angels don't understand men.

Freud's face has altered: he is still sombre but his eyes are shining.

FREUD   What if I weren't capable ...
MEYNERT   If you're not, no one will be.

A silence. He raises his voice slightly.

For six years you've been champing at the bit ... Now charge: it's in your character. Retreat before nothing. If your strength fails you, make a pact with the Devil.

More quietly, but with burning conviction:

It would be splendid to risk Hell so that everyone could live under the light of Heaven.

He has half raised himself, his pillow slips down behind him. Freud rises and repositions the pillow.
Meynert lets himself sink back.

For my part, I lost — through lack of courage. Your turn to play. Farewell.

He is breathing through his mouth. Very slight rattle. Weary, painful expression. His eyes are open and staring. He repeats very softly, as if to himself:

Lost.

Freud looks at him for a moment, impassively.

    Meynert no longer even seems aware of his presence.

    Freud stretches out his hand timidly. Touches the dying man's pale hand with his fingertips, turns on his heel and leaves noiselessly.

7

The Breuers' dining-room.

The guests are awaiting Freud's return, their empty plates before them.
  Conversation continues between Fliess and Mathilde, broken by long silences.
  Breuer and Martha say nothing: the former appears ill at ease, the latter worried and on edge.

MATHILDE   And that avenue in the middle of the Tiergarten ... what do you call it?
  It's so beautiful.
FLIESS   The Siegesallee.
MATHILDE   Oh!

  A pause.

FLIESS   We have nothing to equal your Ring ...
MATHILDE   The Ring is beautiful. But I've seen the seagulls over the Spree ...
FLIESS, *distantly*   The seagulls. Oh yes ... But you have the Danube ...

  A silence. The clock strikes ten. Martha shivers.

MARTHA   Mathilde, ten o'clock! I beg of you, have dinner served! (*Forcing a smile:*)
  We'll give Dr Fliess a very poor impression of Viennese hospitality.
FLIESS   Madam, please ...

  There is an imperious ring at the front door.

BREUER   There he is.
MATHILDE   It's not his ring.

  Martha rises abruptly to her feet; without moving from her place, she peers through the glazed door.

MARTHA, *relieved, almost joyful*   It's him! It's him!

  Everybody turns towards the entrance.
  Breuer, worried, says half-aloud as if to himself:

BREUER   I wonder what they can have had to say to each other.

  The door opens.
  Freud comes in.

He looks distraught, almost exhausted. At the same time, a considerable change seems to have taken place in him; something has blossomed; he appears almost joyful.

MARTHA and BREUER, *almost together*   How is he?

Freud sits down in his place and picks up his napkin.

FREUD, *speaking with a kind of almost naive simplicity, as if he had passed beyond his feelings of grief:*   There's no hope. In my opinion, it's a matter of hours.

He looks at the guests without seeing them. He says mechanically:

Did you wait for me?

Fastening his gaze on Fliess, abruptly, with a kind of burning, suppressed enthusiasm.

He's an extraordinary man.

Mathilde signals to the servant, who goes out, fetches a roast of beef and offers it to the guests during the scene which follows.
     Everyone helps themselves.
     Freud stares into space, he is now almost smiling.

MARTHA, *more worried than curious*   What did he say to you?

Freud makes a gesture of dismissal at this question. He says nothing. The servant has served the two women and Fliess; he bends over Freud, who does not see him.
     The servant remains in this position, trying to attract Freud's attention.
     Martha draws Freud's attention to the dish:

Sigmund!

Freud comes to himself, looks at the dish with a surprised expression and makes a gesture of refusal.

FREUD   Oh! . . . No, thank you.

The servant goes to serve Breuer. There is a moment's silence, then Freud turns abruptly towards Breuer. He has a friendly, respectful expression.

Breuer, I should like to see your Cäcilie.

Breuer looks embarrassed and displeased.
     Freud seems not to notice this.

When you next visit her, take me with you.

MATHILDE, *ironically*   The next visit will be tomorrow morning, never fear!

Freud reiterates ardently:

FREUD   Take me with you.

BREUER   But you said ...

FREUD   Stupidities. I apologize humbly.

BREUER   I don't know if I can ... without preparing her ...

MATHILDE, *laughing*   She'll be delighted. (*To Martha:*) That girl worships the ground he treads on.

BREUER   It's a delicate treatment ...

MATHILDE, *still laughing*   A twosome, you see? With a threesome, the patient becomes difficult.

BREUER   Very well!

Breuer casts a hostile, angry glance at Mathilde.
    He makes his decision swiftly.

(Rather drily, to Freud:)

Come and pick me up here tomorrow at ten o'clock. I think I'll be able to show you the disappearance of two complementary symptoms: psychic deafness and a convergent squint. I promise you won't forget the experience.

(With a constrained laugh, to Fliess:) While we're about it, may I ask you to join us? I'm not entirely sure that Cäcilie's cough is hysterical, and I'd like you to examine her throat.

FLIESS   Very willingly, I'll arrange to be free.

MATHILDE   And now the threesome has become a foursome. The more the merrier! *(To Martha:)* You'd better watch out, Martha: that woman's to be feared! It seems she's an enchantress.

MARTHA, *calmly*   I'm not afraid of anything.

Freud starts to laugh.

MATHILDE   You're very trusting: I admire you.

Freud still retains the distraught expression he was wearing when he came into the room.

FREUD   There's no great merit involved, Mathilde: who could be so crazy as to think I attract the attention of women. *(Pointing to Martha:)* I'm still wondering why this one married me.

He turns to Breuer and, as he speaks, contemplates him with deep and affectionate admiration.

There's the husband who should be watched. If I were you, Mathilde, I'd lock him up: that man is too majestic and too handsome not to steal the hearts of all his female patients.

Everybody laughs, Mathilde more loudly than the rest. Martha utters a cry.

MARTHA   What's the matter with you?

She points at Mathilde's left hand, which is bleeding profusely: deep cuts on three fingers.

MATHILDE, *who is looking at Freud and Breuer and laughing*   Me? Nothing.

   (She lowers her eyes to her hand and utters a faint cry, almost a sigh.)

Mathilde has turned quite pale.
   She speaks in an altered voice, with great effort.

How stupid! I picked up this knife by the blade.

Martha at once rises to her feet and comes over to put an arm round her shoulders.

MARTHA, *tenderly*   Come, Mathilde, come quickly.

She leads her away. The three men have risen. Martha makes a gesture declining their services.

No, we don't need any gentlemen, especially if they're doctors. We shan't be long.

The two women go out. Mathilde is on the point of fainting. Martha supports her.
   When the door has closed, Breuer gives a little false laugh.

BREUER   Well, well! A dinner of upsets.

The two guests do not answer him: they remain standing, their faces turned to the glazed door.
   Seeing Freud's grave and frowning demeanour, Breuer changes his tone; he adds seriously, gesturing towards the door:

A touch of neurasthenia: nothing serious. After ten years of marriage, it isn't good for a couple not to have children.

8

Next morning, around nine o'clock.

In Breuer's barouche.

A fine June morning. The barouche is traversing an outlying neighbourhood — at first poor, then residential: villas and gardens.

Breuer is speaking, in a calm, objective tone. He has evidently reconciled himself in the end to this three-way visit.

Freud listens with the closest attention.

Fliess is more relaxed.

He looks at Breuer from time to time, but we are never sure whether he is listening — and his terrible, flaming eyes never seem to be looking.

BREUER, *continuing a conversation begun long before*   The first disturbances date from her father's death. He had heart trouble and collapsed right in the street. She adored him: you can just imagine the shock. A traumatism, in the most literal sense.

FREUD   What happened to her?

BREUER   Everything, as I told you — even frightful hallucinations. But we've eliminated the symptoms one by one.

Freud pulls out his cigar-case and mechanically takes a cigar.

FREUD   How?

As Breuer prepares to reply, Fliess notices that Freud is going to smoke.

He turns his terrible eyes towards him. He seems interested for the first time.

FLIESS, *imperiously*   You smoke too much.

Freud starts; he hestitates for a moment, but eventually answers amiably enough.

FREUD   You're quite right.

FLIESS, *same tone*   You should at least give up the morning cigars. They are ... terrible.

Freud frowns, hesitates and eventually replaces the cigar in the case and the case in his pocket.

He acts more out of politeness than out of true submission. Breuer regards the scene with amused surprise.

BREUER, *to Fliess*   Bravo! For six years I've been trying to convince him, and you succeed at the first try.

Fliess merely smiles, with the slightest hint of fatuousness. Freud, faintly irritated, turns towards Breuer.

FREUD   Well? This method?

BREUER   From the very first months of treatment, I realized that she was putting herself in a state akin to that provoked by suggestion. In this … self-hypnosis, memories come back to her, she recounts everything which can be of help to her. For example, the events which have accompanied or provoked the appearance of a hysterical symptom. When she wakes up, I remind her of what she has told me and the symptom disappears.

FREUD   It never returns?

BREUER   Some have returned, but that's because she hadn't told me everything. In the evenings, she's forgetful and tired. A lot of patience is needed.

A silence. The three men ponder.
    The barouche passes along a wide road flanked by villas.
    Breuer pensively lights a gold-tipped cigarette.

That gave me the idea of returning every morning and hypnotizing her myself. I ask her to concentrate her thoughts on the symptom she has singled out, and for which she hasn't found any reason.

FREUD   Does she talk?

BREUER   Very easily. She cleanses herself, she hunts out the bad memories lurking in dark corners. Do you know what she calls this? 'Sweeping the chimneys of the brain'.

    (He laughs complacently.)

The barouche enters a park, through an open gate: lawns, groves, ornamental lake; beyond them, a pretty single-storey villa. A perron with three steps leads to the front door.

We've arrived.

[9]

A few moments later.

On the perron, a woman of around forty, dark clothes, austere bearing, awaits them. She must have been very beautiful, and still would be if it were not for the severity and harshness of her countenance.

Breuer appears, climbs the steps and kisses her hand.

BREUER, *introducing*   Dr Fliess, an eminent throat specialist, who is willing to examine our Cäcilie.

Fliess kisses Frau Körtner's hand.

Dr Freud, my closest friend.

Freud bows slightly and shakes the hand offered him.

FRAU KÖRTNER   Come in, gentlemen.

They enter a large, bright room: no furniture. Good taste, but a certain puritanism. A big fireplace, bare walls, a circular table, round the table fine old chairs, but of wood.

As they enter behind Frau Körtner, she turns round towards Breuer who is following her. (Fliess is behind Breuer and Freud brings up the rear.)

Cäcilie worries me. She's awake but she claims she can't open her eyes.

BREUER, *smiling*   I promised I'd open them for her myself.

He indicates Fliess.

Dr Fliess will be so kind as to wait here. Three of us round the patient's bed would be too much. He'll make his examination when I've seen her. Come along, Freud.

They enter the neighbouring room.

Cäcilie's bedroom.

It is the same room that we saw on the previous evening. The shutters are open.

This room, much smaller than the hall we have just left, is furnished with charming taste (eighteenth century). It is the room of a stylish, sensitive young woman. Mirrors, dressing-tables, wing-chairs. Shelves full of books run round the room. The bed is made up and covered with white furs.

Cäcilie is fully dressed. Light-coloured gown. Hair arranged with great care (blonde hair in a coil). She is reclining on a couch, two cushions beneath her head, a blanket over her legs. She is knitting. But her eyes are obstinately closed.

As they enter, Breuer whispers to Freud, with a kind of ecstasy that he barely attempts to conceal:

BREUER, *in a slow whisper*   She's beautiful.

Freud looks at the young patient with a hard, penetrating gaze. He does not answer: manifestly, Cäcilie's beauty does not interest him.

A very faint smile touches Cäcilie's lips, as if she had heard the phrase, albeit uttered very quietly and a long way away from her.

Breuer signals to Freud to stay where he is and goes over to Cäcilie. The latter's smile grows more pronounced.

CÄCILIE, *gaily*   Good morning, Doctor.
BREUER   Did you hear me?
CÄCILIE   I recognized the sound of your footsteps.

Breuer is at the patient's bedside. He speaks to her, throughout the scene, in a tender, passionate but restrained voice. He will demonstrate an exceptional gentleness, as if he were deeply conscious of the girl's fragility.

Pointing to her eyes with the tip of her forefinger, Cäcilie adds:

My poor Mama wanted to dress me, but as you can see I've kept my word.
    Now you must keep yours.

With a slightly teasing emphasis:

Dr Josef Breuer, give me back light.

Breuer bends down. He places his thumbs on Cäcilie's eyes. She opens her eyelids. Her eyes — as we saw on the previous day — are afflicted with a convergent squint.

She raises herself slightly, takes Breuer's hand, holds it between both her own hands and transports it towards her eyes.

BREUER   What are you doing?
CÄCILIE   I want to see your hand. I can only see things close to. It's a big, big hand.

With a kind of stifled cry:

Enormous!

She repulses it, thrusting it far away from her. Fit of coughing. Breuer lays his hand on her head and the fit ceases.

    In a voice still strangled by the cough:

You must cure my eyes.

BREUER   Don't be afraid, Cäcilie. We're going to try. This very day.

CÄCILIE   Are you going to sweep the chimneys of my mind?

BREUER   Of course.

CÄCILIE   Then chimney-sweeping it is!

Breuer signals to Freud to approach. He moves forward heavily — we can tell that he is deliberately making a noise. Despite the sound of his footsteps, Cäcilie seems unaware of his presence.

    He bows. Breuer signals to him to speak.

FREUD   My humble respects, Fräulein.

Cäcilie does not answer.

I'm a doctor too. My great friend Dr Breuer has been so good as to permit me to accompany him.

She lays her knitting down on a pedestal table near the couch, but with the greatest difficulty: her convergent squint prevents her from locating objects precisely. Her hand gropes around blindly, touches the table and lets go of the knitting, which falls to the floor.

    Breuer hastens to pick up the knitting and replace it on the table. He takes Cäcilie's blindly groping hand and replaces it on the couch.

CÄCILIE, *delighted*   You picked up my knitting!

Cäcilie — continuing to ignore Freud — smiles at Breuer without seeing him.

How kind you are. Thank you.

Freud, watching attentively, looks as much at Breuer as at Cäcilie. His gaze travels from one to the other, as if he were discovering a strange and profound bond between them.

BREUER   Cäcilie, you haven't said good morning to Dr Freud.

CÄCILIE   Is there someone here?

BREUER   Yes: one of my friends whom I wanted to introduce to you.

CÄCILIE, *put out*   Oh!

    (A pause.)

What's your name?

FREUD, *loud, clear voice*   Sigmund Freud.

Cäcilie's face remains impassive, she awaits a response.

BREUER, *almost in a whisper*   Dr Sigmund Freud.
CÄCILIE, *repeating docilely*   Dr. Sigmund Freud.

Not very amiably:

Forgive me, Dr Freud, I'm deaf and almost blind. (*Quickly and with asperity*) I don't see in what way I can be of interest to you.
BREUER, *warmly*   Cäcilie! You're not deaf, since you can hear me.
CÄCILIE, *shrugging her shoulders*   Of course I can hear you. And I can hear my poor mother too.

A pause. Smiling to herself:

That's not the same.

Breuer smiles too, with barely veiled satisfaction. He bends over her and puts his forefinger between her eyes.

BREUER   Look at my finger.
CÄCILIE   I can see nothing else.
BREUER   You're going to sleep.

Freud goes and fetches two chairs and brings them up close to the couch. He sits on one of them and looks Breuer up and down. Breuer speaks more as a man in love than as a doctor. He tempers his authority with affection. Cäcilie stirs restlessly.

Go to sleep, please now.

She has difficulty falling asleep.

CÄCILIE   You're not alone. That bothers me.
BREUER   Don't worry about a thing, Cäcilie. Sleep.

She is still restless. He insists. Masterful, like a man who knows he is loved:

Do it *for me.*
CÄCILIE   For you?

She closes her eyes and smiles.
        Freud has frowned. This over-intimate contact between the practitioner and his patient

obviously displeases him, but without diminishing the rapt interest with which he follows the experiment.

> *Cäcilie is already asleep, her eyes closed. She breathes peacefully.*

In the large room next door.

Fliess is seated at the table, on a wooden chair. On the other side of the table, Frau Körtner is like-wise seated.

> *They are both stiff, silent, almost hostile. Both have harsh features, handsome faces with terrible eyes.*

> *Fliess seems irritated by the waiting. He drums with his left hand on the table. A clock strikes. They start and turn round: it is ten in the morning.*

In Cäcilie's bedroom.

Breuer has pulled out his watch and is checking the time. Between his teeth:

BREUER   It's time.

He bends over Cäcilie.

Cäcilie!
> Open your eyes.

She opens her eyes. A silence. Then he questions her:

Your sight problems, when did they appear?
CÄCILIE   I don't know.

She speaks in a hoarser voice. Without gestures or changes of facial expression.

A very long time ago. They come and go.
BREUER   And the deafness?
CÄCILIE   It's the same thing. When I see badly, I hear badly.
BREUER   All the same, there was a beginning.
CÄCILIE   Yes.
BREUER   When?

He has bent over her and waits.

CÄCILIE   Give me your hand. To help me.

Breuer takes her hand.

One day I woke up: I was deaf and half blind.

BREUER   And what had happened?

CÄCILIE   When?

BREUER   Just before that.

CÄCILIE   Nothing. I was asleep.

She makes an effort. She finds a memory.

Oh, yes! I'd taken some sleeping tablets.

BREUER   Why?

She seems surprised by the question.

CÄCILIE   I suppose, because I couldn't sleep.

BREUER   What prevented you?

CÄCILIE   Would you sleep, the day before your father's funeral?

BREUER   So your afflictions appeared on the day of the funeral?

A brief silence. Cäcilie seems astonished.

CÄCILIE   Good Heavens! ... Yes.

BREUER   Did you go to the church?

CÄCILIE   No.

BREUER   How about the cemetery?

CÄCILIE   I couldn't.

BREUER   Did you want to go?

CÄCILIE, *impatiently*   I told you, it was my father they were burying!

BREUER   But you didn't go?

CÄCILIE   That's because I was prevented.

BREUER   By what?

CÄCILIE   By ... By ... *(In a voice of despair:)* I couldn't see a thing any more.

BREUER   What had happened the evening before?

CÄCILIE   Nothing. It was a Tuesday. I stayed by the coffin.

BREUER   How about Monday?

CÄCILIE   That's the day they brought his body back.

BREUER, *in surprise*   On Monday? You must be mistaken, Cäcilie: people aren't buried that quickly.

CÄCILIE, *obstinately*   On the Monday they brought us back his body.

BREUER   I beg of you, child, try again to remember. On Monday, your father has a stroke in the middle of the street and his body's brought home; on Tuesday he's already in his coffin, and on Wednesday he's buried.

Cäcilie weeps quietly. Tears roll down her cheeks. Breuer seems deeply moved.

Answer, Cäcilie. Don't cry.

In obvious agitation:

Don't cry. Don't cry.

A tear has remained on Cäcilie's cheek. Breuer puts out his hand and brushes away the tear, with the tip of his forefinger.
    Freud watches Breuer uneasily, then swiftly turns his eyes away and returns to Cäcilie.
    She relaxes somewhat as she feels the light caress of Breuer's finger on her cheek. She says abruptly, but without intonation:

CÄCILIE   He didn't die on Monday.
    He had his stroke during the night from Saturday to Sunday.
BREUER, *dumbfounded*   What?

Meaning wink from Breuer to Freud.

You never told me that.

Cäcilie's hands begin to flutter again. She closes her eyes.

CÄCILIE   I didn't remember any more.

Breuer takes one of her hands in his own and squeezes it as he questions her.

BREUER   What happened between Saturday and Monday?
    What was done with the body?
CÄCILIE   They kept it.
BREUER   Where?
CÄCILIE   At ... at ... the hospital.
BREUER   At the hospital? Why?

She does not answer. Freud has bent over her: he watches her avidly.

CÄCILIE   Because my mother wasn't in Vienna.
BREUER   Where was she?
CÄCILIE   At Graz. At her brother's.
BREUER   How about you?
CÄCILIE   At home. All alone.

We can see only her head and the pillow. She repeats:

All alone.

She opens her eyes, rises to her feet. It is the same room, but the curtains are drawn. A bedside lamp is burning.

10

Freud and Breuer have disappeared, the chairs they occupied are back in their usual places. Cäci-
lie, whom we now see fully, has normal eyes: the convergent squint has totally disappeared. She is
in her nightdress. She hurriedly takes a dressing-gown, slips it on, ties the belt, puts on some slip-
pers and picks up the lamp.

CÄCILIE'S VOICE OFF   It was past midnight. I thought they were going to break the
door in.

The whole scene is shot with total realism (exactly like the preceding scenes). Simply we hear noth-
ing but the voices off of Cäcilie and Breuer. Not a sound.
  She goes to the door of her room, opens it, passes through into the hall and goes over to the front
door. She seems to be listening.

BREUER, *voice off*   Who?

On the front steps. Moonlight. Two policemen are knocking at the shutters.
  We now see Cäcilie, on the other side of the door, hurrying to open the bolts, then the door, then
the shutters.

CÄCILIE   How do you mean?
BREUER   Who was knocking?
CÄCILIE, *voice off*   Doctors.

As they are opened, the shutters reveal to us two gentlemen — fur-lined coats, flowing beards —
who bow with exquisite courtesy, holding their top-hats in their hands.

CÄCILIE, *voice off*   They were coming to warn me.

Cäcilie listens to them speak (their lips move but no sound issues from their mouths); her eyes
widen, she puts a hand in front of her mouth and sways.
  They rush forward to stop her falling and lead her gently towards an open two-horse carriage.
This whole scene is played with no exaggeration on the part of the actors, but it must appear very
slightly stilted and out-of-date.
  She installs herself on the rear seat, the two doctors on the front seat, their top-hats on their
knees. The driver whips up the two horses, which move off at top speed.
  Here again, nothing should seem false properly speaking, but in the very realism of the scene
something should seem uncanny (unheimlich): the fact, for example, of seeing this beautiful blonde
girl, with disordered hair, sitting in her dressing-gown and nightdress opposite those two bearded
men; the fact, too, that the horses move off at top speed (which in a sense is normal, given that the
case is an emergency, but which can nevertheless produce a jarring effect, by seeming almost like

the start of a wagon race).
Cäcilie, thrown backwards, silent, is beautiful, pale and tragic.

FREUD, *voice off*   Doctors?

The image literally explodes and we return to the bedroom. Freud is speaking:

Usually, they send porters or orderlies.

Cäcilie, her eyes open, does not seem even to hear him.
Breuer lets go of Cäcilie's hand and, with an abrupt, almost violent gesture — that contrasts with his usual behaviour — imposes silence upon Freud. The latter, intimidated, does not insist.
Breuer takes Cäcilie's hand again.

BREUER, *gently*   Go on, child, go on.
CÄCILIE   We arrived at the hospital after midnight.

A corridor. On the walls, frescos representing scenes from mythology: Venus rising from the waves (inspired by the Botticelli painting), Danäe and the shower of gold (inspired by Titian), Spring (Botticelli). To the right and left, plaster statues (half-naked women supporting the ceiling).
Doors (small but sumptuous, fine carved oak, brass handles). Above each door a sign: **Ophthalmology Ward, Neurology Ward**, *etc. etc.*
No sound except that of an orchestra playing a Viennese waltz.

CÄCILIE   They were playing music for the patients.

Cäcilie, between the two doctors who have replaced their top-hats on their heads, walks hurriedly along the corridor.

I remember!
There was a hole in the carpet, I almost tripped over.

We see that the floor is carpeted in red. The carpet is dirty and worn through in places. Cäcilie's right slipper catches in the frayed material at the edge of a hole. She stumbles, her bare foot comes out of the slipper. She recovers her balance. A doctor kneels down, and hands her the slipper. The music swells and becomes vulgar.

I couldn't bear it!
BREUER'S VOICE OFF   What?
CÄCILIE   The music.
(*Sharply:*) You don't play waltzes when people are dead.

A door suddenly opens to her right.
The two doctors place themselves to right and left of the door and usher her in with a bow. She

goes into a little room with silk-covered walls.

A fresco on the (low) ceiling representing Michelangelo's prophetesses (Sistine). Their figures are grouped round a chandelier (glass, gas-lit). The music swells. In the four corners of the room, a headless Graeco-Roman statue.

CÄCILIE   We went in. It was a private room. Statues everywhere. The nurses were shivering, they had goose-flesh.

We perceive, around the bed and hiding its occupant, women dressed in short nightdresses, over which they have hastily thrown nurses' tunics they have not even bothered to button up. They are heavily made up, but with harsh, austere faces and hair pulled back.

BREUER, *amazed*   Goose-flesh? Why?

CÄCILIE   It was late, they must have been dragged out of bed like me. They were wearing nightdresses under their tunics.

One of the nurses turns round and goes towards Cäcilie.

It's absurd.

She is wearing a nightdress. She comes towards Cäcilie and shows her the bed.

CÄCILIE   It's absurd. I can see one who wasn't wearing a tunic at all.

Shot of Cäcilie, who is looking at the (invisible) nurse in astonishment.

My memory must be deceiving me.

The nurse reappears, dressed in a tunic properly buttoned up. Austere face without makeup, nurse's cap.
She has taken Cäcilie by the hand and is leading her towards the bed.

CÄCILIE'S VOICE OFF, *quite altered, slightly vulgar*   Come along now, me darlings, clear off!

BREUER, *astounded*   What?

CÄCILIE   That's what she said.

The women stand back from the bed. It is an iron bed, like the ones we saw in the neurology ward in Part One.
A man — at first we see only his feet and trouser-bottoms. Our view travels up his legs. He is in evening dress, with decorations. His head is not seen.

I saw my father on a hospital bed. Abandoned by everybody.
    Like a dog.

(Calmly:)

He had a death's-head.

We still do not see his head.

BREUER   A death's-head?

CÄCILIE   Yes. Like skeletons. It must have been a mask. They put them on dead bodies in hospitals, don't they?

BREUER   It must have been painful for you.

CÄCILIE, *still calm*   Very painful.

Cäcilie kneels in tears at the dead man's bedside. She takes the dead man's hand and presses it to her face.

CÄCILIE, *serenely*   So I wouldn't see it any more, I flung myself on his hand.

With sudden passion:

I could see only his fingers, those great fingers of his that I loved.

She covers it with kisses. She looks ardently at the thumb of the hand, from close to.
We see her full-face, in close-up. She looks at the finger and her eyes, converging on the thumb which she is pressing against her lips and nose, reproduce the former squint.

11

In the bedroom.

Cäcilie stretched out on the bed (convergent squinting of the eyes). Freud and Breuer. Eloquent wink from Breuer to Freud, signifying: 'Now we're there.'

BREUER   On the following days, you saw the death's-head again.

CÄCILIE   Yes. When I was watching by the coffin. And on the morning of the funeral, when I woke up.

BREUER   And each time you saw it, you thought again of your father's hand and you imagined you were looking at it from right close to.

Cäcilie has closed her eyes again.

CÄCILIE   Yes. I remember ... On the day of the funeral, I woke up with a start. I saw the death's-head. Just above me. And straight away, I began to squint. And I've never seen anything again except right close to.

BREUER, *gently*   And that's everything, Cäcilie, that's everything. The mental chimney-sweeping is over. As you saw the death's head at a certain distance, you began to squint with both eyes, in the way a person looks at something from right close to.

CÄCILIE   Yes. To defend myself.

BREUER, *tenderly*   It's over, Cäcilie. It's all over. You're going to open your eyes and recover the healthy eyesight you used to enjoy in the old days.

She stirs restlessly.

Open your eyes: you'll never squint again.

Cäcilie opens her eyes. The convergent squint remains unchanged.
   In vexation, but almost whispering:

Oh!

He makes a gesture of annoyance, and turns towards Freud, at once bewildered and somewhat aggressive.
   Like someone who has just botched a conjuring-trick.

BREUER, *whispering*   A lot of patience is needed.
   Success isn't automatic.

Freud does not reply.

He seems perplexed and sunk in his own reflections.

I'm going to wake her up.

Freud starts.

FREUD   Allow me to ask her a few questions.

BREUER, *grudgingly*   You won't get anything else out of her. What's more, these sessions are tiring. We mustn't overtax her.

He turns towards Freud, who seems really enthralled. Breuer looks at him for a moment and seems to understand the importance that Freud attaches to this interrogation.
With a gesture of sullen resignation:

Very well! Be brief.

Freud, without leaving his chair, bends over the patient.

FREUD, *bending towards the patient, in a voice choked by timidity*   Cäcilie!

She does not seem to hear him. More loudly:

Cäcilie!

A pause. He leans back in his chair with a certain frustration. Breuer smiles with veiled satisfaction.

BREUER   She hears only me, I told you.

Freud regains hope and turns to Breuer with eyes aflame.

FREUD   Ask her to listen to me. And to answer me.

BREUER, *recovering his authority*   Freud, you've never practised this method and you don't know the patient … We're taking a big risk.

A silence.

FREUD, *impatiently*   I'll be careful.

BREUER   Tell me your questions, I'll ask them myself.

FREUD   Allow me to do it, I beg of you. I should like a direct contact.

Breuer bends towards Cäcilie. At once ingratiating and masterful:

BREUER   Cäcilie, my friend Dr Freud is going to question you.

CÄCILIE   You know I shan't hear him.

BREUER, *insistent*   You'll hear him, Cäcilie. I request you to hear him. And you'll answer him.

CÄCILIE   Very well.

Breuer leans back and invites Freud to begin.
  Freud bends forward.
  Breuer contemplates the scene almost malevolently. We sense that he is watching Freud closely, ready to intervene at the slightest blunder.

FREUD   Cäcilie, tell me again the story of that night between Saturday and Sunday. Try hard to remember.
  There was a knock and you went to open the door.

We once more see Cäcilie in her dressing-gown in front of the bolted front door.
  Cäcilie unbolts the door and prepares to open the shutters as we saw her do earlier.

FREUD'S VOICE OFF   You opened the door, and what did you see?

But at the moment when she is about to push back the shutters, and consequently see her visitors, Freud's voice immobilizes her:

Not doctors, Cäcilie! Certainly not doctors! Doctors on duty do not leave the hospital for a single moment.
  So whom?

Suddenly:

Wasn't it policemen?

With an abrupt movement Cäcilie opens the shutters: the two policemen we glimpsed before are standing in front of the door.
  They look ill at ease, but coarse and devoid of any courtesy.

Answer, Cäcilie! Answer!

They speak brutally, but with an effort at politeness. Cäcilie listens to them, pale with anxiety and grief.
  She turns away and goes off, leaving the French window open.

CÄCILIE'S VOICE OFF   I don't know. I don't remember.

The policemen remain on the perron.

FREUD, *voice off*   Doctors would have given you time to get dressed.

Cäcilie comes back in a suit, fully dressed but hatless. She looks at the policemen in angry indignation and goes out; they follow her.

CÄCILIE'S VOICE OFF   I . . . I did get dressed.

FREUD   A barouche was waiting for you?

CÄCILIE   Yes. One with two horses.

FREUD   There's not a doctor in all Vienna who has a two-horse barouche.

A carriage is waiting in the garden. But it is a common or garden 'Black Maria'. A two-horse one, of course.
    Before climbing in, Cäcilie recoils; then she gets in, followed proudly by the two policemen.

CÄCILIE'S VOICE OFF   Oh, God! *(she sighs in distress).*

We find ourselves once more in the bedroom.

Breuer places his hand on Freud's shoulder and pulls him back.

BREUER   You're tiring her! Just because of a few trivial contradictions, you're not going to . . .

FREUD, *indignantly*   Trivial!

BREUER, *peremptorily*   It sometimes happens that she contradicts herself. It's of no importance. I know her better than you.

He looks at Freud with the jealous anger of a man in love.
    Freud, intimidated, very reluctantly holds his tongue. Breuer bends over Cäcilie to awaken her.

Cäcilie!

Cäcilie suddenly struggles, her hands tremble, her face is contorted.

CÄCILIE, *in a fury*   Leave me alone! Leave me alone! You've insulted me!

Furious glance from Breuer at Freud: 'You see what you've done!'
    Freud, bending over the patient too, pays no attention at all.
    But Cäcilie proceeds, and Breuer, dumbfounded, gives up trying to wake her.

My father was dead and you made me climb into a police-wagon, like a common thief.
    You're lying! My father's a mainstay of the Empire, a man of impeccable morality; the Emperor himself has congratulated him!

A dark street.

A house — shutters hermetically sealed. Red lamp over the door.

The door is open. On the pavement, two policemen are standing guard.

The Black Maria stops in front of the door, Cäcilie gets out, stiff and proud, her eyes sparkling.

CÄCILIE   He was struck down in the street, going about his business; it's overwork that killed him! Overwork.

I'm going to the hospital to identify my father's corpse. It's the hospital, I tell you, the hospital.

She goes in. It is a brothel. To the right, a large doorway leads to a spacious, empty room: the reception-room of the brothel.

In the centre, circular couch. Mirrors on all the walls; a violinist and a pianist standing on a dais, at the far end of the room, are softly playing a Viennese waltz.

Policemen, sitting at a table, are drinking the house cognac and listening to them.

The policemen point out the way to her: she climbs a flight of stairs and follows a corridor.

Stairs and corridor are carpeted in the same material which carpeted the hospital corridor in the first account.

FREUD, *voice off*   Music in a hospital? Music after midnight?

But the carpet is far dirtier. Holes, stains, wrinkles.

CÄCILIE   They were playing in the reception-room on the ground floor. To insult my father.

The walls are covered with crudely executed paintings representing nude women.

There are doors to right and left. With signs, as in the first account. But on these signs, names have been written: **Lily – Daisy – Concha – Francette** *(one name on each door).*

All is silent, but we can hear the Viennese waltz being played as well as might be expected (which is not very well) by the tuneless piano and the squeaking fiddle it accompanies.

All of a sudden Cäcilie, who is marching straight ahead seeming to see nothing, passes in front of an open door.

On the threshold, a blonde woman who resembles her stands motionless. She is wearing the nightdress and dressing-gown which Cäcilie was wearing in the first account.

When Cäcilie passes in front of her, the woman pulls a face, revealing a toothless mouth.

FREUD'S VOICE OFF   Tell me about the nurses.

Cäcilie stumbles (as in the first account), but it is from shock. A little further on, the policemen accompanying her make her enter a little low-ceilinged room (one of the prostitutes' bedrooms).

CÄCILIE'S VOICE OFF, *violently*   They were whores.

BREUER'S VOICE OFF   Cäcilie!

> *The image explodes. We find ourselves back in Cäcilie's room with Breuer and Freud. Breuer looks shaken.*

BREUER   Cäcilie! Child! My ... dear child! You can't ...

> *This time, it is Freud who lays a hand upon his shoulder to silence him. Freud wears a timid, imploring expression. Breuer, pale and nervous, leans back.*

CÄCILIE   There were six of them at the foot of his bed, and some policemen.

> *We abruptly find ourselves back in the prostitute's bedroom.*

I hated them.

> *Women around the bed. The same ones we saw dressed as nurses in the first account.*
> *They were all wearing dressing-gowns like Cäcilie's, which they have slipped on over night-dresses like the one she was wearing in the first account. Except one, the sixth, who is simply wearing a transparent nightdress, with her arms bare.*
> *They look at Cäcilie without uttering a word, but with aggressive, spiteful expressions. Cäcilie looks at them: scornful defiance. Suddenly she perceives the girl in the nightdress.*

CÄCILIE   I saw the one who'd killed him.

> *The girl — a big, amply proportioned blonde, with an enormous bust and firm, plump bare arms protruding from her nightdress — is the living proof of Herr Körtner's somewhat vulgar tastes. Normally, she must be gay and happy-go-lucky. At this moment, she is very worried. A uniformed policeman and another in plain clothes stand at her sides.*

FREUD, *voice off*   How did she kill him?

> *She avoids Cäcilie's eye, but the latter's gaze devours her with a kind of desperate fascination.*

CÄCILIE'S VOICE OFF   How? How? Do you think I know what those women do?

> (*In a strange tone of voice — one almost of jealousy:*)

He died in her arms.

> *The policeman in plain clothes moves forward. The women stand back. We can now see the body on the bed, up to its waist. It is naked. Someone has thrown a blanket over its belly, just hiding the sex.*

Against a background of Viennese music, the policeman speaks and we can hear his voice.

POLICEMAN, *loud voice*   Fräulein Körtner, do you recognize your father?

Cäcilie, very pale, approaches the bed. She does not dare look at her father's face. A silence.

Then she forces herself to glance at it, and with her we discover the face of man of around fifty, who must have been good-looking (blonde moustache and beard, with tufts of grey in them), but who is disfigured by a fixed and almost obscene grimace.

His mouth is half-open and twisted down, and we can see two gold teeth. Traces of lipstick — very visible — on his face and bald forehead give the still flushed countenance a ridiculous, but sinister aspect.

Cäcilie appears to be on the edge of a breakdown.

CÄCILIE'S VOICE OFF   I recognized him! I recognized him! There was lipstick on his
cheeks ...

Suddenly she collapses, falls to her knees, takes her father's hand, kisses it, looks at his thumb from right close to and begins to squint as in the former scene.

I took his hand, his big hand that I loved, and I saw only that, I remembered only that. He used to take me in his strong hands and lift me off the ground.

She sobs, her head bent over her father's hand.

His hands ...
     His hands ...

She is still bending over the inert hand.

BREUER'S VOICE OFF   And that's enough! Cäcilie! Wake up! Wake up!

(The voice swells:)

Wake up, I wish it!

The vision explodes. We find ourselves back in the bedroom.

Freud and Breuer are at the bedside of the exhausted Cäcilie, who lies prostrate with her eyes closed.

CÄCILIE, *natural voice*   I'm awake, Doctor. But how tired I am!
     So what did I tell you?

Breuer hesitates slightly, then, almost shamefacedly, avoiding Freud's eye:

162

BREUER   Nothing.

Freud seems beside himself with fury.

FREUD   Cäcilie!
CÄCILIE   Yes.

Breuer seems angry and terrified, but resigned to the inevitable.

FREUD   Can you hear me, now?
CÄCILIE, *amused, but unsurprised*   Well, well! Yes.
FREUD   You told us that your father died in a bawdy house.

Cäcilie sits bolt upright. She opens her eyes: her eyes are normal.

CÄCILIE, *violently*   Go away!
FREUD   You can see me, Cäcilie.

Cäcilie looks him in the eye.

CÄCILIE, *cold and hard*   Yes. And I can hear you. Leave the house.

Freud does not seem greatly moved. He rises and begins to leave, saying to her very gently:

FREUD   You're cured, Cäcilie.
CÄCILIE, *with a kind of fury*   Cured! Ha! Ha! Ha! Cured!

A fit of coughing convulses her; she doubles forward on the chaise longue.
Breuer — who is standing watching the scene (he too has risen to his feet), gripping in his strong hands the back of the chair on which he had been seated — turns towards Freud and says to him, with an authority full of bad faith:

BREUER   You had better withdraw. I'll try and sort this out.

He seems to be trying, at one and the same time, to condemn Freud for his intervention, while out of politeness hiding this condemnation from him.

(Cough off from Cäcilie.)

FREUD, *somewhat tartly*   What is there to sort out? The symptom has disappeared.
BREUER, *indignantly*   And that cough, do you hear it?

(A pause.)

I beg of you, leave us.

Freud, wounded, bows and goes to the door. As he is leaving, he can still hear Breuer's tender whisperings.

BREUER'S VOICE OFF   Cäcilie! I beg of you, calm yourself!

As he closes the door behind him, Freud sees from afar Breuer bending over Cäcilie, who is still coughing. He has laid a hand on her forehead; we sense that Cäcilie, beneath this gentle pressure, is relaxing slightly.
  Freud finds himself in the hall again: the mother and Fliess are still facing one another; Fliess is drumming on the table.
  He sits down beside Fliess, who looks at him with relief. They exchange a smile of mutual understanding.

FREUD   It will soon be your turn.

Fliess bends down, picks up his laryngological instruments (a small black leather case) and is about to place it on the table. Cäcilie's mother restrains him with a peremptory gesture.

FRAU KÖRTNER   Allow me!

Placed on the table in front of Frau Körtner there was a little circular table-mat. She slides it across to Fliess, who understands and places his case on the little mat.
  The door of the bedroom flies open and Breuer comes out, vexed and upset. He turns to Frau Körtner and speaks to her, with great respect but commandingly.

BREUER   Cäcilie is very nervy, this morning. You're the only person who could calm her. You must stay with her. Don't leave her alone for a moment. I'll come back late this afternoon.

He turns to Fliess.

(To Fliess:) I'm sorry, my dear Fliess, but she's in such a state that you wouldn't be able to examine her.

With forced joviality:

It will have to be for some other time.

Fliess nods in reply, but without concealing his vexation.
  Everybody rises. Breuer hesitates for a moment, then draws the mother to one side.
  During their brief dialogue — which we do not hear — Fliess and Freud exchange a few words.

FLIESS   The symptom?

FREUD   She can see and she can hear.

FLIESS   Then the method is sound.

FREUD   Yes. But it must be followed right through.

12

The barouche.

The three men climb in and sit down in silence. It sets off. Breuer and Freud are seated side by side. Fliess sits facing them. A pause.

    Breuer addresses Freud, with bad grace. We sense that he is displeased, but that his professional duty as a doctor and man of science obliges him to speak.

BREUER   Frau Körtner has confirmed your hypothesis, Freud. Cäcilie's father died in a brothel. The police had the unforgivable boorishness to take the girl there to identify him.

Freud's eyes glow, but he does not reply.
    Fliess seems very interested.

FLIESS   And so?

BREUER   That's all. Since that time, her body has refused to see or hear. I'm worried. I wonder if we were right to touch that particular chord.

FLIESS   Haven't the symptoms disappeared?

BREUER   But how about later? What if they were to come back? Or other ones?

In an objective tone of voice, but really in order to worry Freud:

On several occasions she has tried to kill herself.

FREUD   The chimney-sweeping of the brain must be carried out methodically. The more soot there is, the more we have to sweep.

BREUER   Not with such brutality!

FREUD   She was resisting us.

    (To Fliess:) She no longer even remembered that she'd seen the body. It took two bouts of questioning for the memory to rise to the surface again.

BREUER   A girl of nineteen finds her father naked, dead and surrounded by prostitutes! If you think that situation doesn't present all the circumstances of a psychic traumatism ...

FREUD   Of a traumatism, granted. But why forget it?

BREUER   How many accident victims forget the circumstances of their accident!

FREUD   They forget them, but they don't distort them.

    (To Fliess:) She was hiding the truth from herself. The binocular squint was in order not to see that defiled body, those ladies of easy virtue, any longer; the psychic deafness was in order not to hear the violin playing waltzes any longer. She ... was *repressing* her memory; and her body was her accomplice.

BREUER   Very well. She was 'repressing' it, as you say. That means it was more than she could bear.

FREUD   Certainly.

BREUER   Was it right to bring it back to her by force?

FREUD   It's your method.

BREUER   No. I refuse to violate her soul. And for my part I find it legitimate that a child of twenty should wish to respect her father and that she should make every effort to forget that shameful death. Do you want to know what I really think: I admire her.

FREUD   Admire her as much as you like, but let's cure her: that's our first duty.

BREUER   And you think you'll cure her by inflicting such a terrible humiliation upon her? You've done her only harm.

FREUD   Breuer!

He makes a violent effort of self-control.

Your method is brilliant: it cures by means of the truth! But we must let in all the light, then. We must have no pity.

BREUER   I regret having taken you with me. You distort everything: the goal and the means of attaining it. I was allowing gentle, persuasive forces to act, and you simply hammer away for all you're worth.

Freud forgets even his anger: he looks straight ahead, intently; we sense that he is painfully disentangling the web of his ideas, and that he is nevertheless glimpsing a new truth.

FREUD   Gentle forces ... what good are they?
    Nothing's gentle, with Cäcilie.
    Nothing's tender ...

BREUER   You don't know a thing about it!

(In a more personal tone of voice than he would like:)

For my part, I'm well acquainted with her tenderness.

Breuer's tone has shocked Freud. He replies harshly:

FREUD, *shocked*   It's your own you're so well acquainted with! It's your own that you find in her!

Then he returns to his reflections:

Cäcilie is a field of battle. A fight is being waged, inside her, a fight is being waged night and day ...

He speaks without looking at anyone.

I had the feeling ... when I was listening to her ...

With sudden enlightenment:

Breuer, it's not her father she's defending, it's herself.

Breuer listens to him in stupefied indignation.

BREUER, *in a loud voice*   What?

FREUD   Those unclothed women ... that naked man ... those obscene paintings ... Breuer, she was aroused.

As he speaks, an invisible orchestra (a large number of musicians, playing with talent) strikes up the waltz from the brothel.

BREUER   Aroused? Carnally? When she was shown her father's corpse? Aroused by that sordid caricature of love?

He starts to laugh:

Freud, I no longer recognize you. In my eyes, you were the most austere man I've ever known. More puritanical than a pastor. I can still recall the day when you jumped into my carriage, in full flight, to escape from the clutches of a lady of easy virtue. And do you claim today that a young virgin can experience the sexual attraction of vice?

Freud looks distraught. Breuer's last words have struck home deeply. He turns his head to right and left, as if to escape his thoughts. Then, as if he were asking him for help, he looks at Fliess.
    The latter has refrained from intervening in the conversation — out of simple politeness. But he has not missed a word of it. When he meets Freud's eye, he makes no gesture and speaks no word. But he smiles broadly as a sign of his approval.
    And Freud, looking at him the while as if fascinated by his great, blazing eyes, murmurs in a low, sombre tone:

FREUD   An attraction in horror ... An attraction by horror ... I was wondering ...

Abruptly, without taking his eyes off Fliess as if he were drawing his courage from him, he adds in a louder, more resonant voice:

All neuroses have a sexual origin.

Fliess's smile broadens. He is wearing a truly satanic expression. Breuer starts. With greater violence:

BREUER   That's the first I've heard about it!

He has caught Fliess's smile, and the complicity that suddenly unites Fliess and Freud displeases him.

I see you're becoming a disciple of our friend Fliess: sex is everywhere, even in the nose.

He pretends to poke his forefinger into his nostril, obviously in allusion to Freud's mannerism — which incidentally has not been in evidence since the previous day — but which he must have noticed long ago. Freud does not reply, intimidated by Breuer's anger, but he gives a frown. He no longer looks at anyone; he remains silent and sombre, his head bowed, during Breuer's reprimand.

BREUER   But there it is, you're out of luck. I've known Cäcilie for a year and a half and I visit her twice a day, and in all that time not one of her gestures or one of her words, even under hypnosis, has demonstrated the slightest carnal preoccupation. She is wholly ignorant of love, and never thinks about it. She has but one concern in my experience: to help those in distress. And I'd even say to you, now that I think about it, that her sexual development strikes me as somewhat retarded. Doubtless by her neurosis.

He laughs angrily, rubbing his hands.

Not the least sign of a boy friend. Not even the classic little cousin. Nobody! Ha! Ha! Nobody! The flesh slumbers.
    And there you see, dear colleagues, the dangers of generalization.

To the driver:

Put me down here, Frantz.

The coachman pulls on the reins and the barouche comes to a halt beside the pavement.
    To Freud, more mildly:

I'm going to visit old Dessoir, his condition worries me. Goodbye, Fliess; I'll see you soon, Freud.

He leaps lightly down from the barouche. A wave of his hand.

Frantz! You'll take these gentlemen wherever they wish to go.

13

Freud speaks to the coachman in a natural tone of voice.

FREUD   To the Faculty of Medicine.

Freud addresses Fliess without looking at him.

It's time for my lecture. Come.

The barouche has already moved off again. Simultaneously, Breuer enters the building he had pointed to. Fliess comes and sits beside Freud (in the place vacated by Breuer). The barouche rolls along for a while.
    Freud, with unblinking gaze, torn between the reflections aroused in him by the cathartic method and the resentment that Breuer's conduct towards him has inspired, leans forward in silence.
    After a moment's pause, he hears Fliess's mordant, sombre tones.

FLIESS, *with a certain ardour*   Bravo.

Freud turns with a start and looks at Fliess's face: though still terrifying, it is striving to appear encouraging.
    (It will turn out in the long run that Fliess's face, so constantly handsome and satanic, thanks to the very constancy of its terrifying beauty, presents a rather set and faintly comical aspect.)

FLIESS, *forcefully repeating Freud's phrase*   'All neuroses have a sexual origin.'
    That's right.
    Bravo!

Freud, who was not expecting congratulations, looks at Fliess in amazement. He replies in genuine good faith — and, above all, with great timidity (due precisely to the importance of the idea involved).

FREUD   I don't even know why I said that.
    The idea came to me on the spot. In the bedroom. There was something going on. Something sexual.

Abruptly:

Breuer disgusted me. He seemed too gentle … so fatherly …

He recalls the scene, and appears fascinated by the memory. He is jealous.

He and that child ... they were a couple.

With discreet irony:

Perhaps his method requires one to go that far.

With a kind of rage:

Unaware! Innocent! He's letting himself be fooled.
Do you know what she said, under hypnosis?
'They were whores!' And with what an air!

He calms down, assuming a timid and profoundly shifty expression. Casting a sidelong glance at Fliess:

It's a painful impression: nothing more. He's right: it would be a mistake to generalize.

FLIESS   It's necessary *first* to generalize.
I've watched Breuer: he's jealous of your idea. He'll do you down if you let him.

Freud grows fearful. His face alters: he rediscovers the respect that Breuer inspires in him.

FREUD   I owe him everything ...

Fliess, touching his forehead:

FLIESS   Except *that.*
He's not your father; he doesn't have the right to reprimand you.

Freud winces almost imperceptibly when he hears: 'He's not your father'.

Repeating Freud's phrase:

'All neuroses have a sexual origin.'
I'm fully in agreement with you.

FREUD   I don't have the slightest shred of evidence.

FLIESS   I should hope not.

Freud looks at him in astonishment.

You and I, we're of the same breed.
We're visionaries.

The barouche draws up in front of the Faculty. Students are continually passing in and out through the wide-open main doors.

Freud and Fliess climb out of the barouche and across the courtyard. Freud, followed by Fliess, makes a detour to avoid the crowd and proceeds towards a little side door, obviously reserved for teachers. As he walks, he asks Fliess, without looking at him:

FREUD   What do you mean by visionaries?

FLIESS, *forcefully*   They're people who have ideas before they possess the means to verify them. There must be hidden powers in them.

They have entered; they follow a corridor, then go through a low door into a little chamber reserved for teachers, and which leads to a large amphitheatre.

It contains a table, two chairs, a glass-fronted bookcase, a small washbasin and, over the latter, a mirror flecked with reddish-brown marks.

Freud closes the door carefully. With a gesture that should appear unusual, he turns the key in the lock. He says to Fliess, almost in a whisper:

FREUD   You, you're a visionary. Not me. I'm just a not very good experimenter.

Fliess, by a gesture, rejects this objection with imperious authority.

FLIESS   A visionary can be recognized immediately.

FREUD   By what?

FLIESS   By his eyes.

Pointing to Freud's eyes:

Yours see far. Like mine.

Freud, you're on your way. Don't let yourself be stopped by Breuer's inhibitions. All is sexuality: from volcanoes to the stars, by way of animals and men. Sex: that's what produces the world and what drives it; nature is fecundity run wild.

He pulls out his watch and consults it.

It's time for your lecture.

Freud points out a door to Fliess:

FREUD   Yes. Go through this way: you'll have a seat in the front row.

FLIESS   I shall establish that, even in his smallest actions, man obeys the great sexual rhythms of the universe.

Fliess makes his way towards the door; with one hand on the latch, he turns:

You'll help me, Freud. You'll help me.

He goes out. Freud, subdued for a moment, recovers. He opens the bookcase and takes out a large anatomical work; he leafs through it, finds some handwritten notes between two of the pages and is about to go out likewise, taking them with him. But he changes his mind, goes over the washbasin and studies his bright, hard eyes at length in the mirror.

[14]

Next Tuesday, in Freud's consulting-room *(just as we described it at the beginning of this second part). Dora has just come in.*

She takes off her hat and places it on a chair near the divan. In making this gesture, she is obliged to turn round by the window.

DORA   Well, I never! It's gone.

Freud finishes writing, at his desk. He raises his head.
Freud, innocently:

FREUD   What's that?

Dora points to the site of the 'electric chair', which has indeed disappeared.

DORA   The torture machine.
FREUD   You're pleased, I hope.
DORA   No.

She looks worried. She peers all around.

If you've removed it, that means you've found something better.

Freud begins to laugh. She puts out her tongue at him.

Torturer!

Whereupon she goes off with dignity to undress behind the screen.
Freud has risen to his feet. He stops her with a word.

FREUD   No.

She freezes, astonished.

DORA   No massage today?
FREUD   No.

Dora stamps her foot angrily.

DORA   I've told you it does me good. Thwarting me is all you take pleasure in.

She returns to the couch and sits down, in despair.

Things are going very badly!

She begins to weep.

Very badly! Very badly!

FREUD   What else is wrong?

Freud is wearing an amused, mysterious expression, as if he were preparing some good trick. He listens and registers what she is saying, but we sense that his real thoughts are elsewhere.

DORA, *weeping*   It's horrible! I can no longer … go into a shop.

FREUD, *wryly*   You're very extravagant, Dora. It's a piece of luck for your parents.

DORA, *stamping her foot*   Don't joke. I hate it when you joke. I tell you I'm afraid of going into stores.

Freud goes over to her.

FREUD   Afraid? Why?

DORA   I don't know. Yesterday, I had some shopping to do and I came home without having bought anything.

Each time I put my hand on the latch of a shop door, I'd feel my heart constrict and I'd leave. I *had* to leave.

FREUD   Is it the first time this has happened to you?

DORA, *impatiently*   Of course not! It has happened hundreds of times.

FREUD   Since when?

DORA   For the past four years.

FREUD   Why have you never told me about it?

DORA   It comes and goes. It grips me, then disappears. I didn't think it would interest you.

FREUD   Everything interests me.

DORA   No one who heard you laughing at my misfortunes would think so.

She rises abruptly to her feet.

I don't want to be laughed at. Ever again.

Freud comes up to her. He places his hands on her shoulders and forces her to sit down again.

FREUD   When you want to go into a shop, are you afraid of being laughed at? Is that what stops you?

DORA   Yes.

FREUD   Has it already happened?

DORA   Being laughed at? Of course: I can still hear their laughter.

FREUD   Whose laughter?

DORA   There were several of them. Shop-assistants.

　　It was my fault. I was fifteen years old, my mother had gone out, I had put on one of her dresses and some lipstick.

FREUD   And what then?

She ironically mimics her bearing on that occasion.

DORA   That's all. I thought I was beautiful. A great lady. I went into a confectioner's to buy some candy.

FREUD   And the assistants laughed at you.

DORA   You can just imagine! In that fancy-dress!

She buries her head in her hands. In a sincere and tragic tone of voice:

I loathed myself!

Freud gently separates her hands.

FREUD   Because you dressed yourself up as a lady?

Dora looks at him.

　　At the age of fifteen?

DORA, *forcefully*   Yes.

FREUD   That's not serious, Dora.

DORA   No.

Dora has herself realized that the reason invoked was inadequate. She looks astonished. In worried surprise:

No, obviously not.

A pause. Freud paces up and down the consulting-room. He walks and smokes as he speaks.

FREUD   You were quite right, Dora: Dr Breuer is treating one of his patients by hypnotism.

DORA   You see?

Dora's countenance changes: she stands up, overjoyed to have been right.

You always begin by telling me I'm lying.

Freud comes back towards her.

FREUD, *paying no heed to the interruption*   The results are excellent.

He speaks gently, but his expression is disquieting.

It's a new method.

Dora recoils, and at once falls back to a sitting position on the couch.

DORA, *anxiously*   I don't want it.

Freud comes still closer to her. He towers over her.

FREUD   What is it you don't want, Dora?
DORA   I don't want to be hypnotized.
FREUD, *feigning astonishment*   You were the one who was demanding it, the other day.

Dora slips aside, rises abruptly to her feet and tries to leave. Freud restrains her.

DORA   Apparently it drives you mad, and gives you headaches, and you say any old thing when you're asleep.
FREUD   Oh no! Not any old thing.

He leads her back towards the couch.

You know very well I want to cure you.
DORA   I don't know anything of the kind. I'm only a plaything for you; I'm useful for your experiments, just like some poor frog.

She allows herself to be sat down on the couch.

I don't feel well. We'll begin next time.

Freud has bent over her. He presses down very lightly on her shoulders, to make her stretch out. She looks at him with an expression that is at once provocative and fearful.

Would it make you happy?

He smiles without answering.
    With a kind of plaintive surrender:

Very well then, take her, this poor frog of yours; remove her brain, if it can be of some use to science.

She yields to the pressure of his hands and stretches out on the couch.

In the Freuds' dining-room.

The housekeeper is laying the table. Martha comes in.

MARTHA   Three places, Minna, Dr Fliess is dining with us.
MINNA   Very well, Madam.
MARTHA   Is the Doctor still in his consulting-room?
MINNA   Yes, Madam.
MARTHA   With Fräulein Dora?

The maid nods.

MARTHA   They've been a long time.

Suddenly Martha notices on the wall the print representing Hamilcar and Hannibal.

Oh!

The maid, who was bending over a drawer in the cupboard, lifts her head.

The print. It wasn't there. Who put it back?

The maid looks at the print without understanding her mistress's agitation.

MINNA   It was the Doctor. He asked me for the stool straight after lunch.

Martha looks at the print angrily.

MARTHA, *in a deliberately expressionless voice*   Very well, very well. That's quite all right, then.

She continues to look, more calmly now and with no gesture that betrays her perturbation; but her eyes are filled with tears.

(*Bursts of laughter off.*)
(*Several people.*)

The bursts of laughter begin over the image of Martha looking at the print.

A confectionery shop. Some assistants (three young men, behind counters laden with jars of sweets) are laughing heartily.

One of them is doubled up with laughter, another is slapping his thighs. Their gestures would have nothing exaggerated about them as such — if, for instance, the assistants had been in a group of young men and laughing at one of their comrades.

DORA'S VOICE OFF, *heard above the laughter*   I tell you they were laughing. That's all.

The only strangeness comes from the situation. A woman of about fifty, stern-faced and imposing — the proprietress, obviously — is watching them, without sharing their hilarity but without condemning it.

This whole little scene is viewed by an invisible but fairly tall person (Dora is fifteen).

FREUD   Mocking laughter? Insolent?

The young assistants are still mirthful, but they can no longer be heard. Here again, everything can and must seem normal: they have quietened down, that is all.

DORA   Worse. It made me frightened.

The proprietress, still stern-looking, between two jars. She has turned towards Dora (in other words, towards the camera-lens) and is looking at her. She is not laughing, but we can hear laughter and the laughter seems to come from her.

Laughter (off), strange, slightly panting, almost foolish, with a very faint quaver. It is the laughter of a single individual.

FREUD'S VOICE OFF, *over the laughter*   Frightened or ashamed?
DORA, *voice off*   Both.
FREUD   Why did it make you frightened? It's not very terrible, laughter.
DORA   That laughter was.

The counters suddenly grow taller, as if viewed by an individual of very diminutive stature (a dwarf or a child). The assistants have disappeared.

The camera turns (like a worried glance) towards the door (likewise viewed from very low down) and this movement allows us to see that the store has altered its appearance. It is still a confectioner's, but it is smaller, darker and seedier.

The camera view returns to settle on the place the laughter is coming from. Between two big jars of sweets there appears the head of an old man (plain white moustache, baldness): it is he who is laughing. He wants to reassure. His mouth is smiling, he strives to assume a kindly expression.

But his staring, crazy eyes — which are looking towards the camera — give him an uneasy, sad and almost malevolent expression.

DORA   I was six. The old man said he wanted to give me a candy.

The old man comes round the counter.

I was paralysed. He came round the counter.

Suddenly all the sounds flood back: the old man's steps, his slightly panting breath, the sound of a jar that he knocks slightly as he passes, and finally his voice.

OLD MAN   Are you afraid? Are you afraid? What a silly thing you are! Are you afraid of a kind old grandpa?

As he speaks, he has come out from behind the counter. He walks towards the place where Dora is.

You'll get some candies. As many as you like. A whole bagful.

He bends down towards the unseen Dora.

(*Child's terrified scream off.*)

FREUD'S VOICE OFF   Dora! Dora! Wake up! It's all over!

The scene freezes: the old man remains just as he was: his arms outstretched, in the process of kneeling down. It is a still.

Wake up! I order you to wake up.

In Freud's consulting-room the scene has vanished: when Dora opens her eyes, she sees Freud bending over her.

DORA, *with profound relief*   It's you! It's you! What happened to me?
FREUD   You told me one of your memories. You were six years old, you'd gone into a shop ...

He has straightened up again. She sits up.

DORA, *interrupting him*   Be quiet! (*A pause.*) I remember it all. He was laughing ...

They are both seated, facing one another, she on a couch, he on a chair.

FREUD   You'd forgotten?

DORA, *spiritedly*   Certainly I'd forgotten. You wouldn't wish me to remember that ... filthy episode, after all!

FREUD   And the other story, is that true?

She looks at him in astonishment.

The one that happened to you when you were fifteen. The shop-assistants who laughed.

DORA   That's true as well.

FREUD   That's the one you remembered?

DORA   Yes, because the other one is too ...

Gesture to reject the memory.

FREUD   But it was the other one that counted?

DORA   Perhaps. I don't know. When I thought about the shop-assistants, it was the old man's laughter I heard.

A silence.

FREUD   Come.

He goes over to the window and opens it. She joins him.

You're going to give me a present.

He points out a shop to her.

When you leave, you'll go into that shop and buy me some cigars.
    You'll bring them to me on Monday at five o'clock.

The street, five minutes later.

Dora, in front of the shop. She passes in front of the shop-window, approaches the door, hesitates for a moment, turns round to look at the building (on the other side of the thoroughfare) where Freud's apartment is situated.
    Freud is still at the window. She smiles at him and enters the shop.

In the Freuds' living-room.

Fliess, Freud and Martha are seated in armchairs around a table bearing liqueurs. Freud is not drinking. Fliess is holding a small glass and warming it in his hand. Every now and then he drinks, with evident sensuality. Freud beams as he watches him. Martha is very amiable, but there is something a bit forced in her tone and mannerisms.
    Freud puts his hand into his jacket pocket, to take out his cigar-case. He thinks better of it, removes his hand and places it on the table. He has a childlike, cheated expression.
    Martha, who has seen him out of the corner of her eye, bursts out laughing.

MARTHA   Look at my husband, Dr Fliess, and tell me if he doesn't look miserable.

Fliess turns his great eyes towards Freud in astonishment.

FLIESS   He does indeed. But why?
MARTHA   Because he doesn't dare smoke in front of you.

Freud laughs in turn, with an air of satisfied delight.

FREUD   Good heavens, that's right! That's well observed, Martha. I'm afraid of being scolded.

Fliess smiles with a certain fatuousness: deep down, he finds the thing quite natural.
    Martha is slightly annoyed to see the almost timorous admiration that Freud feels for Fliess.

FLIESS   So much the better, dear Madam. Fear is salutary.

Martha, her eyes sparkling with false gaiety, and with a touch of sadism:

MARTHA   It's the first time …
    I congratulate you.
    If you could use your influence to stop him smoking.
FLIESS   But Madam, don't forget I'm his pupil.

Freud laughs, frankly amused at the idea that this superior individual should have come from Berlin to attend his lectures.

(*Seriously:*) I shall forbid him tobacco when I can be certain of being obeyed.

He has put his little glass back empty on the pedestal-table. Martha rises to her feet, wanting to pour him some more cognac.

Just a drop. Thank you, dear Madam.

He picks up the glass. The clock on the mantelpiece strikes. He turns: it shows eleven o'clock.

It's getting late. You know I work mainly at night.

FREUD   Like me.

A silence. Martha has sat down again. Fliess drinks in little sips, his eyes half-closed. Freud finally plucks up courage to ask him the question which, we sense, has been tormenting him since the beginning of the evening.

FREUD   Have you seen Cäcilie again?

FLIESS   I examined her throat this morning.

FREUD   Was Breuer present?

FLIESS   Of course.

FREUD   I thought he wasn't visiting her any more.

FLIESS   He goes there every day. He claims she's entirely cured, but I'm not convinced of it.

He drinks.

Far from it.

He drinks.

Her throat is inflamed, of course: but it's the cough that inflames it.
    I should be extremely surprised if that wasn't a hysterical symptom.

Martha says nothing, but she has begun to frown: she does not like anything being said against Breuer. Her uneasy gaze travels from Fliess to Freud.

FREUD   He hasn't spoken to you again about my ... hypothesis.

FLIESS   He doesn't mention it: one would think he'd forgotten it. Only this morning he was talking to me about snow, ermine and a host of other things, each whiter than the one before.

Fliess is ironical. His voice has an unpleasant sharpness.

FREUD   In connection with Cäcilie?

FLIESS   Yes, Freud, you ought to have things out with him.

Freud's face darkens. He is himself embarrassed by Fliess's animosity towards Breuer. He seeks to defend him.

FREUD   It's very embarrassing. I've always thought of him as my master. You know he's a man of real worth.

FLIESS   Of course! of course!

Fliess makes not the least attempt to hide the fact that he is agreeing only out of pure politeness.

I'm afraid he's making a serious error of diagnosis.

In a conspiratorial tone, which is very slightly and involuntarily comical.

The case is perfectly clear: you and I both know what's going on ... But he appears so sure of himself ... he's so convinced he knows his patient through and through.

With veiled authority:

So ask if you can see her again.

FREUD   Oh no! Our relationship is not so ... intimate. He'd take it very much amiss.

Fliess's interest fades at once.

FLIESS, *indifferently*   Pity!

He rises abruptly to his feet, very Prussian, very stiff. To Martha:

It's time. You must excuse me, dear Madam.

Clicking of heels, hand-kissing.
   Then Freud chimes in, affectionate and almost tender.

FREUD   Until tomorrow, Fliess.

[18]

The same sitting-room, a few minutes later. The maid is tidying the drinks cabinet, clearing away the glasses. A cloud of smoke floats above her.

MARTHA'S VOICE OFF   I don't like that Fliess of yours.
FREUD'S VOICE OFF   Pooh!

We discover him in an armchair: for the first time since the beginning of the film, and for the last, he seems relaxed — even to have let himself go completely: he is sprawling in the armchair, legs outstretched, and has taken off his necktie and undone his stiff collar. He is smoking a cigar, blissfully.
    In a conciliatory tone and without the least intention of wounding Martha:

You say that because he saw you crying.

Martha is standing; she glances meaningfully at the maid.

MARTHA, *very swiftly*   That's all right, Minna. You can do the dishes tomorrow morning. Go to bed now.

The maid is looking at Freud with a rapturous expression.

(Annoyed:) Do you hear me?

The maid disappears.

That girl irritates me. She looks at you with those swimming eyes ... I'll bet she's in love with you.

Freud merely shrugs his shoulders, he could not care less about the maid's feelings. He exhales a puff of smoke, forms a 'ring' and amuses himself watching it float away.

He doesn't like Breuer, you know. It's obvious.
FREUD   Who?
MARTHA   That Fliess. He frightens me. You're like a little boy in front of him.

She tries to wound him, in the hope of stinging his pride. Freud smiles amiably.

FREUD   True enough, Martha, like a little boy.

Martha paces irritably up and down.

MARTHA   I wonder what you find in him.

FREUD   Couldn't you sit down for a bit? Come here next to me.

She gives him a faint smile and sits down on the arm of his chair.

MARTHA, *pressing her question*   Well?

FREUD   Well nothing. You've seen him. He's a man.

MARTHA   And Breuer isn't one?

FREUD   Breuer's a Viennese. Intelligent, subtle, but sceptical.
Fliess, he's a Prussian.

MARTHA   He certainly does look like one. Stiff as a poker ...

FREUD   Stiff but hard. A soldier. You've seen his eyes.

MARTHA   Yes.

FREUD   I've never seen handsomer ones. *(With conviction, but at the same time mis-*
chievously:) He's the one you should have married.

MARTHA   What a dreadful idea!

FREUD   You'd have had a virile, strong, fascinating husband.

She has bent over him, half-teasing half-tender, and is caressing his beard.

MARTHA   The one I have got fascinates me more, provided he takes the trouble.
And I think his eyes are the handsomest in the world. Once he deigns to look Fliess in
the face, Fliess's great eyes will shatter like glass.

Freud smiles at her, but does not seem to understand this timid exhortation to take cognizance of
his own value. He pursues his own train of thought.

FREUD   You're crazy ... Fliess, you see ... He's an adventurer.

MARTHA   And you approve of that?

FREUD   Yes. No adventurers, no science. The world belongs to them.
Perhaps he'll give me the strength to become one.

He has finished his cigar. She opens the windows.

MARTHA   He isn't even capable of preventing you from smoking. This room stinks.

Freud has risen.

FREUD   I'll see you later.

MARTHA   Don't work too long.

Freud kisses her on the forehead. She adds casually:

What happened with Dora? She stayed almost an hour.

Freud shrugs his shoulders without replying.

Did you hypnotize her?
FREUD   Yes.

Ironical and very mildly jealous (whereas all her allusions to Fliess left him quite unmoved):

You must be pleased: it's your dear Breuer's method.
MARTHA   If you're applying his method, why does Fliess claim that you're not in agreement with him?
FREUD, *smiling*   It's just on a question of detail. A trifle.

He prepares to go off, she gently holds him back.

MARTHA   And Dora?

He answers her — still smiling — but with a touch of bad grace.

FREUD   Well?
MARTHA   Is the method working with her?
FREUD   We must wait and see.
MARTHA   How does it help?
FREUD, *vaguely*   We shall see. We shall see.

Freud sets her gently aside and goes over to the door. When he places his hand on the latch, Martha, for fear he may go off without her having said everything, discloses the true reason for her anxiety.

MARTHA   I saw your mother this afternoon.

Freud turns abruptly. His face has hardened: it appears attentive and anxious.

Do you know your father isn't at all well?

Freud stares fixedly at her, without changing expression or speaking.

You've really been neglecting him recently.

Freud gives a disagreeable pout, which distorts his face. He is not yet irritated, but for the first time since the start of this scene he reassumes the sombre, tense countenance we saw him wear at the beginning of Part Two.

FREUD, *stiffly*   Me? Who said so? Mama?
MARTHA   Your mother, yes. But I'd been thinking it for a long time.

FREUD   What did she say?

Freud lowers his eyes. He looks guilty.

MARTHA   She said: 'I still see my son, because I've got legs and can come here. But Papa can't leave his chair any longer, and it's been over a month since Sigmund last came to see him.'

He says — very quickly, like a child being scolded who, in order to be left in peace, swears he will never be naughty again:

FREUD   I'll go and see them tomorrow morning. I promise you.

He is about to leave. Martha crosses the room nimbly and positions herself between him and the door.

MARTHA   She doesn't trust their doctor.

Freud, in a calm and reasonable tone that hides a growing irritation:

FREUD   He's a first-class doctor. The relatives of patients never trust us.
MARTHA   You treat him.
FREUD   Treat whom? My father?
MARTHA   Why not? When he had that glaucoma in his eye, it was you who operated on him.
FREUD   That's not the same thing … Birnenschatz has been treating him for six years: it's not done to steal a colleague's patients.

Martha, very tartly and swiftly (we can sense both her deep friendship for Breuer and a trace of jealousy):

MARTHA   Yet you're trying to steal Breuer's!
FREUD   Me?
MARTHA   Yes, Cäcilie: Fliess is pushing you to take her away from him.
FREUD   You haven't understood a thing.

She tries to speak, he interrupts her. Very quickly:

I've got work to do, Martha. Tomorrow morning I'll go and see my father, and I promise you I'll examine him. I'll see you later.

He kisses her quickly on the forehead and goes out.
    She remains motionless, uncertain, and we divine that she has some vague foreboding of the misfortunes that threaten their household.

Two o'clock in the morning.

Freud is writing in his study, seated at his desk. He has removed his collar and jacket, but kept on his waistcoat.

FREUD'S VOICE OFF, *as he writes*   Neuroses are pathological defence mechanisms against an intolerable memory seeking to force itself into consciousness. Neurotic symptoms are designed to screen this memory. The patient clings to the delirious symptoms, he loves his delirium as he loves himself. But if we succeed in getting him to discover what he is hiding from himself, he sees the forgotten scene in full daylight, the repression becomes useless and the symptom disappears. Representations of sexual origin ...

He stops writing, seems to be searching and dwells on the interrupted sentence.

He opens a drawer: his night's work is finished. He feels too tired to carry on with it. He puts his manuscript carefully away in the drawer, takes a key from his jacket pocket, locks the drawer, replaces the key in his pocket.

He rises to his feet, goes to the window, leans over the balcony, looks at the sky. He lowers his eyes. In the street, in front of the shop that Dora entered, a prostitute is walking her beat. He sees her and closes the window almost immediately (without haste or emotion — without anything indicating that the girl's presence is the cause of his action).

In the street, the prostitute mechanically raises her head and sees the window close and then the light go out. She proceeds on her way indifferently.

Freud's bedroom. Martha is in bed and asleep. Freud in his nightshirt makes his way towards the bed. He carries a candlestick with a lighted candle in his right hand, and shields the flame with his left hand to avoid waking his wife (Martha occupies the left-hand side — in relation to the spectator — of the nuptial bed).

Freud blows out the candle and slips into bed on the right-hand side. Martha groans slightly in her sleep and shifts over to the left. Freud tosses and turns (we can make out his movements in the half-light and the bed creaks). Then he falls still. He is lying on his back.

In the street, the prostitute tirelessly continues her slow pacing. A cab goes by (open barouche). A fat man of about fifty (flower in his buttonhole) gives an order to the coachman.

(Sound off of an unintelligible voice.)

The cab stops in front of the prostitute. The man smiles at her, she hesitates, then gets in. The cab moves off again and disappears into the distance. The street is now deserted.

A railway compartment. Third class. Freud is sitting there, dressed as an orderly (white coat and cap). He looks young and submissive. Opposite him, stretched out on the seat, a richly dressed old man.

His left leg is stretched out on the seat. The foot is swathed in cottonwool and bandages (it is enormous, like the foot of someone with gout). The other leg is half-extended, the foot (normal and wearing a black bootee) rests on the compartment floor.

He has Breuer's head, but his hair and beard are white. His mouth is open, his lower jaw hangs down: obviously the old man is senile. No suitcases on the luggage-racks. The door leading to the corridor is closed, the curtains drawn.

If the setting appears dreamlike in character, this is solely because it is too sharp, lit by a harsh, white light, with something imperceptibly abstract deriving from its extreme cleanness and from the very noticeable absence of all the props of a railway journey.

Freud and the old man remain silent and motionless for an instant: we would think we were looking at a photograph if, through the window, we did not perceive a procession of vague shapes bearing witness to the train's speed.

All of a sudden, Breuer begins to laugh. His laugh exactly reproduces that of the candy store man (in Dora's story). Freud remains completely motionless. Breur quietens down. He turns his eyes towards Freud and splutters:

BREUER . . . like . . . candy.

Freud answers him in a wholly childlike voice (a boy of twelve).

FREUD Yes, Papa.

He turns to the right and, in the same instant that he catches sight of it himself, we perceive a urinal (classic shape, in transparent glass) filled with candies. Apart from its shape — which is unmistakable — it resembles one of the jars we saw in Dora's story and contains the same candies.

(Eagerly:) Wait a second.

He rises to his feet, takes the urinal, leans out of the open window and empties the urinal outside.

On the outside, every shape has vanished: one would say the train was travelling through fog. (The schematism, in fact, is still the same: in his dream, Freud has not imagined an outdoor landscape. In the dreams reproduced here, we must never find anything except such props as are essential. Moreover, the dreamer discovers these only as he has need of them.)

When the jar is entirely empty, Freud turns towards the old patient and proffers it to him as a urinal.

Here!

He is astounded to discover, as we do a moment later, that the old man has disappeared. In his place, sitting opposite Freud, stiff, with a pointed helmet, there is Fliess dressed like a Prussian officer. He rests his hands on the pommel of his sabre.

FLIESS Let the old bury the old. And let the dead take care of the dead.
   (Imperious and solemn:) Look after Cäcilie, corporal!

FREUD   At your command, Sir.

Next morning, in Freud's bedroom.

Martha is still in bed. The windows and shutters are open. Freud's jacket hangs on the back of the chair.
    We hear Freud's voice, as he completes his toilet in the bathroom.

FREUD'S VOICE OFF, *following on directly from his last line*   I'll be back for lunch.

Martha, still sleepy, opens her eyes blearily.

MARTHA   Are you going to see your father?
FREUD   Later on: if I have time.

He comes back into the room, in his shirt-sleeves, and puts on his jacket.

MARTHA   It's seven o'clock in the morning, Sigmund! If it's not to go and see your father, I'd like to know why you're getting up so early.

He has put his jacket on. He goes over to the bed and kisses Martha on both cheeks.

FREUD   I must speak to Breuer. I want to catch him at home before he leaves on his rounds.

He has reached the door.

MARTHA   You promised me you'd examine your father.
FREUD, *smiling, but categorical*   I won't treat him, in any case. I respect him too much to make myself his nurse.

He goes out. Martha — who had sat up in bed — remains sitting for a moment, then in a kind of despairing resignation allows herself to slump backwards, closes her eyes and, bothered by the daylight, ends up burying her head under the covers.

[20]

In the Breuers' dining-room, a few minutes later.

Breuer is sitting opposite Mathilde. He is ready to leave — as ever, majestic and carefully groomed. Mathilde is wearing a housecoat.

They are taking their breakfast: coffee and toast. Mathilde is watching Breuer fixedly, with a mixture of resentment and love. She tries to attract her husband's attention. In vain.

Breuer remains distant, eyes fixed, sunk in his own silent meditations. He looks at the time (on his watch, which he has taken out of his waistcoat-pocket and which he immediately replaces there), hesitates for a moment, then almost mechanically picks up the large china coffee-pot in the centre of the table and pours himself one last cup of coffee.

Mathilde starts.

MATHILDE   You might have asked me if I wanted any.

Breuer smiles affectionately at her, in faint bewilderment.

BREUER   Forgive me, I was thinking about something else.

He bends over the table to pour her some coffee. She places her hand over her cup.

MATHILDE   I don't want any more. Thank you.

He replaces the coffee-pot on the table with a touch of irritation.

BREUER   What's wrong with you?
MATHILDE   What about you?

She looks at him. He meets her gaze with an embarrassed expression.

You, the soul of politeness, serving yourself in my presence as if I didn't exist.
    It's so unlike you.
BREUER, *trying to smile*   You're not going to condemn me just for one piece of forget-fulness.
MATHILDE   Yes! Because it's me you want to forget.
BREUER, *genuinely indignant*   Your're crazy!
MATHILDE, *with very harsh irony*   Oh! You don't wish me dead! But if I could be very, very happy, anywhere other than where you are ... how that would suit you!
BREUER, *annoyed*   Mathilde!

A footman opens the glazed door.

FOOTMAN   Dr Freud asks whether Sir and Madam can receive him.
BREUER, *delighted to escape a stormy argument*   But of course! Show him in.

> *Mathilde is very discontented, but she recovers at once and smiles gaily.*
> *Freud comes in. Breuer rises and shows him to a chair with great assiduity. Mathilde offers him her hand with a radiant, coquettish smile.*

MATHILDE   You'll take a little cup of coffee, won't you.
    (To the footman:) A cup for Herr Freud.

> *Freud takes Mathilde's hand and raises it towards his lips, but Breuer throws an arm round his shoulder and guides him to a chair.*
> *Freud — who had come in with a firm step — seems quite stunned to be the object of these warm displays of friendship.*
> *The footman has placed a cup in front of Freud. Breuer pours him some coffee.*

BREUER   I'm glad to see you, Freud. And so early: today will be a lucky day.

> *Freud, to stop Breuer, who is filling his cup to the brim:*

FREUD, *very quickly*   Thank you! Thank you!

> *Breuer puts down the coffee-pot and looks gaily at Freud.*

BREUER   Just look at him!

> *He turns towards Mathilde!*

Isn't he a sight for sore eyes?
MATHILDE, *untruthfully*   I've never seen him looking so well. Martha takes good care
    of you, Freud. I hope you appreciate your good fortune.
FREUD, *affectionate but faintly surprised*   Breuer's looking well too.
MATHILDE, *laughing with somewhat wild gaiety*   Yes, everybody's looking well. Every-
    body's looking well! Josef's blooming.
    Only, in his case, he doesn't appreciate his good fortune.

> *Breuer, seeing the conversation is taking a dangerous turn, makes haste to change the subject.*

BREUER   Did you need to speak to me?
MATHILDE   Hang on a moment, give the poor man time to drink!

> *To Freud:*

Drink your coffee in peace.

(He tries to speak.)

Drink!

Freud drinks the whole cup, out of annoyance. He says as he puts it down, in a slightly over-ceremonious tone of voice masking the urgency of his wish:

FREUD   I've come to ask a favour.

BREUER, *gaily*   Granted in advance!

FREUD   Take me to see Cäcilie.

A silence. Mathilde has turned pale. She looks at Breuer with blazing eyes, pursing her lips. Breuer looks embarrassed and very angry. He finally replies, staring at his fingernails.

BREUER, *in a tone of voice rendered almost disagreeable by embarrassment*   But I'm not seeing her any more! She's cured, after all!

Freud looks very surprised. He replies with a naive air — though without our being quite sure he is unaware he is making a blunder — and in the very distinctive tone used by blunderers: a blend of inspiration and ill-will:

FREUD   What? But Fliess told me you'd been ...

MATHILDE, *with brusque rapidity*   To see her? When?

FREUD, *exuding innocence*   Only yesterday.

Mathilde, beside herself with fury, turns towards Breuer.

MATHILDE   You lied to me!

Breuer is furious with Freud, but above all seems very disconcerted.

BREUER, *noble but mild protestation*   Come now, Mathilde!

Mathilde will not be mollified.

MATHILDE, *flood of words*   You who've seen her, Freud, perhaps you could tell me: what has she got, this woman who has taken my husband from me?

It is now the terrified Freud's turn to lower his head, with a doltish look. He certainly was not expecting to unleash this violence.

BREUER, *with a little more authority*   Mathilde!

MATHILDE, *very fast, still furious*   She has taken him from me! He's bored with me, he thinks only of her; we're never alone any more, that girl's between us. All the time! All the time!

This explosion of rage has transformed Mathilde: she looks older and, above all, her charm has been replaced by an almost vulgar violence. She speaks without even knowing what she is saying — and, despite her very real suffering, the exaggeration of her statements makes them faintly comical.

But I warn you, Josef, you'll never get anything out of me. Neither divorce, nor legal separation. You'll have to kill me, it's quite simple, and I really wonder if you won't end up doing it! You're my witness, Freud, you hear me: your friend will end up by killing me!

Breuer is astounded to discover Mathilde's jealousy. As she was talking, he looked at her as if he were seeing her for the first time.

She looks at him too, scarlet with anger. Freud seizes advantage of this moment of silence, during which neither Breuer nor Mathilde is concerned with him, to attempt to take 'French leave'.

He gently pushes back his chair, rises noiselessly to his feet and takes a step towards the door. But Breuer, who has recovered his authority, pins him to the spot with one imperious word:

BREUER   Freud!

Once more very amiable:

Come and sit down again, I beg of you.

Looking sternly at Mathilde:

I'm sorry Mathilde should have taken it into her head to present you with this painful spectacle.

Freud comes back, highly embarrassed, but remains standing behind his chair.

FREUD   I'm the one to be sorry ...

BREUER   I beg of you! I'd have liked to keep you out of this affair, but since you're mixed up in it now, you must stay to hear my explanation.

Mathilde is exhausted by her explosion of rage. She is now staring at her cup, scarlet and embarrassed, with a sombre, numbed expression.

BREUER   I was quite unaware of Mathilde's jealousy. If only she'd spoken to me about it ...

(*To Mathilde:*) Yet you're a doctor's daughter. You ought to know what we doctors feel, when Nature allows us to study a case that is out of the ordinary.

He speaks sincerely and with nobility. His bad faith is far too profound to be detected.

(*He laughs:*) Jealous! My poor darling! If you knew ...

Mathilde — whatever she may think — is ashamed of having shown her feelings. Now she is in a position of inferiority, simply because she has committed what, in this period, any hostess would term a serious impropriety.

But her sullen attitude allows Breuer to introduce his little speech. He has now risen to his feet, and the two men, standing behind their chairs, look at Mathilde with the air of judges.

BREUER   Freud! Tell her that my interest in Cäcilie is strictly professional.
What I like about her, my darling, is the method that has cured her.

A silence. Mathilde does not reply, but she remains tense and ashen, her eyes lowered. Breuer looks at her and takes his decision.

Do you want me to prove it to you? Let's go to Venice.

Mathilde, dumbfounded, raises her eyes and looks at him incredulously. He repeats with great self-assurance:

Let's go to Venice. Let's bring forward the date of our holidays. If Freud will be so good as to keep an eye for me on a few patients who are giving me some cause for concern ...
I need three days to put my affairs in order. You can book the tickets for Thursday.

This time Mathilde's face lights up.

MATHILDE   To Venice!

Naturally, she bursts out sobbing. Breuer moves round the table and comforts her like a child.

BREUER   There! there! there! Are you happy, at least?

She nods affirmatively, her head in her hands, her shoulders heaving with sobs.
Breuer, stroking the back of her neck, tells her very paternally:

I don't want any more tears!
I'm giving in to your foolish fancies in order to cut off the trouble at the root.
Cäcilie's cured.
You won't ever speak of her again! Is that a promise?

She nods and controls her tears.
Breuer adds, very lightly:

I'll call on her this morning to bid her farewell, but you won't be jealous: Freud will go with me.

She turns and looks at him anxiously.

MATHILDE   I can *really* buy the tickets?
BREUER, *paternally*   Of course, child, this very morning.
MATHILDE   Oh! how happy I am!

> *She rises to her feet, turns and throws her arms round his neck.*
> *He frees himself gently.*

BREUER   There now! There now! Let's go off quickly, Freud. Since you're here, I'll make the round of my patients and introduce you to the ones you'll be taking charge of.

> *Mathilde turns towards Freud and offers him her hand, with an apologetic smile.*
> *Freud — a very unusual action both for us, who know his abruptness, and for Mathilde — bends over her hand and kisses it.*
> *Breuer, vexed, drags him away.*
> *They go out, the footman hands them their hats.*
> *On the landing, before they go down, Breuer takes Freud by the arm and says to him confidentially — man to man:*

I consider jealousy to be a neurotic symptom.

[21]

At Cäcilie's.

The French windows are wide open to the garden.
She is seated at her dressing-table, very beautiful, looking entirely normal.
A tall young man of about twenty — also very good-looking, but of Italian appearance, very black hair, black eyes — is standing beside her. He is dressed in workman's overalls and holds a wide straw hat in one hand.

(Sound off of a barouche stopping.)

Cäcilie speaks to him in friendly tones but as to a servant. It is clear that she feels no attraction for him.

CÄCILIE   You promise me you won't drown them?
YOUNG MAN, *respectfully*   Yes, Fräulein.

At the sound of the barouche, Cäcilie has assumed an imperceptibly sly and mischievous air. She prolongs the conversation so that Breuer will find her with the young man.

CÄCILIE   I shall take two for myself and give the others to friends.

At this moment, Breuer and Freud appear at the French window; they have left the barouche and come directly to Cäcilie's room.
Breuer looks at the young man with surprised and somewhat malevolent attention.
On hearing the gravel crunch beneath their feet, Cäcilie has risen unhurriedly to her feet and turned towards the garden. In a very natural and almost indifferent tone of voice:

Good morning, Doctor!

She goes over to them. She is dressed in a loose housecoat that hides her figure. She walks rather heavily. On seeing Freud, her face lights up.

Good morning, Dr Freud. I'm very happy to see you again.

She turns towards the young man. Carelessly:

Good-bye, Hans, I'll see you later.

Hans bows.

HANS   Good-bye, Fräulein.

He leaves by the door leading to the hall.

When the door has closed again, Breuer looks at Cäcilie with a stern, morose expression.

BREUER   Who's that?
CÄCILIE   The gardener's son.
BREUER   What business do you have with him?

Cäcilie replies quite naturally, but she has a faintly sly look. We can sense that she is amused.

CÄCILIE   You wanted me to mingle with people of my own age.
BREUER, *sharply*   Of your own age and your own station.

Cäcilie smiles.

CÄCILIE   Don't worry, Doctor: our bitch is about to whelp, and I was just asking Hans
not to drown the puppies.

She laughs in his face.

That's all it was about. Sit down, I beg of you.

*They move towards the centre of the room. On a table, Breuer notices two little knitted woollen
bootees for a baby, and an unfinished sweater in the same wool—the needles are still projecting from it.*

BREUER   What's that?
CÄCILIE   Baby clothes.
BREUER   You're knitting?
CÄCILIE   Yes. For one of my friends who's expecting a baby.

A silence. They sit down. Breuer looks constrained and gloomy.

BREUER, *with a certain solemnity*   Cäcilie, you are cured.

Cäcilie, smiling and quite straightforward.

CÄCILIE   Yes, I am.
BREUER, *smiling paternally*   I've come to bid you farewell, my dear: you have no further
need of my services.
CÄCILIE, *with a mildness that bodes no good*   I'll be seeing you again, Doctor.
BREUER   Of course you will, Cäcilie. We shall certainly have occasion to see each
other again.
CÄCILIE   When?
BREUER   Later on. My wife and I are leaving on Thursday for Venice.
CÄCILIE, *noting the date*   Next Thursday? Very well.

(Urbanely amiable:) Venice! Is it a kind of second honeymoon?

Breuer seems suddenly furious, as if he had been trying too hard to control himself and now, at the end of his tether, was letting himself go.

BREUER   A honeymoon? After seven years of marriage? You're too grown up to talk such nonsense, Cäcilie, and too young to be talking about marriage.

CÄCILIE, *more and more sly*   Too young? Come, Doctor, I'm twenty years old: I'll be married within a year, thanks to you.

Breuer, ever more ill-at-ease, mops his brow, which is dripping with sweat.

BREUER, *in a perturbed voice*   Marry, my dear child, and be happy. I wish it for you with all my heart.

He rises abruptly to leave.

CÄCILIE, *very swiftly, in sincere and helpless astonishment — but still mildly*   You have a heart?

Breuer frowns.

BREUER, *gravely*   Cäcilie.

CÄCILIE, *laughing*   I'm talking nonsense, Doctor. I know the devotion with which you've taken care of me.

She turns to Dr Freud; with deadly mildness:

Dr Freud, I'm happy that Dr Breuer should have had the very great thoughtfulness to bring you back here.

She offers him her hand, warm and almost tender.

I was afraid I wouldn't be able to thank you.

Freud, bowing, in a pretty stiff and distant tone of voice:

FREUD   I did nothing, Fräulein.

CÄCILIE   You cured me, Doctor! Dr Breuer found the method, but you were the one who applied it.

Freud is genuinely indignant.
  He looks angrily at Cäcilie, and at Breuer with anxious affection.
  He irritably begins a sentence which Breuer interrupts:

FREUD   I find you very ungrateful, Fräulein. I am merely the humble disciple ...

Breuer raises a hand to interrupt him.
   Breuer is still smiling, but underneath he is very bitter. He speaks sharply: it is not Cäcilie against whom his animosity is directed, it is Freud.

BREUER   We shall argue later about our respective merits. Doctors have no pride, Fräulein Cäcilie: the important thing for them is the cure. Wherever it comes from.

He turns towards Freud. Cäcilie goes up to him with a touch of coquetry.
   She offers him her forehead.

... Come!

CÄCILIE   Won't you kiss me!

Breuer looks at her tenderly, but with an unhappy expression.
   He hesitates, before eventually kissing her.
   Cäcilie turns towards Freud with the obvious intention of offering him her forehead.
   But Freud has seen Breuer's face: he looks disappointed (by his master's attitude), unhappy (at seeing Breuer suffer) and furious (with Cäcilie).
   He frowns and casts a glance at Cäcilie that causes her to shrink back.

FREUD   Goodbye, Fräulein.

He turns on his heel and strides towards the French window. Breuer follows him. Cäcilie starts to cough.

(Cough off from Cäcilie.)

We can no longer see anything but the backs of the two men. One would think they had been routed.

CÄCILIE'S VOICE OFF, *punctuated by the cough*   Have a good journey, Doctor! Have a good journey!

In front of the perron.

The two men climb hastily back into the barouche.
   We can still hear the fits of coughing, in the distance.

(Coughing off, a long way away but very clear, from Cäcilie.)

BREUER, *to the driver*   12 Park Avenue. Hurry!

> *The barouche leaves the garden.*
>
> *We hear the gate being closed behind it.*
>
> *Breuer straightens up, turns and looks at the villa as it recedes into the distance and vanishes round the first bend.*
>
> *He slumps back onto the seat beside Freud, whose eyes are fixed in a hard stare and who has found time to light a cigar.*

BREUER   And that's that. They appear, they monopolize our attention, they disappear and thank you kindly: we never see them again.

> *Freud, roused from his reverie, looks at him with so alarmed an expression that Breuer cannot help laughing.*

FREUD   Who?

BREUER, *laughing in his face*   Where were you? I'm talking of our patients.

FREUD, *vague and indifferent*   Oh! yes ...

BREUER, *asserting more than asking*   She's cured, isn't she?

FREUD, *worriedly*   There's that cough ...

BREUER   Just one attack! *(Resentfully:)* She wasn't even coughing, these last few days. It's Fliess's medicines that have inflamed her throat.

> *Freud puffs at his cigar without replying.*

(Categorically:) Finished. The page is turned.

> *A silence. The barouche turns into a street flanked by tall new buildings.*

22

Thursday morning.

It is nine o'clock.
   Fine sunny day.
   In front of the Breuers' house, two carriages have drawn up. In one of them (an open cab — the second carriage), the Breuers' chambermaid and footman are stacking suitcases.
   In front of the other, Breuer, Mathilde, Freud and Martha are chatting animatedly as Mathilde keeps an eye on the cab containing her luggage.
   Everyone looks very gay.

MARTHA   You'll have superb weather.
MATHILDE   My aunt writes that it's raining in the mountains. But in Milan it's hotter than in summer.

She leaves them for a moment and goes over to the servants. Pointing at the last suitcase.

No. That one has my things for the journey in it. Put it next to the driver.

They obey. The driver takes the suitcase carefully and places it beside him. To the servants:

... Goodby, Maria ...
   ... Goodbye, Heinz ...
SERVANTS, *together*   Safe journey, Madam, safe journey.

She comes back towards Breuer and the Freuds.

MATHILDE   It's time.

To the Freuds:

... Are you coming to see us off?
FREUD   Of course.
MARTHA, *laughing, to the two Breuers*   How he must love you! He has a physical horror of railway-stations and journeys.

They laugh. Freud laughs with the others, looking relaxed.

FREUD   Who hasn't got his own little neurosis? *(More seriously.)*

He turns towards Breuer:

Do you know what I dream of writing? A psychopathology of everyday life. I'd show how normal people are just mad people whose neuroses have turned out well.

Breuer listens politely but without real interest.
Mathilde intervenes energetically.

MATHILDE, *with friendly authority*   Yes, well, you'll tell us all about that when we get back. I don't want you to make us miss our train. Get in, Martha.

Martha climbs into the barouche. The cab with the luggage overtakes the motionless barouche.

(Without anxiety: as a mere precaution:) Have you got the tickets, Josef?
BREUER, *automatically*   Yes.

He pulls out his wallet, certain of finding the tickets there. They are not in it. He puts the wallet back in his pocket and searches himself methodically — outside and inside pockets of his jacket, waistcoat pockets, trouser pockets.

No.
MATHILDE, *dumbfounded*   It's not possible! Look properly; you never forget anything.

Breuer obediently searches his pockets for the second time.
He raises the leather band covering the lining of his top-hat. Gesture of impotence.
Mathilde's face turns scarlet with anger.

It's too bad!
BREUER, *to Mathilde*   Get into the carriage. I've left them in one of the drawers of my desk. I'm sure of it. I can still see them.

He is about to go back into the house.

MATHILDE, *sharply imperious*   Not you!

She explains to everyone:

Once you've left your house on a journey, you must on no account go back into it before your departure.
BREUER   Why, pray?
MATHILDE   It brings bad luck!

Freud, with quite spontaneous alacrity:

FREUD   Don't you bother, Breuer, I'll go.

Breuer, beneath his smiles, is no longer quite the same when he is speaking to Freud.

BREUER, *rather disagreeable irony*   Can this be you, Freud, a materialist and an atheist, giving in to my wife's superstitions?

Freud seems not to notice the change.

FREUD, *gaily*   When you're an atheist, you have to be superstitious: otherwise what would be left?

MATHILDE   Thank you, Freud!

MARTHA, *to Breuer*   Let him go!

BREUER   All right, all right!

He takes out his bunch of keys, shows one of the keys to Freud.

… The first drawer on the right.

Freud takes the keys and rushes into the house.

(To Mathilde, feigned indignation:) Aren't you ashamed?

MARTHA   Leave her be! … It's a real honeymoon. You're not going to oppose your wife's wishes right at the start.

At the word 'honeymoon', Breuer's face darkens. A silence.

In Breuer's study, Freud opens the drawer indicated. He takes out a sheaf of papers and hunts for the tickets. He finds them finally: Breuer had put them into a little card-case, which also contains a photograph: it is of Cäcilie.

He hastily bundles the papers together, replaces them in the drawer, locks it and leaves the apartment.

He hurries down the stairs.

In the street, in front of the building.

When Freud comes out of the house, the setting has altered.

Behind the barouche, a heavy two-horse ambulance.

In front of the ambulance, Breuer is talking to an orderly.

In the barouche, the two women are seated, stiff and silent.

Martha is pale with anguish; Mathilde, stiff, her eyes blazing with hatred and anger, seems beyond even despair, in a kind of frenzy of gaiety.

Dumbfounded, he approaches the barouche.

FREUD   What's the matter?

Martha does not reply.
  He looks at them both.

(Insistently:) What's the matter?

MATHILDE, *laughing*   Oh! nothing at all, Freud, a mere prank! Cäcilie has gone into labour.

FREUD, *in utter astonishment*   What?

Mathilde laughs without replying. Martha nods towards Breuer.

MARTHA   Go and join him. And don't leave him.

Freud hastily joins Breuer, who is pale, his features drawn.
  The ambulance door is open.
  Breuer, showing no surprise at his presence, signals to Freud to climb in.
  Freud enters the ambulance and Breuer at once joins him.
  They sit down on a narrow bench — opposite an empty patient's bed — reserved for the orderlies.
  Meanwhile the orderly has climbed up onto the front seat and seated himself beside the driver.
  The ambulance sets off with its two horses at the gallop.

23

In the ambulance.

Freud and Breuer, silent. Breuer is sweating and mopping his brow.
   After a moment, Breuer begins to speak in a jerky voice, punctuated by silences. He seems crushed by this news:

BREUER   It seems that the pains began this morning.   They took her to the St Stephen's clinic. She wants to see me.

He begins to laugh, not in a friendly fashion.

You can be pleased: it's you who were right. Sex! ... I thought she was a virgin, and in the meantime ...

Freud looks at him dumbfounded.

FREUD   But after all ... You ... you can't not have known about it ... You used to examine her.
BREUER   Not for the past year. She didn't like me to touch her.

   (He laughs.)

I thought it was out of modesty.

He turns violently towards Freud and questions him — half-tragic, half-comical:

Pregnant by whom? I ask you! ... That boy, the other day, that gardener ...

Furiously:

I've let myself be fooled by a whore.

In a corridor of the clinic, outside a closed door.

We can hear the characteristic screams of a woman in labour.

   (Voice off of Cäcilie screaming.)

A doctor, a midwife, Cäcilie's mother.

They await Breuer in silence. Cäcilie's mother betrays no sign of emotion. Her face has merely grown still harder. Steps are heard in the corridor.

FRAU KÖRTNER   At last!

Breuer and Freud appear; they are almost running. When he sees Frau Körtner, Freud removes his hat. But Breuer is so overwrought that he keeps his hat on his head.

BREUER, *out of breath*   What's the matter with her?

Frau Körtner, without a word, points to the doctor and the midwife (meaning of her gesture: 'they'll inform you better than I could').
    Breuer turns towards them and looks at them with a perturbed expression; they seem very surprised by the emotion he is showing.

OBSTETRICIAN, *introducing himself*   Dr Pfarrer.
BREUER, *quickly and distractedly*   How do you do?
    (*Continuing:*) What has happened?
DR PFARRER   She's entirely virgin. But she must have been suffering from a nervous pregnancy over the past few months.

    (*Smiling:*)

And, being consistent, today she's giving us a nervous confinement.

Breuer listens to him in astonishment. Then he goes over to the door and opens it. To everybody — including Freud:

BREUER   No. Stay here!

He goes in, shutting the door behind him.
    Cäcilie is in bed. She has her eyes closed; from time to time she cries out or struggles.
    Two nurses are watching over her. With an imperious nod, Breuer dismisses the nurses. They leave noiselessly.
    Breuer sits down at Cäcilie's bedside, on a chair previously occupied by one of the nurses.

Cäcilie!

She opens her eyes. She smiles.

CÄCILIE   It's you? Give me your hand.

Breuer, overwhelmed, takes her hand. She has a contraction, then falls back upon the bed.

(Tremendous scream. She falls silent for a moment, exhausted.)

Are you happy? It's a son, I'm sure of it.

BREUER   Listen to me . . .

She looks at him with an astonishment that is soon effaced by a fresh wave of pain.

(Fresh scream from Cäcilie, then exhausted voice:)

CÄCILIE   What shall we call him, my darling?

She falls back on the bed.

In the corridor.

Half an hour has gone by. The obstetrician paces up and down.
The nurses and the midwife stand a little further off. Freud and Frau Körtner, motionless, stiff, each as hard as the other, wait without looking at one another. Cäcilie is no longer screaming.
Breuer comes out at last, exhausted, sweating. He carefully closes the door behind him. He goes over to Freud and Frau Körtner, who await him in silence.

BREUER, *to the mother*   She is sleeping.
     (A pause.) She recognized under hypnosis that she wasn't pregnant.

Frau Körtner still says nothing.

(Embarrassed by this silence:)

Everything's under control. Leave her in the clinic for two or three days, then you'll be able to take her back home.

Frau Körtner agrees wordlessly, with a stiff little nod.
Breuer looks at her, disconcerted, bows deeply to her and turns on his heel. To Freud:

Come, Freud.

Outside, the ambulance is waiting in front of the door. The orderly approaches Breuer.

ORDERLY   Doctor! *(Breuer turns round.)* We can take you back.

Breuer, very drawn, makes a gesture of refusal.

BREUER   No, thank you. We'll go back on foot.

24

Freud and Breuer are talking, as they walk through sunny, almost deserted streets.
    Breuer has not replaced his top-hat on his head. He walks at Freud's side, mopping his brow. A long silence.
    Freud casts worried, timorous glances in Breuer's direction but does not dare question him.
    They arrive at a crossroads. Breuer crosses the road, with the intention of continuing straight ahead. Freud catches him very respectfully by the arm and compels him to turn to the right.
    Breuer docilely allows himself to be guided.

BREUER   Oh! Yes ...

A few steps more. In genuine distress, and as if to himself:

I'm a criminal.

Freud looks at him in astonishment. Breuer explains, this time turning towards him:

She thought she was pregnant by me.
    This method is diabolical.
    We've no right!

Freud looks at him questioningly. He explains himself:

Man's not made to be omnipotent.
    She obeyed me. I had total power over her.
    There's the result.

They walk on in silence.
    He stares straight ahead of him, into the distance:

When I first knew her, she was innocence itself, I swear to you.
FREUD, *as if to himself*   Innocence ... I wonder if that exists.
BREUER, *abruptly irritated*   If you'd seen her, a year ago, you wouldn't ask that question.

With deep regret:

She didn't know a thing, she was pure as the driven snow.
    Meynert was right: there are things deep down inside us which we don't have any right to touch.

Freud, with a start:

FREUD   Meynert? But he says the opposite, now.

BREUER   Because he's going to die. It no longer matters to him.

> *(Sounds off of a carriage.)*
> *(Horse's hooves, creak of wheels.)*

He turns round: it is an elderly cab. Closed carriage. Elderly driver. He looks at his watch.

I'll take the other train.

Freud cannot believe his ears.

FREUD   Eh?

Breuer signals to the driver, who pulls on his reins.

BREUER, *explaining*   The afternoon train.

The carriage draws up alongside them. Breuer invites Freud to get in. Freud does not get in. He looks indignantly at Breuer.

FREUD   You're not going to …

BREUER   Go away? I certainly am. The further away, the better.

FREUD   But Cäcilie …

BREUER   She's cured.

FREUD   As you can see for yourself, she isn't.

Breuer is lying to himself: he pretends to be quite calm, but he remains deeply upset.

BREUER   It's the last crisis.
      If I remain, I'll only do her harm. If I go away, she'll forget me.

Freud, torn between astonishment and indignation, has lost all his timidity.

FREUD, *forcefully*   Cured! While you were curing her contractures and her visual problems, she was calmly developing a nervous pregnancy and it's you she thought she was pregnant by. She's more ill than ever; you can't abandon her!

Breuer flushes. Freud's tone has antagonized him.

BREUER, *very coldly*   But that's just what I am going to do.

He seeks to climb into the cab. Freud holds him back by his sleeve.

FREUD   Breuer! You're a doctor: it's your duty to ...
BREUER   I know my duty better than you do.

He turns back towards Freud and says forcefully, while the coachman watches in bewilderment:

   (Almost shouting:)

I made her love me, do you understand?
FREUD   She *fell* in love with you. Doubtless because she was already disturbed.
      You had nothing to do with it.
BREUER   Of course not!

   (A pause.)

That would be too easy.

Still with passion, but almost nostalgically:

She was cold. She was pure ... Do you know what I think? Hypnotism is a means of seduction.
      If my colleagues were to insist that I be struck off the Medical Register, I'd have nothing to say against it.

Mounting astonishment on the part of the driver.
      Breuer explodes. He accuses himself, but from his tone and his gestures one would say he was drawing up an indictment against Freud.

I sullied her, Freud, I sullied her by idiotic and criminal practices. I've dishonoured myself.

As he speaks, he jabs his outstretched forefinger into his interlocutor's chest.

A doctor who seduces his patients! A quack doctor! The whole town's going to laugh at me.

In a flat, almost exhausted voice:

I must go away.

He opens the door of the cab and climbs in. Freud does not detain him. He closes the door. Through the open window, we see him sit down. The driver prepares to whip up his horses. Freud stops him:

FREUD, *to the driver*   One moment!

He goes up to the window. Breuer has sat down on the seat, overcome, his eyes half-closed.

(To Breuer, timidly:) If you give me a note for Frau Körtner, I'll treat Cäcilie in your absence.

Breuer's indignation is such that he literally projects his head through the window.
   Freud retreats a step. Breuer's furious face emerges from the open window. His eyes are blazing:

BREUER, *with extreme violence, and for the first time since we have known him with the imperious authority of a tyrant*   Never!
   I know your theories, my poor Freud! I know all your fine ideas about sex.
   You'll steal my method and put it to God knows what use!
   You'll fill that poor girl's head with vileness, you'll drive her stark mad.

Rapping out the words:

Listen well, Freud: I forbid you to concern yourself with her. Is that understood?
FREUD, *in a sharp voice, torn between anger and timidity*   Yes.

Freud takes a step back and signals to the driver to whip up his horses.

(With sombre irony:) Have a good journey!

The cab moves off. Freud, motionless, furious and dismayed, watches the carriage until it disappears.

25

A lecture-theatre at the Faculty of Medicine.

The lecture has just ended. The last students are leaving through the door at the rear, situated behind the highest tier of seats. The camera follows them for a moment, then gives us a high-angle shot of the hall.

From high overhead we can see the lecturer at his rostrum. (It is Freud, who is putting his papers away in his briefcase.) In the front·row, still seated, we can see from behind a strongly-built student who, even from far away, seems older than the very young men — all with beards — who are leaving the hall: it is Fliess.

We are now in front of the rostrum. Fliess has risen to his feet, he is talking to Freud who has just risen too, looking up at him from below.

Fliess wears a sardonic smile; Freud has a bitter, sombre expression: he accepts Fliess's jibes at Breuer's expense, even — reluctantly — joins in, but he does not smile.

FLIESS, *spiteful irony*   And how's our Don Juan?
FREUD, *vexed*   Pooh!

(A pause.)

My wife has just received a letter from Mathilde.
(Bitter:) They are blissfully happy.

He closes his briefcase, climbs down from the stage (a single step) and finds himself on the same level as Fliess again.

With his great, satanic eyes the latter watches him approach. He has not struck up the conversation without a very precise intention. And this is evident.

FLIESS, *same tone*   Is the weather fine in Venice?
FREUD, *sombre irony*   Very fine.
FLIESS, *abruptly*   And what about Cäcilie, in the meantime? Has she been put in a straitjacket?
FREUD   I've no idea.
FLIESS   All the same, it would be very convenient to chain patients up so that doctors could take holidays.

He moves closer to Freud.

So you haven't seen her again.
FREUD, *annoyed*   I tell you Breuer forbade me ...
FLIESS   So what?

FREUD   She's his patient.

FLIESS, *brutally*   And when Breuer isn't there, his patients can kick the bucket?

FREUD, *sharply and with decision*   I won't steal his patients.

FLIESS   She's not his patient, she's in love with him.

Freud, embarrassed, makes an effort to defend his master.

FREUD   Let's drop that, Fliess. It's not Breuer's fault. (*He laughs.*) The man's just too attractive. I've been applying his method to my own patients for two months now, I can swear to you they aren't in love with me.

His face darkens in spite of himself.

What I blame him for is running away.

His eyes are intent and he gazes into the distance.

(*Hard:*) Running away, retreating, I can't accept that. Especially from a Jew.

(*In a half-joking, half-serious voice:*)

In a war, I'd die where I stood.

A silence. Fliess places his hand on Freud's shoulder to compel the latter to look at him.

FLIESS   Freud, Cäcilie's an exceptional case. She can be useful to us...

FREUD, *astonished*   Be useful to *us* ...

FLIESS   I'd find it quite unacceptable for her to be lost to Science.

He lets go of Freud's shoulder and paces up and down in front of the stage.

I need you. You're the only person who can help me in my research. I'm close to success.

With deep conviction, but with a certain pedantry, which gives him a solitary and almost wild look.

I can see. Yes. I've seen the truth. I shall turn biology upside down. My theories are complete: what remains is to prove them. That's the easiest part. Above all, if you give me your help.

Freud's eyes follow him as he comes and goes.

FREUD, *slightly stunned*   What theories?

FLIESS   I'll tell you everything, never fear. But it'll be a real initiation.

(Laughing to hide his deep seriousness:)

We shall make a blood pact! I shall deliver up my secrets only to a brother! We must divide the work.

Without even noticing, he climbs onto the stage.
He moves up and down it as he speaks.
Freud sits down on a tier, fascinated. Fliess, after several journeys back and forth, ends up by stopping behind the rostrum and speaking on his feet, looking down at Freud from above.

Sexuality, Freud. Everything comes back to that. You'll be quite amazed when I let you in on my discovery.
    For the moment, we must go back to Cäcilie.
FREUD   What connection ...
FLIESS   Cäcilie's a proof. I know it.

(In a voice that is harsh, indeed so hard as to be almost inhuman:)

She must be worked on hard and without respite. Until she delivers up her secret to us.

Imperiously, his finger extended over the rostrum to point at Freud:

Let's go and see Cäcilie. In any case I have to go and visit her again, since her throat isn't better.

Insistently:

Let's go and see her! You've no right to hold back the advance of knowledge, just to spare Breuer's susceptibilities.

Freud has risen to his feet, but he does not reply. He keeps his head bowed and wears a stubborn expression.
    Fliess looks at him and — in a measured, almost gentle voice — hurls this poisoned dart:

He's only jealous, after all!

Freud raises his head and turns towards Fliess with some anxiety.

FREUD, *in a changed voice*   Did you have the impression ... ?
FLIESS   It's as clear as daylight. Fellows like that are very fond of showing generosity to their apprentices. It's a very cheap method of forming a good opinion of yourself.

But let the apprentice once become a master ... then he'd better watch out.

FREUD, *thoughtfully*　　I've sometimes felt ...

It is Freud's turn to pace along the stage. He looks thoughtful and malevolent. Above all, unhappy. He no longer looks at Fliess: he is searching within himself.

You see, Fliess, people like me need to provide themselves with tyrants. I don't know why.

Mine was Breuer.

I used to obey him like a child.

Sombre and resentful:

But I wouldn't forgive him a weakness.

Are you sure he's jealous?

FLIESS　　It hits you in the face.

Freud, of course, is not discovering anything at present. Fliess is simply putting into words what he had not dared admit to himself.

FREUD, *sincere and appalled*　　Of me? Of me who's nothing? I admired him so much ...

A pause. It is Freud's turn to be racked by jealousy. In a venomous tone of voice, as if he were taking revenge on his idol by delivering him up to Fliess's mockery:

FREUD　　Do you know that he's in love?

FLIESS　　With Cäcilie?

FREUD　　Of course. I'm none too sure which one of them seduced the other. I've felt embarrassed since the first day of this business.

He'd bend over her, he'd put on a sugary voice, he'd be for ever mopping his brow ...

Fliess does not say a word. He listens with a smile, very well knowing that Freud is entangling himself ever deeper: the trap is working perfectly.

He was like a billy-goat! Everything was *sexual* between them. That's what gave me the idea.

(Abrupt decision:)

Let's go and see Cäcilie.

As he utters these last words, Freud in turn climbs onto the stage, where he finds himself on the same level as Fliess.

26

In an open cab.

The suburbs of Vienna, near Cäcilie's villa. Fliess, sprawled on the seat, is speaking.
Freud, bending forward, his expression anxious, his eyes intent, makes no reply.
It is impossible to tell whether he is attentive or tormented by the decision he has taken.

FLIESS   To conclude, I assert that every individual is simultaneously male and female. That's what I call bisexuality. Naturally, there's one sex which dominates: the other is blocked, masked, but its physiological development continues.

You're a man, Freud, a virile man, yet — as is the case with all men — a part of your make-up is feminine. And your life, like mine, is conditioned by periodic phenomena related to our bisexual make-up. Rhythms ...

The carriage enters the street flanked by villas which leads to Cäcilie's house. Freud shivers and sits up straight. Fliess, furious at being interrupted, looks at him coldly.

You're not listening to me.

Freud, upright, looks at the gate of the villa in the distance.

What's the matter?
FREUD, *between his teeth*   I shouldn't have ...
FLIESS, *furious*   What?
FREUD, *regretfully and with sorrow*   Breuer will never forgive me for it.
FLIESS   So what?
What need do you have of him, now? He provided the method and you perfected it: it's yours.

The carriage has stopped. Freud is the first to jump down.

(Irritated by Freud's silence:)

You told me you never retreated!
FREUD   I'm not retreating. Let's go.

He rings at the entrance-gate. No reply.
After waiting for a moment, Fliess goes over to a little side door and opens it.
He goes in and Freud follows him. They see the villa in the distance. All the shutters are closed. It appears abandoned.
Someone advances towards them. It is the gardener's son. He is wearing a wide straw hat. His respectful air has given way to a certain insolence.

FLIESS   Frau Körtner?

GARDENER'S SON   Gone away.

FLIESS   And her daughter?

GARDENER'S SON   Her too.

FREUD   When are they expected back?

GARDENER'S SON   Never.

(A pause.)

The villa's up for sale.

FLIESS   Where can one write to them?

YOUNG MAN   They've left no address.

FLIESS   Very well.

He is the first to turn on his heel and climb back into the cab. Freud does not follow him at once. The young man closes the door again and Freud remains for a moment, facing the closed door.

FLIESS, *voice off*   Well, Freud?

Freud turns on his heel and makes his way towards the cab. His face has brightened. He says as he sits down:

FREUD, *in a faintly ironical tone of voice, masking his real satisfaction*   Well, Fliess, it's a sign from Destiny, don't you think?

The barouche moves off.

[27]

Freud's consulting-room.

A few hours later, towards the end of the afternoon.
  He is sitting near the couch. On the couch, Dora, under hypnosis. Dora is speaking.
  Freud listens to her, smoking a cigar.

DORA, *in a flat voice*   My poor Mama, I'm never easy in my mind; as soon as she goes out shopping, I have a lump in my throat, I can't help thinking she is going to have an accident.

Dora speaks in a rapid, toneless voice. Without the least intonation, as if she were repeating a part.

FREUD   What kind of accident?
DORA   A runaway horse, for example. Any kind of accident, provided it's fatal.

Freud, who was listening almost indifferently, suddenly becomes interested:

FREUD   What did you say?

Dora's eyelids flutter and she stirs restlessly.

FREUD   What did you say? Repeat it.

Dora closes her eyes.
  In a plaintive voice:

DORA   I can't remember. I'm tired.

Freud hesitates for a moment. Then he goes on, gently but firmly.

FREUD   You said: provided it's fatal.
DORA   Fatal? What?
  I don't know! I don't know!

She tosses and turns, she seems exhausted. Freud sees this: he decides to stop the session.
  He stands up, unhurriedly stubs out his cigar and leaves it in an ashtray, on his desk.
  He comes back towards Dora, but does not sit down. He bends over her.
  Freud lays his hand on Dora's forehead, we sense that he is about to awaken her.

FREUD, *gently*   Dora!

In little Mathilde's room.

She is in bed, very flushed; she is suffocating.
Gasping noises are heard coming from her throat.
Martha is sitting in front of her bed, anxious.

MARTHA, *she speaks gently and with deep love*   Mathilde! What's wrong? Is something
hurting?

The little girl nods, unable to speak.
Her big eyes, open wide, bear witness to her suffering.

Are you suffocating?

More gasps. One would say the child was at death's door, and in order to convince ourselves
that Mathilde is in mortal danger it is enough to see Martha's face.
These new, more violent gasps are all that is needed to throw the young woman into a panic.
She rises abruptly to her feet and runs out of the room.

In Freud's consulting-room.

The two protagonists have remained more or less in the positions in which we left them. Freud,
bending over Dora, repeats gently:

FREUD   Wake up, Dora. You're awake.

Dora's eyes have opened; she is awake.

(There is a discreet knock at the far door.)

Freud, absorbed in what he is doing, does not hear.
Dora smiles at Freud: it is the true smile of a person in love.

(There is a second knock.)

Abruptly, she flings her arms round his neck. She unmistakably offers him her lips.

DORA   My love!

The far door opens. Martha appears, her face ravaged. She sees the scene. Freud, who has not seen
her come in, gently unwraps Dora's arms and straightens up.

FREUD, *embarrassed laugh*   There we have one of hypnotism's little surprises.

Dora, disconcerted, has sat up on the couch.

(In a frosty, but mild voice:)

I'm not your love, Dora. Just your doctor.

Dora, terribly embarrassed, looks at Freud in silence.

MARTHA, *voice off*   Sigmund!

Freud turns round abruptly. He looks angrily at Martha, but sees from her features that she is deeply distressed.
    Dora, crimson, rises to her feet wordlessly and goes to take her hat.

The child's very ill. I don't know what's wrong with her. I'm frightened.
FREUD   I'm coming! Monday, five o'clock!

He turns his head towards Dora, as he swiftly crosses the room. Dora, very timidly:

DORA   Goodbye, Martha.

Martha looks at her coldly:

MARTHA, *icy*   Goodbye.

Freud and Martha go out.

In the children's room.

Little Mathilde is suffocating. Freud and Martha come in. Martha remains in the background. Freud bends over the child.

FREUD   Open your mouth.

Mathilde opens her mouth. Freud bends forward and looks inside.

Has she had her temperature taken?
MARTHA   Thirty-eight point nine.

Freud is still bending over the child. He straightens up.

FREUD, *to Martha*   I think it's croup.

Go and tell the maid to go over to Fliess's and fetch him back at once.

He sits down beside Mathilde, holding her hand. Martha goes out to instruct the maid; then she comes back, takes a chair and sits down on the other side of the bed.

In Dr Freud's consulting-room.

Dora finishes fastening her hat on her head with long pins. She is irritable, grows annoyed when she looks at herself in the mirror, pricks her finger with a pin and stamps her foot.
This task completed, she goes over with sparkling eyes to Freud's desk and tears up — unhurriedly, but systematically — all the papers lying on it. This operation seems to soothe her.
She straightens up and leaves the study with the avenging calm of an executioner.

One hour later (around eight in the evening). In the children's room.

Fliess, still seated at Mathilde's bedside, is putting his instruments away in his bag.

(Gasps off from the little girl.)

Freud and Martha stand watching him in silence. He stands up and goes out. Freud follows him into the corridor. Martha joins them silently.

FLIESS   Diphtherial laryngitis.

Freud is ashen.

MARTHA   Is it … is it serious?
FLIESS   Freud, I'd like to see you for a moment in your study.

They move off. Martha waits, squeezing a handkerchief in her left hand.

(Sound off of a door closing.)

We hear the sound of a door closing, then Fliess's voice:

FLIESS'S VOICE OFF   I'll come back tomorrow morning. If her condition worsens let me know, whatever the hour.

The front door closes.

(Sound off of the front door.)
(Sound off of Freud's footsteps.)

Freud comes back, passes in front of Martha without looking at her. He enters the children's room.

He goes over to the patient and looks at her with deep tenderness. The little girl makes an effort to smile at him.

FREUD   Does it hurt?

What's the thing you'd most like? The one that would give you most pleasure in the whole world?

The child tries to speak. She manages finally, in a stifled voice.

LITTLE MATHILDE   Strawberries.
FREUD   Very well.

He almost runs out of the room. Martha comes in and sits down in his place.

In the street. A greengrocer's shop.

The iron grille is lowered. Freud bangs with his fist on the iron shutter.

On the first floor, a window finally opens. An old man with spectacles leans over the balcony.

OLD MAN   All right now, what do you want?
FREUD   Some strawberries.

28

In the children's room.

Later. Night is falling. Martha is sitting on one side of the bed. On the other we perceive Freud, with drawn features.
    The child tosses and turns and seems delirious. On the night-table, a basket of strawberries. She has not yet touched them.
    Martha gives Freud a hard, cold look.

MARTHA, *whispering*   I've the right to know what he said.
FREUD   Yes. *(A silence.)*

Hard and sombre:

One chance in two.
    Right here . . .

Pointing to his own throat.

. . . she has a false laryngeal membrane that's suffocating her.
    If she can get rid of it during the night . . .
MARTHA   And if she can't? . . .

Freud does not reply.
    Late at night. Martha has been to see her two sons, both of whose beds she has transferred into her own room. They are asleep.
    She comes back on tip-toe to install herself at Mathilde's bedside. The latter opens her eyes suddenly and looks intently at Freud, as if wishing to speak to him.
    Freud bends over her.

FREUD   What do you want, my darling?
LITTLE MATHILDE, *painfully*   Strawberries.

Freud takes the basket and shows it to her. He extracts a strawberry, removes the stalk and places the berry himself in the child's mouth.

FREUD   Gently!
    Gently!
    If you have trouble swallowing it, spit it out.

The little girl begins to chew. Painfully. Martha looks mistrustfully at Freud.

MARTHA   Are you sure it's all right?

Freud shrugs his shoulders sadly.

(Coughing off — the child choking.)

Freud starts up.

MARTHA, *her eyes blazing with anger*   You see what you've done!
FREUD, *to Mathilde*   Spit it out! Spit it out quickly!

Mathilde coughs and chokes more and more. She half sits up and vomits onto the covers.

(To Martha:) Wait! Wait!

The little girl coughs a bit more, then lets herself fall back.

Listen to her breathing.

Her breathing is still wheezy but quieter. Freud and Martha listen for a moment longer.

FREUD   She's out of danger.

The little girl smiles at her father.

Is it hurting less?
LITTLE MATHILDE   Yes.

She shuts her eyes and falls asleep.
    Martha rises calmly to her feet, removes the soiled covers, goes to fetch others from a cupboard and remakes Mathilde's bed, without waking her. She takes away the dirty linen, disappears for a moment, then returns.
    Freud watches Mathilde sleeping with a vague smile of relief. Martha has finished her work. She sits down and abruptly begins to sob in silence, her head in her hands.
    Freud rises and goes softly over to her. He takes her by the shoulders. She frees herself with a movement of almost savage violence.

MARTHA   Don't touch me!

Freud lets his arms drop.

FREUD, *dumbfounded*   Martha!

Martha has recovered. She looks at him stonily.

MARTHA, *in a cold voice*   Forgive me.

I'm letting myself go.

(To excuse herself:) I've been so afraid, you see. Horribly afraid.

FREUD   You don't seem relieved.

MARTHA   I am.

He looks at her with deep anxiety and, discouraged, goes back to his place and sits down again.

The child is breathing almost normally. Martha and Freud, on either side of the bed, their features drawn with fatigue, look straight ahead of them, without seeing each other.

It is dawn. The window brightens. In the street, a milkman's cart goes by.

Freud and Martha still sit mutely at Mathilde's bedside.

The child sleeps. Her sleep is quite peaceful; her face is calm and relaxed. Freud and Martha are aged and hardened by fatigue (wrinkles, circles under their eyes).

Freud seems to be reflecting. Suddenly, he turns his eyes towards Martha.

FREUD, *in an undertone*   Martha!

She looks at him without either affection or hostility.

Are you angry with me?

MARTHA, *coldly but sincerely*   No.

FREUD   Yes you are. About Dora, yesterday evening.

MARTHA   Don't let's talk about that.

FREUD   We must talk about it, Martha! I ...

MARTHA   Why? I know what you're going to say: that you haven't been trying to seduce Dora; that you don't feel any love for her, not even any desire; that her ... symptoms of yesterday evening are a by-product of the treatment; that you'll always be faithful to me?

What's the use?

I'm quite convinced of all that.

Freud speaks to her gently and with sincerity.

FREUD   Well then?

MARTHA   I don't like what you're doing.

FREUD   It's your friend Breuer who gave me the idea of doing what I'm doing.

MARTHA   Yes. And you can see where it got him. Do you really believe it's a scientific method of treatment?

FREUD   What?

MARTHA   To make women fall in love with you in order to cure them.

FREUD   Who talks of doing that?

MARTHA   You. You hypnotize them.

FREUD   Hypnotism has nothing to do with ... that nonsense.

Martha, still stony, raises her voice slightly.

MARTHA, *speaking a little more loudly*   I don't know whether you hypnotize them in order to make them fall in love with you; but what's certain is that they're in love with you because you hypnotize them.

FREUD, *sincerely, without raising his voice*   No.

MARTHA, *taking no notice of this denial*   I find that unsavoury.

Without violence. Almost apologetic. But underneath we sense the inflexibility of a judge.

Mathilde stirs and emits a very faint moan, due probably to the sounds disturbing her sleep. Freud looks at her.

FREUD, *to Martha*   Hush!

He rises noiselessly to his feet and goes to the window. He looks at the street, the people going to work, the rare carriages passing by. He signals to Martha to come and join him. She does not want to. He insists.

(In an undertone:) Please come.

She stands up and goes over to him, somewhat reluctantly. She leans her forehead against the pane, to cool herself down a bit, no doubt.

They talk without looking at one another: both face the street.

FREUD   You know what I think: hypnotism is an effect. Never a cause.

MARTHA   What does that mean?

We sense that Freud is groping for his thoughts. It is a question about which he has never reflected.

FREUD   The first time I hypnotized Dora, she fell asleep in a trice. Because she trusted me; because she already wanted to yield herself up to me.

MARTHA   So she was in love.

Freud begins to laugh: a little, harsh, joyless laugh.

FREUD, *in the ironical, unfriendly tone of voice he invariably adopts when speaking of himself*   In love, yes. But not with me. Look at me, Martha, and tell me whether it's possible ...

She interrupts him wearily and dispiritedly.

MARTHA, *interrupting him*   You always repeat that. If you're good enough for me, why wouldn't you be good enough for her?

Freud starts tapping on the windowpane. He is searching for a reply. All of a sudden, he turns towards Martha and answers her with suppressed ardour: he has just hit upon an idea.

FREUD   Don't let's speak about me. Take Cäcilie. She didn't love Breuer for his own sake. She felt like a child in his hands: he dominated her, he was authoritarian and tender. It was like the reincarnation of her dead father and ...

He gropes for his idea.

She ... transferred to him feelings which she had for her father.

Martha, astonished and indignant, turns towards Freud.

MARTHA   But that's ridiculous!
    (A pause:) What about Dora? Her father's still alive.
FREUD   Then it's somebody else. Somebody of my age ... whom she loves without admitting it to herself. She loves me *instead* of that man.

The two interlocutors are now facing one another.

MARTHA   What man?
FREUD   I don't know. I'll find him. At all events ... it's a displacement of feelings. I'm just an image of the other, a symbol. She has made the same transference.
MARTHA   Transference. What a fine word. It explains everything. My love for you, was that a transference?
FREUD   Why not?
MARTHA   Then we only ever love shadows?
FREUD   I don't know. It's something I've just understood ... I'll see where it leads me ...
MARTHA, *ironical and cold*   No transference, no hypnosis?
FREUD   No trust, in any case. The patient wouldn't talk.

With sudden enlightenment:

Do you know what? Transference is the normal relationship between the doctor and the neurotic patient.
MARTHA   I see.

She leaves Freud, who has turned back to the window and is pursuing his idea with a rapt expression.
    He makes no move to detain her. She glances at the little patient, who is breathing peacefully, leaves the room and goes to have a look at her two sons asleep in her bedroom. We sense that she is deeply distressed.
    One of the children has uncovered himself in his sleep; she pulls up the covers and gently tucks in his bed, without ceasing to reflect. Then she comes back into the children's room and goes over to

rejoin Freud, who has not moved.
    A brief silence. Then:

MARTHA   It's dirty.

FREUD   What?

MARTHA   Those false loves ... those substitutions ... the way in which you exploit them ...

FREUD   How about an illness, do you think that's clean?

MARTHA   I'm a decent woman and you're proud of that. Once you forbade me to go skating; you didn't want me even to greet Irma Stein, because she had a bad reputation; today you still forbid me to read certain things.

I tell you frankly, in the name of what I've always been and what you've made me, I'm revolted by what goes on in your doctor's consulting-room.

It's not jealousy, it's disgust. Reflect carefully, Sigmund: are you sure a woman can live with a husband whose occupation disgusts her?

Freud looks at her worriedly. The daylight illuminates their two faces, furrowed and blackened by the night: their wrinkles and the circles under their eyes help to give their conflict a tragic and irremediable quality.

Won't you give up this ...

With contemptuous irony:

... therapy?

Freud seems deeply distressed. He is all tenderness and warmth, in face of the icy Martha.

FREUD   Martha! You know very well it's impossible to go backwards.

MARTHA   Even if you're in danger of destroying yourself?

FREUD   We're sure of discovering ...

MARTHA   A shameful secret. Something like a family skeleton. In the old days you used to tell me everything ... Now you keep silent, but when you come out of your consulting-room each evening, the look in your eyes frightens me.

Abruptly and impulsively, she puts her arms round his neck. Ardently:

Sigmund! For the sake of our happiness, won't you ...

We hear a bell ring.

    (Bell ringing off.)

Neither Freud nor Martha pays any attention. Freud looks at Martha with a kind of despairing passion.

(Sound of a door opening.)

The maid opens the door.

MAID'S VOICE OFF   Dr Fliess has just arrived.

Martha's face freezes, she allows her arms to drop. Freud straightens up, he is wearing a hard expression.

FREUD   No, Martha. Not even for the sake of our happiness.

MARTHA, *once again stony*   Then don't talk to me about anything any more. Never. There'll be our children, the house, our relatives. As for the rest, I hope I shan't have to know anything about it.

Freud looks at her in anguish.
    It is she who turns away and says to Fliess, whom we do not see:

MARTHA   Good morning, Doctor. I think our child is out of danger.

29

A fortnight later, in the afternoon.

Freud and Fliess are walking on the Ring in bright sunlight; their promenade will take them towards a large stone bridge over the Danube. Many passers-by on the Ring, smart outfits, splendid shops.

Fliess (top-hat, cane, black frock-coat — far more elegant than Freud) looks at the passers-by and the stores with an amusement filled with regret.

A beautiful woman passes and looks boldly at him. He returns her stare with a swaggering expression we have not seen him wear before; he even follows her with his eyes and makes so bold as to turn as she passes. One might almost think she was the object of his farewells . . .

FLIESS, *with faint, self-mocking melancholy*   Farewell! Farewell!

Freud, for his part, is undisguisedly sad. He passes among the people without seeing them. At Fliess's words, he gives a start.

FREUD, *as if roused from a dream*   To whom are you saying farewell?
FLIESS, *gesture*   To all this. To Vienna.
FREUD, *genuinely surprised*   Do you like Vienna? I hate it. Petty people! Petty loves! Petty riffraff!
      And if you count the tourists, more anti-Semites than there are inhabitants.
FLIESS, *jovially*   You couldn't live anywhere else!
FREUD   That's true. But from this evening on, I shall be living here alone. When you've left, nobody, in this city, will take any interest in my research.

For the first time he looks at the passers-by, their tired, preoccupied, inexpressive or foolish faces, and repeats:

Nobody.

Fliess looks sidelong at him and says:

FLIESS   But you've seen Breuer again.
FREUD, *a little embarrassed*   Twice since his return. He's giving up psychiatry.
FLIESS   I should think so! It takes a strong back. What will he do?
FREUD   He's going back to neurology: his special field.
      (*A pause. Timidly:*) We're writing a book together.

Fliess gives him a spiteful look.

FLIESS   About what?

FREUD   About his cathartic method.

(A pause.)

We've agreed to keep away from problems of sexuality.

FLIESS   What's left then? Idle chatter.

FREUD, *gently*   Fliess, when children grow up it falls to them to support their parents. Breuer has helped me: I respect him like my father and I'll respect him whatever happens. He'll just stagnate as a general practitioner and I ... I'd like him to write this book.

FLIESS   Too many fine sentiments, Freud. Far too many. Don't forget that Science is inhuman.

Freud looks at him in friendly fashion and wishes to speak. But he changes his mind. They walk on in silence.

Dora goes by, on the arm of an officer. Freud raises his hat to her, but she turns her head away. Fliess, preparing to raise his hat, changes his mind when he sees Dora's attitude.

FLIESS   Who's that, then?

FREUD   It's Dora, you know. Obsessional neurosis. She stopped coming to see me quite abruptly.

Fliess turns round and looks at Dora, who clasps the officer's arm a little more tightly.

FLIESS   She seems cured.

Freud has not turned round.

FREUD, *little laugh, sharp and vindictive*   She would be completely, if she returned my greeting.

They have arrived beside the Danube. They cross the street and start over the bridge. A few carriages pass by on the roadway. The pavement is deserted. They are in the middle of the bridge. Abruptly Fliess stops Freud.

FLIESS   Here. Above the river, in the middle of the city. It's a dream of a spot.

FREUD   Yes. A dream.

They lean their elbows on the balustrade. To the right, buildings lining the embankment; to the left, above the houses, the big wheel on the Prater with its little cars.

Fliess takes two rings out of his pocket. On the bezels, snakes have been engraved.

FLIESS   One for you. One for me.

With a smile, to show he is not taken in:

A secret society for two.

(*More seriously:*) Today, 13 July 1892, on a bridge in Vienna, there stand two men who are the only ones to know Nature's secret: sexuality drives the world.

He turns nimbly at the sound of a barouche and points to a dignified gentleman (grey beard, row of decorations, a State Councillor at least) passing by in his private carriage.

It drives the world, but he doesn't know it.

He looks insistently at Freud, his large, fascinating eyes flashing.

Let's make a pact.

You in Vienna. I in Berlin. You the psychiatrist. I the physiologist and mathematician. Your patients provide you with the facts and I establish the periodicity of their occurrence.

Rhythm, that's the key. Rhythm and number.

Take the ring.

He proffers him a ring. Freud hesitates to take it.

What's the matter?

Freud looks at the river without answering.

Are you afraid?

Freud turns towards him, cut to the quick. He takes the ring, but instead of putting it on his finger he keeps it in his hand.

FREUD, *in a hesitant voice*   Why, yes: I'm afraid.

He is afraid and allows his fear to be seen. This is something which — as we have seen — he allows himself only with men whom he considers his superiors.

FREUD   It'll be necessary to stir up the slime. Over and over again. That ... that sickens me.

Fliess looks at him without answering. Freud goes on, hesitant and distressed:

And then I'm afraid of losing Martha. She knows nothing but she guesses. And I think she condemns me. I love her because she's like me, strict and chaste. She accuses me in the name of the virtues I hold dear.

He looks at his wedding-ring, and at Fliess's ring which he is holding in the same hand.

She'll live at my side like a stranger.

In this soft, debauched city, which will whisper daily: he's a dirty Jew, he's a pig like all Jews.

A long anxious silence.

FLIESS   There's the Danube. If you refuse, throw the ring in.

Freud, in a harsh near-whisper, as if to himself — as if he had not heard:

FREUD   And then, above all, I'm afraid of myself.

FLIESS, *arrogant scorn*   A marriage, a city, do they really count? We shall have omni-potence, Freud.

Gesture towards the embankment teeming with carriages and passers-by.

FLIESS   We shall know their hidden instincts, the sources of what they call Good and Evil, and we shall dominate them through Reason.

Freud abruptly begins to laugh.

(Somewhat disconcerted:) What's the matter?

FREUD   I'm thinking about poor Meynert. He told me: 'Make a pact with the Devil.'

He slips the ring onto his index finger.

There.

Fliess smiles and does likewise.

FLIESS   We'll write to each other every week. We'll have our own secret meetings.

FREUD   'Congresses' for two.

Freud has recovered his self-control: he is almost gay, now.

FLIESS   In ten years, we shall be able to govern men.

He takes Freud's hand and clasps it in his own.

From now on, we must be as close as brothers.

PART THREE

1

Freud has transferred to the ground floor of the same building. The family has retained the apart-
ment on the third floor, which is now solely a private apartment.

We shall learn this later on through the dialogue. For the moment, we recognize the
consulting-room. It is the same one we have seen hitherto. We simply perceive, when anyone goes
over to the window and glances outside, that the apartment is at street level — which should pro-
voke a certain visual surprise.

The basically identical appearance of the two consulting-rooms derives from the fact that the
new one occupies the same position in the ground-floor apartment as the old one did on the third
floor.

So far as the furnishings are concerned, the only difference comes from Freud's new tastes: same
armchairs, same couch — a little more worn — but, on already existing pieces of furniture (mantel-
piece, desk, occasional tables), small Egyptian figurines (authentic, but fairly commonplace).

A man in a black frock-coat is waiting; very thin, his expression intimidating behind his
pince-nez, his top-hat placed beside him on the carpet, both hands on the pommel of his cane.

(At first, there is silence.)

He has pale blue eyes, cold and clear, a fairly long but sparse pepper-and-salt beard, a fine
head of almost white hair. He is a man of about sixty, 'important' without any doubt (he is
wearing decorations); his thinness and severity give him an air of asceticism.

At present, he seems deeply reproving, but he says nothing.

Then we hear:

FREUD'S VOICE OFF, *harder and more authoritarian*   Speak, Magda, speak! I command
you.

It was about a glove.

MAGDA'S VOICE OFF   What glove?

The old gentleman has picked up an Egyptian statuette from a pedestal-table and studies it
wearily (holding it in his left hand, his right still resting on the cane).

FREUD'S VOICE OFF   The one you dreamed about.

MAGDA'S VOICE, *languid and weary*   I don't know any longer.

(A silence.)

The old gentleman calmly puts the statuette back in its place. After which, replacing his left
hand on his right, he looks at Freud (whom we cannot yet see) severely.

OLD GENTLEMAN   It's pointless. After fifteen sessions, we're no further ahead.

We discover Freud, sitting (as usual) in front of a hypnotized patient. This time it is an old maid (about thirty-five), likewise very thin, entirely dressed in black, with an unprepossessing face (not only is she genuinely ugly, but she seems never to have known either youth or gaiety).

For the moment she has her eyes shut. But even under hypnosis she retains a morose and disagreeable expression. Freud, on hearing the father's comments, has turned round in a rage.

He has regained the sombre expression we saw him wearing in Part One and especially at the beginning of Part Two.

But he has acquired an almost tyrannical sureness and authority, above all with his patients.

In his eyes and the curl of his lips, there is a mixture of scorn and harshness.

He has become what one might call a man of violence, ready to violate his patients' consciousness to satisfy his scientific curiosity.

This is truly the man he would have become if he had really made a pact with the Devil.

At the same time — and this contrasts with his authority — the nervousness of his gestures has increased. From time to time he coughs. A short, dry cough which tears at his throat. He is not smoking.

FREUD, *polite but very hard* Hush!

He rises noiselessly and goes over to the father.

(In a firm tone, but almost whispering:)

It must be said, Councillor, that you don't make my task very easy. I've never once seen Magda on her own. You're present at every single session.

COUNCILLOR, *in the same tone* I'll never let a man hypnotize Magda in my absence. Reputable doctor or no.

FREUD, *impatiently* Then please hold your tongue.

They exchange angry glances and Freud returns to his place. Magda has her eyes open. She says forcefully:

MAGDA I remember everything. The gloves were my father's.

Freud's eyes are shining. With a curiosity devoid of warmth:

FREUD, *in the voice of a policeman in a detective story* When did he wear them?

MAGDA It was in Kitzbühel. Two years after my mother's death.

FREUD How old were you?

MAGDA Six.

We return to the Aulic Councillor. His hands resting on his cane, a faraway look in his eyes, he has not budged an inch.

(Scream off from Magda.)

240

Magda utters a dreadful scream. The old man does not even flinch. He remains upright, staring into space.

MAGDA'S VOICE OFF, *she screams and sobs*   He hurt me!
   He frightened me!
      He wasn't my father any more! I'll never get married, I don't want to see that look.

   (This confession ends in inarticulate weeping.)

The Councillor does not move. The expression on his face does not change, but, all of a sudden, tears flow silently from his eyes. He does not even think of protesting.
   Freud has turned round; he sees the Councillor weeping.
   He looks at him with a mixture of astonishment and contempt.
   The Councillor does not even look at him. Freud bends over Magda. He calms her by the pressure of his hand on her forehead. She stops struggling, and the terrible agitation that had seized her decreases rapidly.

FREUD, *authoritarian*   You are going to wake up, Magda. But I command you to remember word for word what you have just said. Will you obey?
MAGDA, *in a whisper*   Yes.
FREUD   Wake up, Magda. Wake up!
   You're awake.

Magda's eyes are open. She gradually reassumes the sullen, lucid look she must have in everyday life.
   She raises herself and sits on the bed.

Do you remember what you said to me?

Magda's expression does not change. She replies in a faint but natural voice:

MAGDA   Yes.

Freud, though remaining seated, has moved away from her.
   She rises to her feet. She takes her hat wordlessly and fastens it on her head, without turning towards the mirror.
   Her movements are somewhat slow, still numbed one would say, but precise. Freud watches her without saying a word.
   The Councillor has risen likewise. There are no longer tears in his eyes.
   Magda makes her way towards the door and the Councillor joins her.
   He has not taken his hat, which remains on the carpet near the armchair. Magda sees that he is bare-headed. With a very simple and everyday movement she goes to pick up the top-hat, comes back towards the Councillor and hands it to him. Her face expresses no feeling.

MAGDA   Your hat, Papa.

The Councillor takes the hat and keeps it in his hand. Meanwhile Freud has opened the door. They go out.

Magda first, her father follows her. They cross the waiting-room without a word. Magda takes her black parasol from the umbrella-stand, opens the door and goes out, her father behind her.

Freud, who has not left his consulting-room, closes the door again and returns to the centre of the room. Then, as if automatically, he goes over to the window and opens it.

We then perceive that we are at street level. Under a bright sun, Freud sees the father and daughter dressed in black cross the Berggasse, side by side and without a word. They move away, turn into a street on the right and disappear.

Freud closes the window again, returns to the far end of the room. His face expresses a mixture of contempt and despair. He goes up to an Egyptian statuette and subjects it to a lengthy scrutiny. His eyes brighten somewhat. He goes behind his desk, picks up a little open box containing an object surrounded by straw.

He goes out. Through the same door as the Councillor and his daughter. He takes a hat from a peg, places it on his head (he holds the little box in his left hand, clutching it tightly to him).

He goes out of the front door and climbs the stairs.

2

On the third floor, he stops in front of a door and rings three times. The maid comes at once to let him in. She has aged, but when she sees him her eyes still betray a kind of passionate admiration. Freud is unconcerned by it. He gives her his hat and passes into the corridor.

FREUD   No cable?
MAID   No, sir.

The little Mathilde (she is ten) and his two sons (four and six) emerge from the children's room and rush towards him.

CHILDREN, *joyfully*   Papa! Papa!

Freud's face lights up; he smiles at them with deep affection.

FREUD, *gently*   Careful, my darlings, careful.

He points at the box.

You'll break everything.
    Here, Mathilde, take the box and carry it to the dining-room. But be really careful, mind.

Mathilde takes the box carefully and carries it to the dining-room, proud as Punch of her mission.
Freud, his hands free, lifts his two sons one after another and kisses them tenderly.
Mathilde has come back.

MATHILDE   And me! And me!

He takes her in his arms and kisses her.

FREUD   My beautiful little girl! My little angel!

Martha comes out of the kitchen.

MARTHA   Come along! Everyone to table!

Freud takes her by the shoulders and kisses her on the forehead. They smile gaily and affectionately at one another, but without the deep and loving tenderness that united them in Parts One and Two.
Everybody goes into the dining room. The table is laid. As the children are taking their places

round the table, Freud has gone over to a pedestal-table on which little Mathilde has placed the box. From the straw surrounding it he takes out a little Egyptian bust.
    Martha looks at it with the faintest touch of vexation.

MARTHA   Another one! Whatever you do, don't drop bits of straw! They stick to the carpet and it's the very devil to get them off.

Freud has finished the operation. The children and Martha are already seated; Martha serves the two youngest.
    Freud comes and sits down at the family table carrying his statuette.
    He puts it down in front of him but slightly to the left, and contemplates it.

LITTLE MATHILDE, *with childish delight*   It's lovely!
FREUD, *to Mathilde, enchanted by this tribute*   Yes.

The maid brings in a dish of meat. Martha serves Freud.

(To Martha who is serving him:) There hasn't been any cable?

He is really saying it just to make quite sure.

MARTHA   No, darling.

His face has darkened slightly.

Why? Were you expecting one?
FREUD   It's to do with Fliess. We were to meet at Berchtesgaden at the beginning of next week, but he hasn't told me which day.

Martha seems unpleasantly surprised.

MARTHA   You never told me about that. So you're going to leave us?
FREUD   For three days, yes. If Fliess gives any sign of life.

Silence falls. The children eat. Martha watchs them out of the corner of her eye.
    Freud remains sunk in contemplation of the Egyptian bust.

MARTHA, *a moment later*   Eat up, Sigmund. Your meat will be cold.
FREUD, *docilely*   Oh, yes.

He eats without taking his eyes off the statuette.
    A silence.

MATHILDE   Papa!

Martha glowers at her and puts her finger to her lips.

MARTHA   Hush!

MATHILDE, *without paying any attention to Martha*   Papa! Why do you look at the doll
while you're eating?

Freud, without taking his eyes off the statuette:

FREUD, *gently*   Because it's my only moment of rest, darling.

MATHILDE   You could talk to us.

Freud turns his head and looks affectionately at Mathilde.

FREUD   No. Because . . .
       (He hesitates, then with a touch of irony, knowing that he won't be understood:) My job is to
know people as they are. That's not very nice. When I rest, I prefer to look at what
they make.

MATHILDE, *questioningly*   Oh?

MARTHA, *very quickly*   You'll understand later on, Mathilde. Let Papa rest.

Silence once more. Freud has turned back to the statuette and is sunk in contemplation of it.

[3]

Two o'clock in the afternoon.

Breuer gets out of his barouche, enters the building and starts up the stairs.

After a few steps, he realizes his mistake and comes down again. He goes and rings the door-bell on the ground floor.

On the door, a gilded plaque: 'Dr Freud. Neurology. Psychiatry.' It is Freud himself who comes to let him in, a cigar in his mouth.

FREUD, *friendly, but without the timid admiration he had in Parts One and Two*   Good morning, Breuer.

He enters and deposits his hat and stick in the waiting-room.

BREUER   Good morning, Freud. Do you know I was just about to go up to the third floor?

I'll never get used to your new establishment.

He laughs. He is affable and courteous, he has lost his somewhat protective superiority, but suddenly we no longer sense in his voice the generosity that formerly characterized his relations with Freud.

Freud coughs (dry, harsh cough), before replying.

FREUD   You know, I did it mainly for Martha's sake. Up there, it's private life, you see: the children, her domestic chores, the furniture — everthing reflects an image of herself that pleases her. When I was treating my patients on the third floor, she had the feeling I was violating her privacy.

They have entered Freud's consulting-room. Freud waves him to a chair. They both sit down in front of Freud's desk, on the same side. Breuer takes a manuscript out of his briefcase and lays it in front of Freud.

BREUER   There's our introduction.

Freud takes it. He coughs.

What's that cough?

Freud shrugs his shoulders.

I thought you weren't smoking any more.
FREUD   Fliess allows me five cigars a day.

The name of Fliess is not agreeable to Breuer. Visibly.
   Pointing to his cigar:

This is the first one of the day. The best.

He looks at the manuscript, then pushes it away slightly.

If you like, we'll read that later.

He consults his watch.

I'm expecting a patient in ten minutes. Frau Doelnitz. I'm having some trouble with her: I'd like you to see her with me.

BREUER, *politely but without warmth*   Very willingly. But you know that we disagree ...

FREUD, *sharply*   It doesn't concern any point of difference.

He rises to his feet.

It's this: she reacts badly to hypnosis. Or perhaps it's I who am unable to hypnotize her.
   On the other hand, when she stretches out on this couch *without being put to sleep*, it seems to me that she speaks more readily and that she yields up far more of herself.

Breuer listens without benevolence.

Of course, the transference is obvious. So I come back to the question I've been asking myself since that unfortunate Dora business: since it's the transference which allows the doctor to hypnotize the patient, why should hypnosis be necessary at all?

He laughs.

You'll tell me that I'm talking nonsense and that I'm simply a bad hypnotist.

BREUER, *rather sharply*   I shan't tell you that: I'll merely ask you what remains of our method.

FREUD, *warmly*   Everything! Absolutely everything! I ...

There is a ring at the door.

In any case, you'll see her.

The footman opens the door of the consulting-room.

FOOTMAN   Herr Doelnitz.

4

Enter Doelnitz, a giant. About thirty-five. No beard: side-whiskers. Ruddy complexion, huge biceps which swell the sleeves of his jacket. Sports suit.

He looks hale and hearty, cut out for any sporting activity but without much talent for intellectual pursuits. At the present moment, he seems intensely annoyed.

Freud has stood up at the sight of the giant: he will maintain his calm throughout the scene, but we can sense that he is inspired by a cold and powerful anger. He will conduct the whole scene which follows with sovereign authority — but, at moments, with a suppressed violence resembling malice.

FREUD, *coldly*   Herr Doelnitz, it's your wife I was expecting.

DOELNITZ, *responding in kind, but with less control and more outward violence*   Dr Freud, I've come to tell you that she'll never come here again.

FREUD   Well then, your errand is accomplished. You may withdraw.

Doelnitz, far from obeying, takes a chair and sits down.

DOELNITZ   If you don't mind, I've a few little things to say to you.

FREUD   Sir, you are committing what is called a forcible entry. And I could have you thrown out by the police. But out of consideration for your wife, whom until further orders I still consider my patient, I consent to hear what you have to say.

Doelnitz does not seem very impressed. He looks at Breuer in an unfriendly fashion.

DOELNITZ   I don't know this gentleman.

FREUD   It's Dr Breuer, a great neurologist; you'll speak in front of him or you'll leave.

Breuer makes a move to rise.

FREUD   No, Breuer, stay; I beg of you.

The footman opens the far door.

FOOTMAN   There's a person asking for Dr Breuer: he says it's urgent.

Breuer rises to his feet.

FREUD, *to Doelnitz*   You're lucky.

Breuer has reached the door; he goes out. Doelnitz follows him with his eyes.

Speak.

DOELNITZ   You're not a doctor, Sir.

FREUD   I'm a charlatan. A notorious one. Is that all you have to say to me?

DOELNITZ   No.

The far door opens once more. Breuer appears, his hat on his head.

BREUER   It's an emergency. I'll be back in half an hour.

He closes the door again.

FREUD, *to Doelnitz*   You have half an hour at your disposal.

DOELNITZ   Sir, since you have been treating my wife, she has fallen ill.

FREUD   She wasn't beforehand?

DOELNITZ   No.

FREUD   Well then? Why did you send her to me?

DOELNITZ   She was ill. But not so seriously.

FREUD   She had exactly the same illness, Sir. Only her illness bothered you less.

DOELNITZ, *trying to understand*   She bothered me less . . .

He has understood.

Yes, she bothered me less. So what? I don't want her to bother me. I'm the one who's paying, after all.

FREUD   Sir, your wife is suffering from an acute anxiety neurosis. If you're so eager not to be disturbed, tie a stone round her neck and throw her into the Danube.

Doelnitz thumps violently on the arm of his chair, rises to his feet and walks about agitatedly.

You must calm yourself if you want me to take you seriously.

Doelnitz controls himself, then comes and sits down again.

DOELNITZ   She's not my wife any longer.

Freud raises his eyebrows with an air of ironical surprise.

You've forbidden her to have any relations with me.

FREUD, *pretending not to understand*   Any relations?

DOELNITZ   You know very well what I mean. The ones a wife should have with her husband.

FREUD   Oh! I see. Well, yes: I've forbidden her such . . . relations for as long as the treatment lasts.

Doelnitz once again springs out of his chair; he comes and thumps on Freud's desk, and shouts in his face:

DOELNITZ   I'm the full-blooded type, the doctors have told me so; such relations are necessary for me . . .

FREUD   If those doctors said so, ask them for some sedatives. It's not you I'm treating, it's your wife.
        For the time being, such relations are injurious to her.

DOELNITZ   Injurious! They're natural, Sir.

FREUD   You know very well she has begun to detest them.

DOELNITZ, *disconcerted*   Did she . . . Well, all right, she never did like that, but she used to go along with it all the same. Whereas now . . .

FREUD   Each time she went along with it, she had an anxiety crisis. Aren't you ashamed to demand of your wife . . . ?

DOELNITZ, *violent but despairing*   Ach! But I can't help it, Sir. That's our whole sad story.

FREUD, *exploiting his advantage*   Will you please sit down.

Doelnitz, discomfited, goes and sits down.

If you don't obey me, your wife will be locked away within three years.

Freud assumes the tone of a policeman.

Besides, for a long time now you've had other amusements.

DOELNITZ   Eh!

FREUD   Yes. The maidservants.

DOELNITZ   Did she tell you that?

FREUD   Yes.

A pause. Doelnitz remains in his armchair, crushed. Abruptly his anger returns.

DOELNITZ   And you, you claim you'll cure her by filling her head with filth?

FREUD   What filth?

DOELNITZ   I don't know. Her head is full of it!

FREUD   Yours too. And yet I'm not treating you.

Doelnitz has risen. This time he paces round the room.

DOELNITZ   For the past fortnight, each time she comes back from seeing you she talks to us about her uncle Hubert, she goes on about her uncle Hubert and nothing else. I don't want you to remind her about her uncle Hubert.

FREUD   Why not?

DOELNITZ   Firstly because he's dead.

FREUD, *ironical smile*   What else?

DOELNITZ   And then because that's all filthy.

FREUD   Talking to her about her uncle is filthy?

DOELNITZ   Yes.

FREUD   I see! Why?

DOELNITZ   Because he was a filthy pig.

(A pause. Violently:)

You'll get round to it, my fine Sir, you'll get round to it! I can see what you're trying to do, from a mile off!

FREUD   I'll thank you to call me Doctor. What will I get round to?

DOELNITZ   Making her believe that her uncle Hubert raped her.

FREUD, *keenly interested*   Oh!

(A pause.)

Isn't it true, then?

DOELNITZ   Oh yes, my fine Sir! (*Catching himself:*) Oh yes, Doctor! Only as far as she's concerned, it's false!

FREUD   Why?

DOELNITZ   Because they've hidden it from her. All of them, starting with her mother. And ending up with me, when her mother admitted it to me.
     (*Defiantly:*) We've at least got some tact.

FREUD   If someone had raped you, Sir, do you think people could hide it from you, even if they were tactful about it?

At this suggestion, the giant's astonishment knows no limits.

DOELNITZ, *stunned*   Raped me? Me?

He collapses onto the chair and mops his brow.

She was six years old, Doctor!

FREUD   And you think she didn't notice?

DOELNITZ   Oh yes. But she's forgotten it.

FREUD   What does that mean: to forget?

DOELNITZ, *more and more disconcerted*   It means to forget.

FREUD   It means no longer wanting to recall a memory.

DOELNITZ   If you like.

FREUD   And where is it, that memory? Do you think it has flown away? It's still inside her, Sir, unconscious, repressed, and that's what spoils everything. That's what provokes her anxieties! That's what disgusts her with love.

Doelnitz listens raptly: he makes an intense effort to understand.

DOELNITZ   You mean it's not *me* who disgusts her?
FREUD   Of course not: she received a shock in childhood which disgusted her with all men.

Doelnitz's face lights up.

You were afraid your physical person ...
DOELNITZ   Yes. That used to humiliate me.

With sudden violence:

What a filthy pig, all the same!
FREUD, *surprised*   Who?
DOELNITZ   Uncle Hubert!

Freud purses his lips silently, making clear his feelings.

When you've cured her, I won't disgust her any more?

There is a knock at the door.

FREUD   Come in.

It is Breuer. He is pale and sombre, he looks at Freud with a kind of rancour.
    Freud, wholly concerned with Doelnitz, smiles at him without noticing his attitude. Then he turns back towards Doelnitz:

FREUD, *with deep sincerity*   No, you won't disgust her any more.

Doelnitz rises to his feet, quite happy.

DOELNITZ   Thank you, Doctor.

Freud stands up, still authoritarian but relaxed.

FREUD   You've made her miss a session.

As he accompanies him to the door:

Tell her to come tomorrow at seven in the evening.
DOELNITZ, *subdued*   Very well, Doctor.

In the waiting-room, he turns to face Freud, over whom he towers, and asks him timidly:

Doctor, I sometimes wonder if I'm not a neurotic. Would you agree to examine me?

Mysterious and full of promise:

If you hypnotized me, I could tell you about some of those things ... You can't even imagine them.

Freud looks at him: Doelnitz exudes physical and mental health. He begins to laugh, ironical but not unsympathetic.

FREUD, *closing the door*   We'll talk about it again once your wife's cured.

5

Freud comes back to Breuer.

FREUD   The thirteenth case.

Breuer gives a start. He was thinking about something else.

BREUER   Eh?

FREUD   It's the thirteenth case of neurosis in which I've established that the patient had been a victim in childhood of a sexual assault committed by an adult.

Breuer barely listens to him; he has the air of gloomy satisfaction of a man about to work off his hostile feelings by playing the executioner.

BREUER   You saw Magda, this morning?

FREUD   Yes. And precisely . . .

He stops abruptly at the sight of Breuer's face. He is frightened but does not dare question him. Breuer says in a natural voice, but one that barely disguises his malicious triumph:

BREUER   It was her father who summoned me. She has just thrown herself out of the window.

A pause. At last Freud is able to speak.

FREUD, *painfully*   Dead?

BREUER, *taking his time*   No. Fractures and bruises, but if there's no internal haemorrhage, I think she'll pull through.

Freud turns on his heel and goes slowly over to his desk. His face is contorted. He begins to cough.

FREUD, *coughing*   She told me this morning that her father had abused her when she was six.

BREUER, *indignantly*   The Aulic Councillor? She told you a foul lie, and you pushed her into it!

Freud swings abruptly round to face Breuer. But he answers without violence, with deep sadness.

FREUD, *sadly*   Breuer!

     (*A pause.*)

Her father was present. He wept. Without a word of protest.

BREUER, *with almost comical astonishment*   The Aulic Councillor!

We can sense the utter amazement of Breuer, who has always respected the official personages and important people of this world.

It's unbelievable!

He seems overwhelmed too. Freud circles the desk and goes to sit down on his chair in weary despondency. After a moment:

(With conviction:) You must give it up, Freud.

Freud replies without raising his eyes.

FREUD, *drearily*   Give what up?

BREUER   All of it. All that.

FREUD   It's your method.

BREUER   Oh! no: I refuse to acknowledge it.

FREUD   You used to reveal to patients the truth about themselves.

BREUER   When they could endure it.

Freud, in a dull voice and with fixed gaze, as if he were thinking of himself:

FREUD   The real truth about oneself, no one can endure that.

BREUER   There, you see!

FREUD   We're there to discover it and to help people look themselves in the face. With our help, they'll be able to. At cock-crow, vampires disappear: they cannot withstand the light of day.

BREUER   Magda tried to kill herself because she was crazy with shame and horror. There are cases where lies are more human.

FREUD   Was she any less crazy when she was lying to herself?

BREUER   She was less unhappy.

FREUD   The treatment is only just beginning; I'll go and see her and I'll ...

BREUER   You won't be admitted.

FREUD, *stricken*   Oh!

BREUER   Her father told me so.

FREUD   But that's a crime! If the treatment is stopped *now*, all is lost!

BREUER   All is lost, whatever you do.

(A pause.)

You're lucky her attempt at suicide failed.

(A pause.)

If she'd killed herself, I wouldn't like to be in your shoes.

Freud is disoriented; his replies are feeble defences, one would say he no longer believed in them.

FREUD   All doctors take risks.

BREUER   Calculated risks, yes. But not that one. They know where they're going and you don't know.

Freud is crushed by Breuer's harshness. He speaks to him as a friend, with rediscovered deference.

FREUD   I'm going through a ... difficult patch. Breuer, couldn't you ... help me?

Breuer seems somewhat softened by this appeal for aid, which reminds him of the time when he was protecting Freud.

BREUER   I'd be very willing to, but what can I do? You see sex everywhere and I can't follow you ...

FREUD   Magda ...

BREUER   Yes: Magda. Perhaps it's true in her case. And also ... But not in all cases.

With authority, but in a friendly tone:

You trick your patients, Freud, you force them! Stop, if there's still time.
    You can believe me: I know what remorse is.

A perturbed voice. He is friendly enough to reveal his remorse to Freud:

I saw Loewenguth, who looks after Cäcilie's mother. They're ruined. They live in a detached house in Prinz Eugen Gasse. Cäcilie's condition has worsened.

(A pause.)

She'd be better off dead.

Freud has recovered: Breuer's remorse has given him back his aggressiveness.

FREUD   What will become of Science if men of learning do not say what they believe to be the Truth?
    Vienna is rotten! Everywhere hypocrisy, perversion, neurosis!

He rises to his feet and strides up and down.

Do you think I like plunging my hands into this cesspool?

(A pause.)

An Aulic Councillor. With the face of an ascetic! (*Violently:*) He's a cur! If Magda dies, it's he who'll have killed her. Not me.

Going over to Breuer, in a still violent but friendly tone:

We'll cleanse this city or we'll blow it to smithereens.

With deep conviction:

I cannot conceive of a healthy society that's based on lies.

He begins to cough. In a voice strangled by the attack:

An Aulic Councillor!

He drinks, then forcefully, very sombre:

There are days when man sickens me.

Breuer looks at him in silence, disconcerted, partly overawed by this violent, sombre force, partly pitying.
  Freud, with great gentleness:

Would it be a great nuisance for you if we postponed the work till tomorrow?
  (*Confidingly. It is almost a confession:*) I don't feel very well. And then ... I must get my ideas sorted out again.

Breuer smiles affectionately at him and silently clasps his hand. He goes out, turns in the doorway and says in a very friendly tone:

BREUER   Till tomorrow, Freud.

The door has closed again. Freud has not moved at all. Suddenly he calls out, in a worried voice:

FREUD   Breuer!

The apartment door closes: Breuer has not heard him.

  (Sound off of a door closing.)

257

[6]

Freud, left alone, starts coughing again. He returns to his desk: there is no more water in the jug.

He circles the desk, coughs again, presses his right hand to his chest at the level of his heart. He seems to be in pain. He collapses onto a chair, pulls his watch from his waistcoat-pocket and lays it on Breuer's manuscript. Looking at it, he takes his pulse. We sense that an attack may be imminent.

(Sound off, several rings on the bell.)
(Sound of a door opening.)
(A knock on the consulting-room door.)

Freud straightens up.

FREUD, *regaining control of himself*   Come in.

Martha's little maidservant enters. She is carrying a telegram. Freud's face is transformed. He rises to his feet, his eyes shining, fully master of himself.

Give me that.

He unseals the telegram and reads it, while the young maid looks at him with a sly, tender expression. He turns back towards her; his face has lit up.

FREUD   Go and tell your Mistress to be so kind as to pack my suitcase.
I'm leaving for Berchtesgaden tonight.

7

Next day, at about four in the afternoon, in the mountains near Berchtesgaden, at a height of two thousand feet.

Two men appear round a bend on a mountain path, amid a splendid landscape. Above them snowy peaks, around them bare rock and scree, somewhat lower down high mountain pastures and below that the valley.

These two men are identically dressed or almost so (Tyrolean leather jacket, soft Tyrolean plumed hat; they have retained long trousers, but are wearing mountain shoes); each leans on an alpenstock.

They are Freud and Fliess. Freud walks fast, Fliess has to make a slight effort to keep up with him (but without the difference being very marked).

Freud, after a faint hesitation, decides to shorten their route by scrambling down through boulders and scree to rejoin the path two hundred metres below.

Like a practised walker, he goes down sideways across the scree.

Fliess follows him, but goes down with his face to the slope. The result is that he slips and falls on his back, laughing.

Freud turns round at the noise, climbs swiftly back up the slope and tries to help Fliess up. But Fliess has regained his feet unaided and brushes his trousers, laughing at his misadventure. (He is quite sincere: no trace of humiliation. This is not where he invests his pride.)

FREUD   Do the same as me. Go down sideways, you're quite safe and you can brake.

He starts down again and Fliess imitates him this time, quite a way behind.

Freud, reaching the path well ahead, gazes round at the mountains as he waits for Fliess. He fastens his eyes on the peaks rather than the valley. Fliess jumps onto the path, out of breath but happy.

You managed very well.

FLIESS   Yes, but I'm out of breath.
    Let's sit down.

Pointing out a flat rock beside the path.
    They sit down. Admiringly:

What training!
    One would say you'd done nothing else all your life.

Freud looks almost happy.

FREUD   I have done nothing else all my life: whenever I take a holiday, I have to go
    climbing.

The higher I go, the better it suits me.

He speaks without looking at Fliess, his eyes fastened on the peaks.

FLIESS   If I were Sigmund Freud, I'd draw the conclusion that you like to dominate.
FREUD   Maybe.

Pointing at the snowy peaks above them.

The main thing is, it's not alive. Rocks. Snow. Nobody.

He picks up a stone from the edge of the path and looks at it.

It's dry. It's clean. Death!

He throws the stone ahead of him and watches it roll down the slope.

I've often wondered if I didn't wish to die.

As if to himself:

Wish? Fear? I've no idea.

He pulls himself together.

Actually, everyone must be like me.

Fliess looks at him with a smile.

FLIESS   I have no wish to die.
FREUD, *warmly*   Yes, but you're not 'everyone'. You have great things to do.
FLIESS, *with simple conviction*   That's true.

   (*With faint remorse:*) We shall do great things, Freud.

Freud rises abruptly to his feet.

FREUD   It gets dark quickly. Let's go.

A short while later.
   Four hundred metres lower down. The daylight is beginning to fade. The peaks are very high, they seem overpowering. The two walkers enter the shadow of the valley.
   This time it is Fliess who leads the way and Freud who follows him.
   Freud is certainly less tired than Fliess: what delays him is an inner resistance . . .

FLIESS, *friendly but annoyed*   Hey? Are you straggling now? Let's go that way down.

He points to the (waterless) bed of a stream between some trees. And at once he begins to go down (sideways); Freud follows him, effortlessly, nimbly, but with no pleasure.

Come along! Hurry! Hurry!

They reach a fresh path. As they turn onto the path, they see Berchtesgaden at their feet. It is still daylight in the valley, but in Berchtesgaden a few windows are already lit up.
    Fliess wants to press on. Freud stops him.

FREUD   Stop a moment.
FLIESS, *already prepared to enjoy his new superiority*   Are you tired already?
FREUD   Oh no!

Pointing at Berchtesgaden, very sombrely:

We have to go back into that.

Fliess, surprised by his tone, casts an inquiring glance at him:

FLIESS   What's the matter? You don't look quite yourself.

Freud stops. Fliess, irritably, stops too.

FREUD   Listen to me, Wilhelm.

Freud hesitates.

FLIESS   All right, all right! You can tell me about it later. I'm not very keen on being caught in the dark, I don't have your cat's eyes.

He tries to leave.
    Freud detains him.

FREUD   One of my patients threw herself out of the window.
FLIESS, *indifferently*   Oh!
FREUD   I'd brought back a repressed memory: when she was six, her father took advantage of her.

Fliess pulls a notebook out of his pocket.

FLIESS   Interesting. Date of birth?
FREUD   I know it by heart: 6 October 1860.

FLIESS   Date of the sexual attack.

FREUD   It was in 1866.

FLIESS, *impatiently*   Naturally, since she was six. I'm asking you for the day, the month and the hour.

FREUD   I don't know, I tell you she …

FLIESS   … threw herself out of the window, well, so what? How do you expect me to work on such vague data?

Freud shrugs his shoulders and says nothing.

Come along! We can talk as we go!

They continue on their way. Freud looks regretfully at the pure, ice-cold sky high above their heads.
    At their feet, the shadow thickens.

(Condescendingly, like someone preparing to play the role of a comforter.)

It's this death that's worrying you?

Freud speaks confidently. He is full of hope.

FREUD   She's not dead.

FLIESS   She'll pull through?

FREUD   Yes.

He is evidently relying on Fliess's help; he needs to be given fresh heart.

FLIESS   Well then?

FREUD   What if she had killed herself?

FLIESS   What a strange question. There are no ifs in the world. She didn't kill herself: period.

Freud does not reply. We sense that he is disappointed, and that he is struggling against his disappointment.
    Flies realizes this and decides it is necessary to make a further effort.

Very well. Let's suppose she's dead. Is she some relative of yours?

FREUD   Of course not.

FLIESS   If she's nothing to you, I wonder what it can possibly matter to you.

(A pause.)

Hey, it's starting to get dark. I don't want to risk breaking a leg.
    Can't you go a bit faster?

They go faster.

What do you expect me to say? Those are the risks of the trade.

Prussia's greatest general and the best surgeon in Berlin have more or less the same number of deaths on their consciences.

Is it Breuer who has got you all worked up?

Freud nods.

I thought as much. He's the typical representative of Viennese sentimentality. Waltzes! Waltzes! And rivers of tears: you'll never be able to wage a war.

Ow!

He has twisted his ankle. He almost falls, hops a few steps with a grimace of pain, then sits down on a tree trunk.

FREUD, *worried*   What's wrong?

Fliess massages his ankle through the shoe.

FLIESS, *sulky*   I stumbled over a rock. *(Bitterly:)* One can't even see one's own feet any longer. We should have gone back earlier.

        (A pause.)

It's nothing.

He climbs to his feet.

Forward, march.

He walks with a limp. Freud tries to support him, he pushes him away.

Not worth it.

In fact, his gait quickly becomes normal again.

What was she, this good lady?

FREUD   A spinster. She never left her father … she hardly went out.

Fliess listens to him, more and more disappointed.

FLIESS   What a bug-like existence. It wouldn't have been any great loss!

(Conciliatory:)

But I quite agree with you: human lives shouldn't be wasted.

(Forcefully:)

We won't waste them, Sigmund! We're still groping. But for every one we lose, we'll save a thousand later.

Do you know what the Berliners, who are no weaklings, always say? 'You can't make an omelette without breaking eggs'.

Is that what you wanted me to say? Are you happy?

Freud gives a constrained nod, which may be taken as an assent.

Then let's speak no more about it.

They disappear round a bend and night falls on a deserted landscape.

8

We rediscover them a moment later in the dining-room of a second-class hotel.

The 'season' has not begun and the hotel is deserted. In the large dining-room, provided with several small tables (all empty), what strikes one first is a long table d'hôte which, in the season, can accommodate thirty places.

In fact, there are six people at the table. At the far end, four melancholy Bavarians: they must be officials, who have taken daily board in the restaurant. At the other end, Fliess and Freud.

Right in the middle of the table, a seventh place has been laid (bottle of wine already started, boxes of pills for liver-trouble, napkin with a wooden ring engraved with initials).

But this place will be occupied only at the end of the scene, by a hunchbacked old lady wearing spectacles.

Fliess and Freud are on their dessert. Fliess eats his rice pudding with gusto. Freud hardly touches his.

Fliess swallows the last mouthful of his dessert, then turns to Freud with an inquisitive air.

FLIESS   Well, what have you brought me then?

Freud looks wretched and uncertain.

FREUD, *with an air of tender reproach*   Hang on a while; let me thaw out. I'm so alone, down there. Give me time to make the most of your presence.

FLIESS   We've spent the whole day walking. Listen, Sigmund, our Congresses have no meaning if they don't help us advance in our research.

FREUD   The essential thing for me is that they allow us to see each other again.

FLIESS, *amiable but cool*   Yes, of course!

A pause.

Well?

FREUD, *very slightly annoyed*   Well what?

FLIESS   You wrote to me that you had a theory about the sexual origin of neuroses. I'm listening.

Freud rolls a pellet of bread in his left hand.

FREUD   Imagine that a child, in the very first years of its life, is the victim of a sexual assault.

FLIESS   Committed by an adult?

FREUD   Of course.

Its first reaction is fear, to which of course may be added pain and surprise. But, as you may well imagine, it experiences no excitation: there's no sexuality at that age.

Very well. A few years go by; the organs develop. When it evokes that memory, it's excited for the first time. In the meantime, however, society has instilled moral principles into it — strict and unswerving imperatives; it feels shame at being excited, and defends itself by repressing the memory into the unconscious.

Fliess does not seem particularly interested.

FLIESS   All right. What then?

The hunchbacked old lady hobbles to her place; she sits down, unfolds her napkin and opens the box of pills.
She seems content to eat. But little by little she becomes aware of the conversation between the two men, and begins to listen with patent astonishment.

FREUD   The memory seeks to be reborn and the excitation to be perpetuated; but the moral imperatives tend to deny them completely. Defence mechanisms enter into action, the child convinces itself that nothing has happened. It forgets. But since the struggle between these opposed forces is fierce, it's just as if they reached a compromise: the representation no longer appears to consciousness; but something replaces it — something which simultaneously masks it and serves as a symbol of it. This something is the neurosis, or if you prefer the neurotic sympton.

FLIESS   For example?

FREUD   In the obsessional neurosis, the memory of the shock is set aside but what replaces it are phobias and *idées fixes*. Dora had forgotten the old shopkeeper's assault, but she retained her phobia about entering shops.

As for the shame she felt, she'd transferred it onto another object and given it another cause: some shop assistants had laughed at her.

Fliess questions him half-heartedly:

FLIESS   How about hysteria?

FREUD   A special predisposition is needed, which allows the body to make itself complicit with the patient: in order not to see her dead father any longer, Cäcilie squinted with both eyes and saw only at close range. As for anxiety neurosis ...

FLIESS, *annoyed*   All right, all right! I can guess the rest. Repression, transference, that's your field. That's psychology. It doesn't interest me. Do you have any cases?

FREUD   Thirteen.

FLIESS   Thirteen neuroses provoked by a sexual assault?

FREUD   Yes.

FLIESS   Who's the perpetrator?

FREUD   Sometimes an uncle or a servant. In a majority of cases, the father.

The old lady is so astonished that she takes off her spectacles and stops eating.

FLIESS   The father?

FREUD, *sombre and terse*   Yes.

FLIESS   The father?

He rubs his hands with satisfaction, under the stunned gaze of the old lady.

Excellent, that! Excellent! That simplifies the calculations.

So neurosis in children results from the perversion of their fathers?

Freud looks at him in some embarrassment at this crude simplification of his theories.

Well, that seems to me to be entirely solid. At last, we've got some facts.

FREUD, *timidly*   Wilhelm! It's only a hypothesis. Thirteen cases aren't enough to back it up.

FLIESS   Thirteen rapes, thirteen neuroses? And you're not satisfied?

For my part, I'm delighted! But I want dates. If you give me the date of the parents' birth, the date of the child's and the date of the rape ...

FREUD   I've told you it's not so easy.

FLIESS, *indulgently*   Of course. Because mad people are stupid. But you'll manage. You'll perfect your method. When I have the dates, do you know what I'll do? I'll calculate at what stage of the child's feminine or masculine periods the traumatism occurred, and I can assure you from that I'll deduce *with certainty* the nature of the illness. Take anxiety neurosis: I can tell you in a rough and ready way that it's feminine: it's passivity pure and simple. Obsession is active, so it's virile. The former appears in subjects who've been raped at the culminating moment of the feminine rhythm, the latter ...

Fliess is seized by a kind of lyrical enthusiasm.

Freud is more and more nervous: he no longer recognizes his theory; he listens with an astonishment almost equal to that of the hunchbacked lady.

(*Abruptly:*)

The unfortunate thing, in this business, is that it's not possible to make experiments.

In a laboratory, one could determine the time of the experimental rape down to the last second.

The old hunchbacked lady has risen to her feet, beside herself with indignation. She says to the waitress, in a tone of outraged dignity:

HUNCHBACKED LADY   You can serve me in my room, child. I don't wish to sit at the same table as these gallows birds.

She has risen to her feet. After subjecting the two men to a vengeful glare, she disappears.

Fliess bursts out laughing.

9

Next morning, in a modest but pleasant bedroom in the hotel.

Fliess is finishing an examination of Freud's throat.
    Freud is sitting on a chair, his mouth wide open. Fliess gives it a final glance, then goes to wash his hands and put his instruments away in his bag.
    The conversation takes place in the course of these activities.

    (Carrying straight on with Fliess's laughter.)

FLIESS, *laughing*   There's nothing wrong with you. Absolutely nothing. A slight inflammation, that's all.

    (As he goes to the washbasin:)

You can close your mouth.
    Are you being sensible about cigars?

FREUD   Five a day.
FLIESS   And you've never coughed so much?
FREUD   Never.

Fliess has put his instruments away. He picks up his alpenstock and his Tyrolean hat, then slings a rucksack across his shoulders.

FLIESS   Come along.

In a street in Berchtesgaden.

In front of a Tabak Waren. Its windows filled with cigars. Freud waits in front of the shop. He is wearing a rucksack on his back. He glances inside and sees Fliess in front of the till, paying for something he has bought.
    Fliess comes out. As it opens, the door triggers a little musical chime (several different notes forming a melody). Fliess is carrying a rectangular box.
    He hands it to Freud, who opens it.

FLIESS   Here!

Freud takes it in surprise and opens it: enormous 'black' cigars are revealed, the strongest kind.

FREUD   But Wilhelm, what do you expect me to do with these?

FLIESS   I expect you to smoke them.
FREUD   Eh?

He had taken the box; now astonishment almost makes him drop it. Fliess, obligingly, takes it from his hands, stands behind Freud and puts the box into a pocket of Freud's rucksack. Fliess enjoys Freud's surprise and takes pleasure in prolonging it.

FLIESS, *the operation accomplished*   There.

(Smiling:)

Forward, march!

The two men move off again through Berchtesgaden. After a moment's silence:

You can smoke as much as you like.

Freud stops in his tracks. Fliess stops likewise and feigns astonishment.

Aren't you pleased?
FREUD   No. *(A pause.)*
    Wilhelm, this is the first time you've contradicted yourself.

(Sombre:)

You think I'm an incurable case, don't you?

(Fliess smiles.)

Breuer listened to my chest; he spoke of myocarditis.
    Is that it?
FLIESS   Breuer's an ass.

He puts his arm through Freud's and drags him off.

I told you there was nothing wrong with you.

(Smiling:)

The truth is, I've calculated the date of your death.

Complacently and without haste:

So far as matters of that kind are concerned, the rhythm method has been perfected.

Freud seems relieved: we divine that he does not believe very firmly in Fliess's calculation.
Yet he continues to wear an expression of disappointment.

FREUD   Well, then? At what age?
FLIESS   Fifty-one.
FREUD   In twelve years time?
FLIESS   Yes, barring accidents. In twelve years we'll have found what we're looking for, we'll be kings of the earth.

They leave the built-up area and take an ascending road which leads towards the mountains.

FREUD, *wryly*   It's young to die.
FLIESS   Precisely. I told myself twelve years wasn't long enough for tobacco to destroy you.
FREUD   You'll survive me?
FLIESS   By ten years, I think — I die in 1918. But I'd have nothing left to do, apart from a few minor bits of patching up.

He seizes Freud's arm.

Everything's becoming clear, Sigmund. I make new progress every day.
    Do you know why we're right-handed?
FREUD   No.
FLIESS   Bisexuality. The left side corresponds to our femininity, the right is the male side.

Freud is not convinced.

FREUD, *smiling*   So women ought to be left-handed, then?

A silence. Fliess is at a slight loss. But he frowns and gets out of it through irritation.

FLIESS   Of course not! Are you joking, Sigmund? I hate jokes being made about work.

The same day at about five in the afternoon. The station at Berchtesgaden.

Two tracks. Freud and Fliess are sitting side by side on a bench.
    Fliess has put on his top-hat again. Freud is wearing a morning-coat, but has kept on his Tyrolean hat.
    No train. During the conversation, two local trains will stop and the passengers waiting on the platform — fairly numerous — will get in. A quarter of an hour before the arrival of the train to

Vienna, fresh passengers will appear on the platform. Freud and Fliess have their suitcases at their feet.

They have put their rucksacks on the bench beside them. Freud is friendly but sombre. Fliess seems irritated. He pulls out his watch, looks at it and puts it back in his waistcoat pocket.

FLIESS   Your train gets here an hour from now. Mine in an hour and forty-five minutes. I'd like to know what we're doing in this station.

Freud looks at him sadly and apologetically.

FREUD   I have to arrive early. You know very well I have a phobia about trains.

As the conversation proceeds, Freud feels more and more uncomfortable. The attack comes over him gradually. Fliess does not notice.

FLIESS   An idea has occurred to me. Your theory of the neuroses is interesting, but I need dates.

A family is sitting on the other bench. A little girl of five is running around the platform; she passes to and fro in front of the two men, who do not see her.

I recognize that most of your patients are incapable of giving you any.

Do you know what we need? An exceptionally talented person, who would under-stand your research and assist it.

FREUD   I don't really see …

FLIESS   Come now, how about Cäcilie!

Freud gives a start.

FREUD   Cäcilie?

Dazedly:

But she hasn't been raped!

The little girl comes up to Freud and gives him an already coquettish smile.

FLIESS, *peremptorily*   She must have been. Otherwise you've made a mistake.

Freud looks at the little girl and smiles at her.

If your theory is true …

She gives him a little wave and goes off happily, unsteady on her legs.

Freud's gaze follows her and his face darkens.

271

FREUD   If my theory's true, men are swine.

FLIESS, *calmly*   Why not? The only question is to establish it scientifically.

Freud turns towards Fliess.

FLIESS   There's something fishy about the Cäcilie case. Her father's death could very well hide some other memory.

Freud listens to him, keenly interested in spite of himself. His eyes shine, but his face remains sombre.

Is it known what became of her?

Freud nods regretfully.

Ill?

FREUD   Worse than ever.

Fliess claps his hands. He is filled with enthusiasm.

FLIESS   There's what we need. Go and see her. She'll give you the dates, I'm sure of it. And if you cure her, your hypothesis is proved.

Freud does not reply. Fliess looks at him in indignant amazement.

You're hesitating?

FREUD   I can't.

FLIESS   What?

FREUD   Because of Breuer. He has forbidden me ...

FLIESS, *very sharply*   Can Breuer forbid you to do things?

Freud is more and more uncomfortable. One would say he was suffocating.

FREUD   No. But I don't want to quarrel with him ...

FLIESS   What can it matter to you? He's of no more use to us.

FREUD   We haven't finished our book, he and I.

And then I ... I've always needed to be under somebody's influence. Perhaps to escape my own criticisms.

He automatically raises his hand to his chest.

Doesn't it terrify you, Wilhelm, not to have anyone above you?

FLIESS, *placidly*   Good heavens, no.

And in any case, Breuer isn't above you.

FREUD   I don't know. Yes, he is. I still love him.

FLIESS   You wrote to me that you hated him.

Freud speaks almost to himself, very slowly, with silences. He has a flat, dry voice which chokes at times: one would say he was suffocating.

FREUD   I love him, I hate him. It's confused. You know what? I really ought to be hypnotized: perhaps I'd understand it better. I've always needed friends and enemies. It was necessary for my equilibrium. Sometimes the friend and the enemy are lodged in the same person: with Breuer, I think that's the case.

FLIESS, *indifferently*   Bisexuality: hatred is masculine, love is feminine.

Freud turns towards Fliess and looks at him. He does not appear very convinced. But he gazes at length at the face and tall body of Fliess, who has exchanged his Tyrolean hat for a top-hat and his leather jacket for a black morning-coat. He wears a submissive and almost loving expression.

FREUD   Perhaps. In any case, my real tyrant is you.

With a kind of affectionate resentment:

Do you know that you disappointed me when you allowed me to smoke?
    It gave me pleasure to deny myself in order to obey you.

Fliess, a little embarrassed by this too visible affection, replies with a little dry laugh:

FLIESS   Well, the tyrant commands you to find Cäcilie again.

This light tone disappoints Freud and at the same time recalls him to himself. In a more detached tone:

FREUD   After all, why not? One tyrant is enough. Breuer will be the enemy, you the friend.

Fliess looks bored. He stifles a yawn beneath his hand.

Luckily you're worth more than me: as long as I love you, I shan't be obliged to be my own firmament.

    (He laughs with sombre irony.)

What do you say to that? A man of forty who's afraid of growing up? Brücke, Meynert, Breuer, you: so many fathers! Not counting Jakob Freud who begot me.

A local stopping train draws in. General commotion. Passengers get out, others get in.

FREUD, *with decision*   I'll go and see Cäcilie. I'll go tomorrow morning straight from the station.

10

A moment later.

The platform is deserted. Freud is huddled in his corner; his Tyrolean hat — which he has kept on — is tilted over his eyes: he seems to be asleep.

Fliess is frankly bored. He yawns widely, casts a sulky glance in the direction of Freud, then takes a pencil and notebook out of his pocket. He makes calculations on a page of his pad.

A train goes right past the platform at full speed, without stopping. At the sound, Freud starts and sits upright. His hat falls off. His face appears — anxious and wide-eyed.

FREUD, *in a very loud voice* What's that?

Fliess does not reply. Freud looks at the last carriages going by, with a haggard expression.

FLIESS You've woken up?
FREUD I wasn't asleep.

His hands are trembling.

Don't pay any attention to me. I told you I didn't like railway-stations.

He rises to his feet, goes over to the edge of the platform and looks at the disappearing train. He comes back towards Fliess — he is sweating. He sits down again.

I thought it was an accident.

He leans forward and places his clenched fists on his knees.

 (In a strange voice, somewhat husky and as if against his will:)

Or destitution.
FLIESS, *gives a start* What?

Freud looks at him in surprise.

FREUD What?
FLIESS You said: destitution.
FREUD Oh yes?
  Well, trains make me think of destitution, you see.

He casts a rapid, unfriendly glance at Fliess. In an altered voice, harsh, hard and almost bad-tempered:

Twelve patients out of thirteen.

FLIESS   What patients? What are you talking about?

FREUD   The patients I've told you about. There are twelve of them who've never come back. One more suicide and it's all over! I'll be discredited in Vienna. I'll go and sell cloth.

He makes a gesture in the direction of Vienna.

Scandal and destitution: that's what awaits me down there.

(A pause.)

It's Breuer who keeps me alive. If I quarrel with him, I haven't the means to pay him back.

FLIESS, *polite, but irritated*   Yes, well, that's our lot: incomprehension and scandal. So what? We have to press on.

FREUD, *bitterly*   It's easy for you to talk. You treat sore throats, in Berlin. You won't lose your practice.

FLIESS, *wounded*   I'll take my own risks when the times comes: when I write *our* book.

Freud pulls himself together. He is still in pain. Once again he clasps his right hand to his chest, over his heart.

FREUD   Forgive me.

FLIESS, *amiably, though still annoyed*   Of course, dear friend, of course.

FREUD   I don't feel well.

Freud is huddled up on the bench. He is ashen.

FLIESS, *unsympathetically*   What's wrong with you?

FREUD   An attack.

FLIESS   What kind of attack?

FREUD, *mechanically, like a doctor*   Arrhythmia, feeling of suffocation, burning sensation in the region of the heart.

Pointing to his solar plexus:

And a sharp pain there, as in angina.

Fliess starts to rise. Freud checks him.

There's nothing to be done, Wilhelm.

He touches his forehead.

It's in there that there's something wrong. For the past few months, I've been suffer-ing from nervous depression.

Tell me: I'm not a monster, am I?

FLIESS, *patient and distant, as if to a madman*   Come on now, Sigmund, you know very well you're not.

FREUD   Well, whatever possessed me to discover universal vileness?

Almost pleading. He has drawn closer to Fliess and touches his arm, as if this contact ought to give him fresh heart.

Help me.

FLIESS, *coldly*   I ask nothing better, but you tell me there's nothing to be done.

Passengers are arriving on the platform. Fliess is visibly embarrassed to find himself with this man in the throes of a nervous attack. Especially since people are beginning to look at them.

FREUD   If you could . . .

He sees Fliess's priggish, embarrassed coldness and makes a sorrowful gesture. Recoiling and letting go of Fliess's arm:

FREUD   You're right: there's nothing to be done.

(Sound off of a train approaching.)

FLIESS   There's your train.

Freud rises painfully to his feet.
Fliess picks up Freud's suitcase and rucksack. They both move over towards the tracks — at the same time as the other passengers.

FREUD, *humbly*   Forgive me, Wilhelm. I . . . I'm going through a bad patch.
(Timidly:) I brought you something all the same, didn't I?

Fliess seems patently relieved by the train's arrival.

FLIESS   Yes, of course! Of course! If you can give me some dates, it'll be perfect.

The train pulls noisily into the station. It stops.
Freud, helped by Fliess, climbs into a second-class compartment. He shuts the carriage door behind him. Fliess waits for a moment.
Freud, from within, comes back to the window, lowers the glass and reappears. He looks at Fliess with a kind of passion — intense, but disappointed too.
He speaks: he still has a sombre air, but has recovered something of his habitual firmness.

FREUD   When's the next Congress?

Fliess leans his head back slightly to answer him.

FLIESS   Not for at least six months, I think.

FREUD   In six months, I'll have won or lost.
    (Becoming hard again:) Tomorrow, I'll visit Cäcilie. I'll press right on, in the direction we've agreed. I'll have all my colleagues and the whole town against me, but I swear to you I'll continue to the very end.
    If I lose … *(He laughs.)* Well, the next Congress won't take place.

The train begins to move.

    (Truly heartbroken:)

Goodbye, Wilhelm.

Fliess walks along the platform for a few moments, keeping abreast with Freud's compartment.

FLIESS   Goodbye, Sigmund! Give my greetings to Martha and kiss the children for me.

The train gathers speed. Fliess stops.

    (Shouting:) And don't forget to note down the dates.

The train disappears. Fliess returns to his place. He sits down. A young woman has sat down in the place which Freud occupied. She looks at Fliess, obviously finding him attractive. Fliess looks at her boldly and smiles at her.

11

In the train.

Freud leaves the corridor and goes back into his compartment. At the far end, three very ordinary-looking men are silently playing cards on the little table fastened between the two windows. They are the only occupants of the compartment. (It is a smoking compartment; they are smoking.)

Freud sits down in a corner seat next to the corridor. At first facing the rear of the train. But he is made dizzy by the stream of trees and houses: he stands up and installs himself in the opposite corner. He leans against the back of the seat, one hand on the elbow rest, and with his hat over his eyes attempts to sleep.

First tunnel, very short. When the train emerges from the tunnel, Freud stirs slightly, opens his eyes for a moment, then shuts them again.

The players, motionless at first, take advantage of the returning light: one of them throws down a card, gathers up the ones already on the table and takes the trick.

PLAYER   All mine, I think!

At that moment, the train plunges into a fresh tunnel. (The lamps are not turned on.)

ONE OF THE PLAYERS, *who was just about to play*   Damnation!

A moment of total darkness. When the train emerges from the gloom, Freud is fully awake. He removes his Tyrolean hat, takes his suitcase from the rack and extracts a top-hat which he places on his head.

VOICE OFF OF ONE OF THE PLAYERS   Perfect! Well, come and play.

He turns towards them: the three men smile at him engagingly.

We recognize Meynert (as we saw him in the first scene of the film, elegant and still young), Breuer (as he appears in Part One) and Fliess. All three are wearing top-hats.

Freud sits down beside Meynert and takes the cards which Breuer hands him.

MEYNERT, *disagreeably*   You don't know how to play, of course?
BREUER, *indulgently*   We'll teach him the game if he's obedient.

   (Introducing Freud to the others:)

My son.

Freud stands and raises his hat.

MEYNERT, *introducing Freud to the three others*   My son.

Freud stands and raises his hat.

FLIESS, *same pantomime*   My son!

Freud stands and raises his hat.

BREUER'S VOICE OFF   Well, the ice is broken.

They are all amused at Breuer's remark and repeat it, pointing accusing fingers at Freud.

ALL, *except Freud*   Broken! Broken! Broken!

Shot of Breuer, who (in place of the cards he had previously) is tranquilly holding an open book.

BREUER   Everyone has to cheat.

He tears out the pages as he speaks and flings them down on the table as if they were cards.

      (To Freud:) As for you, you pretend not to notice.
MEYNERT   You think he'll know what to do?
FLIESS, *as if he were speaking to a child*   Of course he'll know.
      (To Freud:) Listen, child, you have only to do as I do.
MEYNERT   No, Sir.
      As I do!
BREUER   I beg your pardon: as I do!

Fliess points at Freud.

FLIESS, *laughing*   He's an inquisitive child.
ALL, *laughing, except Freud*   An inquisitive child!
      He puts his fingers into everything!
      Being inquisitive is a nasty habit.

Up till now, Freud has been giving every sign of shame. He has been squirming about like a child.
All of a sudden he bangs on the table and shouts in a thunderous voice.

FREUD   A dead man's needed, for this game.

The three men look at him: they have stopped laughing, they look astonished and terrified.
Meynert leans towards him, affectionately and sadly:

MEYNERT   What, child, don't you know?

It's a game that's played with three dead men!
Three dead men and one living one. The dead men, that's us: you're an orphan.

Freud turns towards Fliess. His place is empty. He turns towards Meynert and Breuer: they have disappeared too.

VOICE OFF   Tickets please!

He turns round: it is Jakob Freud, his father. The latter points at the empty places.

JAKOB   They had no tickets: that's why they're dead.
FREUD, *small childlike voice*   I thought they were going to protect me.

Freud turns back towards the empty places.

JAKOB, *voice off*   What an idea, my darling! And how about keeping a check on yourself? My job is to check tickets, so I'll help you. I'll help you! I'll help you!
     Your ticket!

Freud turns towards the ticket-inspector, who no longer has Jakob's features but a little, thin face with a sparse moustache, and who is shaking him by the shoulder.

FREUD   Here.

He takes it out of his waistcoat pocket and hands it over. While the inspector is punching it, the three men (who have become the real cardplayers again) are holding out their tickets too.

TICKET-INSPECTOR, *his task completed*   Good night, gentlemen.

Darkness has fallen, the lamps are lit. Freud, fully awake now, leaning forward with his elbows on his knees and his head resting on his clenched fists, is engrossed in his own reflections.

FREUD'S VOICE OFF   A dream, that means nothing.
     It's a little neurosis.
     A compromise between the urge to sleep and ...
     And what?
     And what?
     And a deep longing that seeks to be satisfied.
     We at once give it a hallucinatory satisfaction. Just as we give a crying child a rattle.
     What was I wishing for?

We see in front of him, superimposed (because it is now a question of a simple memory, rather than the dream itself), the three 'fathers' (Meynert, Breuer and Fliess) playing cards.

A game for three dead men with one living one.

Accordingly, they can be seen in the depths of the seat opposite him, whereas the three real players continue to play, but to the left and at the far end.

To free myself from them? To move forward under my own steam?

They disappear. Jakob appears in their place, in the guise of a ticket-inspector. He smiles at his son.

I don't need teachers.

It's up to my *true father* to help me. The truth is, I don't want anyone above me. Except the man who made me.

The face of Jakob — who had become imbued with a very great majesty (which we have certainly never seen in him), and who looked like Moses — vanishes.

Freud is still sombre, but his eyes light up.

To interpret dreams ...

[12]

Next morning, the railway-station.

As the passengers are leaving. Freud, with alpenstock, rucksack and suitcase, jumps into a cab.

FREUD   66 Toringasse.

*Landing on a staircase (already described) at 66 Toringasse, outside the older Freuds' front door.
    Freud has just rung. It is Martha who opens the door to him. She looks at him in astonishment. He seems no less amazed.*

MARTHA   What have you come here for?
FREUD   It was last night: I was struck by remorse in the train. I don't see enough of Papa. How about you? Is anyone ill?
MARTHA   Papa's a bit tired.

Made angry by his guilty conscience:

FREUD   Why didn't you send me a cable?

Martha shrugs her shoulders.

MARTHA, *with great weariness*   Pooh!

A very brief pause.

It's not very serious, you know.

The door at the far end has opened. We see Freud's mother appear.

FREUD   Mama!

*She is still beautiful and retains her nobility, but she has aged greatly.
    She looks at Freud with surprise and joy. Freud bends over the hand she proffers him and gives it a long kiss.*

MOTHER   You've come! You've come!

With her left hand, his mother lightly caresses his hair. She steps aside and points to the open door.

Go on in.

He goes in; Martha follows him, after a kindly gesture from Freud's mother. The latter brings up the rear and goes in behind them.

You knew he was worse, then?

FREUD   No.

He turns back towards his mother, with somewhat artificial gaiety.

I'm going through a bad patch: my research is taking me ... Heaven knows where. In such circumstances, a son goes to see his father, doesn't he?

His mother hesitates. Freud looks at Jakob's armchair, which is empty, then looks at his mother, who turns her head away. He insists:

I need to see Papa. That will give me fresh heart.

His mother turns back towards him and looks him in the face. Without the least reproach in her voice:

MOTHER   It has been a long while since you came to see him.

Freud nods: we sense that he is filled with remorse.

FREUD   A very long while.

His mother puts her hands on his shoulders.

MOTHER   You're going to find him changed.

She smiles gently, to soften the shock she is about to inflict on him.

His illness has weakened him greatly.

FREUD, *in a strangled voice*   What's wrong with him?

MOTHER   Everything and nothing. It's age.

She steps aside and points at a door in the background.

Go in and see him now.

Freud is about to leave. In front of the far door, he hesitates. Eventually, he opens it very softly and goes in. The two women, in silence, exchange a look of consternation.
    In his father's bedroom. Between the two windows, a large bed. On the night-table, potions

and a thermometer.

Jakob Freud is sitting up in bed, propped against two pillows. He has retained his extreme gentleness. But he has grown visibly weaker; his mind wanders and — through exaggerated sensitivity — he has relapsed into a tearful mawkishness.

He looks at his son, standing before him in great embarrassment, with deep affection. He speaks in a quavering voice.

JAKOB   You've come! You've come!

His eyes fill with tears. Freud is more and more embarrassed. We sense that he is horrified to see his father weep. Once again, he has been refused the help he was coming to ask of him.

He would like, now, to be able to go away as quickly as possible. But he is caught in a trap. The loving, senile voice resumes, pitilessly.

Stay for a while with me.
     Take a chair.

Freud pulls a chair up to the bed and sits down beside the patient.

The Aulic Councillor himself!
FREUD   I'm not a councillor, Papa!
JAKOB   Oh yes.

Freud shakes his head.

You will be, Sigmund.
     You will be tomorrow.
     It's as if you were already.
     How nice of you to come and see me. An old, ruined tradesman like me. You, an Aulic Councillor, a person of such high position.
     (Laughing:) A bigwig! A bigwig!

He laughs indulgently and stretches out a pale, damp hand to him. Freud takes it in both of his own. He makes an effort at affection. But we can sense his panic. He gives a start when he hears old Jakob say, with senile satisfaction:

Hannibal!
     You were six years old, you wanted to avenge us, you used to say: 'I'm Hannibal . . .' Do you remember?

Flash-back. A street in Vienna.

Jakob is forty-five, his beard is jet black. He is wearing a strange cap. His clothes are clean but poor. He is holding by the hand a little boy of six or seven who trots along beside him, proud as Punch, and looks at him admiringly from time to time.

JAKOB'S VOICE OFF   When I had calls to make, I used to take you with me. Always. You were proud! A little prince!

A fat man, of Herculean build and wealthy appearance, is coming towards them. He is wearing a fur-collared coat and a Russian hat.

    Abruptly he sees them and bears down on them with a quite threatening air. The child notices nothing. When the fat man reaches Jakob and Sigmund, he stops.

FAT MAN   Not on the sidewalk, Jew!

With the back of his hand, he knocks his cap into the gutter.

Pick up your cap and stay in the roadway.

The little boy in a rage tries to hurl himself at the fat man, but Jakob holds him back; the child then tries to kick, but the stranger is already out of reach. He goes off without even turning round.

    Jakob stoops without letting go of the child and picks up his cap. Putting his cap back on his head:

JAKOB   Come!
LITTLE SIGMUND   Where?
JAKOB   Into the roadway.

They both walk along in the road. A carriage passes and spatters them with mud. The young Freud assumes a sombre, stubborn expression (the very one we have so often seen on Freud's face).

JAKOB'S VOICE OFF   You could be very awkward.

At the Freuds' home in 1862.

On the evening of that encounter. Fairly mean accommodation. Some little girls, thin and sickly, are amusing themselves with straw dolls in a corner.

    Large, gloomy room. No furniture. The mother is clearing the table. Jakob in his armchair is smoking his pipe, gentle and weary.

    Little Sigmund goes up to him and looks questioningly at him, with a mixture of amazement and despair.

JAKOB'S VOICE OFF   That evening, you had it in for me! Ach! how you did have it in for me!

In the old Jakob's bedroom. Freud is looking at him and, despite his beard and lined face, we find in his sombre visage the heartbroken amazement of the child.

FREUD   Father, I beg of you ...

(A pause.)

He has let go of his hand.
     The old man attempts to speak, Freud raises his hand to stop him.

Don't talk. You're tiring yourself.
JAKOB   Let me be, child! You don't remember the best part!

We see once more the child with his father. He moves away and goes towards a pile of books.

You went to get your prizes. You had all the prizes. Some lovely books.
     There was one which told the story of Roman history.

The child goes to the table, picks up one of the volumes, sits on the floor, opens it, tears out a page. It is an engraving.
     He comes back towards his father and hands it to him.

JAKOB, *astonished*   What do you want me to do with that, my little one?

He puts on his spectacles. He looks at the engraving.
     Reading the inscription beneath the engraving:

'Hamilcar makes his son Hannibal swear to avenge the Carthaginians.'

He props his spectacles up on his forehead. He looks at the child, who is wearing an impatient, obstinate expression.

Well?
CHILD   You're Hamilcar, Papa.

Jakob laughs gently.

JAKOB   Oh! no, I'm not Hamilcar.
CHILD, *warmly pleading*   Oh! yes, you are! You have to be.
JAKOB, *to humour the child*   All right, I am then.
CHILD   Make me swear.
JAKOB, *amused*   Very well, swear!
CHILD, *with savage fervour*   I swear to avenge my father, the hero Hamilcar, and all the humiliated Jews. I shall be the best of all, I shall beat everybody and I shall never retreat.

The harshness of his intonation, so rare in a child, makes Jakob jump.

He stops smiling, looks at the child, understands that he is struggling not to be ashamed of his father. His face becomes profoundly sad, as if he were able to divine, remorsefully, that his action would weigh on his son's entire life.

OLD JAKOB'S VOICE OFF   You've never been the same since.
(*A pause.*) Could I have got back onto the sidewalk?

Father and son look at one another in silence, after Sigmund has sworn the oath.

Then we find ourselves back in the bedroom. Old Jakob is looking at Freud with anguish. He is wearing exactly the same expression as in the 1862 scene, when he was looking at the child Sigmund.

JAKOB   It was the time of the pogroms. They were just waiting for a pretext to set fire to the whole neighbourhood.

He smiles weakly and stirs in his bed.

FREUD, *gently*   No. You couldn't. You had to be careful.
(*Still more gently:*) Calm yourself, Papa. Calm yourself. You couldn't.

The old man smiles. His eyelids flutter.

JAKOB, *laughing and waving a threatening finger at Freud as if he were a child*   My little Hannibal!

He closes his eyes. He is not asleep. His hand stretches out towards Freud. The latter recoils sharply and pulls his hands away.

(*In a childlike voice:*) Give me your hand.

Freud, by dint of a violent effort, forces himself to take Jakob's hand. The old man smiles without opening his eyes and gradually dozes off.

Gradually Freud's face recovers its fixed and almost vicious hardness (such as we have seen it wear at the beginning of this Part Three).

VOICE OFF OF THE ANTI-SEMITE, *faraway and almost whispering*   Dirty Jew, pick up your cap.
JAKOB'S VOICE OFF   I'm not Hamilcar.
LITTLE SIGMUND'S VOICE OFF   I shall avenge all Jews. I shall never retreat. I shall never go down into the roadway.

He looks at his sleeping father with bitter scorn, and takes advantage of the sick man's drowsiness to free his hand.

As he rises to his feet and turns on his heel, the voice off of the child he once was repeats:

Never!
  Never!
  Never!

He goes out, closing the door noiselessly. He is wearing a vicious, pitiless expression. His mother and Martha start towards him, but his gaze halts them.

MOTHER, *timidly*   How do you find him?

Freud smiles without answering, kisses his mother on the forehead and says to Martha in a neutral voice:

FREUD   Can you take care of my suitcase and rucksack? I'm going to visit a patient.

He gives her a thin smile and goes out before they can make a move. Once the door is closed:

MOTHER, *shrugging her shoulders*   And there you are!

  (A pause.)

I wonder if he loves his father.
MARTHA, *bitterly*   Apart from you, Mama, I wonder if he loves anybody.

13

A little later that morning.

A street in the suburbs of Vienna. To the left, small three-storey houses (lower middle class), some waste ground and, very far away in the background, some factory chimneys.

To the right, a six-storey apartment-building, fairly old, inhabited from the second floor up. (On the mezzanine, broken panes, windows open onto empty premises.)

After this building, a gate protects a fairly large garden which seems abandoned. (The grass is invading the paths, the bushes have not been trimmed for a long time or the trees pruned.) At the far end of the garden, a two-storey lodge, comfortable, clearly better built than the other little houses: perhaps an old hunting-lodge.

This is Prinz Eugen Gasse. Freud starts along the street. He has kept on his Tyrolean hat. He walks along the right-hand pavement, striving to recognize the lodge Breuer has told him about. As soon as he has passed the apartment-building and finds himself in front of the gate, no further doubt is possible: this must be where the Körtner ladies live.

He goes up to the entrance and, before ringing, takes off his hat, removes the Tyrolean feather and stuffs it into his pocket, then replaces the hat on his head.

He rings. Long silence.

Then an old woman appears on the threshold of the lodge and shouts to him from a distance, in an unfriendly manner.

OLD WOMAN, *shouting*   What do you want?
FREUD, *shouting*   Frau Körtner.
OLD WOMAN, *same style*   Not there.
FREUD, *same style*   Fräulein Körtner, then.
OLD WOMAN   She doesn't see anyone.
FREUD   Ask her.

The old woman shuts the door of the lodge. Freud remains motionless in front of the gate, stooping slightly, but obstinate.

After a moment, he presses the bellpush once more. The door of the lodge does not open. Freud twists the latch of the gate — which does not open. It is locked.

He remains outside the gate; he waits without moving — like a beggar who relies on his persistence to convince people to open their wallets.

A tall woman dressed in black glides past the apartment-building in the bright sunlight, with a short shadow at her feet (it is about ten in the morning). She comes noiselessly up to Freud and places a hand on his shoulder. It is Frau Körtner.

FRAU KÖRTNER   What do you want, Sir?

Freud starts and turns round. She looks hard at him, vaguely surprised.

I recognize you.

(A pause.)

You're the doctor ...

Freud takes his hat off.

FREUD   Sigmund Freud.

He transfers his hat to his right hand.
    He takes out his wallet and extracts his visiting-card, which he presents to Frau Körtner.

FRAU KÖRTNER, *reading the card*   I see.
    (In a harder voice:) What have you come here for?
FREUD   Is your daughter cured?
FRAU KÖRTNER, *in an expressionless voice*   No.
FREUD, *very simply*   I should like to treat her.
FRAU KÖRTNER, *almost insulting*   Useless.

Frau Körtner looks him full in the face. She has aged and hardened, since we last saw her. The corner of her mouth has an ill-tempered, scornful crease. Her black clothes are well cut, but the material is cheap.

It was doctors who made my daughter ill.
FREUD   Frau Körtner! You know very well that's not true. Dr Breuer ...
FRAU KÖRTNER   My daughter is an insufferable child, and Dr Breuer made the unpardonable mistake of taking her seriously. She thinks herself a martyr, Doctor, and her misfortune is that her father spoiled her too much.

She rummages in her bag, pushes Freud rudely aside, takes out a bunch of keys, inserts a key into the lock and turns it.

Goodbye, Doctor.

She goes into the garden, Freud follows her. When she turns round to shut the gate, he is already inside.
    She glares at him out of her fine, hard eyes, but without managing to intimidate him: the man standing before her is even harder — and more determined — than she is.
    She grows annoyed and the incisive sharpness of her voice gives way to violence.

FRAU KÖRTNER   Get out!
FREUD, *without raising his voice*   You don't love your daughter, Madam.

Anger transforms Frau Körtner's face; she suddenly has the vulgarity of a fishwife.

FRAU KÖRTNER, *vulgar and violent*   Bastard!

She raises a hand to Freud and tries to strike him. he catches her wrist in mid air and restrains her for an instant. That instant is enough for her to recover her poise and her outward appearance of a distinguished bourgeois lady.

   (Very cold and imperious:)

Let me go!

Freud lets her go with the faintest of bows, as if in apology.

You take me for a bad mother, don't you?
FREUD   No.
FRAU KÖRTNER   It shows in your eyes.

   (A pause. Defiantly:)

Look at me. In four years, I've aged twenty. I can't stand up straight. I sleep four hours a night. Do you know why? Because I've made myself the devoted nurse of a daughter who loathes me and would like to see me dead.
FREUD   So what? You look after her, but you don't want to cure her. You've thrown the doctors out and you foster her illness, because it allows you to dominate her.

The mother looks at him, furious but uncertain. Freud is improvising: it is an attempt at bluff. He presses ahead because Frau Körtner seems cut to the quick.

FRAU KÖRTNER, *cold and lucid*   I haven't thrown the doctors out.

   (Bitter laugh.)

They don't come any more because we're ruined. Do you understand? They stopped calling as soon as they realized we hadn't a penny left to pay them with.

In an ironical challenge, sure of the response:

Dr Freud, do you agree to treat Cäcilie free of charge?
FREUD   Yes, Madam.

Seriously and with force:

I'll undertake it.

(A silence.)

Well?

Frau Körtner looks at him, disconcerted.

Cäcilie has a chance of being cured. Are you going to deny her that chance?

FRAU KÖRTNER   I know men, doctors or no: they don't do anything for nothing. Don't you imagine I take you for a philanthropist.
     What's your interest?

Frau Körtner speaks to him in a tone that is too lucid and too knowledgeable simply to be that of a 'woman of the world'. We can sense, behind her self-assurance, a profound experience — which society, at that time, generally denied to women of her condition.
     Freud looks at her sternly, but not without a certain sympathy. We realize that he finds this kind of woman attractive.

FREUD, *simply*   I've got an idea about neurosis and I want to verify it.

FRAU KÖRTNER   And you're looking for non-paying patients to turn inside out? My daughter will be your guinea-pig?

FREUD   I shan't turn anyone inside out, Madam. And your daughter isn't a guinea-pig: I consider her the most intelligent patient I've known.

Frau Körtner hesitates in silence. After a moment, she goes to the front gate, closes it again and turns the key in the lock, then puts the key back into her bag.

FRAU KÖRTNER   Follow me.

They cross the garden. As they climb the three steps up to the lodge, she turns towards him.

It's for a trial period. If I see that you're doing her harm, I'll interrupt the treatment.

He nods in silence.
     They enter a poorly furnished room, made dark by the trees in the garden. The old maid-servant is sitting at a table, darning.
     We recognize a few pieces of furniture from their old residence, that by some miracle have escaped the family's financial disaster.
     The maid lifts her cold, grey eyes to Freud; she looks at him indifferently, then goes on working.
     Frau Körtner has stopped in the middle of the room, leaving Freud to close the door himself. When he turns back towards her, she asks:

Shall I be present at your sessions?

FREUD, *polite but firm*   No, Madam.

FRAU KÖRTNER   Very good.

Frau Körtner points to a door at the far end.

Well, it's there. Go in.

As he crosses the room, she gives a little harsh laugh, full of resentment.

The worst part's still to come. She has still got to accept you.

Freud knocks on the door.

CÄCILIE'S VOICE OFF   Come in!

14

Cäcilie's bedroom.

Narrow, poorly furnished room. In one corner, a water-jug and a washbowl on a table. Two chairs, a rocking-chair.

Cäcilie's bed is to the right of the door and against the wall; the foot of the bed is near the door, the head away from it.

Two windows: one to the left as you enter, the other at the far end. Cheap prints attempt — with varying success — to disguise the stained and mouldy condition of the wallpaper. A bedside table heaped with books.

When Freud comes in, Cäcilie, lying with her head propped up on two pillows, is reading. She lowers the book she was holding in front of her eyes and looks at the new arrival. Her eyes are perfectly normal. A long silence, then:

CÄCILIE   I recognize you.

Freud has closed the door and stands facing her.

Haven't I been punished enough, then?
FREUD, *gently*   I haven't come to punish you, Cäcilie.

Cäcilie shrugs her shoulders.

CÄCILIE   I must be punished, because I'm guilty.

She gives a mysterious smile of secret complicity. She is still looking at him; slowly:

You're Dr Freud. Your friend was called Fliess.

With a vague and distant air:

And that other one, who was so cowardly, what was he called?

Cäcilie no longer has the air of innocence that captivated Breuer. She remains a young girl, but with a knowledgeable, contemptuous look which is that of a woman. A bitter crease at the corners of her mouth — which will remain in the following scenes up until her cure.

FREUD, *imperceptible complicity*   The cowardly one? Breuer.
CÄCILIE   Breuer. That's it. His wife's name was Mathilde. Apparently he gave her a baby?
FREUD   A daughter.

CÄCILIE, *smile of contempt*   In Venice, of course. The child of the lagoon.

Almost proudly:

As for me, I've got both legs paralysed.

Freud starts to move over to her.

Useless.

She tears off her blanket. Her nightdress is raised to her knees: her legs present the same features already noted in the hysterical patient of Part One, and in Jeanne (Charcot's subject).

CÄCILIE, *with an ironical smile*   Hysterical contractures. Anaesthesia on both sides.
    I know all about it, as you may imagine: considering how long it has been going on.

Freud draws near, this time without her making any move to stop him. He raises the covers and tucks her in.

So very kind.
    Exactly like Mathilde's husband. What's his name, again?
FREUD   Breuer.
CÄCILIE   That's it. What's the name of your wife?
FREUD   Martha.
CÄCILIE   God bless her.

With sudden and terrible violence, but without raising her voice:

Go away!
    Go away!
    Tell his wife that I'm atoning for my sins and that I'll never have children.

Unmoved, Freud goes to fetch one of the chairs, carries it to Cäcilie's bedside and sits down.

FREUD   Cäcilie, I want to cure you.

Throughout the scene he will be gentle and persuasive, but there is a disturbing sparkle in his hard, intent eyes: we sense that he has no particular feelings for Cäcilie, and that he is ready to do anything in order to test out the truth of his theories on her.

CÄCILIE, *bursts out laughing*   Yet again!
    And then you'll run off as fast as your legs can carry you, once you've made me really ill?

I'm perfectly all right like this. If you gave me back the use of my legs, I'd go and walk the streets of the town and ...

FREUD   And?

CÄCILIE   Nothing. Just nonsense.

She picks up her book again and pretends to resume her reading.

Freud does not move. From time to time, she casts him sly glances over her book. Laying down the book, all of a sudden:

(Calm, smiling inquiry.)

Are you quite sure that I'm suffering from hysteria?

FREUD   I've no idea. Let me treat you: then I'll see.

CÄCILIE   Because, you see, I have fits of anxiety. According to the books, hysterical patients don't suffer from anxiety.

FREUD   You read stupid books. Hysterical patients can be anxious, just as normal people can.

He picks up the book which she has dropped onto her blanket.

Charcot! I was the person who translated him.

CÄCILIE   I know.

FREUD, *in the partly scornful, partly nostalgic tone of voice people use in speaking of a very old love affair:*   Pooh! that's old stuff!

Freud turns the book round and round in his hands, quite disconcerted.

CÄCILIE, *pursuing her idea*   Because, you see, I don't want you to touch my legs. But so far as my anxieties are concerned, I'd like you to get rid of those.

(Smiling to herself.)

If you can.

FREUD   Let's try.

He draws his chair very slightly nearer. She recoils in quite genuine alarm.

CÄCILIE, *shouting out suddenly*   Leave me in peace! Leave me in peace! Help, Help! Mama, Mama!

The door opens abruptly. Her mother appears.

FRAU KÖRTNER, *coldly*   What's the matter?

Freud turns towards her for a moment.

Do you want him to go away?

CÄCILIE   No. But I don't want him to hypnotize me.
Enough! Enough nonsense! Enough!

Freud turns back to Cäcilie

FREUD   I won't hypnotize you, I promise you in front of your mother.

CÄCILIE, *to her mother, in a tone of voice whose mildness conceals an intense malevolence:*
Good. Then, my dear Mama, you can go away.

Her mother closes the door again. Cäcilie, to Freud, incredulously:

You won't hypnotize me? That's all you know how to do.

FREUD   Yes, up till now I've done nothing else. But something has happened which has made me give it up.

CÄCILIE, *quite naturally*   You've killed someone?

FREUD, *calmly*   Almost.

CÄCILIE   It was bound to end up like that.

FREUD   When people are awake, they defend themselves with all their might against the memories they want to forget.

CÄCILIE, *ironically*   And when they're put to sleep by hypnotic suggestion, they remember anything you like.

FREUD   Exactly so. Then we tell them what they've said under hypnosis. But once they've woken up, they've rediscovered morality, taboos, prohibitions, all the mechanisms of repression. The repressed memory fills them with horror when they recall it: they'd constructed themselves with the precise aim of repressing it. The confrontation is too brutal. We must proceed gently, talk to patients when they're wide awake, attack and break down their defences gradually.

CÄCILIE, *laughing*   How about Mathilde's lover? What's left of his method? He was so proud of it!

FREUD   Breuer? In all essentials, his method remains unaltered. There'll simply be no more hypnotizing.

CÄCILIE   What shall we be doing?

FREUD   Well, you'll talk about whatever you like. You'll say everything that comes into your mind, however preposterous it may seem. Nothing's accidental: if you think about a horse rather than a hat, there's some deep reason for it. We'll search for that reason together; and the nearer you get to it, the weaker your resistance will become and the less painful it will be for you to discover it.

CÄCILIE, *amused*   It's like a parlour game.

FREUD   Yes. The truth game. Begin.

CÄCILIE   What with?

FREUD   I've told you, whatever you like.

Cäcilie, with a certain coquetry — very aware of her charm:

CÄCILIE   Just this first time, you could help me.
FREUD   Very well. Do you ever dream?
CÄCILIE   Every night.
FREUD   Last night?

Nod from Cäcilie.

Well then, tell me what you dreamed.

Cäcilie is obviously enjoying herself. What counts, at the moment, for this lonely woman is the presence of a man and the game she is playing with him.

CÄCILIE, *vivaciously*   That's easy; last night's dream was one I have three or four times a week. With variations, of course. I'm sure it's a punishment.
      I was ...

She tilts her head to one side and feigns shame. In reality, it is coquetry.

You're going to think I have very odd ideas.
      I was a prostitute. One of the kind who walk the streets.

15

As she describes her dream, we see it as she describes it. We see a street at night: a gas-lamp illuminates it dimly. In the distance a woman who is Cäcilie, but whom we can barely make out, paces to and fro on the pavement. From a distance, she seems to be dressed like a classic prostitute.

FREUD, *voice off*   Have you ever actually seen women walking the streets?
CÄCILIE, *voice off*   Of course.
FREUD, *voice off*   Were you dressed like them?
CÄCILIE, *voice off*   No.

Abruptly we see Cäcilie emerge from the shadows; she is wearing a wedding-dress, pure white, white veil, orange blossom. But her face is horribly painted, aged by a hard, exaggerated make-up, almost hideous.

I had a wedding-dress on.

The wedding-dress, moreover, has an enormous tear in front, and through the rent her leg can be seen to above the knee.

It's funny. It had a tear. That made me ashamed.

She paces to and fro on the pavement, in front of the street-lamp.

FREUD, *voice off*   Think a bit, Cäcilie. When did you see a torn wedding-dress?

Cäcilie stops under the street-lamp and seems to be thinking.

CÄCILIE, *voice off*   Never.
FREUD, *voice off*   Or other dresses?
CÄCILIE, *voice off*   Oh! yes. My mother's black dress. It got torn yesterday, and Mama sat beside me mending it while I was reading.

The prostitute Cäcilie, as if satisfied by this reply, starts pacing up and down again.
She passes in front of a carriage-entrance. In a dark corner, we suddenly perceive an alarming shadow: a motionless man waiting.

CÄCILIE'S VOICE OFF   I had a funny name. Potiphar. You know, like that queen in the Bible.

The shadow is clearer now. It is a very well-dressed Gentleman, whom we see from behind. He is wearing a top-hat.

GENTLEMAN, *whispering*   Potiphar! Potiphar!

Cäcilie, who had passed him by, comes back towards him. When she is level with him, she takes a gold ring from her bag and offers it him.

CÄCILIE'S VOICE OFF   I had a client.

The Gentleman, still with his back to us, stretches out his forefinger and we see Cäcilie slip her gold ring onto his finger.

FREUD, *voice off*   What was he like?
CÄCILIE'S VOICE OFF   I didn't see his head.
     I gave him a gold ring. It was too big for his finger.

The Gentleman's hand is lowered towards the ground and the ring falls off. The Gentleman runs away as fast as his legs will carry him, and in his alarm pushes Cäcilie so roughly that she falls over.

He ran away and knocked me over.

At the moment when she falls, we hear a burst of laughter. On the first floor of the building in front of which she has fallen, a window is open and a woman is laughing. She is wearing classic prostitute's garb.

A woman laughed. She said:
THE WOMAN, *speaking while we see her, very vulgarly*   ... weren't worth killin' me.
CÄCILIE'S VOICE OFF   I didn't care about anything she said. But I'd hurt myself badly, falling on the perron.

We leave the woman in the window and return to Cäcilie. The scenery has changed while we were looking at the woman.
     Cäcilie has in fact fallen on the perron of her old villa. The carriage-entrance has disappeared. What is left is three steps leading to an open French window.
     Cäcilie is still in the wedding-dress, kneeling on one of the steps. French window, windows, steps are brightly lit: it is broad daylight.
     We can glimpse the interior that we know.
     Cäcilie is crying like a very young child, screwing up her face and sobbing violently.
     She has tears running down her cheeks.

FREUD, *voice off*   Which perron?
CÄCILIE'S VOICE OFF   The perron of our old villa.
FREUD   What then?
CÄCILIE'S VOICE OFF   That's all. I woke up.

The dream dissolves. We are back in the bedroom. Freud is still bending forward. Cäcilie is enjoying herself.

CÄCILIE   It's great fun telling someone your dreams. But it's idiotic. It doesn't mean anything.

FREUD, *with conviction*   It means *a great deal!*

Cäcilie appears incredulous.

CÄCILIE   All right, why for example was I called Potiphar?

FREUD   Potiphar was the name of Pharaoh's wife. She was in love with Joseph.

(A pause.)

Josef was Dr Breuer's first name.

Cäcilie stops smiling and looks hard and with mistrust at him.

In your dream, the client ran away like a Joseph.

Thin smile from Cäcilie. Freud returns her smile. Neither of them looks well-disposed.
   Freud, smiling, with intent:

FREUD   It was a nightmare, in fact?

Cäcilie, relaxed by this complicity:

CÄCILIE, *smiling*   The story of Potiphar, of course, is all to Joseph's credit — but it's a nightmare for Potiphar.

(A pause.)

FREUD   Do you have this dream very ofen?

CÄCILIE   Very often; but so far as Potiphar's concerned, it's the first time.

FREUD   Prostitution: does that recur often?

CÄCILIE   Yes. And the woman at the window and the fall on the perron.

FREUD   When did you dream about that for the first time? Long after your father's death?

CÄCILIE   Long *before.*

Freud appears dumbfounded.

FREUD, *with an astonishment that causes him to raise his voice:*   *Before?*
   Before you found him ...

Cäcilie is hard and vulgar: she is playing a role but we do not know what it is.

CÄCILIE, *very hard*   In a brothel?
    Long before!
    Years before!
FREUD   Why?
CÄCILIE   I loved my father very much. But I had a big grudge against him, because he was unfaithful to my poor mother.
FREUD   With prostitutes?
CÄCILIE   Of course. All men like prostitutes, don't they? Luckily!

In a simpering voice that is not her own:

Decent women wouldn't dare set a foot outside their homes, if girls like that didn't exist.

With an air of deep sincerity:

I adore my mother, Doctor. She'll tell you the opposite, because we both have bad characters. But it's false. I know all the trouble she puts herself to. And I love her more and more. Even today, I can't forgive my father for the hellish life he made her lead.

Cäcilie speaks almost with hatred.

He deceived her even under her own roof. The woman who was looking at me from the window, in my dream: I know who she is. A former governess — Papa's mistress. Mama threw her out, and a good thing too.

She doubles up with laughter.

He was one who certainly didn't deserve his first name!
FREUD   Who?
CÄCILIE   Papa. He was called Josef too.
FREUD   Oh! *(A silence.)* He pushed you when you were little. And you fell over?

Cäcilie looks at him in astonished mistrust.
    Freud is pursuing his idea and returning to his main line of inquiry.

CÄCILIE   How do you know?
FREUD   It's in your dream.
CÄCILIE   Oh! That's just a bad memory; as you can imagine, I didn't hold a grudge against him for that.

The little Cäcilie runs into the former villa.

I must have been six. I was running. It must have been my fault.

She bumps into her father, a powerful, majestic man, who is leaving the villa through the French window at the same moment. She falls over.

FREUD   And then? What happened.?

The image dissolves.
    Cäcilie's room.

CÄCILIE, *who is giving signs of weariness*   Nothing more. Absolutely nothing.
FREUD   Yet you still remember that fall, twenty years later. And you've forgotten so
    many things! Even my friend Breuer's name.
        Why do you remember it?
CÄCILIE   I've no idea. Does anybody ever know why they recall one event rather
    than another?
        I won't tell you anything more, I'm too tired.
        Your method's exhausting. Much more than hypnotism. I feel there's nothing
    more to be got out of me today.

    (With a certain complacency:)

You've squeezed me like a lemon.

Very nicely:

Come back tomorrow.

Freud rises to his feet, amiable but cool. He is totally preocupied by his investigation.

FREUD   I'll come back. Try to think about that business of the fall on the perron.
    Any details you can give me will be useful.

Cäcilie looks at him attentively. She smiles, but without any liking.

CÄCILIE, *half-joking, half-serious*   I don't like your eyes.

Freud looks at her inquiringly.

They're a murderer's eyes.
    You're planning some dreadful trick.

He jokes too, but his eyes remain hard.

FREUD, *same tone of voice as Cäcilie*   Or perhaps a fine trick, a very fine one, that will net me all the monsters in the depths of the sea. Did you know there are some that live under such pressures they explode when they're brought to the surface?

He bows. She smiles at him. We discover between them an odd complicity, but one that is very different from that which united Cäcilie and Breuer.

This time, one would say they were trying to deceive each other. She watches him go out with an ironical smile, as if she were vaguely aware that she had fooled him.

[16]

Next day, after lunch in the Freud household.

Martha bustles to and fro. She is hard at work, the maid is helping her.

Freud is sitting in an armchair; the two boys are crawling on the floor; Mathilde, already a little lady, stands upright beside her father. Martha, very busy, passes close to Freud. He catches her by the arm:

FREUD, *smiling affectionately*   Martha, sit down. Come and keep me company.

MARTHA   Impossible.

FREUD   Why?

MARTHA   I'm tidying.

FREUD, *playfully threatening*   Take care, Martha! Remember the story of Martha and Mary. It was Mary who had the best of the bargain.

MARTHA, *rather sad smile; faintly ironical, but without any disagreeable intention*   I doubt whether your teaching bears much resemblance to that of Jesus Christ.

She disappears, leaving Freud alone with the children. Mathilde takes advantage of this to draw a little closer to Freud.

MATHILDE   Is it true we'll be getting it?

Freud speaks to her with very great gentleness. His face has lit up, and he looks joyful.

FREUD   What, my darling?

MATHILDE   I don't know its name, that machine.

FREUD   Oh! the telephone? Yes, indeed, Mathilde: they're installing it in the next few days.

MATHILDE   I talk in this house and you're in another house and you can still hear me.

FREUD   Yes.

MATHILDE   And if I kiss you, you'll notice that in the other house?

FREUD   No.

Mathilde, jumping up on Freud's knees and kissing him impetuously.

MATHILDE   Then I'd rather you were here.

Freud allows himself to be kissed, and even returns her kisses. But then, all of a sudden, his face becomes hard and almost vicious.

He frees himself and sets Mathilde back on her feet, without violence, but forcefully. Mathilde looks at him, flabbergasted. Freud stares into space.

Mathilde, frightened by this hard, expressionless countenance that she has never seen on her father before, bursts out sobbing.

Martha, who was just coming in, has seen the entire scene.

MARTHA, *in distress*   Mathilde!

The child glances furiously at her, then runs from the room. Martha goes over to Freud, who has not moved. She studies him sorrowfully, in silence.

Freud eventually raises his head. He looks at Martha with an expression of deep sadness. After a moment he rises to his feet.

FREUD   I have to go and visit a patient. I'll see you later.

He kisses her mechanically on the forehead and goes out. She stares for a long time at the door through which he has left.

In Cäcilie's room.

Half an hour later. Frau Körtner is sitting sewing at Cäcilie's bedside, still dressed in black with a chemisette up to her chin. Cäcilie lies unmoving in her bed, propped up on pillows like the day before. Her staring eyes seem dilated by anguish. From time to time her hands clasp the blanket lightly.

The two women do not exchange a word, but, from time to time, Frau Körtner glances at Cäcilie.

These brief glances are cold and objective. No affection. When she lowers her head to her work, Cäcilie gives her a quick, sly look out of the corner of the eye.

Between the two women we can sense an extreme, if silent, tension. We divine that this is a daily scene. Every day, Frau Körtner comes to 'mind' her daughter in silence.

There is a knock at the door.

Without waiting for an answer, the old maidservant opens the door.

She stands to one side to let Freud pass. Then she shuts the door again.

OLD WOMAN Dr Freud.

Freud bows silently to Frau Körtner. She gives a slight nod, without a word. She rises to her feet, tidies her things unhurriedly and goes off.

Before she has crossed the threshold, Freud has turned towards Cäcilie and smiled at her. She blinks to show that she has noticed his presence, but not a word is exchanged. Frau Körtner closes the door.

Cäcilie's face changes at once. She remains pale and anxious, but she masters her anxiety. She manages to smile and holds out a hand to Freud, in a cordial but weary gesture.

Freud shakes her hand and sits down in Frau Körtner's place.

His eyes are so hard and intent that they look like glass. He does smile, but his smile looks false.

CÄCILIE You have a wolfish smile.

FREUD Wolves don't smile.

CÄCILIE Hasn't anybody ever told you the story of Little Red Riding-Hood? There was a wolf, and he smiled. But Little Red Riding-Hood was in your place and the wolf in mine.

FREUD, *very curtly, to cut her short* I won't eat you.

(A pause.)

What's the matter with you? Anxiety?

She nods

You had nightmares?

CÄCILIE   No. Not nightmares.

I didn't sleep.

Hallucinations. Always the same: a bleeding head.

FREUD   Whose head?

CÄCILIE, *vaguely*   A head ...

Cäcilie shrugs her shoulders without replying.
After a moment:

CÄCILIE   It was somebody I'd killed.

Freud stares intently at her without replying.

Doctor, I must have done something very bad.

He does not reply. She insists:

I feel so guilty.

Perhaps you know what I've done?

Freud's expression grows harsher and harsher: he has decided to strike a great blow, this very day.
This is evident: we sense in his movements and voice a kind of unaccustomed precipitancy. Seizing
the opportunity:

FREUD   No. But we're going to find out this very day.

CÄCILIE, *in alarm*   Who, *we*?

FREUD   You and I.

CÄCILIE   If it's serious, you won't say anything to Mama.

FREUD   No.

A pause. He is preparing his attack, then suddenly:

So you fell over on the perron at the villa.

How old were you?

CÄCILIE   Eight.

FREUD   Of course, you don't remember the exact date?

CÄCILIE   Well, yes I do, as a matter of fact, because it was my governess's birthday: 6
June 1878.

Freud has taken a notebook out of his pocket. He notes down the date carefully and puts the note-
book away in his jacket pocket.

FREUD   You can still remember the date of her birthday. So you liked her a lot?

CÄCILIE   Yes, a lot.

FREUD   And your father deceived your mother with her?

Cäcilie gives a thin smile.

CÄCILIE   Well, yes! But that wasn't my business.

FREUD   You said your mother was quite right to throw her out.

CÄCILIE   She was quite right! She was absolutely right. From her point of view, of course.

FREUD   So? Your father bumped into you and you fell over?

In front of the villa, a little girl is climbing the steps of the perron. A man (Herr Körtner) rushes out and knocks her over.

CÄCILIE, *voice off*   Oh! no.

FREUD, *voice off*   You told me so yesterday.

CÄCILIE, *voice off, touch of cynicism*   Then I must have been lying.

Herr Körtner and the little Cäcilie have disappeared.
The three steps and the sitting-room visible through the French window are deserted.

Didn't anyone tell you I was a terrible liar?
I was running, I fell down; that's all.

A little girl arrives running; it is Cäcilie.
She is wearing ringlets and a crinoline. She trips over one of the steps of the perron and falls over. Herr Körtner appears at the sitting-room door.
He rushes forward and picks the child up in his arms. As soon as she sees him, she stops crying.

My father carried me to the couch.

The father carries his daughter in his arms. He climbs the steps and is about the enter the sitting-room when Freud's sharp voice stops him in his tracks, with one foot in the air.

FREUD'S VOICE OFF, *sharp and menacing*   Is that all?

CÄCILIE, *voice off*   That's all.

FREUD, *voice off*   You're a liar, Cäcilie.

The image disappears. We rediscover Freud sitting on his chair and bending forward, looking severely at Cäcilie.
Cäcilie, mesmerized, begins to protest. But Freud does not give her time.

A liar: you admitted it yourself.
When you were on the couch, what happened to you?

CÄCILIE   He wanted to look at my knee.

Cäcilie looks at him with strange eyes; she seems at once terrified and tempted by the story Freud tells.

FREUD   In those days little girls used to wear very long knickers under their skirts. Your father must have ...

     (A pause.)

CÄCILIE   He pulled up the first leg of the knickers ... gently ... gently ...

The sitting-room of the Körtners' villa. A couch. Herr Körtner has his back to us, he is bending over the couch. He is pulling up the left leg of a baggy pair of cotton knickers that reach down to the ankles — thus unveiling first a white sock, then a bare calf, then the knee, then the beginning of a thigh.
     This slow and almost voluptuous gesture seems lascivious to us for one reason only: it is because the leg thus laid bare is not that of a little girl of eight, but the very beautiful leg of a young woman.
     We then see that the person stretched out on the couch is not a child: it is Cäcilie at the age of twenty-five — the same who is talking to Freud — but dressed in the style of 1878 (crinoline, ringlets, long knickers). We can now see her terrified face.
     The man bending over her frightens her dreadfully.

FREUD'S VOICE OFF   He was rubbing your leg.
     You're afraid of my eyes. How about his? Weren't you afraid of them?

Cäcilie, lying on the couch, looks in fascination at the eyes (invisible to us) of Herr Körtner, of whom we can see only the shoulders and the powerful neck.

Remember, Cäcilie! Remember your terror. That's what made the date impossible to forget.

All of a sudden Herr Körtner bends down brutally over Cäcilie's face, which he masks: we can now see nothing but his head and broad shoulders. But it is obvious that he is kissing her on the lips.
     The vision, in any case, lasts only for a split second. At once Cäcilie's voice off rings out.

     (Great scream off from Cäcilie, terror — and in the terror itself a certain consent.)

     The vision disappears: we find ourselves back in the bedroom. Cäcilie is lying back on her pillows, terrified; Freud is bending over her.
     (In a certain way, these positions reproduce those of Herr Körtner and Cäcilie in the story just recounted.)
     All of a sudden, Cäcilie's face changes: it no longer expresses terror, but a kind of angry shame.

CÄCILIE   It's not true! It's not true!

Freud straightens up slightly. He presses both hands to Cäcilie's forehead.
She blinks, then closes her eyes.

FREUD   Close your eyes.

(In an authoritarian and persuasive voice.)

You know very well that it's true. You know it.
    I realized it straight away, even yesterday, when you said your father knocked you over.
    You invented that false memory to mask the other one.
    Say that it's the truth.

Cäcilie opens her eyes. Her face has changed. Her eyes are now sly and wicked, her smile disturbing and almost smug.

CÄCILIE, *in a too consenting, almost ironical tone of voice*   It's the truth.

[18]

A post-office.

Telegram counter. Freud, head bowed, is listening to a clerk reading back the wording of his telegram to him.

CLERK   Wilhelm Fleiss.
FREUD   Fliess: F.L.I.E.S.S.

The clerk puts on his spectacles and reads slowly, without giving any meaning to the words he reads back:

CLERK   Wilhelm Fliess 16 Marienstrasse Berlin. Cäcilie traced spectacular confirmation born 16 March 1870 ass ... ass ...
FREUD   Assault.
CLERK   Assault 6 June 1878. Fourteen cases. Decide give paper Medical Society on six ... sex ...
FREUD   Sexual.
CLERK   Sexual origin neuroses. Greetings. Sigismund.

19

Freud's consulting-room.

Two workers are finishing installing the telephone. One of them is fixing the wiring, behind the desk.

The other has taken off the receiver and is calling the operator. The instrument is placed on Freud's desk. Freud watches the installation with enjoyment. He is wearing a hard, nasty expression, yet looks happy and, for the first time, sure of himself.

His three children appear to be greatly enjoying themselves. Mathilde in particular is at the peak of over-excitement. She has slipped close up to the desk, right next to the instrument, and is watching the technician telephoning.

TECHNICIAN   Hullo. Exchange? This is 16–82. All right.

He hangs up.
   To Freud:

They'll ring back to check the line.

Mathilde has assumed an imploring expression:

MATHILDE, *to Freud*   I'll talk to them. Please, Papa! I'll talk to them.

Freud smiles. The technician says amiably:

TECHNICIAN   Of course, my little lady, you'll only have to say: this is 16–82.

A telephone-bell rings.
   Mathilde rushes over and picks up the receiver.
   She is too little to talk into the instrument; the technician takes the receiver gently from her.

MATHILDE, *trying to reach the instrument by standing on tip-toes*   This is 82–16.
TECHNICIAN, *paternally*   You have to wait for them to speak.
   There.
   And it's 16–82.

He hands Mathilde the receiver and lifts her up to the telephone.
   Freud's face darkens but he says nothing.

MATHILDE   Yes. This is 16–82.

The technician puts her back on the ground.

> *(Proudly, to Freud:)*

D'you see? I talked.
FREUD, *smiling*   I heard.
TECHNICIAN, *to Freud*   Everything's in order, Sir.
FREUD   That's fine.

He shakes his hand.

TECHNICIAN   Goodbye, Sir.

He goes out. His colleague has rejoined him and goes out too, nodding farewell.

MATHILDE, *ecstatically, to her two little brothers*   It talks into your ear!

> *(There is a knock at the door.)*

FREUD   Come in.

Breuer opens the door. He wears a friendly but embarrassed expression.

BREUER   I'm sorry I came in without ringing. Two post-office men let me in.

Spotting the telephone:

Oh! I understand!
FREUD, *with naive pride*   I'm among the first of us doctors to have one.
      Do you want to talk to me?

He turns to the children:

Off you go, children!
      Off you go, quickly. Mama's waiting for you.

The children run towards the door.
      Breuer goes up to Freud.

BREUER   I must admit I'm very surprised.
      You're giving a paper this evening to the Medical Society and I heard about it only
this morning, from an invitation card.

He takes out a card and shows it to Freud.

FREUD, *polite, but not excessively so*   I was given short notice.

BREUER, *wounded by his coolness of tone*   Well, why were you in such a great hurry?

FREUD   The time has come to strike a great blow. I'm ready.

Breuer, reading the card:

BREUER   Sexual origin of the neuroses.

(Sniggering:)

The fathers have raped the daughters: is that still it?

FREUD, *cold and calm*   When the daughters are neurotic, yes: always.

BREUER, *vicious irony*   Do all sexual assaults cause neuroses?

FREUD   Most assuredly not: the patient has to be predisposed.

BREUER, *same manner*   So there are far more unworthy fathers than there are neurotic children?

FREUD   Inevitably.

BREUER, *same manner*   Man really is loathsome!

(A pause.)

Seriously, Freud, you're not going to embark on that subject in front of our colleagues.

FREUD   Why not, since it's the truth?

BREUER   Freud, I beseech you to be careful. We've just finished a book together, it'll be out in a few days and this isn't the moment . . .

FREUD   On the contrary. Out of respect for you, I've accepted that we should make our exposition of your methods without breathing a word about sexuality.

Today, I'm making up for that.

BREUER   But you've no idea, you poor devil, of the scandal you're going to unleash.

You'll be speaking to elderly men, most of whom are fathers and some grand-fathers, and you'll venture to cast doubts on their relationships with their children!

FREUD   I don't say that all fathers are guilty!

BREUER   No. But for there to be so many guilty ones, if you're telling the truth all must have been tempted.

FREUD   I know nothing about that. I say what I know.

BREUER   If you say what you *think* you know, my poor Freud, you're ruined. And I don't want you to drag me into your ruin, on the pretext that I've put my name to a book with you.

FREUD   So that's what it is!

BREUER   Yes, that's what it is! I don't want to lose either my practice or my repu-tation.

FREUD   In short, you're afraid.

BREUER   And you, preparing your blows on the quiet, I suppose it's not fear which stopped you giving me any warning.

I've no reason to risk my good name, as a doctor and as a man, for some idiotic theories which I don't share.

FREUD, *beside himself with rage*   Idiotic perhaps, but proven.

BREUER, *scornfully*   I know: thirteen cases!

FREUD   Fourteen since the day before yesterday.

BREUER   One more? Bravo!

FREUD   One more. And of capital importance. That of Cäcilie Körtner.

BREUER, *deeply wounded*   What?

(He controls himself.)

My dear Freud, she was *my* patient. If you've committed the professional impropriety...

FREUD   There's no impropriety in helping an unfortunate woman whom you've abandoned. What justifies me, in any case, is success: she's on the way to recovering the use of her legs.

BREUER   Helping Cäcilie! Poor girl, you've now besmirched her completely. Helping! You! You've never helped anyone, and you'd kill your patients to verify one of your theories.

(With a kind of sexual jealousy:)

So? Cäcilie was the object of an assault?

FREUD   Yes. At the age of eight.

BREUER   And it was?

FREUD   Her father.

White with anger they face one another, staring into each other's eyes in silence.

20

The Freuds' sitting-room, on the third floor.

Martha and Mathilde are sitting close together. They are frightened.

MATHILDE BREUER   This time, I think it's finished, Martha. When he received the invitation ... I've never seen him in such a state.

MARTHA, *tenderly*   I loved you so much.

MATHILDE, *timidly*   Won't we be able to see each other any more?

MARTHA, *shaking her head*   Sigmund is too unyielding. If he quarrels with your husband, he won't allow me to see you any more.

MATHILDE   Without his knowing?

MARTHA   I won't do anything without his knowing. Even if it's all his fault.

(With a kind of anguish:)

But what will I have left, if I lose you!

She throws herself into Mathilde Breuer's arms. The two women remain for a moment locked in each other's embrace. Mathilde is weeping. Martha, harsh and despairing, does not weep.
    The door opens abruptly. Breuer comes in first, with a savage tread that we have not seen him use previously. Freud follows him. Both men are beside themselves with anger. The two women part and look at them in dismay.

BREUER   My regards, Martha. I admire and pity you.

Martha sits bolt upright.

MARTHA   No one has the right to pity me. I love Sigismund and I'm proud of him.

BREUER, *brutally*   So much the worse for you.
    (To Freud:) And mark my words: I'll dissociate myself from you publicly, starting *tomorrow*!

FREUD   Very well. You'll be abandoning me at the most difficult moment, but I'll go on alone.

BREUER   Alone! You're never alone, my poor friend. In order to work, you need a master. You'll fall under the influence of Fliess, that's all.

(To Mathilde, brutally:)

Come along!

Mathilde stands up. The two women exchange a look of deep affection and distress. Mathilde turns round and follows Breuer; they go out.

Freud is ashen. When the door closes again, he staggers. Martha rushes to support him. He has already recovered. Standing there beside him, Martha looks at him. He is having difficulty with his breathing.

FREUD   Ten thousand guilders.

MARTHA, *in surprise*   What?

FREUD   I owe him ten thousand guilders and I can't pay him back.

(To Martha, menacingly:) We'll save it up penny by penny. I'm counting on your help.

21

The same evening, in front of the 'Medical Society'.

The façade of the building. It has not changed since 1886. Just as old, just as baroque.

But this evening the whole building is resounding: through the open door and the windows can be heard howls, indistinct shouts, whistles.

From time to time the voice of Freud, taking advantage of a precarious lull, pronounces a few words — anyway unintelligible to us — and the hubbub abruptly begins afresh.

Two men go by — well dressed but vulgar — merry-makers. They listen and laugh. As they pass the door they notice the doorman, who is sitting peacefully astride a chair and smoking a cigarette in the most total relaxation.

ONE OF THE TWO MEN   Some shouting-match going on in there.
DOORMAN, *philosophically*   Certainly is!
    (By way of explanation:) They're scientists.
OTHER MERRY-MAKER   Well, I'm glad to know they shout at each other just like everyone else.

They go off.

A cab has now drawn up to the sidewalk, just short of the door. The driver is old, the horse very thin, the carriage none too clean. We learn later that this is the rented cab Freud sometimes uses for paying calls on his patients.

Martha is in the cab, white and drawn. She hears the shouts and realizes the situation is even more serious than she feared.

MARTHA   What time is it?

The driver looks at his watch.

DRIVER   A quarter past ten.
MARTHA   It's just about to finish. When he comes out, I'll go and fetch him. As soon as he's up on the seat, whip up your horse and we'll leave.
DRIVER   Very good, Madam.

The hall.

Since Freud's first address (1886), it has not changed.

There are new faces, but the youngest are not below forty. Two people have disappeared: Meynert and Breuer. Breuer's place has been left empty.

Around the hall, on the wall, we perceive a series of busts (they are those of the greatest

Viennese doctors since the eighteenth century). One of these sculptures, a very recent one, repro-
duces the head of Meynert. His name is engraved under the bust in gold letters.

Same arrangement of the hall: a chairman, seated; Freud is standing — pale, but smiling con-
temptuously. The hall is in an uproar. Everybody is howling: we can hear words and snatches of
phrases. Whistles. People are stamping their feet. Etc., etc.

(From amid the hubbub:)

'... psychiatry for pigs!'
  '... old maids' fancies.'
  '... scientific fairy-tale.'
  '... and what fairies!'
  Etc.

During this outpouring of anger and violence, Freud looks calmly at Meynert's bust.

He takes advantage of a lull to conclude his lecture by these words, flung down with con-
temptuous irony:

FREUD   I thank my colleagues for their kind attention: not for one moment have
they failed to show the calm and objectivity appropriate to true men of science.

Fresh boos. A few doctors, among the youngest, exchange looks then slip out.

Freud, entirely at ease (which makes a striking contrast with his bearing at the first lecture),
turns towards the chairman of the meeting and says a few words to him that we cannot hear (but
whose meaning we divine: 'no point, under these conditions, of starting a discussion').

The chairman (a bulky man — who is, moreover, just as indignant at Freud as his colleagues
are) rises to his feet and declares amid the hubbub (we guess at, rather than hear, what he is say-
ing):

CHAIRMAN   The meeting is closed.

Freud tidies his papers. His eyes remain sombre and hard, but a smile of triumph has appeared on
his lips, as if he rejoiced at the idiotic attitude of his colleagues.

Outside.

From the cab where she is sitting, Martha observes with disquiet the stratagem of a number of doctors
(the ones we saw leave the hall), who have lined up on both sides of the door with the evident inten-
tion of booing Freud or roughing him up.

The doorman, worried likewise, has just left his post and is running off: apparently intending
to warn a policeman whom we can see a hundred metres further on, doing his nightly round.

The doctors seem to be putting their heads together. One of them, the biggest and strongest
(black side-whiskers, ruddy complexion, florid appearance), seems to be the improvised leader
chosen by the little band.

He is speaking (from where Martha is sitting, it is impossible to hear what he is saying) with a nasty smile and very excitedly. (He carries a walking-stick.)

Freud (top-hat, tail-coat) comes out of the hall, on his own. At once the doctors start shouting:

DOCTORS, *all together*   Dirty Jew!

Dirty Jew!

Filthy yid!

Back to the ghetto! Back to the ghetto!

Freud stops for a moment, his eyes shining with a joyful and almost invigorating anger. Then he passes between the two rows (spread fairly thin, in fact: a mere ten individuals) as if it were a triumphal procession.

Arriving in front of the leader of the demonstration, who is orchestrating the booing with his stick like a musical conductor, he stops deliberately and with the back of his hand knocks his top-hat into the gutter.

FREUD, *in icy tones*   Dirty anti–Semite, pick it up.

The other raises his stick. But already the doorman and two policemen have run to separate them.

The other members of the little band, disconcerted, say nothing.

Martha, who has hastily climbed out of the cab, tugs at Freud's arm and drags him away. As soon as they are seated in the cab, the driver whips up his horse and the carriage moves off.

Freud has the simultaneous air of a soul in torment and a conqueror. He turns round and sees the anti-Semite with the side-whiskers stoop to pick up his top-hat from the gutter. He sits back at Martha's side, cold and silent. He says with a calm smile:

FREUD   I've just settled an old score.

22

On the ground floor of the building in the Berggasse, a few minutes later.

Freud and Martha outside the door of 'Dr Freud's Consulting-room'.

FREUD, *pleasantly*   Thank you Martha.

  (A pause.)

Go upstairs without me and go to bed. I've a letter to write.

Martha, in the tone of chilly irony that has become habitual to her:

MARTHA, *ironically*   To Fliess?
FREUD, *tonelessly*   Yes.

He pulls out his bunch of keys, bends over the lock and opens the door. Martha turns and goes towards the stairs. Freud enters.
  Freud in his doctor's consulting-room. He lights a kerosene lamp, transfers it to his desk and takes off his tail-coat. Then, in his waistcoat, his collar open, he goes and sits down in front of his blotter.
  He muses for a moment; his face retains a triumphant air, but at the same time pain and fatigue have left dark rings under his eyes. Soul in torment or martyr? Both at once.
  He takes a sheet of paper, dips his pen in ink and begins to write. His voice off recites what he is writing.

FREUD'S VOICE OFF   My dear Wilhelm.

The telephone rings. Freud picks up the receiver.

FREUD, *breaking off*   Hullo?
A VOICE, *from the receiver*   Dirty Jew!

Freud, with no sign of concern, hangs up unhurriedly and picks up his penholder again.

FREUD'S VOICE OFF   I broke with Breuer a short while ago. The lecture caused a scandal. Tomorrow all the papers will be talking about it. I have lost all my patients, except Cäcilie whom I am treating gratis.
  All this proves to me that we are on the right track.
  Society is resisting. It wants to suppress the troublesome person who uncovers its secrets — just as the individual represses unbearable truths.

You may rest content: I have burned my boats. Now I must win or die.

He is interrupted by the ringing of the telephone. He hesitates for a moment, stretches out his hand to pick up the receiver, but then with an ironical smile takes up his pen again and returns to his letter.

FREUD'S VOICE OFF   I have cut out hypnotism …

But the ringing continues, for a long time.
    He puts down his pen in annoyance and decides to pick up the receiver in his left hand, while with his right pulling the telephone itself across and placing it on the blotter, beside his letter.

FREUD, *in an aggressive tone*   Hullo?

    (Still aggressive but surprised:)

Who's speaking?
    Oh!
    What is it?

Frau Körtner in the basement of a café. She is bending over a telephone.
    Male and female customers come and go, entering or leaving the lavatories. The telephone lady looks at Frau Körtner in mute astonishment. The latter speaks quite naturally, in a dry, precise voice. Her face is lined with fatigue, but it remains hard.

FRAU KÖRTNER   About twenty minutes ago. It was the sound of the door which woke me up.
    I went into her room, she wasn't there any more.
    A message, yes. On the bed.

She rummages in her bag, takes out a scrap of paper and reads:

'I'm going back to our old profession. Don't be alarmed: I'll earn lots of money.'
    Oh, prostitution. She imagines she was once a prostitute. She could talk of nothing else, this morning. She was saying she'd go onto the Ring, because the clients are more distinguished there.
    Yes. Normally — since this morning. She even walked in the garden.
    Should I notify the police?

Shot of Freud, in his consulting-room, bending over the telephone.

FREUD   On no account.
    She said: on the Ring?
    Very good. I'll go myself.

Go home: I'll bring her back to you.

He hangs up. His air of satanic triumph has entirely disappeared. The corners of his mouth droop, his wide eyes betray his anguish.

He refastens his collar, pulls up his tie, hastily dons his jacket and goes out of the room.

[23]

In a neighbouring street, a few minutes later. A window on the first floor of an apartment-building.

(Violent knocking at a door.)

FREUD'S VOICE OFF   Hirschfeld! Open up! Open up!

The window opens. The coachman who shortly before was driving the old barouche with Martha inside now appears at the balcony, in his nightshirt.

HIRSCHFELD   Who's there?
     (Recognizing Freud:) It's the Doctor.

Shot of Freud, who was knocking at the coach-house door.

FREUD   I need you, Hirschfeld. At once!
HIRSCHFELD   Well, the fact is, Doctor … I'm asleep.
FREUD   Well wake up, then, it's an emergency.

The window closes again. Freud paces up and down in front of the door.
     A little further on, a prostitute — with her back to us — waits under a gas-lamp.
     After a brief hesitation, Freud makes up his mind; he crosses the street. A passing cart covers the sound of his footsteps. The prostitute does not hear him coming.
     He goes up to her: her blond hair is visible under a little straw hat. He taps her on the shoulder. She turns round: it is not Cäcilie. She is ten years older, and very ugly.

PROSTITUTE, *turning round*   Want to make love, darling?

As soon as he sees her, Freud loses all interest in her.

FREUD, *stiffly*   No, Madam.

He raises his hat politely, and moves away.
     As he crosses back over the road, the coach-house door opens and Hirschfeld's ancient horse emerges pulling the ancient barouche.
     The carriage draws up to the sidewalk. Freud leaps in. Hirschfeld bends down to him, while an old woman refastens the coach-house door.

HIRSCHFELD   What address, Doctor?
FREUD, *distractedly*   No address.

HIRSCHFELD, *surprised*   I mean: where does your emergency case live?
FREUD   I don't know. Drive round the Ring.

The Ring.

Late merry-makers, with women. It is about one in the morning.
   Elegant carriages drive past on the roadway. In their midst we see Hirschfeld's cab make its appearance, creaking and rattling, very much the 'phantom cart'.
   Hirschfeld talks all alone as he drives. In reality, he is addressing Freud, but without turning round (apart from one or two occasions, which will be indicated) — so that he seems to be talking to his horse.

HIRSCHFELD   The truth is, I wouldn't have wanted to be a doctor for all the money in the world, because I like to sleep, I do, and doctors never sleep, or at least when they do sleep they get woken up all the time.

As he talks, Freud is peering intently at the passers-by: through his eyes we see groups of night-birds, both sinister and merry.

Being a coachman, on the other hand, anyone'll tell you that's a job for sleepyheads, you can even grab a nap during the day. But then, Doctor, that's just like me, I go and hire my carriage out by the month to a doctor. Result, I'm woken up by the emergency cases and I don't even have the honour of treating them.

He turns round to Freud.

Isn't that Fate for you?

Freud, without looking at him:

FREUD   Drive slower.

A group goes by, bearing along a blonde woman who, from afar, looks like Cäcilie.

Stop!

Hirschfeld, in amazement, stops the carriage. Freud stands up and is about to climb out. Meanwhile the group has come closer: the blonde woman is not Cäcilie.

Drive on!

Hirschfeld, more and more surprised, gives a crack of his whip and the carriage starts up again.
   Half an hour later. A café: men and women, in couples. But no woman on her own.

Freud enters and stares into the faces of the couples. A young man raises his head angrily (he had been caressing the throat of a beautiful, highly made-up girl), but Freud's frosty gaze intimidates him. He says nothing and even — as if the disgust signalled on Freud's face were contagious — drops his hand and stops caressing his partner.

Freud has already gone out.

He climbs back into the barouche.

FREUD   Drive on!

Hirschfeld looks at him with a surprise which at any moment might change into outrage. Whipping up his horse, he turns round.

HIRSCHFELD   Is she in a café, this emergency case of yours?
FREUD   Perhaps. Unless she's under a street-lamp.

A bar.

At the far end of the room, some gypsies are playing a waltz. Prostitutes with their gallants for the night — or in each other's company.

All are dressed in garish, low-cut dresses. None is very beautiful or very young. They look tired, but disguise their tiredness with professional laughter.

Sitting rather limply beside them, the men smoke without making any effort to converse with them.

Three prostitutes, Lili, Daisy and Nana, are alone at a table; they yawn as they wait for a client.

Lili has turned towards the door.

LILI, *astonished*   Oh!
   Will you just look at that!

The two other women turn round.

NANA, *simply*   I'll be damned.

Cäcilie has just come in. She is dressed entirely in black, down to her hat, her gloves and her stockings. She has a mourning veil, thrown back from her face. But her dress is cut outrageously low. Actually, she has cut out her décolleté from a high-necked dress, with scissors.

DAISY   What's that doing here?
LILI   Get an eyeful of that neckline!
   She's cut it out with scissors!

Her hat is put on crooked. She has made herself up clumsily: her lipstick spills over the outlines of her mouth, giving her at first sight enormous, sensual lips; she has dabbed rouge on her cheeks haphazardly, and these scarlet patches stretch almost to her ears.

Over her blonde eyebrows, she has drawn two sooty black lines which do not even coincide with the line of the eyebrows. Despite this masquerade, she appears a hundred times more beautiful and young than all the other ladies of the assembled company.

She comes in boldly, spots an unoccupied table and sits down at it. She looks simultaneously like a little girl who has dressed herself up and like a tragedy queen, thanks to her comically daubed cheeks and her great, tragic, madwoman's eyes.

CÄCILIE   Waiter!

The waiter, a handsome boy with dark hair and a moustache, comes over to her. She flashes him a cheap smile and endeavours to give him a flirtatious wink, by closing her left eye and raising the left corner of her mouth.

(Laughter off from the prostitutes.)

The waiter, who has seen all kinds, waits unconcernedly. But we can hear the laughter of the three girls observing her.

CÄCILIE   A liqueur!
WAITER   What liqueur?
CÄCILIE, *mysterious tone, pregnant with innuendo*   You should know.
WAITER   Kirsch?
CÄCILIE   Very well.

He goes off. She turns her head, sees the three women and smiles at them. The three women respond to her smile with censorious sniffs and turn away.

In the street.

A row of gas-lamps, and under each one a prostitute.
Freud, on foot, passes beneath each lamp, looks each prostitute in the face and continues on his way.
The barouche keeps abreast of him and Hirschfeld watches him with unbounded astonishment.

A café.

The door opens, a customer comes in. He is a burly, prosperous-looking man with white hair.

LILI'S VOICE OFF   There's my Karl!

Cäcilie sees him go by. She stands up and catches him by the arm.

CÄCILIE   Hey!

She confronts him, thrusting out her young bosom.

I'm beautiful, aren't I?
KARL, *in a hurry*   Of course you are, my dear.
CÄCILIE, *in a hard voice*   You'll die of love in my arms!

Karl pushes her away almost brutally and goes to sit down at the three girls' table.

KARL   What's got into that kid?
LILI   No idea what's got into her, but she's a prize hussy trying to pinch my sweet-heart from right under my nose.
    (To Cäcilie, who seems not to hear:) Watch out, kid, 'cos I could get annoyed.

Cäcilie seems not to hear. She turns towards a young man who has just come in and ogles him.

CÄCILIE   Come here!

The man, thirtyish, fair moustache, blue eyes, at first sees only Cäcilie's plunging neckline and allows himself to be tempted.
    She drags him by his sleeve to her table and he sits down beside her.

CÄCILIE   You're very young. I prefer the old ones. But I take anything: that's part of the job.

He looks at her with faint unease.

You'll be well taken care of, I can promise you that. Our family have been whores from mother to daughter.
    (Declaiming:) I'm a filthy slut, Sir, a harlot. Everyone must know it. I'll make love to punish myself.

The young man's unease grows.

Carry me off in your arms.

    (In a sombre, pathetic tone of voice:)

And then you'll die in mine.
    (Laughing:) With lipstick all over your face.

Gradually he slides to the corner of the table and then, with a single movement, rises to his feet, takes to his heels and exits.

    (Sound off of indignant voices.)

NANA, *furiously*   And into the bargain she frightens off the customers.

She has risen to her feet and moves towards Cäcilie.

Tell me, kid, has no one ever given you a good hiding?
LILI, *to Nana*   Oh, come on! Drop it.
NANA   Are you crazy? She needs to be taught about life.

    (Turning back to Cäcilie:)

Well then? Has no one ever given you a hiding?

Cäcilie has risen to her feet. She really does look simultaneously tragic and sinister.

CÄCILIE, *with the humility of a madwoman*   Beat me! With a horse-whip!
    That's all I deserve!

Nana, disconcerted, recoils a step. Her face registers almost fear. But her anger is stronger. After a moment's pause:

NANA, *in a menacing voice*   Right. If that's the only thing that'll make you happy.

She is about to hurl herself at Cäcilie. The customers, cheering up, watch the scene without any thought of intervening.
    At this moment, the door opens and Freud appears.

FREUD   Cäcilie!

Cäcilie looks at him without apparent recognition, and ogles him as she did with the waiter and the two 'clients'.

NANA, *seizing her arm across the table*   Again!

Freud, sizing up the situation at a glance, strikes Nana a sharp blow on the arm and makes her let go.

Hey now!

Nana turns to face him. But Freud's expression impresses her.

(More feebly:) There's no room here for trespassers, and she's got no right to come awhoring.

FREUD   You can see her, can't you?
    Didn't you realize?

Swift glance from Nana in Cäcilie's direction. She shrinks back a little.

NANA   You should have said!

Freud takes a step towards her to complete her rout.

FREUD   Well, I'm telling you now. And I'm her doctor. Leave us alone.

Nana, somewhat discomfited, resumes her seat.
    An intense embarrassment has overcome her friends and even Karl. No one breathes a word.
The four individuals bend over their glasses in silence.
    Freud gently approaches Cäcilie.

FREUD   Come along, Cäcilie
CÄCILIE   No, why? I've ordered a kirsch.

Freud flings a coin onto the table.

FREUD   Come along: the kirsch is paid for.

She looks at him with an uncertain air.

CÄCILIE, *coarsely*   You're in a big hurry! D'you think I'm beautiful? You're not bad either.
    Where shall we go? To your place? To a hotel?
FREUD   We'll go back to your own home, Cäcilie.
CÄCILIE   To my own home? I'm quite willing. But you'll have to pay me a lot of money.

Freud waits in silence.

Say you'll pay me a lot of money!

He hesitates.

I'm not doing anything for nothing, my friend.
FREUD   Very well, that's agreed. Come along.

In the street, in front of the café. Hirschfeld, dumbfounded, from up on the box of his cab sees Freud come out of the café with his arm round a young prostitute, who is laughing crazily.

CÄCILIE, *approaches the barouche laughing uproariously* You know, I've never made love: you'll have to tell me how.

Freud pulls her along and hoists her almost forcibly into the barouche. He sits down beside her. Hirschfeld points at her in disgust with the tip of his whip.

HIRSCHFELD   Is that your emergency case?
FREUD, *very sharply*   Mind your own business and take us to 7 Prinz Eugen Gasse.

Hirschfeld turns round and whips up his horse.

CÄCILIE   How do you know my address?

When she hears the name of her street being given, Cäcilie abruptly stops laughing and looks at Freud with attentive mistrust.

You're not a client: you're Dr Freud. For you, it'll be free.

Violently:

Let me follow my trade.

She tries to jump out of the moving carriage, he restrains her and forces her to sit down.

Let me go or I'll call for help.
FREUD, *authoritatively*   If you call for help, we'll be taken to the police station, I shall explain your case and you'll be taken back to your mother in a Black Maria.
CÄCILIE   So much the better: it's what I deserve.
   (*Coldly:*) Listen carefully, Doctor: I won't go home to my mother. I'll make any kind of scene rather than go home.

   (*Explaining in a calm tone of voice:*)

I'm a monster.
FREUD   You want to punish yourself, don't you?
CÄCILIE   Of course. What would you do in my place?
FREUD   I don't know. What have you done?
CÄCILIE, *very simple, but utterly distraught*   I had the best, most loving and noblest of fathers and I've accused him publicly of a base crime.
   Only a whore could do such a filthy thing. So there you are, that's what I am, everything's fine.

She looks intently at him, then begins to laugh.

In any case, you know all that by heart: it was in your presence that I accused him.

Freud is surprised by the turn events have taken.

FREUD   Wasn't it true then?

But it is obvious that he still believes Cäcilie's declarations. What disconcerts him is the fact that her confession, instead of calming her, should have plunged her into such disarray.
    Cäcilie looks at him; in a cold, biting voice:

CÄCILIE   Of course not.

(A pause.)

He was kissing the governess.
FREUD, *disconcerted*   What?
CÄCILIE   Luckily the memory has come back. I ran up the steps of the perron and fell over because I saw them kissing.
FREUD   And then?
CÄCILIE   That's all. They didn't even see me. That was no concern of mine, Doctor. It's my mother's affair.
    You have a daughter?

Freud nods.

I swear to you I'm telling the truth. I swear it on your daughter's head.

Freud is dumbfounded. He strives to understand.

FREUD   You were speaking bitterly about him, the other day. And you seemed to hate him in your dream. Why?
CÄCILIE, *laughing nervously*   It's because I'm losing my head. Recently, I've begun to confuse him sometimes with your friend. You know, Josef? When they're ... condensed into the same person, I hate them for it — it's only natural!

Passionately:

You do believe me, don't you? You do believe me?

Freud does not answer.

(Sly smile:) If you don't believe me, I'll kill myself. You'll have to believe me.
    Say you believe me.

Freud retains the obstinate look of a man convinced that he knows the truth. He still does not answer.

Very well.

The barouche is passing along a road flanking the Danube. The horse, exhausted, is hardly moving. Cäcilie eludes Freud, jumps into the roadway and runs towards the parapet that borders the Danube.

  Hirschfeld pulls on his reins, the horse stops and Freud jumps down in turn. But he has hardly set foot on the pavement before Cäcilie is standing on the parapet. Below her, five metres of empty space, then the embankment. If she jumps, it is clear she will kill herself.

Say you believe me or I'll jump!

Freud hesitates an instant longer, so great is his revulsion from lying. But he is defeated. He makes a violent effort to control himself, then declares reluctantly:

FREUD   I believe you, Cäcilie. Come down.

Cäcilie has turned towards him triumphantly. With a malicious smile:

CÄCILIE   Come down? Why? You can see what a monster I am. The best solution is to jump.

Freud very softly draws closer. He speaks almost in spite of himself: the words escape him. He wants, above all, to calm her.

FREUD   Cäcilie, you never *wanted* to slander your father. It was I who forced you to do it. You resisted me as long as you could.
CÄCILIE   Why did you force me to do it?

Cäcilie, very surprised, is off her guard for a moment. Freud takes advantage of this.

FREUD   Because I was mistaken.

At these words, he throws himself upon her and, catching her above the knees, succeeds in toppling her over on the street side. He restrains her in time to prevent her falling and carries her to the cab, helped by Hirschfeld.
  She does not resist. He sits her down in the barouche.
  She remains sitting, upright and silent; the tears run down her cheeks.
  Freud sits down beside her and takes her by the arm; he holds her firmly, but his gaze is elsewhere. The sombre harshness of his countenance bears witness to his inner conflicts.

Three o'clock in the morning. On the stairs of the Freuds' apartment-building.

He steals up. Reaching the landing, he slides a key into the lock and opens it noiselessly. But as soon as the door opens, he discovers that the hall is lit, as indeed are all the other rooms. The doors are open, voices can be heard from the kitchen.

MARTHA'S VOICE OFF   You'll take good care of the children.

Freud closes the door behind him.
    Martha — who has doubtless heard the sound — comes out of the kitchen. She is wearing her hat.
    Freud looks at her in surprise.

FREUD, *forcing a smile.*   What's going on? Are you going dancing?

Martha comes up to him. Her eyes are red and swollen.

MARTHA, *with a great deal of renewed affection*   My darling.

She seizes his left forearm in a tight grip and squeezes it with all her strength.

FREUD, *smiling gently at her*   You're hurting me!
    (Becoming serious again:) What's the matter?
MARTHA, *in a meaning tone*   Your father.

Three days later. A barber's shop.

It is morning.

Freud, in deep mourning, comes in and discontentedly contemplates the customers awaiting their turn, who will be served before him.

The owner comes up.

OWNER   Good morning, Doctor. Sit down.

FREUD, *discontented*   What a lot of people today. There's normally nobody at this hour.

OWNER, *surprised*   At ten o'clock? It's always full then. You *normally* come at half past nine.

(A silence.)

Freud pulls out his watch, looks at it in surprise and sits down, resigned to waiting.

A BARBER'S ASSISTANT, *bending over his client, to whom he is administering a head rub* Close your eyes, Sir: it's spirit.

The building where Freud's father and mother live.

In front of the entrance, a hearse. Several people are already waiting. The children of the neighbourhood find the presence of the funeral carriage highly entertaining. The door of the building is draped in black.

In the older Freuds' apartment.

The family has assembled. Sisters with their husbands, nephews, etc. The bonds of kinship are close, but will not be specified. Freud's mother is present. Pallid but dry-eyed. Martha is at her side. She has been weeping.

An undertaker's assistant appears at the door of the room (it is the living-room we saw on the occasion of Freud's first visit — in Part One).

ASSISTANT, *very respectfully, to the mother*   Madam, our times are fixed very strictly. Believe me, I'm sorry but ...

The mother, very politely, but with an authority of which she is not even aware.

MOTHER   Wait a moment longer.

He bows, not best pleased, and withdraws.
     A young woman (to the mother's left) bursts out suddenly (it may be Rosa Freud, but her name will not be mentioned):

YOUNG WOMAN   He's right, Mama! We can't make them wait any longer; it's just too bad about Sigismund.

Martha seems worried and very disconcerted.

MARTHA   Be patient a little while longer, I beg of you. When I left him, he had to go to the barber's ...

A gentleman dressed in black, no doubt the husband of the young woman:

GENTLEMAN   Sigmund's half an hour late! I just can't understand him. His first duty towards our poor father ...

MOTHER, *cutting him short*   *Your* first duty towards your poor father is not to raise your voice when his coffin's in the next room.

An embarrassed silence. A moment later, the door opens: it is Freud. He rushes towards his mother and takes her in his arms without a word.

A WOMAN IN MOURNING, *in a disagreeable tone of voice*   I hope we're going to be able ...

His mother smiles at Freud, then frees herself.

MOTHER   One moment.
     (*To Freud:*) Come.

She takes him by the arm. She leads him to the far end of the room and ushers him into Jakob's bedroom. Freud obeys with the faintest trace of repugnance.

MOTHER   Go in.

They go in. Jakob's coffin is standing on a kind of trestle. Lots of flowers.

Come close.

Freud and his mother are right next to the coffin. His mother lays her right hand on the coffin lid; with her left hand, she takes Freud's right wrist and compels him to put his right hand on his father's coffin.

(Gently:) He never knew what you thought of him.

FREUD, *very embarrassed*   Oh, Mother, I didn't ...

MOTHER   Let me speak ...

He adored you. He was sure that you loved him. Only last Monday, he was saying: 'If I'd done nothing else but bring a man of genius into the world, I wouldn't have wasted my life.'

You made him happy, Sigmund: don't reproach yourself for anything.

Sigmund, his face drawn, his eyes dry and staring, remains for a moment before the coffin. Then, as if he cannot stand it any longer, he turns away almost brutally.

His mother looks at him with deep sorrow, then moves away, opens the door and goes out.

Freud's features contort, as if he were about to break into sobs. But no: his face becomes impassive and he follows her.

In front of the building.

The number of people waiting for the funeral procession has increased considerably.

Among them, we recognize Fliess, who has pushed his way into the front row. Four under-taker's assistants go by carrying the coffin, which they place inside the hearse.

Behind them, with their faces hidden by mourning veils, Freud's mother, Martha and two other women; then Freud and three other male relatives.

When Freud goes by, Fliess, who has taken off his hat, touches his arm. Freud turns round: he sees Fliess and looks at him with an astonishment that is faintly tinged with hope.

FREUD   You!

FLIESS   I was summoned by cable yesterday morning, for an urgent consultation.

FREUD   I've never had such great need of you. I'll see you later.

The carriage has moved off. The group of close relatives — first the women, then the men — begin to follow it; other people join the procession.

A little further on, in another street: the traffic has come to a temporary halt to allow the funeral to pass.

In his closed carriage, drawn up at the side of the road, Breuer is waiting; he watches the funeral procession through the window-pane. When the last ranks are passing the carriage, he opens the door, climbs out and follows the funeral at a distance, hat in hand. His carriage follows him at a distance.

A shop —

Topographically identical to the barber's. There are even armchairs in front of mirrors.

But the barber's assistants, standing between the mirrors and the armchairs and facing the camera, instead of shaving or cutting hair (there is not a single customer in the chairs), are passing from hand to hand (three armchairs, three assistants) some round balls wrapped in white paper (with pink ribbons and bows), which end up in the hands of the owner, seated behind his till.

The latter sticks on each of them the label 'Sold', then throws them one after another onto the floor. What is most striking, however, is not this odd game but the huge enamel plaques that have been fastened on all the walls (in place of the advertisements for perfumes or shaving-creams that could be seen there when Freud went in).

(Sound off of a machine working, which in a ridiculous and almost nightmarish manner provides the rhythm for the progress of the goods from one assistant to the next.)

On all these plaques there is written (printed characters, block capitals or italics or roundhand, etc. as if they were writing-patterns or advertisements for an engraver):

YOU ARE REQUESTED
TO CLOSE THE EYES*

The noise of the machines is drowned by an imperious ringing and, all of a sudden, the dream dissolves.

(Imperious ringing.)

---

*See *The Interpretation of Dreams*, Harmondsworth 1976, p. 429 [Trans.]

27

Freud is at his desk, jolted into wakefulness by the ringing. It is the day following the funeral. He had dozed off.

The door opens.

MAID   Dr Fliess.

Fliess appears. Freud jumps up to meet him. They exchange a vigorous handshake.

FREUD   I can't get over the fact you're in Vienna. You were the only person who could help me. Wilhelm, I'm in a very bad state.

FLIESS, *with genuine interest*   Did you care about him a great deal?

FREUD   My father?

Can you imagine, I've no idea!

Well, yes, I did. With every fibre of my being. His death is driving me mad.

He turns away from Fliess and looks towards the window.

And yet, I wonder if I loved him.

Sombrely:

Sometimes I thought I hated him.

He shakes his head, as if to rid himself of a worry, then turns back to Fliess and looks at him with sparkling eyes.

Whether he hates him or loves him doesn't matter: the event that counts most in a man's life is his father's death.

Fliess smiles gently.

FLIESS   I can't believe it was possible to hate Jakob Freud. I saw him only twice, but he appeared to be such a fine man ...

Freud paces agitatedly up and down the room.

FREUD   Oh, yes, so far as that goes, he did appear to be. What does that prove?

He comes back towards the worried Fliess, takes him by the shoulders and looks at him with an almost threatening air.

FREUD   Sometimes I've said to myself: it's not *normal* to hate him so much; one of us two *must* be a monster; if it's not me, it's him.

Fliess is immediately embarrassed by the psychological and moral turn which this conversation is taking.

FLIESS, *too hastily to be of comfort*   Oh come on now, you did love him!
FREUD, *sombrely*   Yes. I loved him too.

   (Sudden violence:)

One more reason why those surges of hatred are incomprehensible to me.

Without looking at Fliess:

What makes you think I'm not repressing, in the depths of my unconscious, some childhood memory that is ... vile?
   I ought to apply my own method to myself. If only I could squeeze myself like a lemon ...
   (Slightly distraught:) Who said that? 'Squeeze like a lemon.' I've heard someone ... Oh, yes. Cäcilie.

   (Harsh laugh.)

There's a total success for you! She tried to kill herself.
FLIESS   Did you stop her?
FREUD   Yes.
FLIESS   Thank you for the dates; my calculations establish definitively and irrefutably that she's suffering from a hysterical neurosis.

Freud, with a touch of irony — for the first time since he has known Fliess:

FREUD   So much the better. I already suspected as much, just fancy.

   (A pause.)

And her mother has telephoned me. The child is out of her mind with anxiety. I really think her neurosis is in the process of changing to nothing less than an incurable psychosis.

Pointing wildly to his own head.

Whatever can have got twisted in there, to make me do nothing but harm to people?

Abruptly, he appears calm and resolute. He looks long and hard at Fliess, then all of a sudden:

You're going to help me.

FLIESS   To do what?

FREUD   Come along!

He leads him over to the couch. Pointing at the chair placed in front of it:

Sit down there.

He restrains him.

No.

After a moment's hesitation, he takes the chair and transfers it to the head of the couch, to the position that has become classic for the analyst's seat.

There! It's better if I can't see you: I know you too well.
    You'll play my role. I'm the patient.

Fliess resists, ill at ease and indignant.

FLIESS   Are you mad? I'm not a psychiatrist.

FREUD   So what? If I want to analyse my case, I must speak in someone's presence.

He forces him to sit down. As he himself stretches out on the couch:

You don't have to do anything except listen to me. I don't know where I'm going. But I need a witness.

With a shrug of his shoulders, Fliess has sat down, bristling. Freud speaks relaxedly.

First, the dream.
    It was a barber's shop. Yesterday I went for a shave: there were lots of people and I arrived late for the funeral. I was ashamed.
    All right. Dream reflecting shame and remorse. I can see the enamel signs in my dream: 'You are requested to close the eyes.'
    That means: 'Sons must close the eyes of their fathers. But you arrived too late to close your father's eyes.'

FLIESS   Listen, Sigmund.

Freud tosses about on the couch, like a real patient.

FREUD   Keep quiet. Keep quiet, can't you? There's something else. A dream is *always* the satisfaction of a wish. Where's the wish?

Wait! Wait a minute!

To close your eyes, that also means: to die. I wanted to die; for years I've been summoning death in my dreams: I've got a sort of death instinct, it's a feature of my character I can't close my eyes to.

He speaks these last words quite naturally and without thinking. Then he gives a start and sits up suddenly on the couch.

Eh?

(Very quickly:) Bankers defraud the tax authorities, but the government closes its eyes.

That woman finds the shrewdest thing is to close her eyes to her husband's infidelities.

(A pause.)

He turns towards Fliess.

You see: the expression recurred of its own accord, without my seeking it. And in a third sense. The deepest of the three, the one that explains the whole dream. In the name of filial respect, I want to close my eyes to some action of my father's.

He rises to his feet and paces about agitatedly.

FREUD   An action that I don't want to see. That I hide from myself. That I repress from my consciousness.

Fliess tries to stand up likewise.
Imperiously:

Stay where you are.

I'll find that memory, even if I have to spend my whole life searching for it.

He sits down again.

It happened during that journey, I'm sure of it!

FLIESS, *grudgingly*   What journey?

FREUD   I was born at Freiberg, in Bohemia. My father used to sell cloth. He was rich. The growth of anti-Semitism frightened him. We left for Leipzig, then for Vienna, ruined. It was during my earliest childhood.

What did he do? What happened?

Suddenly he bursts out laughing. Fliess jumps.

FLIESS, *furiously*   Sigmund …

FREUD, *still laughing*   Hang on a minute! Do you know why I'm laughing? I was busy saying to myself: 'Old Jakob must have raped one of his daughters before my very eyes!' And now I've just remembered that my sisters weren't born.

Fliess looks at him almost with horror.

Freud is too absorbed to notice. He is sitting on the couch, bending forward. A moment later, he relaxes somewhat, swivels round, sits up straight and raises his legs onto the couch, preparing to stretch out as he had done before.

FREUD   Let's continue!

Fliess rises to his feet at the same moment and plants himself in front of Freud, fiercely determined to call it a day.

FLIESS   Oh no! Once is enough.

This method's stupid: it just involves puns and leaping about from one subject to another.

FREUD   It's not a method: I'm searching. Help me.

FLIESS   I can't help you, because I disapprove. I prefer hypnotism.

Freud moves towards him, with an almost homosexual air of provocation.

FREUD   All right, hypnotize me.

Fliess turns abruptly away.

FLIESS   I don't know how to. Anyway, you're not neurotic.

FREUD   Why not?

FLIESS, *spiritedly*   We're a team, Sigmund. And you've got no right to have problems of conscience.

At Berchtesgaden, you offered me something solid: a method, hypnotic investigation; a result, sexual traumatism. But now, I no longer follow you. Why on earth do you need to analyse your every state of mind?

FREUD   I'm not sure of anything any more. With Cäcilie, I forced her to make those confessions of hers …

FLIESS   There are still thirteen other cases.

FREUD   Perhaps I forced them too, or else the patients lied to me.

FLIESS   What interest could they have had in besmirching their fathers' reputations?

FREUD   What interest can I have in besmirching mine?

FLIESS, *alarmed*   What?

He tries to minimize matters.

Sigmund, you've just received a terrible shock and what's more you've been over-working lately. I know that. Abandon your patients for a fortnight; take Martha and the children, have a holiday, you need one.

FREUD   As far as my patients are concerned, it would be easy to abandon them: I haven't got a single one left ...

But I can't abandon myself.

FLIESS, *recovering his authority*   Listen to me, Sigmund: we're working together; I need your theory of traumatisms for my calculations; you *must* preserve it. I grant you may have made errors of detail. Very well, find them. Correct them! Take all the time you need. But our collaboration no longer has any reason to exist if you repudiate the facts upon which it is based.

FREUD, *uncertain; docile rather than convinced*   Errors. Yes ... maybe ...

FLIESS   Look for them. But don't dig down into yourself any more. You'll go mad if you try to know yourself; we're not made for that.

Freud looks at Fliess with fresh curiosity. He becomes more detached.

FREUD   And you, haven't you ever tried, Wilhelm?

FLIESS, *firmly*   To know myself? Never.

Freud shakes his head without taking his eyes off him.

FREUD   I see.

28

A few hours later.

Cäcilie in her room, worried and nervous. She is dressed very simply, but very elegantly.
   She is sitting near the window, reading. But from time to time she gets up to look at the clock.
   No trace of make-up. But she is very pale, with rings under her eyes.
   There is a knock; she turns eagerly towards the door.

CÄCILIE   Come in.

Freud comes in, with a little doctor's bag. His face has altered. Still sombre, he has lost the aggressive moroseness that we have come to associate with him. And he no longer has the stubborn, impenetrable and slightly satanic look of recent days.
   He is sad, but seems open. And beneath his deep anxieties, a new self-assurance is beginning to show through, though it is not conscious of itself.
   Cäcilie smiles at him. He goes over to the chair where she is sitting.

FREUD   Good morning, Cäcilie.

She offers him her hand gracefully. He takes a chair and sits facing her.

How do you feel?
CÄCILIE   Unwell.
FREUD   Anxiety?

She stares into space.

CÄCILIE   Yes.

Freud looks at her in silence. She turns abruptly towards him.

You're not going to tell me that you're abandoning me?
FREUD   I don't know.

She looks at him in alarm as he speaks.

I was mistaken, that's certain. But when? How?
   It's the method which isn't good ... Or else ...
   I've nothing to suggest to you. Nothing further.
   (Forcefully, all of a sudden:) And yet, I've the feeling I'm getting close.
   Are you angry with me?

She looks at him, long and hard, hesitating. And then, all of a sudden, firmly:

CÄCILIE   No.

FREUD, *tonelessly*   Cäcilie, I think I'm sick myself. I project my own sickness onto my
patients.

CÄCILIE   What sickness?

FREUD   If I only knew.

What's certain is that I won't be able to know them until I know myself.

Or to understand myself until I understand them.

I must discover in them what I am; in myself what they are.

Help me.

Cäcilie looks at him rather more sympathetically. She seems amused and flattered.

CÄCILIE   It's a collaboration that you're asking of me?

FREUD   Yes.

CÄCILIE   What do I have to do?

FREUD   You accuse me of having forced you to reply, the other day.

Well, I won't ask any more questions. Tell me whatever you like.

CÄCILIE   And then?

FREUD   Nothing is accidental. If you think about a horse rather than a hat, there's
some deep reason for it. You must tell me everything. Everything that comes into
your head, even those ideas that strike you as most preposterous.

We'll search together for the reason behind such associations of ideas; the nearer
you get to it, the more you'll weaken your resistance and the less painful it will be for
you to discover it.*

CÄCILIE   It's a parlour game?

FREUD   Yes. The truth game. Well?

Cäcilie lays her hand on his arm in a friendly manner.

CÄCILIE   You want us to be cured together?

FREUD   Yes. And by one another.

CÄCILIE   Let's try.

FREUD   Come along!

She stands at his invitation.

FREUD   Lie down on the bed.

While she stretches out, he positions a chair behind the bed and sits down.

---

*The text of these remarks by Freud is almost word for word the same as the passage at the end of Part Three, Scene
14 above.

CÄCILIE   Where are you?

    I don't like not being able to see you any more.

Freud stands up.

FREUD   When I'm cured, I'll place myself behind my patients. I'll no longer be any-thing but their witness, then.

He picks up the chair again and replaces it in front of Cäcilie.

It's still too soon, you're right.

Sitting down at her bedside.

Begin.

CÄCILIE   What with?

FREUD, *faint smile*   Free association. With whatever you like.

A pause. Cäcilie, lying on the bed, begins to speak without looking at Freud.

CÄCILIE   Haven't you ever had the feeling of being guilty, without knowing why?

FREUD   Oh, yes. All the time.

CÄCILIE   Well, there you are. When I'm crippled or paralysed, it's not too bad: it's as if my body's taking responsibility for my sins. But when I have the use of my limbs, I torment myself.

    I must have done something very bad. In the old days. I've got no excuse, Doctor: I had the most beautiful childhood. My father used to take me everywhere.

A luxurious dining-room.

Guests are sitting down. The mistress of the house is addressing Cäcilie's father.

MISTRESS OF THE HOUSE   Josef, you'll be on my right.

    Your daughter opposite me.

Cäcilie sits down. She is six, cushions have been placed on her chair to raise her up. She looks like a little lady.

    A gentleman of about fifty — who has just sat down on her right — bows humorously to her.

GENTLEMAN   Fräulein, my humble respects, I'm delighted to be your neighbour.

Cäcilie bows her head gravely and holds out her hand to be kissed.

FATHER'S VOICE OFF   Later, Cäcilie. Much later! Gentlemen will kiss your hand when you're married.

GENTLEMAN, *smiling*   Oh, but you must permit an exception.

He bends his head and kisses her hand.

FREUD'S VOICE OFF   Where was your mother?

The image disappears. Cäcilie's room.

CÄCILIE   At home.

     (Disagreeable laugh.)

She was a domesticated woman.

A drawing-room, in an apartment.

Frau Körtner, much younger (eighteen years less) but perhaps even harder, comes in, followed by two servants (women). She surveys the room like an officer inspecting troops.

FRAU KÖRTNER   Give me my white gloves.

A servant hands her a pair of white gloves. She puts them on, goes over to a sofa, stoops and passes her gloved hand beneath the sofa.
She stands up, looks at her glove, notices traces of dust on it. She turns towards the servants.

Who swept this floor?

ONE OF THE TWO SERVANTS   I did, Madam.

Frau Körtner displays her gloved hand.

FRAU KÖRTNER, *imperiously, but without anger*   You'll do it all over again.

Cäcilie (aged twelve) runs into the drawing-room. She is wearing a hat and carrying a satchel. She makes as if to kiss her mother.
Behind her we can see a very pretty woman, austerely dressed. It is her governess.

FRAU KÖRTNER, *scolding tone*   Cäcilie!

Frau Körtner points to two cloth pads in the doorway to the drawing-room — allowing us to perceive that the large, luxurious room has no rugs: the parquet floor — admirably and magnificently polished — is bare.

Cäcilie puts her feet on the two pads and goes to kiss her mother, dragging her feet; she has lost not only her vivacity, but also the genuine feeling that had impelled her towards her mother. She puts up her forehead sulkily, makes a little trained curtsey.

Go and do your homework, child!

*Turning her back on her mother, she goes to rejoin her governess, who smiles tenderly at her.
As they both disappear:*

FREUD'S VOICE OFF   Did your mother ever give elegant parties of that kind at home?
CÄCILIE, *voice off*   Never.
  One evening, my father gave a big dinner-party. That was in Mama's absence.

A big table.

Guests are dining. We notice her father, sitting opposite his daughter.

CÄCILIE, *voice off*   My father had said to me: you'll be the mistress of the house.

*Cäcilie (she is ten) occupies the place of the mistress of the house; serious and solemn, she plays the role of her mother.
  A servant is going round with the food. A gentleman, on Cäcilie's left, is just helping himself. He is youthful and shy.*

LITTLE CÄCILIE, *to the gentleman*   Oh! you haven't taken a proper helping! Come now, I'll help you myself.

The servant moves to the guest's right and holds the dish for Cäcilie; she deftly spears a fine piece of roast and puts it on the guest's plate.

GUEST, *overawed and abstracted*   Thank you, Madam.

All the guests burst out laughing.

HERR KÖRTNER, *heartily*   Not yet, my dear Sir.

A woman of about forty.

WOMAN   Oh yes! Yes. he's quite right: the child is an accomplished hostess. She's more than a match for any of us.
ANOTHER WOMAN   Suppose we call her Frau Honoris Causa.

Herr Körtner, very flattered, protests for form's sake.

HERR KÖRTNER   Oh! you mustn't spoil her for me.

Cäcilie, with blushing cheeks and a rather sly look, receives these compliments with a sovereign calm that cannot disguise her pride.
   Against the shot of Cäcilie:

FREUD'S VOICE OFF   Where was your mother then?
CÄCILIE'S VOICE OFF   In the mountains: she had a lung condition.

The image dissolves.

It was a bad year. I was afraid she was going to die. All the time.
   At night, I had nightmares. I used to see her in a coffin.

(These words are interrupted by a loud scream off from the child Cäcilie.)

A bedroom.

It is night-time. A night-light burning on a bedside table next to Cäcilie.
   Cäcilie sitting up in bed, in her nightdress. At the far end of the room, another, larger bed. The governess Magda has just woken up. She still looks half asleep.

LITTLE CÄCILIE   Magda! Magda! I was so frightened.

Magda sits up, propping herself on one elbow, kindly but somewhat annoyed. She is wearing a very low-cut nightdress.

MAGDA   Well, what's the matter?
LITTLE CÄCILIE   Magda, I had a horrible dream: Mama was dead.
MAGDA   How silly you are!

She turns over in bed, fully determined to go back to sleep. She is reckoning without Cäcilie, who begins to scream.

LITTLE CÄCILIE   Magda! Magda!
MAGDA   Don't shout so loud; you'll wake up the whole house.

Cäcilie stands up.

What do you want?
LITTLE CÄCILIE   Let me come into your bed. Oh! yes, Magda, please do! I'm too frightened, let me come into your bed.
MAGDA, *trying to be strict*   You're too big, Cäcilie.

Cäcilie has already crossed the room, she is standing in front of Magda's bed. She begins to cry.

(*Sound of Cäcilie weeping.*)

MAGDA   All right! All right! Get in!

She holds the sheets open, Cäcilie slides in. As soon as she is in the bed, she cuddles tightly up against Magda.

MAGDA, *laughing*   Watch out, you're going to suffocate me.
CÄCILIE   I'm fine.

She very gently caresses Magda's bare shoulders. Her tears have stopped.

You smell nice, Magda.
    You're so soft.
    When I grow up ...
    Do you think I'll be as beautiful as you?

Magda smiles and lets her go on.

MAGDA   You'll be much more beautiful, Cäcilie.

Cäcilie caresses her neck and shoulders; Magda, tickled by the child's light fingers, laughs and shivers.

You're tickling me.
CÄCILIE   Shall I have skin like yours?

Magda smiles without answering.

Then Papa will look at me like he looks at you?

Magda is stunned.

CÄCILIE'S VOICE OFF   Ugh!

The vision disappears.

CÄCILIE   I don't like memories of that sort.
FREUD   Why?
CÄCILIE   He used to come into our room, at night. Once I saw him when he was leaving.
FREUD   Who?

CÄCILIE   Why, my father, of course!

FREUD   You were jealous.

CÄCILIE   No. Not of her.

In the beginning, it amused me. I used to watch her, I was fascinated, I used to say to myself: *that's* the face he loves.

I had the impression a good trick was being played on somebody.

But I soon realized that he didn't love her. He just used to amuse himself with her when he had free time and nobody else to hand.

It was she who loved him.

Such a discriminating, sensitive man! And he only liked prostitutes.

FREUD   He didn't love your mother?

At this question, Cäcilie literally springs up.

CÄCILIE, *shouting*   What do you mean! He adored her!

Freud half stands and forces her to lie down again.

She had only to give a sign … She spent her whole time rejecting him.

She twists and struggles.

She was really nasty to him.

With loathing:

Cold and nasty. Never a smile. She was the one who forced him to be unfaithful to her.

Do you know they had separate rooms?

He always gave in to her, poor man. With a look that used to make me ashamed.

At these words: Frau Körtner, Herr Körtner, are sitting in the garden, under a bower. Cäcilie, at their feet, is playing with a doll.

The memory is obviously distorted by Cäcilie's passionate feelings: Frau Körtner, very beautiful, is harder than ever. Herr Körtner, ill at ease, casts her cringing glances.

The scene is seen from below: we are viewing it from little Cäcilie's level.

FRAU KÖRTNER, *harshly*   Josef, I've dismissed Magda Schneider. She has packed her things and will leave within the hour.

(*Nastily:*) Do you agree?

Herr Körtner, after an almost imperceptible hesitation.

HERR KÖRTNER, *submissively*   I agree entirely.

354

Shot of little Cäcilie, sitting on a small chair in the bower, who lifts her face towards her mother and looks at her with an expression of deep hatred.

CÄCILIE'S VOICE OFF   After that, she chose my governessses herself: cripples, old women, real frights.

The image dissolves.
    Cäcilie — lying on her bed — to Freud, violently:

I hated them!

Shouting:

It was she who ruined my father.

In the drawing-room.

Frau Körtner, sitting at the table opposite the old serving-woman, is mending. The serving-woman is darning. Repairs, dressmaking.
    But Cäcilie's voice, raised in anger, can be heard through the door. Frau Körtner listens, without her face expressing the slightest emotion.

CÄCILIE'S VOICE OFF   In the old days, we lived in Graz. We came to the villa in Vienna only for the summer. She forced my father to move here, he obeyed her as always, he entrusted his business to others and it collapsed.

Frau Körtner puts her work away unhurriedly and goes towards the door.

In Cäcilie's bedroom.

Cäcilie is pale and haggard. She is having trouble breathing.

CÄCILIE   That's it.
    The vice.

Freud looks at her intently.

I feel anxious. I feel that way whenever I think about her.

In the shrill voice of a madwoman:

She killed my father.

And I'm sure she pushed me into committing some crime.

Suddenly she sits up. Looking Freud in the eyes.

Is it a crime to condemn one's mother?

Freud too has turned pale. He does not answer.

And you, did you love your father?

He still does not answer, though his wide eyes betray his anxiety. After a moment's pause:

FREUD   Why do you ask me whether I love my *father* and not my *mother*?
CÄCILIE   I don't know. Let me speak. I find it hard to explain, as you can see.
     Your father, is he a decent man?
FREUD   He was a decent man.
CÄCILIE   Then you're lucky. Respect is easy for you.

Violently:

In my case, I have to respect a whore.
FREUD   What?
CÄCILIE   Didn't you know?
     I told you: he only liked prostitutes.

She gets up, goes over to her desk, takes a key from her pocket, opens it, brings back a roll of paper and gives it to Freud, who unrolls it.
    We see a coloured poster, portraying a so-called Spanish dancer, almost naked. The picture — very stylized — does not allow us to recognize Frau Körtner. Under the picture: Conchita de Granada.
    Cäcilie bends over him and stabs with her left forefinger at the poster he holds in his hands.

CÄCILIE   There you are.

A moment earlier, the door has opened noiselessly. Frau Körtner has appeared in the aperture. She listens.

He picked her up in a saloon.

Freud is quite flabbergasted.
    Frau Körtner comes in.

29

FRAU KÖRTNER, *icily, to Cäcilie*   So you kept it?
I didn't know you liked family keepsakes.

She turns towards Freud; in the same tone of voice:

Are you happy?

He does not reply.

You're not a priest, Doctor. Only priests have the right to know our secrets.

With an inflexible authority, but without raising her voice:

I must ask you to leave.

FREUD   Madam . . .

FRAU KÖRTNER   Don't insist. You've done enough harm.

FREUD   We're nearing our goal, Madam: it's the most dangerous moment. It's quite impossible to interrupt a treatment when it enters this phase. Cäcilie may do anything.

CÄCILIE, *soft and sly*   I'll do nothing at all, Doctor. My mother knows what I think of her and I know what she thinks of me.
We'll carry on living. As in the past.
Please leave, since she asks you to.

With deep resentment, which shows through her soft manner:

She's throwing you out just as she threw out Magda. And all my friends. What can I do about it?
She's my mother, isn't she?

Freud looks Frau Körtner in the eye. He sees that her decision is unshakable. He bows and goes out, after collecting his bag.

FREUD, *to Frau Körtner, on his way out*   I hope you'll never live to regret what you're doing.

On the other side of the door, the old woman is no longer there. He is about to leave when he hears violent noises from Cäcilie's room.
He hesitates for a moment, then runs back in. None too soon.
Cäcilie, younger and stronger, has flung Frau Körtner back onto the bed, grabbed her throat in

both hands and is trying to strangle her.

She would probably succeed if Freud did not hurl himself upon her and free Frau Körtner, not without difficulty.

The latter stands up, without a word. She is breathing with the greatest difficulty; but she at once recovers her sombre dignity and, with a swift gesture, refastens her bun, which has become disarranged.

Cäcilie is dazed. She looks at her mother in almost bemused amazement. In a toneless voice:

CÄCILIE   Come, come ... I killed her long ago!

With these latter words, she begins to howl and thrash her arms around in all directions. If Freud were not holding her, she would roll on the ground. He leads her back to her bed, where she collapses screaming in panic.

FREUD, *to Frau Körtner*   Keep her from falling.

He opens his bag, takes out a needle and ampoule, grasps Cäcilie's arm, rolls up her sleeve and, with a swift, accurate movement, gives her an injection.

In two minutes, she'll be asleep.

Night has fallen. In Cäcilie's room, Freud and Frau Körtner are at the patient's bedside: she is sleeping.
Frau Körtner speaks in an undertone, without taking her eyes off her daughter.

FRAU KÖRTNER   I used to dance in a saloon, yes. So what?
Cäcilie knows that.
Now you know it.
How will that help you to cure her?

Freud looks at Frau Körtner sympathetically, and without the least trace of puritanism.

FREUD   I don't know. It will help me.
I'm on the point of finding something.
It's not the first time she has tried to kill you.

Frau Körtner looks at him in astonishment: he knows that too.

FREUD   When she was a child, you spent some time in a sanatorium.
She used to dream every night that you were dying.
Dreams reveal our wishes to us.
FRAU KÖRTNER   She used to tell her father they were nightmares. I didn't believe it.
FREUD   They were nightmares. In her dreams she had the vague feeling that she wished for your death, and she reacted against that forbidden wish by becoming

358

anxious.

I too have dreamed on countless occasions that I was killing my father.

Frau Körtner, still hostile but interested.

FRAU KÖRTNER   But why?

FREUD   I don't know yet. I shall know.

     (A pause.)

Why did Cäcilie …

FRAU KÖRTNER   Out of jealousy: she wanted to become mistress of the house.

FREUD   Everything always comes back to that strange father she had … to your husband?

FRAU KÖRTNER   He wasn't a strange man, oh! no. He wasn't even bad. He was just a coward. Like everybody else.

At this moment, the image is transformed. We are returned twenty-five years into the past.

In a third-rate saloon at Graz (dingy tavern with floor-show), a very beautiful young woman, half-naked, is performing an extremely daring dance routine: 'Leda and the Swan', as indicated by a sign propped on an upright stand facing the audience, which is changed after every act.

(A wretched orchestra playing out of tune: a violin, a cello and a piano.)

She is dressed in a brassiere and frilly knickers; transparent stockings reach up to the knickers. Her right arm is entirely hidden by swan feathers, her hand — all that can be seen — has shaped itself into a bird's beak (with the thumb placed against the other fingers).

This hand, playing the part of the Swan Jupiter, roves boldly over the dancer's shoulders and bosom. She expresses her turmoil by dancing. The beak-hand reaches as far as the dancer's lips and mimes a swan's kiss on Frau Körtner's lovely mouth.

Her senses in turmoil, she droops backwards beneath the ardour of the prolonged kiss.

Her head touches the ground, while her knees and legs are still straight (classic gymnastic pose: the bridge); then she gently extends her legs to lie on her back while the swan assails her, kissing every part of her body.

The little curtain which half conceals the scene (it is suspended — at a man's height — by rings from a string crossing the scene from one side to the other) is drawn shut by two stagehands (whose shoes can be seen under the fringe of the curtain), when the swan's beak slowly approaches the swooning dancer's belly.

During the dance, we have seen the audience several times. A few 'toughs' of the period: bowler hats, moustaches and stiff collars. But above all soldiers (conscripts and re-enlisted men).

One man alone (top-hat, carefully trimmed beard, elegant outfit), who applauds more loudly than the others, is out of place in this purely male and very mixed audience: it is Herr Körtner.

FRAU KÖRTNER'S VOICE OFF   Just one unusual thing about him: he only liked prostitutes.

The wretched dressing-room where Frau Körtner is removing her make-up. She is sitting in front of a cracked mirror and looking at herself with intense sadness.
    There is a knock at the door.

    (Sound off of discreet knocking.)

DANCER, *turning round*   Come in!

A dance-hall attendant, seedy and shabbily dressed, slips into the room: he is carrying an enormous and splendid bouquet.
    She takes it, in astonishment. A little envelope containing a visiting-card is pinned to the bouquet. She opens the envelope, glances at the card.
    In a vulgar, knowing tone of voice:

The flowers are fine.
    How about the fellow?
ATTENDANT   He's right behind them.

In the glass, through the door left ajar, we can see Herr Körtner approaching.

Will you receive him?
DANCER   Yes.

He comes in and moves to kiss her hand.

VOICE OFF OF A PRIEST   And you, Ida Brand, do you take Josef Körtner as your lawful wedded husband?

A church. The young couple are taking their sacramental vows. Ida Brand is wearing a wedding-dress. White dress with orange blossom.
    In a firm voice:

IDA BRAND   I do.

Behind them, there are three or four individuals. But all the other benches are deserted.

FRAU KÖRTNER'S VOICE OFF   He married me because I was a whore. It was his vice. In the first stages of our relationship, I used to be unfaithful to him. He adored that.

The vision disappears: Freud and Frau Körtner, side by side.
    Frau Körtner speaks without looking at anybody. Freud looks at her as he listens.

When he told me he'd marry me, I began to love him; I swore to be faithful to him. I'd come to loathe my life: I wanted to be his true wife. Decent. Pure. I needed respectability.

Herr Körtner, in the drawing-room we have already seen, is reading his newspaper.

Frau Körtner appears: it is impossible to recognize the former prostitute in this austere, hard woman, her hair drawn back, without a speck of powder, dressed up to the chin (dark clothes, chemisette, lace cuffs).

(Sound of Frau Körtner's footsteps.)

He hears the sound of the footsteps, raises his head and puts down the paper. An almost comical disappointment is reflected in his face.

HERR KÖRTNER   Ida!

He stands up and takes a closer look.

What's that?

IDA   That? It's my dress.
Would you, perhaps, wish Frau Körtner to dress up as Leda?
Your friends wouldn't receive me.

Herr Körtner looks at her with deep unease.

HERR KÖRTNER   At all events ...

Ida Körtner gives a start and her face hardens.

IDA   What?

Herr Körtner, to change the drift of the conversation:

HERR KÖRTNER   It's Leda that I married.

She goes over to a mirror and looks at herself. But it is the image of Leda she sees there, with a haggard, despairing face.

Frau Körtner stares hard-eyed at this image of her past. The image vanishes. What remains is the present-day reflection of Ida Körtner, still very young but growing gradually harder.

We can see this hardening of the features taking place as the voice off of Frau Körtner explains:

FRAU KÖRTNER'S VOICE OFF   They never received me. They never came to my house.
They used to say 'that woman' when they spoke of me. Josef's best friends.

Ida Körtner turns away from the mirror and goes over to the window. She leans out and sees a barouche disappearing, carrying Cäcilie and Josef Körtner.

He was a coward!

He used to visit them without me. When my daughter was five, he'd take her with him.

The vision disappears. Frau Körtner is speaking to Freud in Cäcilie's room.

FRAU KÖRTNER   So I cleaned.

I tidied. I hated dirt and dust.

Sometimes I used to do the sweeping myself, or I'd scrub the floor.

Everything had to be clean. Everything.

Freud asserts rather than inquires:

FREUD   And your husband was unfaithful.

FRAU KÖRTNER   With every prostitute in Graz.

In the summer, in Vienna, he was sleeping with Cäcilie's governess. My daughter knew, but I didn't. Everybody was in league against me.

Cäcilie didn't love me.

FREUD   Why not?

At this question, the scene changes, we see Cäcilie, aged twelve, looking at the tall, dark shape of her mother with deep bitterness.

FRAU KÖRTNER'S VOICE OFF   I don't know.

Perhaps I was too strict. I didn't often smile. The governess was pretty, my husband was charming, weak and fickle. Cäcilie had taken his side.

The woman and the little girl are standing face to face. Cäcilie eventually lowers her eyes. We see that she is nervously shredding a flower (snapping the stem, tearing off the petals).

The scene is taking place in the garden of the villa, during the summer. Ida Körtner looks at her daughter sternly.

IDA KÖRTNER, *in a calm but frosty voice*   Don't destroy the flowers, Cäcilie.

Her voice makes Cäcilie jump, and gives her courage to speak.

CÄCILIE   You've sent Fräulein away?

IDA KÖRTNER   I've dismissed her, yes.

At these words, Cäcilie, white with anger, flings down the flower she was holding in her hands. Then:

CÄCILIE   Why?

Frau Körtner looks at her without emotion.

FRAU KÖRTNER   Pick that flower up, Cäcilie. I won't have untidiness. You can throw it away behind the greenhouse.

Cäcilie looks at her without moving.

Do you hear?

Cäcilie bends down and picks up the flower.

CÄCILIE   Why did you send her away?

FRAU KÖRTNER   That's my affair, Cäcilie.

CÄCILIE, *beside herself with fury*   Five years I've known her, I don't spend even my nights away from her, yet you dismiss her without saying a word to me and when I ask you why, you tell me it's your affair. But I love her!

FRAU KÖRTNER   Precisely.

She looks at her almost spitefully.

I engage governesses and I dismiss them: that's my role. You're not supposd to love them. Nor to hate them. You do what you're told. That's all.

　　You're still a child, Cäcilie. That girl wasn't serious enough to take care of you.

The sermon enrages the little girl; her eyes sparkle, she goes red in the face. She tugs nervously at one of her ringlets.

　　Cäcilie takes her time before replying. She lowers her eyes and tugs at her ringlets, her face working. With a serious, very sly air, as if she were agreeing with her mother:

CÄCILIE   Oh! so a governess needs to be serious.

She shifts from one foot to the other, sensing that she is about to take an irretrievable step, intimidated but determined. At last she adds:

But for a mother, it's not obligatory.

Frau Körtner appears irritated rather than surprised.

FRAU KÖRTNER, *still calm*   What do you mean by that?

Cäcilie is still jogging from foot to foot. But she has burnt her boats. She lifts her head and says, with a bright smile:

CÄCILIE   When Papa married you, you used to dance in front of gentlemen stark naked.

Frau Körtner just restrains herself from striking Cäcilie. But she goes up to her and takes her by the shoulders.

FRAU KÖRTNER   Was it Fräulein who told you that?

Cäcilie does not reply.

Your father must have whispered it to her under the sheets.

Cäcilie, suddenly, looks terrified by what she has said.

FRAU KÖRTNER   Poor Cäcilie! Magda wasn't lying to you. Your father takes you to visit his friends in my place, and when I'm not there you act as mistress of the house.
     That doesn't stop you being the daughter of a whore, child. You wanted to hurt me, but you're the one I pity! You'll see: it's a bad start in life.

Cäcilie, who has been listening to her in horror, wrenches herself free and rushes away. She has dropped the flower which she was shredding in her hands.
     Frau Körtner remains motionless for an instant, staring fixedly; she then notices the broken flower, picks it up and carries it over to a rubbish-heap behind a greenhouse.

FRAU KÖRTNER'S VOICE OFF, *to Freud*   That's all.
     Magda Schneider left and we carried on living.

In Cäcilie's room. Frau Körtner is still just as hard and implacable.

FREUD   Have you ever talked to Cäcilie again about the affair?
FRAU KÖRTNER   Never.
FREUD   Have you continued to hold a grudge against her for …

Frau Körtner shrugs her shoulders.

FRAU KÖRTNER   Pooh!
FREUD   Yet you don't love her?

Frau Körtner hesitates.

FRAU KÖRTNER   I could have loved her.

A long silence. Freud, who is looking at Cäcilie, turns towards Frau Körtner: her facial appearance has not altered, but tears are rolling down her cheeks. Silence. Not the faintest sob.
     She rises to her feet.

Are you planning to sit up all night with her?

FREUD   Yes.

FRAU KÖRTNER   Then please excuse me. I feel my nerves are failing, and I don't want to make an exhibition of myself.

I'll come back. In the early hours of the morning.

She goes out, without Freud making any move to detain her. We follow her into her bedroom. She sits down on a chair in front of her dressing-table, then suddenly lets herself go, plunges her head in her hands and begin to sob.

[30]

Little Mathilde Freud's bedroom.

She is playing serenely with her dolls, all alone, sitting on a little wooden chair. Suddenly, she gives a start: she has heard footsteps. She seems to be afraid.

(Sound of footsteps in the corridor.)

The door half opens; she is watching. Since the door opens inwards, we cannot see what she sees. But from the little girl's terrified eyes we can guess that it is some frightening spectacle.
The door opens wider: Freud appears. He smiles sweetly, unctuously, but his eyes have the maniacal stare characteristic of perverts in similar situations. The contrast between his smile and his eyes gives him a hideous expression.
Little Mathilde stands up. She remains pale and motionless, clasping her doll to her chest.
He advances towards her, very gently.

FREUD, *in a sugary voice*   How big you are! Good morning, my little wife.
When you were small, do you remember? You used to say: I won't marry anyone but Papa?
Well, we're going to get married, Mathilde. We're going to get married!

She tries to run away, he catches her roughly by the arm. In a brutal tone of voice:

You're my wife and my daughter: I have full power over you.

He presses her to him. At this moment, laughter we were barely able to hear — in the background — breaks out, ironical and relieved.

(Laughter off from Freud.)

It is Freud's laughter; but the Freud we see in the image, fierce and brutal, is not laughing.

(Louder and louder.)

The vision disappears as the laughter continues. And we find ourselves back in Cäcilie's room. Freud is laughing in his sleep.
But almost immediately the laughter wakes him up. He sits up on his chair, opens his eyes, looks around him and finally returns fully to his senses.
He looks relieved, almost cheerful. We have never before seen him wear this bold, calm expression. After checking that Cäcilie is sleeping peacefully, he fastens his gaze on the wall.
He still has a faint smile on his lips as his voice off tells us his thoughts.

FREUD'S VOICE OFF   That's it!
Did I want to seduce my poor little Mathilde?

(Forcefully:)

Certainly not!
Yet that dream hides some desire. What is it?

(A moment later:)

If *I* feel desire for my daughter, that means all fathers do.
I dreamed I was committing that sexual assault because I wanted my theory to be true.
It's false.
It's certainly false.

He stands up and goes over to the window; a very faint luminosity seems to indicate that dawn is about to break. He remains for a moment standing with his forehead against the window-pane, dreaming.

I wanted to sully my father's name. To degrade him.

(Abruptly:)

How about those thirteen cases?
Women … They were lying …
Why?

He turns round towards Cäcilie, whom we can see sleeping peacefully.

Because they were entertaining an unconscious desire. They'd have liked it to be true.
From her earliest childhood, Cäcilie was in love with her father …

(Almost angrily:)

What about me, then?

(A pause.)

There was that journey … that journey …

It is night — forty years before.
A very old railway carriage, crammed with passengers.
Jakob Freud, still quite young, is sitting beside Frau Freud, who is holding a two-year-old

367

child (Sigmund) on her lap. The train is passing some smelting-works, and we can see red flashes in the darkness.

The child, who was sleeping, wakes up and screams. The dozing passengers abruptly open their eyes.

FRAU FREUD   Sigmund! Sigmund, darling! Hush!

The child has seen his mother. He caresses her throat and chin with his little hand, then, satisfied, goes back to sleep.

Meanwhile, the train has arrived at a station. It comes to a halt. The passengers stand up and take their luggage down from the rack.

In front of a hotel reception counter; a sleepy clerk is unhooking two keys from the board.

JAKOB   No double rooms?

The clerk shakes his head.

(To his wife:)

You take the bigger one with the baby, I'll make do with the attic.

A little while later.

The child, tired out, is already asleep in the bed of a small hotel room. We are right beside him, at his pillow, and can see Frau Freud undressing in front of the washstand.

The hotel must be near the station: we can hear the puffing of locomotives and, suddenly, a violent whistle which wakens the child.

(Puffing of locomotives.)
(Sudden whistle.)

The child, his eyes open, and we — almost with his eyes — see in the distance, half in shadow, a tall woman with a very lovely figure slip off her last garments and, standing there naked, soap her face, shoulders and neck. Then put on a nightdress.

There is a knock at the door.

(Sound of cautious knocking.)

She hastily slips on a dressing-gown.

FRAU FREUD, in a whisper   Who's there?

She opens the door. Jakob appears.
He is aroused by the sight of his wife.

JAKOB'S VOICE OFF   How lovely you are!
    Do you love me?
FRAU FREUD   Yes.
JAKOB, *with an authority that is really very rare in him, and that is rooted in sex*   Do you
    belong to me?
FRAU FREUD   Yes.
JAKOB   Come! I've got the next-door room.
FRAU FREUD   I can't leave the baby on his own.
JAKOB   The baby?

He turns his head towards little Sigmund, who at once closes his eyes.

He's asleep.

(Aroused and insistent:)

For a moment. Just for a moment.
    Come!

He carries Frau Freud along and they go out, closing the door gently behind them.
    As soon as they have left, the child opens its eyes, flails the air with its little arms and begins to howl.

CÄCILIE'S VOICE OFF, *drowning the child's howls*   Doctor! Doctor!

31

The vision disappears. In Cäcilie's room. She has just woken up. She looks at him in anguish.

CÄCILIE   What are you thinking about?
FREUD   My past.
CÄCILIE   Did I try to kill my mother?
FREUD   Yes.

Or rather, it wasn't you who tried to do that, it was the child Cäcilie who came back from the dead and thought Magda was being sent away.

CÄCILIE, *disgustedly*   The child Cäcilie was a little monster.
FREUD   No. She was a child. That's all.

I've won, Cäcilie. Thanks to you, I think I understand both of us. And that I can cure us.

(*A pause.*)

Do you know the story of Oedipus?

CÄCILIE   He killed his father, married his mother and put his own eyes out, so he wouldn't be able to see what he'd done any more.

FREUD   Oedipus is everybody.

(*A pause.*)

I must talk to you a bit about myself.

In neuroses, I've viewed the parents as guilty and the children as innocent.

That was because I hated my father. It's necessary to reverse the terms.

CÄCILIE   It's the children who are guilty!
FREUD, *smiling*   Nobody's guilty. But it's the children who ...

At these words, the hotel room.
His mother opens the door softly, she glides noiselessly across to the bed.

I loved my mother, in every way: she fed me, she cuddled me, she took me into her bed and I was warm.

She slips between the sheets next to the child, after divesting herself of her dressing-gown; with his eyes closed and as if in his sleep, he cuddles up against her and clutches her round the neck with a jealous movement.

I loved her in the flesh.
Sexually.

The image disappears.
   We find ourselves back in Cäcilie's room.

CÄCILIE   You mean I was in love with my father?

He speaks as if to himself.
   He seems to be almost asleep.

FREUD   I was jealous of mine because he possessed my mother. I loved him and hated him at the same time.

Cäcilie listens to him, but translates as she does so: it is her own story she hears.

CÄCILIE   Jealous. Yes …
   It was her he loved. I was glad about Magda: he didn't care about her and at the same time it humiliated my mother under her own roof. I connived at it.
FREUD   He was kind and gentle, decent through and through.
   I reproached him for his weakness. I treated him in my mind as a coward.
   I'd have liked a father as strong and hard as Moses.

In a quite ill defined room, old Jakob, serene and gentle, sits on a chair with his pipe in his mouth.
   As Cäcilie's voice makes itself heard off, Frau Körtner, with an expression of profound sadness, comes and sits down on the other chair.

CÄCILIE'S VOICE OFF   She was unhappy. She seemed hard to me because she had to control her feelings all the time.
   I preferred Magda, who might be malicious but was affectionate to me.
FREUD'S VOICE OFF   I searched for other fathers: my teachers, my colleagues. As soon as they gave any sign of weakness, I'd abandon them. It was his weakness that I hated in them.

Freud's father and Cäcilie's mother appear to be listening to these confessions with a kind of mild benevolence.

I was jealous! Jealous! And out of jealousy I accused him of having been incapable of raising or even feeding his family.
   But it wasn't true: it was anti-Semitism that ruined him.
CÄCILIE'S VOICE OFF   My father had mistresses, but I was jealous only of her. Because he shared her bed. Magda drove me mad.

We see the child Cäcilie once more, in her bedroom watching Magda pack her bags. Magda has knelt down to close one of them.
   Tears are streaming down her cheeks. She speaks between hiccoughs of rage.

MAGDA   She threw me out and he didn't lift a finger. He's a weakling.

Do you know why she dominates him? Because she was dancing in the nude in some saloon when he picked her up. Look!

She rises to her feet, goes to fetch a roll of paper from another suitcase and hands it to Cäcilie, who unrolls it. It is the poster we saw previously.

He only likes prostitutes, that's his vice.

I can't put up a fight: I'm a decent woman.

Little Cäcilie looks at the poster.

CÄCILIE'S VOICE OFF   He only likes prostitutes! He only likes prostitutes!

I wanted to become a prostitute so that he would love me.

A sudden dreadful scream, followed by sobbing.

(Scream off from Cäcilie.)

Against the background of this scream and sobbing, the image breaks up. Another takes its place.
Frau Körtner alone, in the light barouche she is driving.
The sounds of the carriage (horses' hoofs, wheels turning, etc.) cannot blot out the sobbing.
The barouche (a single horse at the gallop) is bowling along beside a lake, on a fairly narrow road, twenty metres above the water. Suddenly the horse stumbles; Frau Körtner, far from pulling on the reins, lets go of them: without making the least move, she allows herself to be buffeted about by the barouche, which jolts along until eventually it overturns at a bend.
The carriage topples over towards the lake and Frau Körtner's body is flung out onto the slope descending to the water.
A bush checks her fall, but she is left unconscious.

(Scream off from Cäcilie:)

I've killed her! I've killed her!

Freud and Cäcilie in the bedroom. Freud is looking at Cäcilie, who just before seemed calmer, but who is now for the second time giving signs of violent emotion.
He stretches out his hand, in a brotherly gesture (the first time we have seen him do such a thing).

She threw herself into the lake three days after Magda left. She couldn't stand my knowing the truth.

Freud bends over her.

FREUD, *gently, tenderly*   It was an accident, Cäcilie.

CÄCILIE   It was suicide. She escaped death, but she wanted to kill herself. And I was the one who drove her to it.

I remember! I remember! For more than a year, I had fits of anxiety that I told nobody about. And then I forgot, but my physical disabilities began!

I'm a monster!

She has doubled up and is sobbing.
Freud touches her shoulder.

FRAU KÖRTNER'S VOICE OFF   It was an accident!

Cäcilie sits up with a jolt. Dawn is breaking. Frau Körtner has opened the door noiselessly and is looking at Cäcilie with a kind of serene benevolence.

I swear to you.

I never thought of killing myself. We're used to hardship in my family, and we live with our misfortunes.

With an ironical smile, but without malice:

On the day after our quarrel, I polished all the floors myself.

Cäcilie is looking at her with a mixture of fear and relief. To Freud:

Was that her neurosis, then?

FREUD   That was the fortuitous cause. She could no longer endure the idea that she'd driven you to suicide. Her body helped her to forget it.

Frau Körtner looks at Cäcilie with affection: the idea that her daughter was punishing herself for having harmed her seems to relax and please her.
Freud looks first at one, then at the other.

FREUD, *gently*   The thing now is to try to live.

He takes Frau Körtner's hand and places it upon Cäcilie's.

32

Six months have passed.

It is winter. Snow is falling. We are at Achensee, near the lake.
Two individuals (fur-lined coats, Tyrolean hats) are walking in the snow, and talking without regard to the weather.
They are Freud and Fliess.

FREUD   She's well on the way to being cured.

Freud is wearing an open, tranquil expression: he speaks calmly, with conviction but no passion.

The case is quite clear: Oedipal love for her father, jealousy of her mother, whom she wanted to kill. When she found out that Frau Körtner had been a prostitute, she had dreams and phantasies of prostitution to identify with her. All the more so because she'd been told: your father only likes prostitutes. At the same time, of course, she was repressing those desires deep inside her and they appeared to her consciousness only in symbolic guises.

Fliess listens with a sulky air.

On that notorious night when I found her on the Ring, she wanted to prostitute herself both in order to punish herself and in order to become the chosen mate of her dead father.

FLIESS, *tartly*   In short, you were mistaken?
FREUD   Totally. But I'm glad of it. That's what led to the whole thing collapsing.
FLIESS   No more traumatism, then?
FREUD   Oh, yes. That's the shock preventing the liquidation of childhood.
         In Cäcilie's case, it was Magda's revelations and her mother's false suicide.
FLIESS   Then the child's first relations with its parents are of a sexual nature?
FREUD   Yes.
FLIESS   So there is infantile sexuality?
FREUD   Yes.
FLIESS   Six months ago, you were saying the opposite.
FREUD   But this time I'm right.
FLIESS   What proof do I have of that?
FREUD, *slowly*   What proof do you have?

He stops and looks Fliess in the eye.

I'm cured, Fliess …

Fliess shrugs his shoulders.

FLIESS   You weren't ill.

FREUD, *calmly*   I was a hairsbreadth away from neurosis.

They walk in silence. Then Fliess suddenly explodes.

FLIESS   I don't believe it! Children being raped by perverted adults, that yes! That was something solid! A basis for my calculations. But I don't care two hoots about psychology. It's just words.

FREUD   Yes, words!

FLIESS   Your patients lie down on your couch, they tell you whatever they like, and then you come along and project into their heads whatever ideas you've got in yours.

They arrive near a railway-line.
    A child of about four comes out of a house and runs towards the station, which can be seen in the distance.
    Fliess points at the child with a shrug.

That little mite over there desires his mother and dreams of killing his father?

(Laughing:)

Luckily it's not true: otherwise I'd be horrified.

FREUD   Do you think it fills me with delight? But that's how things are. And we must say so.

During this conversation, Fliess grows more and more angry.
    Freud remains perfectly calm.

FLIESS   They've not done with laughing at you, in Vienna! One day, it's the father who ravishes his daughter; the next, it's the daughter who wants to ravish her father.

FREUD   Oh, they'll laugh.

FLIESS   Where does Science come into all that? It's nothing but cock-and-bull stories; I can't build anything on it. Thinking means measuring. Have you taken any measurements? Established any quantitative ratios?

FREUD   No.

FLIESS   Then it's all quackery!

FREUD   Take care, Fliess. You can talk of nothing but figures, rhythms and periods. But when it comes down to it, I wonder whether you don't tailor your calculations to produce whatever final results you've been aiming at from the outset.

Fliess stops dead.

FLIESS   What does that mean?

The road happens to be sloping up gently towards the station. As Freud has taken a step forward, Fliess finds himself slightly below him (which recalls — but in reverse — the scene at the Faculty, when Fliess, standing on the stage, towered above Freud).
   Fliess looks at Freud from below, but with a threatening air.

You no longer believe in what ... what we established together?
FREUD, *gently*   In what *you* established? I don't know.
FLIESS   Bisexuality, its two rhythms, their *absolute* importance in every human life — don't you believe in that any more?

Freud looks at him with distress and some astonishment, as if he were waking from a long and fascinating dream.

FREUD   If I didn't believe in it ... completely, any more ... or if my investigations led me into another world ... would we stop being friends?
FLIESS, *firm and unequivocal*   Yes. Friendship is work in common. If you're no longer working with me, I can't see what we're doing together.
FREUD   If I'm not working *under your orders*, there are still lots of things to do: see each other, talk to one another, give one another encouragement ...
FLIESS   And you really think I'd come from Berlin to the Achensee for that sort of idle chatter?
FREUD, *gently*   You're my friend, Fliess.
FLIESS   I'm your friend if you believe in me.
FREUD, *very warmly*   I do believe in you.
FLIESS   'Me' means my ideas. You believe in them or you lose me.

Freud looks at him. He hesitates for a moment.

FREUD, *sadly*   I don't believe in them.
FLIESS, *in the tone of one drawing the appropriate conclusion from Freud's reply*   Very well.

   (*A pause.*)

He points to the station. Ironically:

You'd better hurry. You'll miss your train.
FREUD, *quite naturally*   No, no. It doesn't go until three twenty-two.

He pulls out his watch.

I'm ten minutes early.
FLIESS, *taken aback*   Oh?

(A pause.)

You had only one father left, Sigmund. And I wonder whether you didn't come here with the intention of liquidating him.

Freud begins to protest. Fliess checks him:

(Ironically:)

Oh! an unconscious intention, as you would say.

Freud looks at him attentively.

FREUD   Perhaps.
FLIESS, *very coolly*   Well, it's done. Farewell.

He turns his back on him and goes back off down the road, through the snow. Freud follows him with his eyes, then continues on his way towards the station.

33

In the Freuds' drawing-room, the same day.

Freud, in the same costume, has just returned from his journey. Martha is alone. She kisses him.

FREUD, *tenderly*   Hullo, darling.
MARTHA   Did that congress of yours go all right?
FREUD, *in an absolutely natural voice*   Oh! yes, as usual.

(A pause.)

I'd like some coffee.
MARTHA   I've just made some. Here.

He follows her into the dining-room. A cup of coffee and a coffee-pot on the table.
He sits down. Martha pours for him.

FREUD   What's new?
MARTHA   Nothing much.

She has automatically picked up a duster and begins to dust the furniture.
Freud watches her with sad concern.

FREUD, *smiling to hide his concern*   Watch out, Martha. Like all house-proud women,
you're under threat from neurosis. Come and sit down.

Martha stands upright.
She smiles at him, but her face remains expressionless.
She does not sit down.

Well, then? No news at all?
MARTHA   Breuer lost his elder brother, the day you left. I don't think they really saw
much of each other. I think the funeral must be taking place just about now.
FREUD, *without the least expression*   Oh?

He unhurriedly finishes drinking his coffee.
Then he stands up and looks out of the window.

It's not snowing any more.

He turns back towards Martha.

I'll see you later.

MARTHA   Are you going out already?

FREUD   I'm going to visit Papa's grave.

34

The cemetery.

Freud is walking among the graves.
  In the distance, a group of people beside a newly dug grave: the coffin is being lowered in.
  Freud stops in front of Jakob Freud's grave.
  He is carrying a wreath, which he lays clumsily on the stone, amid flowers some of which are still fresh while others appear wilted.
  In the distance, the ceremony is over, most of the participants are dispersing. They pass along a paved walk not far from Freud.
  Breuer passes by with Mathilde Breuer. He glances towards Jakob's grave and sees that Freud, who has raised his head, is looking at him.
  Freud takes a step towards him. But Breuer has already turned onto the side path leading to Jakob's grave.
  The two men clasp hands.

FREUD   I only learnt ...
BREUER   Oh, don't ... My brother and I hadn't been on speaking terms for thirty years. I'm here purely for propriety's sake.

He goes up to the grave and looks at it.

I loved your father. His death grieved me more than Karl's ...
  How are you?
FREUD   Changed.

Freud points at the grave.

A part of myself is buried there.
  It's all my fault, Breuer.

He turns towards Breuer — calm, devoid of warmth, but utterly sincere.

BREUER   No.
  Cäcilie separated us.

He looks at the grave and lays one hand on the fence surrounding the stone.

And then ...
  I've often thought this, Freud: I saw myself as your spiritual father. And even though I'm not envious ... when I sensed that you'd go beyond me ... I ... that set me

against you and your ideas.

(With an ironical laugh.)

You looked like a young boy, whereas I felt like an old mother hen.
Pooh!

He shakes his head, to show it is all over.

How is Martha?

FREUD Martha loves her children, she's a wonderful housewife, and I think she loves me just as much as on the day we were married.

But there used to be something between us ... that will never come back.

Never again.

Please forgive me, Breuer.

Do you know that since the funeral I'd not dared revisit my father's grave?

I came back today because I was hoping to see you.

I've applied your method to myself, Breuer. All alone. And I'm going to continue.

I loved my father, but I was jealous of him. I couldn't even see him without feeling within myself a terrifying aggressiveness ...

BREUER Aggressiveness? Against a man as gentle as that?

FREUD Precisely. His gentleness disarmed me. I'd have liked a Moses as my father.

The Law!

BREUER So you could revolt against it?

FREUD And obey it.

Meynert played that role for a time.

He smiles.

It was ... a transference.

BREUER And did I do so too?

FREUD Yes. For ten years. I hated Meynert, who'd cursed me. For you, I had only love and respect. Meynert is dead, he begged for my forgiveness, that delivered me from him; you were my only father, the object of my dual feelings.

I thought you weak, and that drove me out of my mind with anger. But it wasn't your weakness I was hating, it was Jakob Freud's.

He points at the grave.

BREUER, *sincerely* I am weak.

FREUD No. You're kind.

BREUER How about Fliess?

FREUD A mirage. I took him for the Devil: he was just a book-keeper. No matter: I respected his strength — what I took to be his strength — and that allowed me to hate what I took to be your cowardice.

BREUER, *smiling*   What a lot of fathers! Most of the time, you had two of them at once.

With this remark, the two men disappear; we see Meynert once again in his study, feeble and timeworn, under the vast statue of Moses.

FREUD, *voice off*   Yes. I was afraid of myself, I refused to grow up. To look at the truth.

    I was perpetually tearing myself apart, Breuer: I was taking all those fathers to protect myself against myself, and I had no respite until I'd destroyed them.

    You all obsessed me and I wanted to kill my father in you!

We return to Jakob Freud's grave.

He's dead. And my adoptive fathers are buried with him. I'm alone face to face with myself and I no longer hate anyone.

BREUER   Will you be able to love again?

FREUD   Yes. My children ... and adopted sons — men who'll believe in my words — if any such can be found. I'm the father now.

    Breuer, I used you as a means to lose myself and to find myself. Will you forgive me?

Breuer takes his hand affectionately and clasps it in his. A silence.

BREUER, *gently*   I don't suppose we'll be seeing much of each other any more.

FREUD, *in a friendly tone*   Not much, no.

BREUER   You've won the right to be alone.

FREUD, *with deep sadness*   Yes.

He points to the sky: the clouds have disappeared; bitterly cold winter sun.

I'm alone and the sky has emptied.

    I'll work alone, I'll be my sole judge and my sole witness.

    Luckily we always die in the end.

Abruptly:

Breuer, I don't want my wife to be the victim of that solitude.

    She isn't happy; she worries me.

    Would you allow Mathilde to see her again?

BREUER   Mathilde asks nothing better: it was Martha who wouldn't see her, for fear of displeasing you.

FREUD   It would have displeased me ... once!

Jakob Freud made my mother happy.

(With a smile of melancholy humour:) But I can't believe it's much fun being the wife of Sigmund Freud.

BREUER   Mathilde will write to her this very day. Goodbye, Freud.

FREUD, *with friendly affection, but sorrowfully, as if the separation would be a very long one*   Goodbye.

Breuer moves away.

Freud remains alone before the grave. He does not turn round: his gaze is fixed upon his father's name (engraved on the tombstone). After a few moments, without his making the least movement to wipe them away, tears begin to roll down his cheeks. He stays there for a few moments longer, then turns round and walks towards the monumental gateway, between the graves, his eyes still moist.

VERSION II
(1959–1960)
— *extracts*

PART ONE

[In the first version, Cäcilie Körtner makes her appearance only when Freud is already established as a doctor in Vienna. In the second version, Freud enters into contact with her before his stay in Paris.]

[8]

Frau Körtner has remained quite motionless, upright and implacable: a statue.

But she takes advantage of the fact that Freud has lowered his eyes to scrutinize him from head to foot, without the least trace of sympathy. Neither does she display any real curiosity.

Freud does not interest her, that is all. He is poor. She studies him out of a habitual mistrust (which we can sense has deep roots).

She says nothing. There are more than fifteen chairs and armchairs in the room, but she does not invite him to sit down.

Freud, more and more ill-at-ease, strives to find a subject of conversation. But Frau Körtner is no longer looking at him and has moved over towards the piano.

She looks at the furniture with the same expression she wore when looking at Freud — mistrustfully, and in order to see whether the brasswork is shining and the furniture has been dusted.

Freud, too absorbed in his investigation, has not noticed her leaving her place. He raises his head and says (facing the spot where he believes her to be):

FREUD   Your husband ... er ... is indisposed.

Frau Körtner, continuing her inspection, replies without raising her head.

FRAU KÖRTNER   Yes.

A silence. Freud is in agonies. He has now realized Frau Körtner is at the far end of the room, so he turns towards her. In a final effort he says, understandingly:

FREUD   He must work very hard.

Frau Körtner is no longer concerned with her guest. She replies just as laconically, but with a kind of intense spite which — as we shall learn much later — is in fact directed at her husband:

FRAU KÖRTNER   No.

Freud, offended, raises his head and looks straight at her; his displeasure erases his timidity. But Frau Körtner is not even affected by his anger: she is unaware of it.

She adds, in a cold, calm voice:

I'll have some coffee brought in to you.

She is standing near a door. She opens it, goes out and utters her final words with her back turned:

Forgive me: I've got things to do.

Freud remains alone, bristling with rage. At first rooted to the spot, he grows bolder and crosses the room, looking at the furniture and ornaments with the greatest interest. But this interest has nothing aesthetic about it: it is more like that of a policeman searching for clues.

A footman — a tall fellow of about forty, in livery — opens the door just as Freud has picked up a little Chinese vase from a table.

He is carrying a tray (coffee-pot, sugar, a cup) which he deposits under Freud's nose, on the very table from which the latter has taken the vase. As he straightens up, the footman sees the vase in Freud's hands. He gives a warning scowl and says haughtily:

FOOTMAN   Fragile.

With this single word, he withdraws.

Freud, furious but intimidated, at once replaces the vase beside the tray.

This incident sparks off the explosion. Furious at his own docility, he suddenly grabs the coffee-pot, pours himself a cup of coffee, then, deliberately — and in order to reciprocate one show of discourtesy with a discourteous gesture of his own — extracts a cigar from his case, takes his box of matches and lights up. He then stands with the extinguished match in his fingers, searching for an ashtray. There are none. Whereupon, in a very offhand manner, he throws the match into the Chinese vase.

A few moments before, Cäcilie has entered the room through the French window. She observes Freud in silence, curiously but without the least sign of sympathy: she is shocked to see him light a cigar and throw the match into the vase.

But she seems still more shocked when Freud — more interested, as ever, by men than by furniture — sets down his full cup on the piano, installs himself comfortably in an armchair with his legs crossed, and looks at Herr Körtner's portrait, taking deep puffs on his cigar.

At this moment the camera, like Cäcilie herself, can see nothing of Freud but an abundant head of hair resting on the back of his chair. Above this head (Freud and the armchair have their backs to Cäcilie) copious wreaths of smoke are rising.

Cäcilie approaches noiselessly. She is an odd creature, at once charming and faintly monstrous. But it would be hard to put one's finger on the exact source of this monstrous quality.

Actually, it is due to the fact that this very beautiful, shapely girl is dressed like an adolescent. She herself behaves like a little girl; and though her ravishing face shows remarkable intelligence and exceptional sensitivity, it simultaneously displays a rather sly infantilism. In her arms, moreover, she is holding a huge doll.

When she is quite close to Freud, but still behind him, she says with a mixture of false naïveté and mischief (her aim is evidently to make this coarse person staring so impudently at Herr Körtner jump):

CÄCILIE   It's Papa!

But Freud does not jump. He raises his head slightly, turns towards the girl, casts her a cold glance and says, with provocative and studied indifference:

FREUD   Oh?

The two individuals clearly take an instant dislike to one another.
    She approaches to discover Freud sitting there with a frown. He straightens up slightly and looks at her with frigid interest. She, however, looks shiftily at him, with sly curiosity (that of a child rather than a young lady).
    She nods towards the picture.

CÄCILIE   Do you think I look like him?

Freud answers at random (and with deliberate terseness):

FREUD   Yes.

Cäcilie gives a laugh of gentle mockery (the laugh of a child of thirteen or fourteen: her manner seems childish — in other words, she is acting the child).

CÄCILIE, *ironically*   That's just what you shouldn't have said. I don't look like him at all. Take a good look:

Her eyes are black.

He has blue eyes. Hadn't you ever seen him?

Freud shakes his head and takes a puff on his cigar.

CÄCILIE   What do you think of that portrait?

Freud takes a fresh look at it.

FREUD   Somebody's very unhappy: if it's not your father, it's the painter.

With these words, he rises to his feet.

CÄCILIE, *curtly*   It's the painter.

Uneasy, all the same, about smoking in front of the girl, he again looks for an ashtray, does not see one, goes to stub out his cigar in his coffee-cup and throws it into the Chinese vase.
    He accomplishes these last actions provocatively, transforming his clumsiness into a challenge.

But Cäcilie does not allow herself to be disconcerted. She surveys him smilingly.

He turns back towards her and looks her up and down, still the policeman but to some degree imitating Frau Körtner's inspection. She is not embarrassed. Still hostile, however, she speaks to him in a soft, childlike, venomous tone of voice:

CÄCILIE   My name's Cäcilie.

A pause.
   (Her meaning is clear: You've got the particulars; all right, here's the name.)

I don't know what you're called.
FREUD   Sigmund Freud.

Cäcilie draws closer; she looks at him guilelessly, but we can tell she is preparing some really 'dirty trick'.

CÄCILIE   I wonder how old you are. Wait, I'll guess. Thirty-five.
FREUD   No.
CÄCILIE, *faintly surprised*   Thirty-eight?
FREUD   Twenty-nine.

He pulls a bulky watch from his waistcoat pocket, looks at the time and automatically raises his eyes towards the first floor.

CÄCILIE, *who has watched him doing this*   Twenty-nine. And already you've got your
father's watch?

Freud shakes his head.

Is he dead, poor man?

Same gesture.

No? Nor your mother?

Same gesture.

Well, then? You've no right to be so serious!
FREUD   I'm going to guess your age, Fräulein.

Pretending to reflect:

Thirteen? Fourteen?

Cäcilie, offended, takes a step back. In a curt voice:

CÄCILIE   Seventeen.
FREUD   Seventeen.

Medical scrutiny of Cäcilie.

Normal physiological development. Body has undergone puberty. You've no right to be so childish.

She stamps her foot.

CÄCILIE, *indignantly*   What insolence!

Freud touches the doll with his index finger; Cäcilie, with a brusque gesture, pulls it away and hugs it to her.

FREUD   You play with dolls.

She stiffens and acts the young lady.

CÄCILIE   I can speak English, Russian, Spanish and French fluently.
FREUD   A person can play with dolls in any language.

Cäcilie looks faintly distraught: he has put his finger on her little fad.

CÄCILIE, *belligerently*   What doll?

She cradles her doll (or rather her baby, a chubby boy who shuts his eyes when tilted backwards).

This is my son.

Its eyes are closed: she lifts the doll so that its eyes open and presents it to Freud.

CÄCILIE   Look at his eyes. China blue. Like Papa's.

She laughs and goes back to cradling it. The viewer must not at any time take her for a neurotic. He must ascribe her attitude to infantilism and defiance.
  Yet there is something very faintly suspect in her expression and tone of voice when she says: They're Papa's.
  At this point, Freud studies her with still greater curiosity. He has the air of some diabolical detective.
  Cäcilie is unsettled by his scrutiny. She changes her tone. Sullenly:

I'm only saying that for a joke. You don't like joking.

FREUD   On the contrary. It always gives more away than a person thinks.

Cäcilie shrugs her shoulders and pouts.

CÄCILIE   There you are: seriousness will be your downfall.

Very gay and carefree:

I've a cousin of your age who's always laughing.

FREUD   I've a sister of your age who never laughs.

They stand facing each other defiantly.

CÄCILIE   I pity her. Why?

FREUD   No time. Last year, she took a job as a maid in France and used to send all her wages back to my parents.

This is an admission that would normally cost Freud a great deal. But he senses that everybody, from Frau Körtner to the footman, sees his poverty and reproaches him for it. Out of sadism (even more than masochism) and wounded pride, he goes one better: he wants to compel these people to despise him utterly, in order that he may himself quite intentionally be the cause of their contempt (through his revelations about himself) and so in turn despise them more radically.

CÄCILIE   You're poor?

Cäcilie scarcely seems concerned.

You should have said so.

Freud points to his clothes (clean but worn and slightly outmoded).

FREUD   Anyone can see that.

CÄCILIE, *rather haughtily*   I don't see such things.

Cäcilie turns slightly away.

FREUD   Your esteemed mother notices them at once.

CÄCILIE   Before her marriage, she was poor.

(With a faintly suspect laugh.)

Very poor.

She picks up a watercolour from the piano and shows it to Freud.

There she is. At the age of twenty. She has the same serious expression as you.

FREUD   Poor people have no youth.

Here, by force of circumstance, Freud becomes a spokesman for all poor people.

CÄCILIE   Didn't you have one?

FREUD   No.

CÄCILIE, *gesturing at the portrait*   Isn't she adorable?

FREUD, *faintest hint of black humour*   Adorable: that's the very word.

Freud gives the slightest of bows.

CÄCILIE   If I reach thirty, I'd like to help poor people.

FREUD   Our thanks to you.

CÄCILIE   Oh, but by that time you'll be rich. You're a doctor, aren't you? And Dr Breuer's friend? Your career is made.

She looks at the portrait for a moment, then puts it down again.

CÄCILIE   It's funny, poor people who become rich! They're harder than we are.
    Dr Breuer has always had money, for his part, and look how kind he is. And yet he's a Jew.

Freud, who had eventually begun to relax somewhat, abruptly stiffens, sombre and hard.

FREUD, *curt, frosty tone of voice*   I'm one too. So what?

CÄCILIE   That's exactly it: I meant that it's all the more to his credit. It can't be much fun being Jewish, with all those people hating you.

Cäcilie assumes a naïve, childish voice, but one that is rather too self-possessed; she relishes this gaffe she is making (deliberately, of course). She surveys Freud with a limpid gaze and speaks solicitously, soulfully.

Papa says we shouldn't be anti-Semitic, and that there are some very good Jews: decent and patriotic and so on; he always mentions Dr Breuer, who's such a fine man.

Freud's gaze has become unendurable. She turns away, delighted but alarmed.

You have funny eyes. I wouldn't like to have you as my doctor.

FREUD   Set your mind at rest, Fräulein, that will never happen.

He bows; suddenly, he appears at ease and assumes his 'good manners'.

Would you be so kind as to inform my friend Breuer that I'll be waiting for him in his carriage?

He takes her hand, bends and kisses it.

Farewell, Fräulein.

Cäcilie snatches it away, shocked and alarmed (we shall see later that this salutation reminds her of a childhood memory).

CÄCILIE   It's not proper to kiss a girl's hand.

Freud touches the doll with his index finger.

FREUD   Of course. But you're already a lady, aren't you?

He strokes the baby's head.

Goodbye, little rich boy. Goodbye, you poor little goy.

He straightens up and goes out quickly.

[This scene follows the last one. It shows Freud reacting against the prevailing anti-Semitism.]

[9]

Breuer's barouche, outside the Körtners' villa.

Freud is smoking a cigar. He has retained the sombre, angry expression he was wearing in the Körtners' house, and seems to be sunk in his own reflections.

He does not notice that the door of the villa has opened and Breuer is hurrying towards him, with Frau Körtner. The latter retains her sour expression, but seems intensely embarrassed.

Breuer is looking unhappy, but there is a gleam of mischief in his eye.

BREUER, *unhappily*   What on earth happened, my dear fellow? You mustn't be cross with the poor girl: she's only a child.

He steps aside for Frau Körtner. Freud at once removes his hat.

Frau Körtner would like a word with you.

She makes her apologies haughtily, and without shedding any of her curtness.

FRAU KÖRTNER   You must forgive me, Doctor: my husband's condition was worrying me and I hadn't realized you were the friend ...
BREUER   The *best* friend.

Breuer interrupts her with a hint of harshness that is very rare in him. He is not displeased (as we shall see better in a moment) with the turn matters have taken, but he is nonetheless indignant (and astonished) at the way in which Freud has been treated.

Clearly, he must have rebuked Frau Körtner and asked her to apologize.

FRAU KÖRTNER, *docilely*   ... the best friend of our dear doctor.

(*Very much the woman of the world:*)

Next time he comes to dine with us, we should be delighted if you would accompany him.

Freud bows with stony politeness.

FREUD   It would be a pleasure, Madam, but I'm leaving tomorrow for Paris. As to the rest, I'm the one who should apologize: a poor Jew has no business in a family of rich Christians.

Visibly wounded likewise, Frau Körtner stands motionless and silent.
Breuer bows hastily. He more seizes her hand than she offers it him. He kisses it. She turns away and goes back into the garden. Breuer climbs into the carriage.

BREUER, *to the coachman*   Drive on.

The carriage passes between villas all resembling that of the Körtners. Freud looks at them all with a kind of loathing.

FREUD   Every one of them, all the same. I pity you.
BREUER   The Körtners aren't anti-Semitic, my dear Freud.
FREUD, *bitter irony*   Really?

> (*A pause.*)

You'd better watch out for that girl.
BREUER, *in surprise*   Why?
FREUD, *curt and vindictive*   Neurosis.
BREUER   Cäcilie?

This time, Breuer laughs heartily.

You say that because she teased you.
She's a child, that's all.

> (*He laughs affectionately.*)
> *Laying a hand on Freud's shoulder.*

You don't know children yet.

Freud remains sombre. Breuer stops laughing, casts a mischievous glance at Freud, who does not see it, and says to the driver:

Stop here. You can wait for us.

He climbs down from the carriage. To Freud:

I'm going to call on General Mathausen. It's only three hundred metres, let's go on foot.
FREUD, *bristling*   Breuer, I don't ...
BREUER   You can do as you please, but see how lovely the weather is: come with me

at least as far as the gate, you don't take enough exercise.

Freud climbs down from the carriage. They walk along side by side, past the gardens and the villas. (Children in the gardens; gardeners.) Sometimes, at an open window, a maid doing the housework.

A little while later, a big door swings open and a barouche emerges from a park (two horses), carrying an official personage in uniform and wearing decorations.

Freud and Breuer will stop for a moment to let it go by.

A moment later, Breuer turns towards Freud and says to him affably:

BREUER   You told Frau Körtner you were leaving us?

FREUD   I did.

Freud's countenance has changed: he no longer has that tortured face that used to betray his inner contradictions. His decision has been taken, this time, in the joyous intoxication of anger.

He has an inflexible, mean and almost gay air. For the first time, we see the true Freud, the one whom neither Meynert nor Martha has seen.

BREUER, *amused*   You've changed your mind again.

FREUD   Yes.

He smiles at Breuer.

But I won't change it any more.

BREUER, *with calm certainty*   I know.

FREUD   In the old days, they drove our family out of Germany. During my child-hood, they drove us out of Moravia. Tomorrow, they may drive us out of Vienna.

He looks at Breuer with an expression of passionate fury.

One can never be sufficiently bitter.

(Full of spiteful irony at his own expense:)

And I wanted to work my way up: student, Privatdozent, Professor. When they'd given me their title, I thought they'd accept me.

What gullibility!

He points to the villas with an expansive gesture.

Those people keep us in quarantine; they always will.

He smiles and points at himself:

I'd be the leper Professor, I'd have a bell to warn people I was coming.

The gate of a villa. He goes up to it: two children are playing on a lawn with a dog.

Their brothers hate us, they'll hate us. And when they have sons ...

One of the children, hearing this harsh, shouting voice, raises its head and looks uncomprehendingly at the stern finger that Freud is pointing at him.
He does not even know — doubtless — that Freud is a Jew, but he assumes a hostile, fearful air because of the latter's hostility.
The dog, alerted, bounds towards the gate, comes to a halt, fixes its eyes on Freud and begins to growl. Freud laughs mirthlessly:

Even their dogs are trained.

Breuer tries to drag him away, he resists for a moment. To the dog:

Yes, old fellow, that's right: a poor Jew makes a dainty dish. Never fear: one day they'll open the doors for you and you'll be allowed to get a taste.

Breuer manages to tear him away from the gate. They walk in silence.
The gate of another villa has opened; the barouche (which was mentioned earlier) emerges slowly and crosses the pavement with caution. Inside (it is open) we can see a man wearing decorations and in official costume (academician). Commonplace features. Blend of pride and authority.
The two friends stop to let him pass.

FREUD   Who's that?
BREUER   Hartmann-Asveet, Professor of Law, Aulic Councillor, Academician.

As the carriage passes slowly in front of them, Freud bursts out laughing.

FREUD   There's my career passing by.
     Don't you admire it?

Breuer, more reserved, nods smilingly.

I should say so! Christians have the right to be commonplace: the whole world belongs to them. And what do they have to prove: they *are* Humanity. At any rate, they think they are.

Turning towards the carriage, which is making a half-turn onto the roadway leading in to town:

How supremely comforting! I shall never be *that*: I *cannot*. It took two thousand years of Christianity to produce that bloodless bigwig.

Freud's voice off against a shot of the barouche moving away (horses at a trot).

He's a goy: the goys honour him because he reflects their own mediocrity.

We come back to the two friends resuming their walk.

FREUD   But me they wouldn't accept. I'd go to their homes, in my carriage with its two horses, they'd be all smiles, and when I'd left them they'd say to each other: 'For a Jew, he's not too bad.'

Violent:

I won't be a *good* Jew, an honorary goy.

Sombre:

To be like everybody else: sometimes that's my dream. Ruled out! Everybody else — that means the goys.
   If we aren't the best at everything, they'll always say we're the worst.
   Do you know that a Jew is condemned to genius?
   Seeing that I'm damned, I'll make them afraid. Since they reject me, I'll crush them. I'll revenge myself, I'll avenge all our people. My ancestors have bequeathed to me all the passion they used to put into defending their Temple.

Breuer listens to him contentedly, with an affectionate smile on his lips.

Do you have faith in me?
BREUER   Yes.
   I'm the only one — apart from Martha, I suppose — who knows your strength.

He puts the question for form's sake:

Meynert too?

Freud's face darkens slightly and he shrugs his shoulders.

FREUD   We shall see.

He stops for a moment, struck by an idea, and looks at Breuer in admiring astonishment.

Breuer, you brought me along on your rounds ... to restore me to my senses.

Breuer smiles without answering: it is an assent.
   Freud looks at him admiringly.

401

How wonderfully intelligent! You hardly say a word, but you know how to pull our strings.

Breuer's smile fades; he speaks with discreet melancholy.

BREUER   What do you expect: I'm just an honorary goy.

Pointing at the villas:

Those people adore me, but I can read the easy-going superiority of the Christian in the eyes even of their menservants.
   I'm never at my ease. Besides, when I play the part of the *good Jew* for anti-Semites, I have the feeling I'm betraying my brethren.
   That's another reason why I regret having abandoned a life of Learning.
   So there you are! I wanted to show you what awaits you. You didn't take long to understand.

Freud looks at him; he has an agitated, but almost gay, air.

FREUD, *little laugh*   Oh no.

They have arrived outside the general's villa. Over the entrance, an Austrian flag. A soldier on the perron of the villa, standing sentry.

BREUER   Come and see my general. A real anti-Semite, that one, a butcher.

Pointing to himself:

But it's a Jew who treats his gout.
FREUD   No. Your sham anti-Semites were quite enough for me.

He looks at Breuer seriously and with deep trust. He offers him his hand:

Encourage me to be of good heart.

Breuer takes his hand.

BREUER, *affectionately*   Be of good heart.

Breuer keeps hold of Freud's hand during the entire time he is speaking to him.

Perhaps there's nothing to be found there. But you'll become what you are: an adventurer, a damned soul. You're choosing the arduous road and I thank you for it.
FREUD, *in distress*   You'll write to me often? Every week?

Breuer, smiling, promises it with a nod.

I'm going to feel so alone there.

Freud recovers.

Goodbye. Go and visit your gout case.

He smiles at Breuer, turns on his heel and walks back past the villas.
    Breuer has put a finger to the bellpush and, before pressing the button, he looks at his friend (from behind) with an affectionate smile.

[The student Wilkie, who occupies only a fairly unimportant place in Version I, here receives a more developed role. An example of the burgeoning of Version II.]

[16]

The square in front of Notre-Dame.

Two or three weeks later, on a fine, cold December day, an omnibus has drawn up in the square and the two friends climb out.

Freud still has the same overcoat. He has grown thinner, he is nervy, but despite the rings under his eyes he appears in better physical and mental condition than in the last scene.

Wilkie, for his part, is wearing different clothes from those we have just seen on him. He is clearly very well off. He radiates self-confidence: he will be sustained until the end of the following scene by his absolute certainty of possessing the truth.

Freud and Wilkie climb down from the top deck. Freud walks quickly: he is in a hurry to see the portals and sculptures once more. Wilkie takes him by the arm and slows him down.

WILKIE   What is this church, Dr Freud? And why are you taking me there?

It is Freud's turn to struggle to drag him along. They both move forward very slowly.

FREUD   It's Notre-Dame, Mr Wilkie.
WILKIE   Dr Freud, you're a Jew and I'm a Protestant: what have we to do with this Catholic building?

Freud, full of sympathy for Wilkie, answers him with a seriousness whose humour escapes his interlocutor:

FREUD   We have to look at it.
WILKIE, *understanding*   Oh! Like a monument? All right.

For a moment he allows himself to be dragged along, then he halts at the edge of the central area, still quite a long way away. He looks Notre-Dame up and down, with pursed lips.

The thing is, I don't like that at all.
    God didn't create stone so that it could be made into lace.

Freud resigns himself to remaining for the time being on the area in front of the church. Wilkie looks for a moment, then gives free rein to his indignation. Pointing to the statues on the portal:

Those ... Oh!

Raising his finger:

Such indulgence towards evil: it's Papism's final twitch; immediately afterwards, decadence sets in.

FREUD, *irritated by this prattling*　　You've got cathedrals in England, and very beautiful ones too.

WILKIE, *with crushing scorn*　　Anglican, Dr Freud.

With pride:

But I'm a Presbyterian. Do you understand?

FREUD, *ironical but still polite*　　Poorly, since I'm a Jew.

WILKIE　　Yet it's simple. The Anglicans are the ones who go to Hell; the Presbyterians are the ones who don't.

FREUD　　I see!

He makes Wilkie cross the roadway and conducts him from one portal to the next, taking advantage of the sermon the latter has begun.

WILKIE　　Rejoice, Dr Freud!
　　Rejoice!
　　Sing Hallelujah, for the Jews will be chosen. Be sure of that.

Freud looks at one of the portals. He replies, still distracted:

FREUD　　Why?

WILKIE　　If God had wanted to damn you, he'd have made you an Anglican …

Some passers-by go past in the other direction. A shopgirl brushes against them, very provocative (they pay no attention). An elderly beau is hot on her trail.
　　Once again, the carvings on the portal.

SHOPGIRL'S VOICE OFF　　Old swine!

Wilkie turns round. The old man has attempted to clasp her round the waist. She swishes off, a living embodiment of offended Modesty.
　　Wilkie concludes his sentence with a forefinger pointed at the discomfited old beau.

WILKIE, *triumphantly*　　… or a Catholic!

The elderly beau inserts his monocle and looks at them with studied hauteur. He is about to speak. But Wilkie goes up to him and towers over him.

(To the elderly beau:) God will heed your wishes, Sir! In the pigsty of Hell, you'll be a

hog *ad aeternum*!

Freud drags him away.

What are we going to do?

FREUD, *pointing to the church's first platform*   Climb *up there*!

He drags him along.
    A stone staircase, just before it reaches the first landing.
    Freud is in front, Wilkie follows him. Wilkie is out of breath, but is speaking. Freud's breathing is normal.

WILKIE, *continuing his speech*   I'm afraid she may be a sow.

FREUD   Eh?

WILKIE, *still panting*   In Hell.

FREUD   Yes, but who?

WILKIE   The girl being pursued by a hog.

FREUD, *understanding*   Oh!

He starts to laugh. A younger and more spontaneous laugh than all his Vienna sniggering (even though it still has its roots in irony amd mockery).
    They emerge onto the platform.

WILKIE, **with impressive assurance**   In this world, the damned-to-be can sometimes recognize one another.

FREUD   They ought to form a club .

It is Wilkie's turn to jump out onto the platform. The sun dazzles them, as they emerge from the dark stone stairway. He blinks.

WILKIE, *sadly*   Dr Freud, your behaviour is exemplary. I'm only sorry that you don't believe in Hell.

FREUD   I believe in it very strongly. But I don't see it as you do.

He shows Wilkie a group of visitors leaning over the parapet. We see them only from behind; the wind tugs at their coats and skirts.

In any case, I don't like the French. Too small, too quick-tempered, too artful, too mean. Monkeys or pigs.

A young boy of ten is playing ball with his nanny. He throws it, she catches it and throws it back, and he traps it deftly in mid flight. This scene, given the height and the sacred character of the spot, seems at least out of place.
    Freud and Wilkie notice the roof attendant, who is just beside them. They look at him. This

attendant (grey moustache, no beard; a war pensioner — he has a limp) looks gloomily at the little boy's antics.

    He says, with melancholy indignation:

ATTENDANT   It's dangerous, isn't it?

He shakes his head gloomily.

Very dangerous. And that child comes back here every day.

Wilkie listens to him and sees his uniform.

WILKIE   Tell his nanny that!
ATTENDANT   I have told her.
WILKIE   Well then?
ATTENDANT   She answers that he comes from the mountains and enjoys playing only in high places.
WILKIE   Stop them coming here.
ATTENDANT   I can't, Sir, that's the worst thing about it. I can't, because she pays me five francs every day. And I'm a war pensioner: I don't have any right to refuse a contribution.
    Oh!

The child has stopped playing for the past few moments: he listens to them, angry and indignant. A moment later, he goes over to the parapet with a determined expression and throws his ball over the balustrade.
    The attendant grabs the little boy by the arm and speaks severely to him, but — in spite of everything — still like a respectful inferior.

How can you have the audacity, my young Sir, ...
CHILD, *grinning*   My nanny has got two more.

The nanny, smiling broadly, can indeed be seen in the distance displaying another ball.
    The attendant releases the boy and goes over to engage the nanny in animated conversation (which will end — whether we see this or not — with a gift of money that she will bestow on him). However, Wilkie has grasped the child by both arms; he lifts him up and shows him to Freud.

WILKIE   They get away with anything: there's Catholic education for you. Where I come from, my young friend, you'd have been whipped till the blood ran.

The child, frightened, pulls his head away. Wilkie thrusts his forward.

Look at his eyes: I can see the stigmata of vice.

(Terrifying to the little boy:)

I can see the lustful old man he'll become.

FREUD   In half a century.

WILKIE   What does it matter how long: that spool will unwind as it must unwind.

The child has begun to scream. The nanny stands up and comes over, with a calm but fierce expression, to seize him from the hands of Wilkie, who gives him to her unresistingly.
   To Freud:

Are you convinced? It's necessary to repress! repress! repress! The whip, the bit and the spur. How could we exist without subduing nature? You obviously don't believe in original sin.

FREUD, *sincerely*   Yes, I do.

WILKIE   But you don't believe in God?

FREUD   No.

WILKIE   Just fancy!

FREUD   In any case, I think the natural man is a bloodthirsty animal ...

WILKIE, *finger raised*   And a lustful one, Dr Freud! And a lustful one!

A fresh ball, thrown by the nanny — and which the child catches in mid air — just misses Wilkie.

Oh!

FREUD   Come!

He drags him to the edge of the parapet, they survey Paris.

It's beautiful.

WILKIE, *convinced*   Yes.

Freud drinks in the view.

FREUD   I like seeing things from on high. Did you know I was a climber? In Austria, I've been up all the mountains.

WILKIE, *with an indulgent smile*   Nearer to God.

Freud has leaned out: following his gaze, we can discern tiny, black human figures at the foot of the cathedral.

FREUD'S VOICE, *ironical*   Or further away from people!

He speaks without taking his eyes off the square. Gradually, the void over which he is leaning will become fascinating and vertiginous.
   He picks up the conversation that was begun, but then interrupted:

FREUD   I admire English education. You crush the instincts, you relegate them to the darkness; if they lift their heads, you gag them or break them. That makes real men. Adults. Worthy of the freedom they've won.

With a kind of exaltation:

My brother, who has lived in London for years, hasn't met a single anti-Semite.
   Yet I sometimes wonder ... Instead of denying those instincts, if we tried to get to know them.

Wilkie jumps.

WILKIE   Get to know them? Why on earth?
FREUD, *uncertainly*   Perhaps they can be used ...

The square, seen from on high, seems truly like an abyss.

WILKIE   The iron heel! The iron heel on the loins of the beast. That's all. Whoever thinks himself stronger than other Christians, whoever imagines he can look the beast in the face and subdue it, he shall be doubly damned. For his pride, first of all. Then for the demoniacal fascination that pagan pleasures will exert upon him!

Freud does not reply. Wilkie turns towards him. Freud is pale, with huge eyes that appear almost mesmerized; he has collapsed against the parapet and is clinging onto it.

WILKIE, *in astonishment*   What's the matter?
FREUD   Nothing. Hold me up: I can't stand looking into the void any longer.

Wilkie holds him up: he almost carries him in his Herculean arms. Freud leans for an instant against a wooden hut placed in the middle of the platform (it is the hut of a restoration contractor). He 'recuperates'. Before long, he laughs in amazement.

Do you know what the matter with me was? Vertigo.
   A mountaineer!
   It's the first time in my life.

Wilkie has positioned himself between Freud and the parapet, to shield him from the view.

WILKIE, *solemn and triumphant*   You've seen the Devil, Dr Freud. He's Lord of the Abyss.

Gesture at the square, at the foot of the church.

He was awaiting you, at the bottom of that yawning gulf; just as he awaits you at the

bottom of your own self.
Let that serve as a warning to you.

Freud's face grows harder and darkens during Wilkie's speech. He grits his teeth and says with a brusque, determined air — the same one he had after his visit to the Körtners:

FREUD   The Devil, really?
Let's see if he's as strong as people say.

He eludes the astonished Wilkie, jumps onto the rim of the parapet and, in spite of the wind, walks the entire length of one side.
The little boy stops playing; he is highly entertained.
The attendant — who is at the other end of the parapet — rushes over as soon as he sees Freud balancing on the balustrade.

ATTENDANT   Everybody's mad, this afternoon.

Wilkie's iron grasp restrains him.

Let me go: if he falls, I lose my job.
WILKIE, *in an undertone*   He will fall if you speak to him.

Freud jumps nimbly down. He seems satisfied. His eyes are shining, his cheeks have become rosy.

FREUD, *to the attendant, very politely*   Forgive me: it was a stupid wager.

He turns towards Wilkie, who has not recovered from his astonishment.

It's the Devil who lost.

[Freud in his family circle, worried about his future.]

[24]

Evening of the same day.

The main room, which doubles as drawing- and dining-room. In Jakob Freud's apartment.

The room is quite large, but dingy and poor (straitened circumstances rather than absolute penury). The furniture is sparse and ill-assorted (cane armchairs stand next to a shabby easy-chair). The sideboard, on the other hand, is a commonplace modern piece. At the far end, two windows; not against the wall but quite some way away from the room's geometrical centre, between the two windows, a fairly large oval table covered with a checkered oilcloth. No carpets. Jakob is sitting in a big rocking-chair, set at an angle to the table upon which he has laid down an almanac. From time to time he very gently imparts to the chair a slight rocking movement. A blanket is wrapped round his legs and half his body. He has aged since we saw him at the station. His complexion is waxy. His nose somewhat pinched. Nevertheless, with his snow-white beard against that very pale face, he has the unconscious majesty of a patriarch.

Mitzi, Frau Freud and Martha are clearing the table and washing up: the open door allows them to shuttle continually back and forth between the kitchen and the living-room: they are in no sense absent and never stop listening to, or taking part in, the conversation. The camera must be able to follow them right into the kitchen. It is Mitzi who clears the table; she removes the last plates and the fruit basket, then, with a brush, she sweeps the crumbs and morsels of food remaining on the table into some improvised receptacle (for example, a plate or the bread-basket). When she carried what she has just removed from the table into the kitchen, she finds Frau Freud washing up, while Martha, at least initially, seated on a stool with a coffee-mill between her knees, is busy grinding coffee for the Freuds and for Breuer, who has not yet arrived.

Freud is the only person — apart from his father — not to leave 'die gute Stube'. Apparently, the two men are conversing while the women work. But in fact Freud, embarrassed to remain seated next to his father and meet his eye, walks up and down in front of the old man. He tells the whole family about his problems with Meynert. He appears deeply upset, and is very obviously on edge: any interruption, especially when it comes from his father, makes him jump.

Mitzi takes the receptacle full of crumbs off to the kitchen, not without having first cast an ironical glance at her brother. We follow her and discover, at the same time as she sees them, Frau Freud at her washing up (back turned, standing in front of the sink) and Martha in profile busy grinding. It is at this moment that Freud's voice reaches us.

FREUD'S VOICE OFF   He'll drive me out of medicine just as he drove me out of scientific life: it's an excommunication.

Martha seems haggard: she believes what Freud is saying. But his mother, still facing the other way, gives a loud, unperturbed laugh.

FRAU FREUD, *without turning round*   I suppose he'll put it in the papers: 'Austrian patients, don't go to Dr Freud'?

(With the calm assurance that makes her presence so soothing to Freud:)

He'd need a very long arm!

Mitzi empties the contents of her receptacle into the rubbish bin. She goes back into the room. During the continuation of the dialogue, she will take the coffee cups, the sugar bowl, etc. from the sideboard and place them on the table (the first cup is for her father).
     Her return to the living-room discloses Freud to us, pacing before his father with his hands clasped behind his back and head bowed.

FREUD'S VOICE OFF   He can do anything!
     I shall leave Vienna!

It is obvious that Freud is wantonly exaggerating Meynert's power and ill-will. Mitzi out of animosity, Frau Freud out of almost mystical faith, do not believe him. Martha half believes him (she is the one who understands him best at this moment). But poor old Jakob takes his son's declarations as articles of faith. He will follow his son's pacing like a spectator at a tennis match. He has an air of consternation.

JAKOB, *utterly crushed*   You mustn't ... What will become of you, my poor child?

Freud, pacing the room, has arrived at the right-hand wall; he makes an about-turn and continues, without looking at his father:

I'll sell cloth.

These words shatter Jakob, who has done everything to ensure that his son will become an intellectual. Raising a hand, he shouts out:

JAKOB   Not that!
     It was all right for me — and, as you see, I didn't succeed any too well.

With a gesture to indicate the poverty of the room.

But *you!*

Mitzi is looking angrily at Freud. She shrugs her shoulders slightly as she comes back to the table.

FREUD   Well, I'll be a country doctor. Pity poor Martha!

In the kitchen, Martha protests rather tartly, because she can sense the exaggerated character of these statements.

MARTHA, *shouting a bit to make herself heard*   I love the country, there'll be no need to pity me.

MITZI, *laughing uncharitably*   Especially since you'll be staying in Vienna.

Freud turns furiously towards Mitzi; he looks at her, his brows lowered, like a bull. Jakob, who has noticed nothing, questions Freud gently, almost humbly, with very great anxiety.

JAKOB   Please explain to me, dear child, this Meynert knows so many things ... If he's not good, who can one expect to be?

Freud turns away from Mitzi and gives up the idea of saying anything to her. But he does not answer his father either. It is obvious that Meynert's goodness is the least of his concerns. He shrugs his shoulders and goes back to his pacing (from the right-hand to the left-hand wall). Mitzi waits for a moment, then, convinced he will not reply, she frowns, positions herself behind Jakob's arm-chair and speaks in a clear, hard tone of voice:

MITZI   Our father is speaking to you, Sigmund.

Freud stops without turning round. Annoyed, and violent — but to Mitzi:

FREUD   What do you want me to say to him? I've no idea.

Jakob, with a somewhat smug air that he allows himself only when speaking of his Sigmund.

JAKOB   At all events, he lacks judgement.

Freud, astonished and offended, turns clear round, this time towards his father.

FREUD   Eh?

JAKOB   He was incapable of recognizing your value.

FREUD, *violently*   That's because I don't have any.

He starts pacing again. Taken aback, old Jakob falls silent. Freud feels vague remorse: when he reaches the left-hand wall, he makes an about-turn but this time makes his way to his father's chair and plants himself in front of Jakob. Yet he cannot bring himself to look at him. More conciliatory:

You'd need to have known him: he's renowned for the sureness of his eye. And as for his judgement, in the hospital he sometimes makes his diagnosis simply at a guess — and the diagnosis is accurate.

With solemn respect:

He's a great mind.

JAKOB   If he knows you, my Sigmund, he must be jealous of you: you're younger than he is and you'll go further.

Freud laughs bitterly.

FREUD   Jealous! Jealous of me!

A pause. He makes an about-turn and resumes his pacing.

I'm a rat; he's a Golem. I made the mistake of squeaking. Yesterday evening. He noticed me 'Hey, a rat!' A stamp of his heel: 'Squashed the creature! Good riddance.'

Jakob is utterly crushed by this fit of 'self-deprecation', of which he can understand nothing.

JAKOB   Listen ...
FREUD, *interrupting him*   It's true!

Mitzi lays a hand on her father's shoulder as if to protect him.

MITZI, *irritably*   If only you'd let our father speak, instead of spending all your time contradicting him!

Freud has stopped, taken aback. The fact is that he cannot at this moment bear anyone either attacking or defending Meynert: his humiliation and his respect are making him almost crazy; he is possessed by the most contradictory emotions.
     But Jakob has not noticed this violence or else he is unconcerned by it. He raises his pale hand and lays it on his daughter's. Mitzi has laid her hand on Jakob's left shoulder. (The latter has laid his right hand on that of Mitzi.) Jakob is utterly sincere. He speaks with no trace of irony.

JAKOB, *calming Mitzi*   You must listen to Sigmund, my dear.

     (His voice remains amiable, but it is cooler when he is speaking to Mitzi.)

We don't know these gentlemen, Mitzi, and we cannot understand them: they are men of learning.

     (With a simple, kindly little laugh — modest without being humble:)

While we're just donkeys.
     That Professor Meynert, you used to love him, Sigi.

Freud twists his head nervously and groans: this conversation is unbearable to him. Without the least bitterness:

Once you called him your spiritual father.

Freud loses his self-control, at this memory: he forgets that he is in Jakob's presence.

FREUD, *bitter and slightly demented laugh*   Well, I'm an orphan.

Spreading his hands as if he were dropping some object:

No father left at all!

Mitzi stiffens and stares indignantly at Freud. Their mother, in the kitchen, turns round serenely, advances to the doorway and in a tone of voice that is calm but stern:

FRAU FREUD   Sigmund!

Freud comes to his senses: he grasps the enormity of what he has just said and tries to make amends. But it is stronger than him: he cannot turn towards his father, and it is Frau Freud whom he addresses:

FREUD   Father will forgive me. He knows I'm unsure of myself: I need a master.

Jokob has turned towards his wife and speaks to her mildly.

JAKOB, *to Frau Freud*   He's right. Begetting isn't enough. The true father takes his son at birth and guides him to manhood.

Deeply moved, filled with remorse, still gentle but seized by a terrible, old man's sorrow:

I didn't know how ... couldn't — I married too late; I became too poor; I remained too ignorant.

With a little distressed gesture of his left hand:

And there you are.

His eyes have filled with tears which will not flow. The three women seem overwhelmed. Mitzi, with a kind of scream of anger, abruptly pulls away the hand she had laid on her father's shoulder, runs across the room, opens the left-hand door and vanishes, slamming the door behind her.
    Freud, his legs apart, motionless, his eyes fixed on the floor, has not moved a muscle.
    Luckily, a ring on the doorbell comes to break the tension. Frau Freud quickly crosses the room and goes to open the main door (which leads directly onto the landing). It is Breuer. Freud has given a start and turned round, but his perturbation is so deep that he has not had the presence of mind to go and open the door. Breuer holds his top-hat in his hand. He bends over the hand which Frau Freud proffers him and kisses it respectfully, then goes in a lively manner towards Jakob. He

is carrying a packet, which he puts down on the table.

BREUER   There's some Dutch tobacco for your pipe. How are you?

Jakob smiles at him with an expression of trust and gratitude.

JAKOB, *sincerely*   Quite all right. It's Sigi who worries me.

Breuer has put his top-hat down on a chair. He turns towards Freud and smiles at him. Freud smiles back at him affectionately.

BREUER   I've been told the whole story.
JAKOB, *very worried but trustful*   Is it . . . is it serious?

Breuer has come to reassure the whole family. He speaks gently, but with strength and conviction.

BREUER   Of course not!
JAKOB   My son says he won't be able to practise any longer.
BREUER   Haven't you noticed, my old friend, that your son is a bit crazy?
     I don't know what's happening: all Vienna is ill, the doctors don't know which way to turn. I've got twice as many patients as I can look after.
     I'm glad your son is starting a practice: he's the only colleague I have any confidence in. We shall share our clients.

He puts his arm round Freud's shoulders.
     The two women and Jakob look gratefully at him.
     Freud, moved, suddenly radiant, but at the same time embarrassed, turns towards Breuer. They are very close to each other, and face to face. But of course this fondness must — at least in appearance — exclude any homosexual affection.

FREUD, *filled with gratitude and confusion*   Breuer!
     (To the two women:) You understand I cannot accept.

Breuer lets go of Freud's shoulder, goes over to Jakob, pulls up a stool (whose seat is a little lower than Freud's father's), and sits down next to him (not facing him, but by his side). He is the only person, when it comes down to it, who addresses Jakob as a real head of the family, and quite straightforwardly: the others only pretend.

BREUER   My dear Jakob, listen to me.

One would think he was trying to convince him, as if Jakob still had the right to decide in Sigmund's place.

I'm the cause of everything.

I pushed your son into going off to France.

When he took the train for France, I told myself: whatever may happen, I'll answer for it.

Forcefully:

I am answering for it!

My practice is his. As for science ...

In Freud's direction, with a mischievous smile:

That laboratory is a symbol and Sigmund knows it.

In a little while I shall have another proposal to make to him.

He turns back to Jakob. Warmly:

We shall have work, never fear.

A long silence. Sigmund, eyes lowered, chewing his moustache, looks at once furious and happy. Breuer seems embarrassed himself by this mute gratitude; he leaps at the first subject that comes to mind.

And ... and your leg? How is it?

He tries to stand. Jakob puts a hand on his shoulder and compels him to remain seated.

JAKOB, *without paying any attention to this last question*   Sigmund, take the other stool and come and sit down here.

Freud raises his head, somewhat distraught. His mother, from the kitchen door, continues with gentle authority:

FRAU FREUD   Sigmund! Did you hear?

Freud, absent-mindedly — but not without revulsion — pulls up a stool next to his father and sits down. These two tall men are somewhat comical, though not ridiculous, on their stools, with their long legs and their knees at the level of their chins. Old Jakob is a head higher.

At first, smiling and familiar. Slapping Freud — who endures this contact with no pleasure — on the shoulder:

JAKOB   God has been too good to me.

When he was only three, I'd already realized there was more intelligence in his tiny shoe than in my entire body.

I've never been able to follow him.

That world of learning seems so hard to me ... and Sigmund is so young!
He'll be broken!

Breuer, I give you my son. Treat him as I should have liked to treat him. With
your help, he'll not fear anything.

*Freud has stiffened. Everybody is slightly embarrassed by this transfer of power. In Jakob, there is
in fact a mixture of senility and deep goodness which makes his words always inopportune and
embarrassing, without their ever being ridiculous.*

BREUER   My dear Jakob, you're ageing me: I'm only sixteen years older than he is.
(He laughs.) Meynert and Josef Breuer, don't you think that makes rather too many
fathers, old friend, for the son of Jakob Freud?

*Glance from Breuer at Freud, who seems terribly ill-at-ease, and at Frau Freud, who smiles at
him as if encouraging him to pacify Jakob by accepting. Breuer pronounces these words with the
evident intention, if he accepts, of first asserting Jakob's inalienable rights.*

JAKOB   Of the three, you're the only one who's worthy. Accept, I beg of you. I'm ill,
as you know, and I worry about him. If he's in your hands, I'll feel less remorse.

*Breuer searches for a formula to reassure the old man without reverting to the subject of ceding
paternity. But all of a sudden, after a glance at his mother, Freud rises to his feet, stiff and formal,
even paler than Jakob. He bows stiffly, almost clicking his heels, and speaks painfully, in a broken
voice but one which to the end remains deferential and courteous.*

FREUD   I owe everything to you, Father, and I know it.

When I was born, you were rich and it was the anti-Semites in Bohemia who
drove us out of Freiberg and took all your money. You have been and always will be
the exemplary Jewish father. But don't worry: I'll obey you.

Turning towards Breuer — who has remained seated— and smiling affectionately:

Dr Breuer will have the authority over me that you have been pleased to give him.

[Freud with Karl, the old general's son. The scene is the counterpart of the one (19) in Version I, but the treatment is very different. We give the scene here as an example of the divergent orientation that Sartre's work can take, even when the subject and situations remain the same. It could also be compared with certain scenes in *Les Séquestrés d'Altona* (Franz and the dummy).]

[29]

In the same apartment: on another floor.

Door, at the end of the corridor. Fritz, bending over a lock, inserts a key, turns it and opens the door. A large room appears, which serves as an office and a dining-room.

It contrasts with the room we have just left, thanks to the discreet, sure, very feminine taste (is it the young man's or his mother's?) which has presided over the furnishing (German rococo furniture and hangings). The ensemble, lit by three oil lamps, seems all in all very gay. Vast glass-fronted bookcase full of books. A large desk.

FOOTMAN'S VOICE OFF   When the Doctor is ready to leave, the Doctor has only to
ring.

In front of the desk, something utterly out of place — the only thing — a female dummy (a bust on a varnished ebony stem). On top of the bust, in place of the neck, a kind of appendix in polished ebony which takes the shape of an inverted pear standing on a disk.

On this bust, a red Austrian uniform jacket (that of a general) and a general's kepi. The jacket, far too broad in the shoulders, hardly stays up on the dummy. One button of the uniform is inserted into a buttonhole — not the one corresponding to it, but the one immediately above — in such a way as to reduce the jacket's girth and enable it to stay up on the dummy.

A man of about thirty, dressed in black, is sitting on a chair and huddling into the right-hand corner of the far wall, as if to be as far from the door as possible and also like a child in disgrace. When the door opens, we think we are seeing Freud himself: the beards are trimmed and the hair cut in a virtually identical way in the case of both individuals. As Freud approaches Karl, however, we see the differences grow sharper and blot out the similarities. Karl's hair and beard are lighter in colour: dark chestnut. The features of his face are fine but somewhat soft, his lips are thick and in other circumstances might appear sensual. But, above all, their attitudes are quite different. Karl's shoulders are hunched; his gestures are easy, deft, effortlessly polite, but he makes them out of habit and almost reluctantly; we can sense that he feels a perpetual urge to drop his arms. Above all, the ardent gaze that Freud has fixed upon him encounters only mournful eyes expressing an infinite grief. Freud enters the room, looking round for Karl. The latter at once rises to his feet and politely comes over to meet him. Apart from the incurable sadness of his gaze, nothing indicates that he is mentally ill.

(Sound off of a key turning and relocking the door.)

KARL, *approaching*   Dr Sigmund Freud?

He takes Freud's hand in both his own and presses it warmly. Freud appears astonished. Karl speaks affably: in recognizing Freud, he has managed for a moment to escape from the circle of his worries.

You don't recognize me but I know you: I saw you at Professor Brücke's. Oh, you were already in your second year. He was talking to you about your future; he was advising you to establish yourself, to build up a practice. And you, you were refusing.
That struck me so forcibly. You had such good reasons ...
And there we are.
You wanted to be a scientist and you're only a doctor.
I wanted to be a doctor and I'm only your patient.

(Wretched smile.)

That's life.

But at once he relapses into his habitual grief. The 'you're only a doctor' is not insolent: on the contrary, it is a certain way of linking Freud's supposed disappointments to his own misery.
Freud has remained impassive: he has not even frowned. He studies the patient intently; he examines his every gesture and article of clothing like a policeman looking over a suspect. From time to time his gaze moves away and travels round the room as if searching for clues there.
But what distinguishes him from a policeman is his neutral air, devoid of mistrust, almost benevolent: he is not dealing with a rival or enemy but with a patient, and we sense that he is determined to give him of his best. For the first time, we must sense the couple relationship between mental patient and doctor.
His eyes are drawn to the uniform and kepi on the dummy.

FREUD, *pointing to the uniform*   What's that?

Karl replies carelessly and without turning round:

KARL, *very naturally*   It's my father's uniform.
FREUD   He was a colonel?
KARL, *imperceptible irony: we cannot tell if it is directed at Freud and his ignorance of ranks or at Herr Schwarz:*   A general, Doctor!

(In a very simple tone:)

It's an honorific title the Emperor gave him, when he was responsible for the Under-secretariat of War.

Freud goes over to the dummy and looks at it.

(*Sharply:*) Don't touch it.

(*Natural tone. Apologizing:*)

Forgive me: it's too big for that bust. If anybody touches it, it falls off.

Freud, with his back turned, continues to look at the dummy. Without turning round:

FREUD, *neutral voice*   Your father has told me that you tried to stab him.
KARL, *in a faint, sombre voice, but firmly*   That's correct.

Freud turns round swiftly. Since Karl has turned towards him in order to reply, they find themselves face to face. Freud takes a step towards Karl and looks him in the eye.

FREUD, *not harshly, but with intensity*   Why?
KARL   I don't know.
FREUD   Were you angry?
KARL   No. (*Trying to be helpful:*) Well, yes. When I tried to stab him. Not beforehand. Nor afterwards. (*A pause.*) It was an ... impulse.
FREUD   An impulse? Have you had others of that kind?
KARL   Of what kind?
FREUD   Homicidal?
KARL   Never. I'm not a violent person, Doctor. Of course, my mind often isn't free. There are things I *have* to do.

(*With sincere revulsion:*)

But not that!
FREUD   What, for example?
KARL   I have to count.

(*Little apologetic laugh to show the foolishness of his pastimes.*)

When you came in, I counted the buttons on your jacket.
FREUD   And then?
KARL   I multiplied by 22 and divided by 3.
(*Mirthless laugh:*) I know my ailment.

He goes over to the bookcase, takes out a large volume on mental pathology and shows a chapter (pages dog-eared). Freud is able to read: 'Obsessional neurosis'. Freud gives the book back without comment, Karl goes and replaces it in the bookcase: we can tell that he is a meticulous, orderly man. He questions Freud, his back turned:

You've come to have me committed?

Freud does not answer. Karl turns back towards him. He is ashen.

Fritz told me. It's my sister who's insisting on it, isn't that right?

He awaits Freud's reply, which does not come. A hint of resentment:

She loathes me.

   (But at once he is seized anew by his feeling of guilt.)

I know I deserve a punishment. Parricide ... there's nothing worse, is there?

He has spoken firmly, looking Freud in the eye. And it is Freud, ill-at-ease, who turns his gaze away. Karl insists:

Is there?

FREUD, *in a strange tone, at once stern and perturbed*   Nothing!

KARL, *very sincere*   You see, I plead guilty, I'm horrified by myself. But I've seen asylums when I was a student. If I've got to be committed, tell me straight away: I'll kill myself.

FREUD, *gently*   That's blackmail, Sir, and you won't gain anything by it.

KARL   Isn't it enough to keep me under lock and key?

FREUD   And what if you strike the servant who brings you your meals? You'll be committed instantly, with the aggravating circumstance that you'll really have killed someone.

KARL, *astonished*   The servant? Why on earth should I attack the servant?

Karl's astonishment should strike both Freud and the spectator forcibly. Freud should be roughly thinking: if he really does not know why he attacked his father, if his action really seems absurd to him, he should not be astonished at the idea that he could kill anybody.

   Freud looks attentively at Karl. This time it is Karl's turn to drop his eyes. He goes over to the table, picks up an ivory paper-knife and starts tapping the table with it (groups of sounds, almost like Morse). He picks up an open newspaper from the table: it is the Medical Bulletin. A six-line paragraph has been circled in red ink.

Couldn't you cure me?

He holds out the paper to Freud, who refuses to take it.

FREUD   I've already received it.

KARL   It's the summary of your lecture. I haven't read anything so enthralling for over ten years.

FREUD, *sardonically*   Six lines: you're very kind.

KARL   I find a reason to hope there.

Freud's eyes suddenly shine. He cannot disguise his excitement.

FREUD   Do you want me to hypnotize you?

KARL   That's just what I want.

FREUD, *objectively*   Only today, I attended some experiments proving that hypnotism is a valid therapy for hysterical patients.

But I have *absolutely no idea* whether the method is applicable to obsessional neuroses.

These words are spoken in a neutral voice: Freud is seeking to warn the patient, in order to maintain an easy conscience whatever may occur.

KARL   Try it on me: you'll see then.

FREUD   That was my intention, before I ever entered this room.

This admission is made very cordially. But at once the tone changes: Freud goes up to the patient and his imperious voice betrays his fierce need to dominate.

But I warn you: I shall leave at once if you don't put your trust in me *completely*.

You must surrender yourself to me like a child.

KARL, *submissive and full of hope*   Like a child, I swear.

For a moment, Karl seems radiant: his acute anxiety and feeling of guilt give him, conversely, a need to be dominated. To surrender himself is all he asks. From their exchange of looks, we this time gain a radical insight into the bond between patient and psychiatrist (and into the genesis of transference and counter-transference). This image must be powerful enough — and, in a certain way, disturbing and disagreeable enough — for us to recall it when Freud, much later, broaches the problem of transference. And the unpleasant thing about the couple which has just formed is precisely the very faintly homosexual appearance of domination and submission.

Freud takes Karl by the arm, leads him to the bed-settee standing against the bookcase, and with a light pressure of his fingers wordlessly compels him to sit down and then stretch out on it. Karl obeys.

FREUD   Loosen your tie.

Clasp your hands together.

Fingers laced.

Freud places the index finger of his left hand on Karl's nose, between his eyes.

Look at my finger.

Karl squints slightly, binocular convergence, towards Freud's finger.

Very well.
    Now you are going to sleep ...
    Sleep.
    Sleep.
    You are sleepy.
    Sleep.
    Your eyelids are heavy, heavy.

Karl's eyelids blink slowly.

They are going to shut.
    They are shutting.

Karl has closed his eyes.

You are asleep.
    You cannot separate your hands.

Karl tries and does not succeed.

You can't any longer, because you're asleep.
    Sleep deeply.
    Deeper.
    Deeper!

Freud has been bending over Karl for the past few moments — giving him orders in an undertone. Now, satisfied, he straightens up, goes to fetch a chair, pulls it up to the bed and sits down. He asks his questions in a normal voice, quite loud and imbued with gentle authority.

The day before yesterday at lunch-time, where were you, Herr Karl?

KARL   In the dining-room.

FREUD   What did you do?

KARL   I tried to kill him.

FREUD   Why?

KARL, *with a kind of groan*   I don't know! I don't know! I don't know!

FREUD   Herr Karl, you know it perfectly well, you know why you struck him.

KARL, *docilely*   I know.

FREUD   Why?

KARL   To defend myself.

FREUD   Against whom?

KARL   I don't know ... Yes ...

FREUD   Was he threatening you?

Karl groans and stirs slightly. Freud grows irritated.

Was he threatening you?

More to himself than to the patient:

Let's go about things differently. What did you eat?

KARL   There were some hors-d'oeuvre.

FREUD   And then.

KARL   Roast pork.

FREUD   When did you strike your father? (*A pause.*) While you were eating the hors-d'oeuvre?

KARL   While he was carving the roast.

FREUD   Do you recall the scene?

KARL   I held out my plate. He had a fork in his left hand and in his right hand a big knife. (*Violent and almost mechanical:*) I'll have your blood, you dirty swine!

A pause. Freud's eyes are shining. Karl's face has completely changed. His mouth is twisted into an unpleasant, spiteful grimace, his brow is furrowed. He now speaks in a coarse voice, harsh and often obscene. Explaining:

He wanted to chop them off, with his carving-knife!

   (*Abrupt halt.*)

Freud stiffens slightly, surprised. But he wants to carry through the test.

FREUD, *gently*   Go on, Karl, go on. Tell me what happened.

KARL   He wanted to chop them off! Chop them off!

In a coarse voice, heavy with innuendo:

He wanted to chop off my ... ears! And what good would my nose have been to me, if the ears were missing?

More and more vulgar:

He's learnt that to his cost, the old bastard, since he's deaf as a post. The fun's over: no more ears, so no more nose.

FREUD   He wanted to castrate you?

KARL   Yes! yes! yes!

FREUD   When did it start?

KARL, *suddenly exhausted*   I'm tired.

FREUD   When did it start?

KARL, *tossing about, muttering*   I'm tired, tired, tired ...

He looks dismal and wretched. He keeps his mouth open and breathes noisily and with difficulty.

FREUD, *authoritarian*   You will answer me, Karl, you will answer me!

(He repeats his question with suppressed violence.)

When did it start?
KARL, *muttering*   You ... (*moans:*) Oh!

(In a clearer tone, as if to rid himself of it:)

It has always been that way!
FREUD   And when did you start wanting to kill him?
KARL   I always have ... I always have!

He falls back exhausted, then tosses feebly, with painful gasps. Freud seems exasperated. He opens his mouth to question Karl, but realizes as he bends over him that he will get nothing more out of him, even if he does go on with his interrogation.

Freud's face is hardened by his will to dominate and by a growing disgust. Visibly, Karl's jibes at his father, as well as the clearly sexual aspect of the neurosis, have greatly displeased him. He bends over Karl, lifts one of his eyelids, examines the whites of his eye. Then, changing his attitude but retaining his tense, malevolent expression, he speaks to him in a soft, penetrating voice.

FREUD   Calm yourself, Karl. Peaceful! Peaceful!
      You are peaceful.
      You are asleep!
      Fa–ast aslee–eep.

A pause.

Sleep!
      Open your eyes.
      You are still asleep.
      Sit up.
      Stand up
      You are asleep on your feet and with your eyes open.

Karl makes the appropriate movements.
      Freud feels in his pocket. He pulls out the Swiss knife.

Hold out your hand.

Karl has held out his hand. Freud places the Swiss knife in the outstretched hand.

What is it?

(No reply.)

Look!

KARL, *same coarse, sleepy voice*   My knife.

Freud takes Karl by the shoulders and turns him towards the dummy bearing the uniform.

FREUD   What do you see?

Karl starts laughing with a disturbing, spiteful expression.

KARL, *vulgarly*   I see the general.

Freud lets him go and takes a step back.

FREUD   You've got the knife, Karl.
   And the general is there.
   Go on!
KARL   What should I do?
FREUD, *very emphatic*   Whatever you like.

A pause. Karl looks back and forth from the knife to the uniform. Then he starts laughing and opens the knife by scratching clumsily with the nails of his left hand. He closes his right hand on the haft and walks towards the dummy.

FREUD   Where are you going?
KARL   Have at the old swine!

He is in front of the dummy.
   His left hand holds the uniform by one of its facings; his right hand, behind his body, holds the knife low with its point raised.

I've got him.
FREUD   Wait! Why do you call him a swine?
KARL   Because he raped a little girl.
FREUD   Who? Your father?
KARL   Didn't you know? It's public knowledge.

(In shocked disgust.)

A little girl of seventeen! Every night!
 I know to my cost: she's my mother.

Freud begins to understand.

 He has suddenly turned pale and now appears more agitated than his patient: his hands move clumsily around him, as if he were torn between his desire to stop the experiment and his curiosity. At Karl's last utterance — and more precisely at the words: 'She's my mother' — a kind of growl escapes from his mouth and he clenches both fists as if he were about to hurl himself at Karl.
 Karl seems to hesitate for a moment, one hand on the jacket.

The product of a rape can only be a monster.
 Seventeen and fifty!
 Seventeen and fifty!

Freud has regained control of himself; he speaks, gritting his teeth:

FREUD   Well then? What are you going to do? Continue!

All of a sudden, Karl thrusts forward his knife, passes it between the two lapels of the uniform and cuts the thread of the sole button fastened into a buttonhole. The button falls to the ground and rolls tinkling away. Karl releases the uniform, which opens and slides down the bust to collapse at the foot of the dummy.
 The dummy revealed by this protracted slide is the bust of a woman. A clumsy hand — that of Karl, obviously — has marked the tips of the breasts with a brush. At the bottom of the bust, black lines endeavour to represent the hairy triangle of the pubis (in fact, this triangle is placed too high, since the bust stops at the level of the groin).
 As the uniform slides to the ground, Karl speaks in his coarse voice. Pointing at the uniform:

KARL   Fifty over seventeen.
 Take away fifty, what's left? That filthy hunk of offal has collapsed.
 And what was it covering, that slab of meat?
 My mother!

With a flick he sends the kepi flying, and seizing the ebony head swivels the dummy round to display its back to Freud. The beginning of the cleft of the buttocks is marked by a black line (the shape and nature of the dummy mean that its naive unclothed state can have only a purely symbolic character).

My mother *au naturel.*

Freud watches the scene in horror. He is pale and sweating. He seeks to stop it, but the word barely escapes his clenched teeth and Karl does not seem to hear it:

FREUD   Enough!

The patient has gone up to the dummy. He places his left hand on one of the two 'breasts' represented on the dummy. The index finger is lifted, the four other fingers seem to be squeezing an imaginary breast (in fact, this type of dummy presents the form of an already corseted bust). The index finger is placed on the tip of the left breast, or more precisely on the black spot that represents it, and titillates it gently while Karl licks his lips with a sensual, aroused expression.

KARL   The breast which suckled me!

Freud takes a step forward. At this moment, the patient goes into ecstasy. He throws back his head. It is an orgasm, and simultaneously with Freud we discover that the point of his knife — which remains open and is still held in his right hand between finger and thumb — is touching the triangle drawn on the dummy, while its handle is touching Karl's fly, from which we could even imagine it to be protruding. With slight movements of his loins, Karl alternately draws away from the dummy and back towards it. When he moves towards it, the point of the knife strikes the pubic triangle. Freud, forgetting that he is dealing with a patient in a state of induced somnambulism, hurls himself upon Karl and, in order to get him away from the dummy as quickly as possible, strikes him in the hollow below his shoulder.

  Karl recoils, with the dazed face of a man under hypnosis incapable of confronting the events occurring around him. Freud seizes him by the shoulders. Karl's right hand moves to the side and backwards, as if to strike Freud in the abdomen. But the latter, without even noticing this, has already regained control of Karl.

FREUD   Enough!
  Give me your knife.

Without looking at the knife, Karl checks the movement of his arm, holds out his hand and surrenders the knife.

You are asleep.
  Fast asleep.
  You are lying on your bed. With your eyes shut.

He supports Karl to the bed-settee and helps him lie down.
  Karl has lain down.
  Karl groans and shuts his eyes. Freud looks at the knife in disgust, releases the safety-catch, folds the blade and puts the knife into his pocket. His face stony, his eyes hard, in a hard, scornful tone of voice:

You said nothing but absurdities.
  Do you hear: absurdities.
  Forget everything!
  I command you to forget everything.
  Nothing happened.
  Nothing.

Do you hear?

Karl has shown considerable agitation since he lay down. Freud's commanding voice gradually calms him. He eventually falls still as if he were sleeping naturally.

KARL, *unintelligible mumblings.*

FREUD, *authoritatively*   You have never despised your father! You have never dreamed of killing him. *Do you hear?*

This utterance and the following one (about the mother) are pronounced with such force, and betray such inner anguish, that it is impossible to know whether Freud is trying to convince the obsessed man or himself.

KARL, *vague growl of approval.*

FREUD   There isn't ... there can't be ... a child in the whole wide world who's so unnatural as not to respect his mother. *Do you hear?*

KARL   Yes.

Karl sleeps. Quieter breathing.
   Freud turns away from him.
   He goes over to the dummy, without looking at it, as if it were his own mother and she was naked. He stoops, picks up the uniform and throws it across the dummy's shoulders, as if he wanted discreetly to cover its nakedness. But the uniform slips off. With nervous gestures, as if he were afraid of the dummy's nakedness, Freud pulls the uniform up again and fastens another button (crooked, of course) in order to tighten the jacket round the bust again. Then he stoops, picks up the kepi and puts it back on the dummy's head. All these operations are carried out with nervous haste. Relieved, Freud goes over to a little table (not far from the bed) that carries the bell the footman showed him (when he said: 'You can ring for me'). He rings, then returns to Karl. He passes his hand across the latter's forehead (we sense that he has to overcome his disgust).

FREUD   Wake up!
   Wake up!
   Open your eyes.

A moment's wait.
   At this moment, the footman, outside, inserts the key into the lock.
   Sound off of the key turning in the lock.
   Karl has opened his eyes.

You've woken up.

His task accomplished, Freud no longer conceals his disgust: he looks at his patient with a mixture of horror and severity.
   Karl sits up on his bed and looks at Freud in surprise. Then his gaze travels round the room: he

recognizes it.

KARL, *hesitating*   Did you put me to sleep?
    What did I do?

Freud gives a vague nod of assent.
    Karl is very slightly uneasy. He does not suspect the seriousness of his trouble. Freud shrugs his shoulders without replying.
    Karl has risen to his feet. He speaks softly, sincerely: he would like nothing better than to show his gratitude.

It has been a long time since I felt so well. (*With a shy smile:*) You see: hypnotism can be used for obsessional neuroses too.

Freud looks him in the eye, with a scornful, stony expression. His countenance, and his accompanying silence, seem to disconcert the patient. His smile fades and the corners of his mouth begin to tremble.

(*In an affable tone, through which we can already sense his anxiety breaking:*) Is the session over?
FREUD   Yes.

Karl takes a step towards Freud, as if he wished to clutch onto him. But he does not dare. We sense that he is afraid to see him leave.
    He raises his hands slightly, then lets them fall again.

KARL, *in the same tone of voice*   When will you come again?

Freud has not managed to restrain himself from recoiling. He assumes an expression of deep revulsion.

FREUD   I don't know.
    Goodbye, Sir.

Curt bow. He turns on his heel. The footman with the bandaged arm is waiting for him outside the door. He goes out. The footman follows him. Just as Freud has left and the footman is getting ready to close the door behind them, Karl addresses him from the far end of the room.

KARL   I'm feeling a bit better, Fritz, there's no need to lock me in.

In the corridor Fritz, who has just closed the door, has a key in his hand — the key to Karl's room — and turns to Freud as if to ask him if he should obey his young master.

FREUD, *with a violence that surprises Fritz, as if he wanted to make Karl disappear for ever*   Under lock and key! Under lock and key!

[A nightmare of Freud's. This scene follows the preceding one in Version II.]

[30]

In the mountains.

A narrow path winds round a sheer peak. On the left-hand side, a crag blocks the view; on the right, a vertical precipice. The path is cut into the rock. As in the previous dreams, the decor is notable for its schematic character: the contours of the mountain (those of the crag rising on the left, those of the precipice) are absolutely sharp and real.

But what is missing (as in certain cartoons) is the rocky substance. It is not a question of mist, or blurred images: there is actually nothing. The film does not appear to have been obliterated. What characterizes the decor is, on the left, ascending lines and, on the right, falling ones. It is, in any case, not so much a decor as accessories required by the dramatic content of the dream. The other accessories appear as they are needed — and they never exist except insofar as the oneiric action requires their properties. A hoarse voice very close at hand is singing a yodelling song, with no other words than 'la-la-ee, la-la-e-tu': the voice is that of Karl.

   (Karl's voice singing.)

The latter comes into sight, mounting the path easily, moving freely and without bothering about the precipice. Tyrolean hiker's costume: hat with a feather, green jacket, lederhosen. Thick stockings, a woman's high-heeled shoes which in no way impede the agility and ease of his gait.

At first he is alone. But the camera — which has first seen him full length, then fastened upon a detail of his person (close-up of that bearded face, with the black hole of the mouth singing) — as it draws away slightly discovers a thick rope, which did not exist a second before: it loops his waist, is knotted behind his back and extends straight and taut out of the frame — as if he were hauling something or someone.

In fact, at the moment when the young man turns and disappears to the right, we see Freud appear in a Tyrolean costume identical to that of Karl, with the rope looped round his waist in the same way (except that it does not extend behind him after the knot).

Same high-heeled shoes; the stockings are exactly like those of Karl. Freud is not singing the yodelling song, but he whistles it; he follows the path and disappears round the bend.

The same path, after the bend. The rope linking the two men has shortened considerably, as has the distance separating them. This distance, which must have been about two metres, now suddenly appears to us to be no more than half a metre.

The path is still just as narrow. It makes a bend a few metres further on; the precipice is just as sheer, the mountain just as steep. But Karl, turning his head, discovers in the rock-face to his right a deep, shadowy anfractuosity (1.8 metres high, two metres wide). Karl enters this cavern. Freud begins to scream.

FREUD   No! No!

Karl seems to possess Herculean strength: he drags Freud along effortlessly. Freud resists in vain, the taut rope hauls him forward willy nilly. Freud passes in front of a professorial lectern that has appeared within the cave, but facing the entrance. Meynert is seated at the lectern: top-hat, morning-dress, flower in his buttonhole. Meynert looks at Freud without uttering a word. Freud notices ants in Meynert's beard and emits a terrible scream.

(*Scream from Freud.*)

Luckily for him, as he turns away from Meynert he sees, opposite him, at the far end of the cave, his own mother, Amalia Freud, sitting on a real throne, dressed like a Byzantine empress, with numerous jewels, her arms, neck and shoulders bare. The throne stands upon a step cut into the rock.

Freud smiles at his mother and, still hauled along by the young man, gives her a wave of the hand. But Freud's mother, who has recognized him perfectly well, remains impassive and reticent, her hands placed on the golden arms of the throne; a living snake is coiled round her wrist.

Karl draws closer to Frau Freud, who sees him coming and makes no gesture to repulse him. He climbs onto the step leading to the throne and begins to caress Frau Freud's arms and shoulders in a very sensual manner. The latter, without a word, looks at Freud with a distant and vaguely mocking expression. Karl takes Amalia Freud's head in both hands and is about to kiss her.

FREUD, *to Karl*   I'll have your blood, filthy swine!

He flings himself upon him, pulls him back and strikes him (in the hollow beneath his shoulder, as he did in reality in the previous scene). Karl does not resist: he is wearing a malicious, ironical smile. Freud, furious and deeply disgusted, pushes him back towards the entrance of the cave, still hitting him with all his strength. We do not hear the sound of the blows, only the low, mocking laughing — at first very faint — of Meynert.

(*Laughter off from Meynert.*)

They pass in front of Meynert, Freud pushing and hitting Karl who retreats smilingly.

Meynert rummages in his beard, hunts for ants in it, catches them and puts them on his desk. All this without looking at his hands: he does not take his eyes off Freud and laughs louder and louder.

Laughter from Meynert (*crescendo*): *Freud pushes Karl out of the cave and throws him down the precipice (still smiling). Karl disappears.*

Laughter from Meynert (*very loud*): *but the rope which girdled the two men, suddenly tautened by Karl's fall, drags Freud down and projects him likewise into the abyss. The precipice is vertiginous: the wall beneath the path is actually vertical. There is nothing to catch hold of. Yet Freud finds himself clinging to a rock that has providentially appeared just below the path. The rope, still taut, pulls him with such violence that it will soon be impossible to resist; however, Freud abruptly frees his right hand — which all of a sudden turns out to be armed with Karl's knife, open and with its blade locked — and starts sawing at the rope. But no sooner has the blade touched the cord than it too turns to rope. Instantly a disk of red light appears in the sky (the same one we saw in the dream about* *the derailment), Meynert's laughter becomes deafening and Freud, letting go of the rock, falls headlong into the abyss, screaming.*

(Laughter from Meynert, deafening. Scream from Freud.)

Martha, woken with a start by this cry, lights a candle on her night-table. Freud has woken up too. His eyes are wide open and demented. The bedroom is spacious and still sparsely furnished (bed, night-tables, a chair, a Dresden clock on the mantelpiece). The couple look lost in that big bed and that huge empty room. Shadows moving on the ceiling (draughts cause the candle-flame to flicker).

MARTHA, *worried*   Sigi!

Freud looks at her, at first without seeing her.

FREUD, *semi-conscious*   I must make a clear break. Did I cry out?

He recognizes her.
    She nods: she is frightened — Freud frightens her.
    He looks at the clock as Martha takes the candlestick and lifts it at arm's length to shed some light.

What time is it?
    Five o'clock. I'm getting up.
MARTHA   Are you mad?
FREUD   I've got a file to read. A patient's file.
MARTHA   Sigi! He's your *first* patient: there's no hurry.

Freud looks at her malevolently: he wears a fearful, stubborn expression.

FREUD   I have to get it done *at once.*

PART TWO

[In Version II, Dora is a young woman who has marital problems. Her role has been expanded.]

[8]

In Freud's consulting-room.

The next day, at five in the afternoon. Dora is lying on the couch, having been put to sleep. Freud, sitting by her bedside, is smoking a cigar. The cathartic session is in progress. Freud holds a notebook in his left hand. When he takes notes (with a pencil), he puts the cigar into his mouth and leaves it there. For the ash, he has taken care to position the spittoon-cum-ashtray at his feet, and he makes use of it. He looks at Dora as if he were about to devour her, his eyes shining with excitement and curiosity — from which, of course, all sexual desire is banished.

FREUD   You're no longer suffering from flatulence?
DORA, *sleepily*   No.
FREUD   But you've bought more candy?
DORA   Yes.
FREUD   Do you have any in your bag?
DORA   Yes.
FREUD   Take one.

Dora picks up her bag, which is on the couch beside her (she picks it up without raising her body, groping cautiously for it with her left hand), she takes out a bag of candy, and from this bag she takes a little stick of barley sugar.

What is it?
DORA   A boiled sweet made with apple-juice, from Normandy.
FREUD   Eat one.

Dora removes the paper in which the barley sugar is wrapped and begins to suck it. Sometimes she barely grazes the barley sugar with her lips, nibbles it, or even, without inserting it into her mouth, puts out her tongue and gives it little licks. At other times, she thrusts it deep inside her mouth. In the former case, we have the impression of a sexuality that is somewhat cold, curious, perhaps slightly depraved (symbolically: clitoral); in the latter, of a deep sexuality that is only now being awakened (vaginal).

    The point is to show how Dora, perpetually aroused and perpetually unfulfilled, is torn between the superficial excitements of onanism and the deeper arousal of coitus.

    Freud observes her and takes notes (as if he were describing this behaviour).

Is it good?

DORA, *with respect*   It comes from France.

Freud looks hesitantly at her, then seems resolved to embark on a fresh approach. At least for a while.

FREUD   And you like France, don't you?
DORA   Yes.
FREUD   Have you been there?
DORA   No.

Freud deliberately repeats the usual banalities.

FREUD, *sententious, almost absurd air*   French women are so beautiful!
DORA   No more so than our women.
FREUD   Perhaps, but they know how to dress.
DORA   No.
FREUD   They don't?
DORA   They're frumps: I saw some last year at our Exhibition.
FREUD   Luckily, there are the French men.
DORA   Yes.
FREUD, *taking his direction from her reactions*   They're no better looking than Austrians.

Dora smiles with a rather knowing air and shakes her head.

DORA, *knowingly*   No.
FREUD   Nor more intelligent, nor wiser, nor braver, nor stronger.

She shakes her head at each qualification. For an instant she remains with her mouth half-open, smiling: at this moment, Freud risks all. In the same amiable tone of voice:

But the thing is, they're wonderful lovers.
DORA, *in a neutral voice*   The best in Europe, aren't they?

Now that he has got what he wanted, Freud lets his disgust show.

FREUD, *sternly*   Who told you such a foolish thing?
DORA   Irma.

Dora thrusts her candy-stick deep into her mouth, through pouting lips.

FREUD   Irma has impure fancies. She's bad for you.
     Have you had any French lovers?

She shakes her head, withdrawing the candy-stick slightly only to thrust it into her mouth anew.

What about others?

She has removed the candy-stick from her mouth. She shows it to Freud:

DORA, *sincere and indignant*   Never! There's my lover. I give him little bites and I kiss him.

He takes twenty minutes to melt.

Loud laugh (which betrays her resentment against some person about whom she says nothing).

Twenty minutes! It's so lovely it's like a dream.

And when I've crunched that one up, I take some more. I start again as often as I like.

She nods in approval of each fresh element on the list:

FREUD   You also eat meat smothered in sauce.

Pâtés.

Between meals, buttered bread with honey.

Or with jam.

Or cakes. Why?

DORA   It fills me up. It stuffs me full.

It sates me.

It's transformed into my blood; it becomes flesh of my flesh.

Freud leafs through the notebook.

FREUD   The compulsive eating begins six months after your marriage. Why?

DORA   I had an appetite.

FREUD   Before your marriage, you had none?

DORA   No. Oh, no!

FREUD   What happened?

DORA   My appetite was stimulated, and then, when I was hungry, no trouble was taken to satisfy me. *(She laughs uproariously.)*

FREUD   Why are you laughing?

DORA   I'm thinking about what he says at official dinners: 'Industry creates needs, but only in order to satisfy them.'

FREUD   Industrialists are not like industry.

DORA   No. He gave me that need — which I hadn't had ... he fosters it by kisses and caresses.

But he never satisfies it.

Sharp, violent bite at the candy-stick, which snaps.

FREUD   Why?

DORA   I wish you'd find out!

    It's always all over so quickly. He's there before I've even started.

FREUD   So you eat?

DORA   As much as I can. I give myself pleasure.

FREUD   Food's a substitute, Dora, for the love he doesn't give you and the child he hasn't provided you with.

He stands up, his eyes shining, and goes to sit at his desk, where he writes at length in an exercise book. We can read only the title of his comments: **Dora: sexual frustration.** *Suddenly he raises his head and notices that he has totally forgotten Dora. He stands up, goes over to her and wakes her up.*

Wake up, Dora. And remember what you've told me.

She opens her eyes. He is in front of her, austere and formal. Imperious:

All will turn out for the best, Madam. Tell your husband I want to see him.
    I'll expect him tomorrow at six o'clock.

[A treatment by Freud. Magda and her father also appear in Version I]

[12]

Next morning. Freud's consulting-room.

Freud is bending over Magda, whom we can barely see and who is asleep, stretched out on the couch.

The camera is pointing at State Councillor Schlesinger. Around sixty, with snow-white hair, the latter is sitting on a chair.

His top-hat is placed on the ground beside him, both his hands are resting on an ivory-knobbd cane and his chin is propped on his hands. The councillor is tall and extremely thin. His face is ascetic. Cold, pale-blue eyes, hollow cheeks, thin lips, no beard; side-whiskers. Lined features, tortured but cold; protruding veins at the temples. He seems ill-at-ease and outraged, but is assuming the attitude of the man of his word who has promised to remain silent and will do so, despite his indignation. We can hear Freud's questions, and can make him out vaguely in the background (or perhaps not even see him).

Magda's replies are slow, hard to understand. Her resistance can be measured by her delays in answering. We sense that this cathartic session is disturbed at once by Magda's resistance and by her father's presence.

FREUD   Your back pains, when did you feel them for the first time?
MAGDA   Ten years ago.
FREUD   When did you begin to hunch forward and hobble?
MAGDA   Ten years ago.
FREUD   Was he dead?

(Silence from Magda.)

Come on now, answer.

(Silence. Between his teeth:)

This is unendurable.
(More loudly:) Was he dead?

Freud turns partly round. He glances irritably at the councillor, who is staring wordlessly into space.

COUNCILLOR, *from his place, in a soft, dull voice*   Yes.
FREUD, *polite exasperation*   I'd be most obliged, State Councillor, if you'd refrain from

answering on your daughter's behalf.

(To Magda:)

For how long?
MAGDA   What?
FREUD   Dead for how long?
MAGDA   Six months.
FREUD   How did he die?
MAGDA   Fell.
FREUD   Fell where?
COUNCILLOR   Frantz fell over a cliff during a climbing expedition.

Freud has spun round towards the old man with blazing eyes. But just as he is about to explode, he hears Magda's voice behind him and it is almost intelligible. His face lightens at once. He turns on his heel.

MAGDA   His spine …
FREUD, *turning towards her*   What did you say?
MAGDA   His spine … *(Almost malicious laugh.)* … broken. He'd fallen on his back.
FREUD, *he has picked up a trail; he bends over Magda*   Did he ever kiss you?

Her father is revolted by this question and the ensuing ones. At each of them he frowns, or else he raises his chin slightly and taps his cane on the floor.

COUNCILLOR, *indignantly*   Kissed? *(Little cough of disapproval. Without raising his voice, to himself:)* Come now! Come now!

Freud pays no attention to these interruptions.

FREUD   Did he ever kiss you?
COUNCILLOR, *rather more loudly*   Of course not!
FREUD   Did he ever kiss you?
MAGDA   Once.
FREUD   Only once?
MAGDA   Ten times.
FREUD   Ten times?
MAGDA, *ironical laugh*   Ten thousand times. Often.
     (She recovers her poise. Sincerely:) Often.

Her father seems flabbergasted.

FREUD   Where?

(Silence.)

Where did he kiss you?

Her father taps his cane on the wooden floor.

MAGDA   In the garden.
FREUD   No, Magda. I'm asking you: whereabouts on your body?
MAGDA, *as if she were replying to his question*   In the garden!

Magda's face changes. Without opening her eyes, she smiles with a kind of depraved malice.
    The councillor has turned his head; for the first time he looks at Magda and seems speechless with surprise at his daughter's sly air of depravity.
    His indignation overcomes his self-imposed restraint, and he raises his voice for the first time.

FATHER   Enough!

He stops, taken aback, fearing lest he has gone too far. Magda tosses about; she emits a series of little yelps, as if her father's intervention had affected her even in her sleep. At once Freud bends over her and calms her.

FREUD   You're sleeping, Magda.
    You're sleeping peacefully.
    You're in your room, all alone.
    It's dark.
    It's the deep midnight of slumber.

Magda relaxes and buries herself more deeply in her slumbers. Freud abandons her for a moment to go over to the councillor. This movement reveals Magda completely. She is dressed in black, and is buried in the pillows in an odd manner, as if she were simultaneously hunchbacked and twisted. She is an old maid who is not, in fact, more than thirty, but who appears ageless. Genuinely ugly, flabby, grey cheeks, over-prominent nose, her father's thin lips. A black parasol has been laid down beside her, which she often touches in her sleep with a gesture that resembles a conjuration.
    Freud halts in front of the councillor. He waits. The man we see today is (at least in his relations with his patients and their relatives) rid of the doubts, the passions and the shyness which we associate with him (and which he will recover — though less intensely — when he is personally involved). On the contrary, he displays a calm, deep-rooted authority (which derives from his work and his knowledge), radically contrasting with that of the councillor (based on the habit of command and on his social influence).

FREUD   Well, Councillor?

The councillor, furious, but regaining his self-control, continues to speak in a hushed voice, as if he were nonetheless afraid of waking his daughter. He points to Magda, with an expansive, indignant gesture.

FATHER   She's a maiden.

FREUD, *with serene brutality*   I've no idea if she is, and neither have you.

The councillor rises to his feet in outrage. He leans on his cane and looks stonily at Freud.

FATHER, *outraged*   What do you mean?

FREUD   I mean that in order to assert that a woman is a virgin, one must have sub-mitted her to a medical examination. As far as I'm concerned, virgin or no, she's a patient. That's enough.

A pause.
   The councillor looks at him with the same hard, angry expression, but without uttering a word.

On the other hand, I acknowledge that we're wasting our time.

FATHER   You're saying so of your own free will.

FREUD   You've no business here, Councillor.

FATHER   Oh yes, I have, Sir!

FREUD   What?

FATHER   I'm keeping an eye on you.

Freud is faintly amused by this mistrust.

FREUD, *faint smile, after a glance at Magda; almost relaxed*   Are you afraid I might take advantage of her?

FATHER   Why not?

FREUD, *fresh glance at Magda*   Why not, indeed?

He becomes hard once again.

When Magda goes to see a gynaecologist, do you go with her?

FATHER   Of course.

FREUD   Right into his consulting-room?

A brief silence. Freud looks the councillor full in the face, his eyes flashing: he is a policeman discovering a clue that he still cannot decipher but whose importance he divines. For a moment, it is not enough to say that he looks at the councillor — he observes him (like a detective or like an entomologist: dispassionately).
   The councillor seems disconcerted by Freud's attitude, more than by his question. He feels obliged to explain, which he does majestically, in his frosty, sharp-edged voice.

FATHER   Are you married?

   (Vague grunt from Freud, which may be taken as assent; clearly he thinks it is up to him to put questions, not up to his clients. The father takes the grunt for assent.)

I hope for your sake you'll spend your whole life in ignorance of the fact that a widower's first duty is to act *also* as mother to his children.

Freud still looks at him as before; in his eyes, we discern the probing gaze of an analyst. (Hitherto, we have hardly ever seen him observe, rarely seen him look. This contrast — between the blind look of the private individual and this pitiless light — must make us understand how Freud is, simultaneously, the man who will subsequently decipher the case of Cäcilie and the man who will live his entire life with Martha without knowing her.)

After a moment's silence, he turns away from the councillor and goes back to Magda.
Freud has laid his hand on Magda's forehead.

What are you going to do?
FREUD   Wake her.
     I give up.

The councillor has fully recovered his self-control; he speaks sternly to Freud.

FATHER   Take care, Dr Freud! You told me this morning you were changing your methods. That you'd put my daughter to sleep, that you'd go back to the source of her symptoms and that on waking she'd be cured.
     You've found nothing: what can I do about that?
     Is it honest to cast the responsibility for your failure onto me?
FREUD   Even under hypnosis your daughter is controlling herself, because she can't forget you're listening to her.

Regretfully:

We needed to go down! Down! Plumb the deep recesses ...
FATHER, *outraged*   Dr Freud. A Schlesinger *has no* deep recesses.

Freud stares at him wrathfully. He is exasperated by Schlesinger's incredulity and stubbornness — as he is by the sad necessity of abandoning a catharsis which held out great promise. His pride leads him to take a false step: he reacts to scepticism with a need to crush the unbeliever — in other words, with an unfortunate bragging.

FREUD   What do you know about your daughter? (*Treacherously:*) She hid her relations with Frantz from you!

The councillor shrugs his shoulders indifferently: in fact, he is appalled by this discovery.

How can you be sure I haven't got hold of what's needed to cure her?
FATHER   That passing fancy ... do you attach any importance to that? Two children exchanged kisses. It happened twelve years ago.
     Two years later, the boy died ...

FREUD   Died, yes, with his spine shattered — and six months later the doctors summoned to Magda's sickbed diagnosed a curvature of the spine, because she displayed all the symptoms of one. But they were mistaken: it was a case of hysterical contractures — she was imitating the curvature. As if she'd wished to make real *in her body* the death of the person she loved, in order to keep him within her for ever.

A silence. The father does not like these conjectures at all.

FATHER, *harsh, unpleasant irony*   Her illness, you're saying, is just an ... original ... way of wearing mourning for her cousin?   *(Quite convinced that Freud is going to lose face.)*

If you're right, Magda will be cured this very morning.

Freud realizes that he has been boasting.

FREUD, *beating a slight retreat*   I didn't say that.
FATHER   You've just said so.

Freud looks hesitantly at Magda: he knows he has not gone far enough; he is afraid to wake her.

FREUD   I repeat, I'd have needed ...
FATHER, *frankly unpleasant, with authority*   Wake her up, my dear fellow; we'll soon see.

He raps the floor with his cane: it is an order.
     Freud shrugs his shoulders and takes the decision to wake Magda. Bending over her:

FREUD   You're going to wake up, Magda.
MAGDA   Yes.
FREUD   You're going to remember everything you've told me, aren't you?
MAGDA   Yes.

Freud presses his palm very lightly on Magda's forehead.

FREUD   Wake up.

She cannot have been very deeply asleep: she wakes up instantaneously. At once her lips purse and she assumes the Schlesinger family expression; that expression — harsh, puritanical, gloomy, not devoid of real distinction — is precisely the one Schlesinger himself is wearing at the same moment. Her first glance is not directed at Freud, but at her father. Father and daughter look at one another; we sense that something is passing between them but cannot tell what it is. It obviously has to do with Magda's feelings for Frantz and the fact that she kept them hidden. Immediately after this, with the authority given him by wealth and the habit of power, the councillor takes control of operations — as if he wished to eliminate Freud (and perhaps compromise any chance of a cure).

FATHER   Dr Freud thinks that you're cured, child, so sit up.

Magda sits up with an effort. We see her: stooping, bent forward, almost hunchbacked. Without taking her eyes off her father, she gropes for her parasol, grasps it and sets it down at her side. Her right hand moves back and forth along the parasol. It seems to serve as her magical protection.

FREUD, *annoyed and replying directly to the councillor, though looking at Magda*   I don't think anything.
    Leave that parasol alone, for heaven's sake.

Magda takes her hand away from the parasol for a few moments, but soon goes back to it. Schlesinger speaks to her with a kindliness belied by the coldness of his blue eyes.

FATHER   Sit up straight, Magda.
    Come on! Hold yourself upright.

She makes vain efforts. Her father, in the tones of a judge:

You've told me a great many lies, child, as I've just learned.
    But if that can help you, very well, I forgive you.

Freud listens — somewhat withdrawn, uncomfortable, furious. But the failure of his attempt (a failure which he provoked in any case by his bragging) deprives him of the taste and the means for violent protest.

FREUD, *harshly, but feebly*   Allow me.
FATHER   I'm her father, Doctor. She'll obey me better than she will you.
    (With a touch of playacting:) Stand up and walk.

He places himself conspicuously in front of Freud. The latter says nothing: he observes the other two. Magda takes hold of her parasol; she leans on it with all her strength to help herself up. She is now upright on her feet, her neck and shoulders bowed, her torso twisted, her nose hardly higher than the knob of the parasol. She begins to walk, supported by the parasol, with tiny, hobbling steps, barely parting her legs and dragging her feet. Without the parasol, it seems obvious that she would fall headlong. But at the same time it seems that this parasol is more of a magical incantation, a talisman that has become indispensable, than a real crutch. Freud has eyes only for the parasol.

FREUD, *beside himself with annoyance*   Again that parasol! It's just playacting, Magda. It can't support you. Let go of it!

Freud's position has become intolerable, through his own fault: he knows very well that it is

Schlesinger himself who, by his presence, has rendered the session quite useless. But he also knows that the latter will take advantage of Freud's bragging to show — in bad faith — that the cathartic method is a failure. Freud sees, in fact, that all the symptoms have returned and that Schlesinger is obliging his daughter to walk so that the evidence of failure will be irrefutable.

FATHER, *deliberately adopting Freud's command in order to show that he is putting his paternal authority behind this experiment*　　Do what the doctor tells you. Let go of your parasol.

Magda is afraid to let go of the parasol, but her father's toneless voice seems to terrorize her. She opens her hand, the parasol falls to the ground. For a moment Magda teeters as if about to walk, but eventually she dips her head and would fall headlong if Freud and Schlesinger, each from his respective side, did not rush to catch her in mid air and prevent her. Dragging her forward:

Try again. We'll hold you. As far as the window.

When she gets to the window, she struggles slightly, her face expresses an intolerable anguish and she mutters to herself:

MAGDA　　　　I can't! I can't!
　　I want my parasol. I can't! *(Shrill, crazy scream.)* My paraso-o-ol!

The councillor appears strangely delighted by his victory: is he pleased because Magda is still ill or because (in his eyes, at least) the futility of the cathartic method has been proved? He speaks indulgently to Freud: he is a magnanimous victor.

FATHER　　　　Yes, my darling. *(To Freud:)* Be so kind as to hold her for a moment, Doctor.

He goes to pick up the parasol and holds it out to Magda, who grasps it eagerly and leans on it.
　　Magda, reassured by her parasol, moves away from the window, doubled up and hobbling.

You can let her go.

(Sad smile.)

So there we are!
　　Nothing has changed.
　　(A pause; magnanimously:) I move with the times, Doctor. Electrotherapy, I understood that! Our century has tamed electricity: so much the better, let it be used for medical treatment.
　　But hypnotism! That old rubbish! And in out good city of Vienna, which over a century ago had the honour of driving out Mesmer, the first magnetizer.
　　Do you have a taste for such phantasmagorias? That astounds me: I know men,

and I'm convinced you're no charlatan.

Freud submits to this reprimand without moving a finger or uttering a word. But it is clear that he is furiously angry (particularly at himself, for having fallen into a trap). He smiles, bows quickly and digs his nails into the palms of his hands.
  He is beside himself with exasperation. But he still suppresses it.

FREUD, *in a flat tone, very calm*   You're right, Councillor. A charlatan would go on with the treatment. He would dazzle you with conjuring-tricks. As for me, I refuse. I'll not treat your daughter any longer.

Magda, trotting and hobbling along, leaning on her parasol, comes back towards them. She looks at Freud ironically (as if to say: 'So what?'). He catches that look. This time the breaking-point has been reached. He says with irresistible authority:

(To Magda:) Come on!

To the councillor, who wants to protest and is already opening his mouth to do so, Freud adds — without even looking at him:

(To her father:) Silence!

With a vague movement of his hand, but in an inflexible tone of voice. He places his hand on the forehead of Magda, who is still bent — indeed almost doubled up — over her parasol. Forcefully:

Go to sleep.
  Yes, instantly.
  Standing up. With your eyes open.
  That's an order.

Magda goes to sleep like a lamb, on the spot.

(With extreme violence:) I'm sick to death of your parasol.
  I loathe it.
  I command it to break in half in your hands, *before nightfall.* Do you hear me?
MAGDA, *with a sigh*   Yes.
FREUD   Good. Wake up.

Magda has woken abruptly. Her first glance once again is for her father. The latter, moreover, does not take his eyes off her: one would say they were suspicious of one another. The councillor turns towards Freud, with ironical affability:

FATHER   And do you hypnotize objects too!
  Which are more suggestible?

Parasols or umbrellas?

It is Freud's strength to admit his mistakes calmly.

FREUD, *hard and sincere*   I've committed two stupidities, Councillor: the first is to have believed, even for a moment, that the symptom would disappear after this grotesque session; the second is to have so far lost my head as to have given hypnotic commands to a parasol. But you exasperated me! I'll do nothing worthwhile with Magda and that's *your fault*. It's as if you didn't want . . .

The councillor has risen to his feet, superb in his outraged majesty. All of a sudden, a sharp crack, a scream from Magda, the two men turn towards her and we see, at the same moment they do, the broken parasol. It has half broken at the precise point at which its leather handle joins the central stem — along which the rib-mechanism slides. The occurrence has taken place outside our field of vision and outside theirs. Magda, bent forward, surveys the parasol in astonishment. It has, of course, ceased to be of any use to her as a crutch: it is at the end of Magda's (horizontal) arm, like some mysterious, disturbing object held at a safe distance while it is studied.

At the same time, Magda's head tips forward and we have the feeling she is about to fall flat on her face. Her father wants to rush forward — as he did a little earlier — to support her. But Freud stretches out his arm and bars his way.

FATHER, *furious at his progress being checked*   What did you do, my poor child?
MAGDA   I didn't do anything.

She straightens up suddenly, with a swift, firm movement raises the arm holding the parasol and releases it; it strikes the ceiling and falls back to the ground near her father's top-hat. Magda's face has lit up. Without being beautiful, it is transfigured by the passion it expresses. Her body, for its part, released from its contractures, is beautiful. Beautiful according to the canons of the period, in other words somewhat heavy but tall, majestic, narrow-waisted. We can sense long, shapely legs and fine, rather heavy breasts. Magda smiles at her father and sticks her tongue out at him, with a childlike air devoid — at least apparently — of any hostility. She catches her skirt between two fingers of her left hand, raises it — on the left — to the beginning of her calf and starts to dance. In a contralto voice, she sings a saucy refrain which, emerging from that tall, passionate woman, seems strange and almost sinister.

The curtains of our bed are made of linen red. (*twice*)
And when we are within,
Our belly-dance we begin —
It all moves,
It all moves,
It all mo-oves.

As she repeats 'It all moves', she flings her entire body into a frenetic dance.
The councillor's first reaction is one of shock.

COUNCILLOR, *imperious*   Enough!

She stops singing, but looks him in the eye without halting her dance. Freud observes both of them, frowning and enthralled.

Where did you learn that?

MAGDA, *bursting out laughing, in a voice that is still sleepy:*   How do we know what we know?

This obscure phrase seems to shatter Schlesinger.
    Dancing with fresh vigour — around her father this time.

Freedom, hurrah!
Freedom, hurrah!
All come in!

There is a knock at the door; she dances across to open it.
    The door opens to admit Breuer, who surveys the scene unblinkingly (she is a patient; he has seen others). She bows and goes back towards her father, walking quite normally, without dancing. To Schlesinger, looking him straight in the eye:

I'm cured, Father.

In an ambiguous tone of voice:

Aren't you glad?

COUNCILLOR   Glad isn't the word, child: I'm *wonder-struck!*

He stresses the word 'wonder-struck'. But his voice, though gracious, remains terse and sad.
    He finds a degree of warmth when addressing Freud.

(*To Freud:*) I'm a Doubting Thomas, Doctor, and I can't believe what I see.
    But I've seen it.
    I offer you my humblest apologies, and all my gratitude.

Freud's face has darkened. He looks at Schlesinger with very decided hostility — for the first time since the beginning of the scene. He can more easily forgive him his scepticism than his present credulity.

FREUD, *curt and hard*   What have you seen? What have you seen? Nothing.
    A piece of charlatanry.
    I've known it for ages: sceptics of your kind are the first victims of charlatans.

To Magda, who is listening with a serene smile:

You're not cured, Magda. And you won't be until you've unburdened yourself.

The councillor, annoyed, tries to cut him short.

COUNCILLOR   You'll be so good as to let me know ...

Freud, with terrible anger and real malevolence:

FREUD   Later, Councillor. When you come back to see me again. For you'll be back within six months. And on that day, my poor Magda, you'll be walking on crutches.

MAGDA, *dazzling smile*   We shall see. Father, your hat.

She stoops and picks up the top-hat the councillor deposited by the chair he was initially occupying. She hands it to him. Her father takes the hat in his right hand and gives his left arm to his daughter. Breuer opens the door for them (Freud has remained near the window). The councillor recognizes him as he passes and bows.

COUNCILLOR, *politely*   I hadn't recognized you, Doctor. My respects.

To thank him for holding the door open:

Thank you.

They go out. Breuer closes the door behind them. Breuer and Freud, at opposite ends of the room, look wordlessly at one another, waiting until the patient and her father have left the outer office. Almost immediately we hear the sound of the apartment door opening and shutting again.
    At once, Freud doubles up and — for the first time since the beginning of the film — bursts out laughing. This wild laughter, of course, is as violent as it is rare: it is harsh and swift as a mountain stream, and we do not know whether Freud is laughing out of anger or amusement. In fact, we should sense that he is relieved at the providential manner in which he has been extricated from a terribly delicate situation.
    Breuer looks at him in amusement and begins to laugh too.

BREUER   I'm laughing because I see you laugh, but I don't know what I'm laughing about.

FREUD   Breuer, that girl's admirable! She's the equal of your Cäcilie.
    When I'm angry, I do nothing but stupid things, you know. I began by boasting of having cured the patient, and ended up hypnotizing a parasol.
    He was laughing up his sleeve, the old fox, and I almost lost face.

With real exultation:

Magda saved me with an *admirable* sense of the situation and her illness: she broke her parasol, she freed herself from her chains ... for only a week, perhaps, but it's a victory

452

over herself. I've got her, she's ready: when she comes back, with or without her father, I'll squeeze her like a lemon.

Breuer hears these declarations with unease: this mild, liberal man prefers to disguise from himself his friend's tyrannical violence and despotism. He smiles vaguely and hastens to turn the conversation.

BREUER   Will you come and see Cäcilie with me?

FREUD   At once!

He turns and glances out of the window. We see father and daughter round a street corner and disappear. Magda, upright and steady, is a head taller than her father. As if to himself:

What an odd couple. They horrify me.

[Discussion between Freud and Breuer about Cäcilie.]

[14]

Breuer and Freud in Breuer's carriage.

Very busy street. The carriage passes in front of a pretty Viennese café whose name is inscribed in gold letters above the windows: 'Aesculapius Coffee House and Doctors' Club'. Breuer signals to the driver. The barouche comes to a halt; Breuer climbs out first.

BREUER, *to Freud*   We'll be able to chat more comfortably.
FREUD, *slight resistance*   It will be full of doctors.

Breuer looks at his watch:

BREUER   At a quarter to twelve?

Freud gets out: they go inside. the café is indeed still deserted. During the conversation, a few doctors will appear, wave at the two friends and go to sit down quite some way off. Over some tables at the far end, a sign: 'Medical Whist Club'.
    Freud and Breuer go and sit down in a little isolated booth. Above them, on the wall, the head of a magnificent ten-pointer. Beneath the stuffed head, the words: 'Donated by Dr Hergisheimer. 1870.'

Freud, I must apologize.

The waiter has come up, respectful but familiar.

WAITER   Doctors, gentlemen?
BREUER, *still affable*   Good day, my friend.
    Bring us two cafés au lait.

The waiter goes off. Freud looks at Breuer uncomprehendingly.

FREUD   Apologize?
BREUER   The symptoms have well and truly disappeared.

He muses.

I know her too well, you see. And then, after all, it's she who found the method.

In fact, I let her say whatever she wants.

He bends closer. Confidingly:

Frau Körtner confirmed your hypothesis to me: Cäcilie's father died in a Neapolitan brothel.
It's unbelievable.

Shrugging his shoulders:

The women were all crazy about him.

A silence. Freud has been looking at him from the outset with timid apprehension, as if he expected and feared a rebuke. Breuer is staring into space, but his face becomes glum and anxious.

FREUD, *with affection, but shyly*   You're not pleased?
BREUER, *very cordial*   Half and half.

It must be clear that he is in no way reproaching Freud: he accepts his responsibilities and, if he is worried, it is because he is afraid of harming Cäcilie.

Were we right to touch that particular chord?

Breuer adds — soberly and without comment, his gaze still fixed:

She has tried to kill herself several times.

FREUD, *insinuating rather than asserting*   The more soot there is, the greater the need to sweep the chimneys.

Freud speaks to Breuer with considerable circumspection. He is glad to have intervened, of course, but Breuer still frightens him.

BREUER, *distracted, speaking to himself*   Not with such brutality!

Freud takes this remark (which, obviously, applies to both friends) as being directed only at him.

FREUD   I ... *(Somewhat pitiful excuse:)* ... she was resisting.

Breuer looks at him and Freud's piteous expression makes him laugh, very affectionately moreover.

BREUER, *without malice*   'She was resisting me, so I killed her.' I can't remember what melodrama that's from.
It must be admitted, dear friend, that you really went at it with a will.

Freud looks very crestfallen.

That's your way, my friend. And above all don't think I reproach you for it. I let you question her, so if anyone was to blame ...

Freud can at a pinch stand Breuer holding him to blame, but he cannot bear for his master to accuse himself.

FREUD, *with lively indignation*   In any case, it wouldn't be you, Breuer.

A pause. It is his turn to reflect ...
   All of a sudden, the words come almost without his knowing it; yet, to his mind, the argument is fundamental.

She was *repressing* her memories. Even under hypnosis.
BREUER   So?
FREUD   Strong methods were the only thing you had left.
BREUER   If she was repressing them, it's because they were unbearable for her.
   Will she be able to bear them any better now?

He looks at Freud with sad uncertainty.
   Freud takes Breuer's forearm and squeezes it.

FREUD, *warmly and with conviction*   But it's *your* discovery, Breuer, it's *your* method: curing by means of the truth.
   Let's shed light fully and everywhere!
BREUER, *with a touch of violence*   Take care! When dawn's approaching, I'm very willing to help the day break through.
   But I refuse to violate people's souls!

He is ashamed of his outburst and at once lays a friendly hand on Freud's shoulder.

Isn't it legitimate for a child of twenty to want to respect her father's memory? Wasn't she right to bury within herself a memory that dishonours her?
FREUD   In order to forget what she saw and heard, she made herself blind and deaf: that's too steep a price to pay. Now she knows: she can see, she can hear, she's going to live.
BREUER   Let's hope so!

   (A pause. With passionate sincerity:)

I wish it with all my heart.

They finish drinking their coffee, each deep in thought, their eyes intent.

They greet one or two newcomers. Breuer summons the waiter. Freud lays a hand on his arm and, with an insistent air, heavy with implications (No; Not you; You've already settled this, that and the other bill, and so on):

FREUD   Please.

BREUER, *tactfully*   Is it your turn? Fine.

As Freud gives the waiter a coin, Breuer, certain that Freud's eyes have been opened, adds with a smile:

How about you, Freud? *(Freud looks at him.)*
      Has that treatment by truth cured you?

FREUD, *bewildered*   Cured?

BREUER, *still careless*   Yes. Of the bee in your bonnet ...

Freud looks uncomprehendingly at him; Breuer presses on, but his aim is not to point out a scientific error: he would quite simply — against Mathilde and Freud — like to prove Cäcilie's innocence. Still smiling:

That girl's as white as snow.

Freud, who still does not understand, casts a glance around him in search of the girl to whom Breuer is alluding. Breuer, faintly annoyed, waits until the waiter has given back the change and gone off, then:

Cäcilie: sex has nothing to do with her problems.
      You established their source yourself: that terrible night in Naples. A good old traumatism, Charcot-style.

He rises calmly to his feet, certain of his reply. He adds:

We'd have a hard time finding your 'frustrated or repressed desires' and your 'over-accumulation of nervous energy' in this particular story.

Freud has not risen; he looks up at Breuer with a mixture of sadness, resolution and true affection. Breuer, who was not looking at Freud, notices that he is remaining at the table. He bends over towards him, very faintly annoyed.

Eh?

FREUD, *warm and insistent*   Sit down again, Breuer.
      Just for a moment. I'd like to say ...

Breuer makes a very faint grimace and sits down again.
      Breuer is not prepared to let Freud speak.

He outlines the case again, with the aim of pitting Freud against Charcot.

BREUER   A young girl from high society is woken up at night in a foreign city by two policemen, who take her to a brothel in a Black Maria. There among the whores she finds her father's body, naked and defiled.

As a nervous shock, isn't that enough for you?

Freud listens to him, very ill-at-ease. He sincerely believes in the traumatism, but he does not know Cäcilie well enough to decide whether her father's death is the primary traumatism.

He replies timidly that he does not know, in order to avoid displeasing Breuer by revealing his true thoughts to him.

FREUD   I don't know ...
BREUER, *rather aggressively*   So you're abandoning the theory of traumatism?

For Breuer, it is necessary to choose: either accumulation of nervous energy or traumatism.

FREUD, *sincerely and forcefully*   Never!
BREUER, *insistent*   Where's the traumatism in Cäcilie's story?
FREUD   I don't know. *(He hastens to add:)* In any case, her father's death was certainly a traumatism.

For Freud, there can (he does not know how) be some way of reconciling these two aspects of the question.

Freud lays a hand on his arm and, with a pleading expression, obliges him to remain seated.

The policemen lusted after her, and she sensed it. God knows what they did or said.

Then she saw all those naked women. And to cap it all her father — the old male — in his nakedness, surrounded by the females he'd been caressing. *And killed by sex.*

(A pause, then Breuer finds an answer.)

Breuer, at first disconcerted, recovers his animation as soon as he grasps what he believes to be the mistake Freud has made. He screws up his eyes, exchanging his unwonted air of majesty for his habitual expression of lively intelligence and subtlety.

BREUER   I know where the mistake is, Freud.

Yes, the whole story is *sexual.*

But for whom?

For the father — who, God knows why, liked prostitutes.

For those girls — who live off their looks and sometimes, it's said, get a certain pleasure out of it.

For the policemen even — foul brutes.

For everybody *except* for Cäcilie.

FREUD   Cäcilie? Do you think she could have lived through an event whose sexual charge was so powerful without herself being imbued with it?

BREUER, *seeing that Freud is not disconcerted but is maintaining his stance, relapses into an irritation that will grow with each reply*   Sexual charge, sexual discharge, that's very fine-sounding.

In practical terms, what does it mean? Surely you don't think she envied the inmates of the establishment?

This irony falls flat. Freud, absorbed in his thoughts, answers him seriously:

FREUD, *seriously*   It's your job to find out: you should question her about those women. Very directly. But under hypnosis, of course.

BREUER   God forgive me, did you think I was serious?

A doctor comes in and looks over towards them. Breuer points out the newcomer and starts smiling in his direction.

Watch out!

(*Smiling at the doctor, he whispers to Freud:*) Smile.

The doctor smiles and bows; Breuer gives him a broad smile and a wave of the hand.

The doctor goes and sits down at the far end.

In an undertone, still smiling at first but then serious and even stern, without looking at Freud:

Now don't be so stubborn! Try to understand other people for once.

The treachery of this 'for once' must be perceptible: Breuer undoubtedly has Martha in mind.

She has just learnt of that shameful death; now she can *see* the shame: in the faces, on the corpse. She's crazy with grief and anguish; crazy with *loneliness*. The whores, for her, are criminals: they've besmirched, they've killed the man she revered.

What were her feelings?

Intense sorrow and revulsion. Those are no aphrodisiacs.

FREUD   Most assuredly not.

(*He muses.*)

Revulsion, that's right.

A mixture of revulsion and arousal.

A doctor has just come in.

Breuer almost knocks over his glass.

BREUER, *in a voice almost like thunder*   *Sexual* arousal?

To avert the storm, Freud draws his attention to the newcomer:

FREUD, *very quickly*   Smile! Smile! It's Rumpelmayer.

Breuer and Freud smile at the doctor. The three men exchange bows.

RUMPELMAYER, *very loudly, from a distance*   It was a paraplegia.
BREUER, *cordially*   You must be pleased!
RUMPELMAYER, *quite proudly*   I'm sending a report to the Medical Association.

He goes and sits down at the far end, opposite one of the newcomers. They embark on a game of dominoes. Freud takes advantage of this lull to continue in an undertone, without looking at Breuer.

FREUD   No revulsion without a forbidden desire.

He has picked up his empty cup by the handle. He tilts it to the right, to the left, forwards, backwards, watching a drop of coffee flow across a little half-dissolved sugar at the bottom. The impression is of a precipice, miniature but still vertiginous. He speaks in a neutral, restrained, careful tone of voice, which is enough to make us understand that, perhaps without realizing it, he is doing some soul-searching — although the 'I' he uses is obviously abstract and universal.

This desire grows since it is unappeased; the forces of repression grow with it; when the number of rioters doubles, the government doubles its regiments.
    A desire that is crushed, anathematized, but *alive!* Outside me, the bottom of the precipice, vertiginous, fascinating. Inside me, that unmoving, pitiless struggle, the certainty that I'm a monster ... I lean over, I want and do not want to fall: I'm afraid. That's revulsion: arousal hating itself.

    (Laughter off from Breuer.)

At the end of this line of thought, he is suddenly interrupted by a burst of laughter, quite devoid of malice, from Breuer, who is looking at him in a friendly fashion. Freud appears disconcerted.

BREUER, *still friendly*   Forgive me, dear friend, may I ask you a question?
    (At a nod from Freud:) How many times, in your life, have you been to a brothel?
FREUD, *firmly and clearly: matter of principle*   I've told you: not once.
BREUER   I went three times between the ages of seventeen and twenty, out of bravado. They're my three nastiest memories. Those women are hideous, Freud. They filled me with revulsion, to be sure; but with so little desire that, on each occasion, I left just as I'd come.

He has now calmed down and at once shows himself conciliatory. With no trace of hypocrisy: apart from his relations with Cäcilie, his reservations derive in fact from the distrust he feels for all

460

theories and systematizations.

There are traumatisms whose origin is sexual: I'm convinced of it.

But why do you want that to be the case with all of them?

Nature is varied, Freud, infinitely varied. And Cäcilie is nothing like your Dora.

Freud looks uncertainly at Breuer. He eventually makes up his mind to confide something of capital importance:

FREUD, *in a hollow voice*   Dora doesn't count.

Breuer, astonished at Freud's voice, looks at him attentively. Freud is once again wearing the haggard expression he had at the end of Part One.

Do you remember the Schwartz boy?

BREUER   He wanted to kill his father, didn't he?

FREUD   He wanted ...

Freud gives a sudden smile: a customer has just come in. The customer, astonished, takes his hat off without smiling and moves away. Breuer has turned rather belatedly and sees only the back of his neck.

BREUER   Who was it?

FREUD   Nobody. I'd taken him for a doctor. *(Returning to his story:)* On that day I understood.

The smile has disappeared. Freud is wearing his haggard expression again.

BREUER   What?

FREUD   Something horrible. The world perhaps ... or perhaps myself. It's of no importance — I've forgotten everything.

BREUER   You hypnotized him.

FREUD   I suppose so.

BREUER   What did he say? What did he do?

Freud shrugs his shoulders.

A pause.

FREUD   I know that he filled me with revulsion — because he fascinated me ...

With an odd laugh:

And then I saw the Great Devil!

BREUER   *Sex.*

Freud utters no word, makes no gesture, but his very silence is an assent.

BREUER, *with affectionate irony*   In yourself, such a puritan?
FREUD   A puritan is a repressed person.

They look at one another. Breuer's discretion prevents him from insisting. But it is clear that he is rather worried. Freud smiles at him.

I'll try to remember. I'll talk to you ...

(A pause.)

Freud has turned towards Breuer; he is a little less sombre — his face expresses hope and trust. Very gravely:

You'll help me, won't you?

Breuer smiles at him and squeezes his hand silently. Some doctors come in as the two friends are looking at one another; they bestow salutations and smiles to which neither Freud nor Breuer responds. Freud recovers and lets go of Breuer's hand.

(Smiling:) As for Cäcilie, I relinquish her to you. The evidence isn't there — it would have been necessary ...

Glimpsing Breuer's reviving annoyance, he hastens to add:

All right, all right! Tell Mathilde that she's an angel and I've lost my wager.

PART THREE

[The 'You are requested to close the eyes' dream. Freud attempts to interpret it with Breuer.]

[5]

A waste land. No horizon. It is bounded by a kind of mist or lucid non-existence. Mute, eyes closed, men in black wearing top-hats walk alone or two by two. They all share one characteristic: they drag their feet, which produces the only sound we can hear — a very unpleasant scraping. Posts rise from the ground, in quite large numbers and a variety of sizes. They all carry signs, of which we can see only the backs. On the other side, these signs most assuredly display directions or signals — but we cannot see them. The walkers no doubt would see them if they opened their eyes, since for the most part they are moving in the direction of the camera-lens. But all their eyelids remain shut. In the foreground, motionless, facing us, we recognize Freud — he is wearing a top-hat and has his eyes shut like everybody else. Yet he has stopped in front of a sign — which is fixed on a post about 1.6 metres high — and is bending slightly towards it as if he were reading. And he does in fact abruptly open his eyes and see what is written. His face expresses no particular sentiment, but at the same moment we hear a yell — without Freud's lips having moved.

FREUD'S VOICE OFF, *yell of a sleeper terrified by a nightmare.*

The scene we have just described (the posts, the walkers, etc.) lasts hardly more than a 'flash'. In fact, it is almost a tableau and we see Freud at once in front of the sign.

What lasts a little longer (barely a second, though) is the scream.

With the scream, the image disappears but the scream remains. This is what establishes the connection between Freud's nightmare and the reality seen by him on waking.

The disappearance of the image, in fact (which takes place brutally and with no transition: we were on that waste land, we are in Freud's room), reveals to us the bedroom of the young Freud couple just as the patient sees it from his bed — or almost. Almost: because in the foreground we see Freud himself in his bed. He has just sat up. The camera-lens is positioned to the right of the bed, a little behind Freud: what it sees is what would be seen by a witness standing at the head of the bed, on the right-hand side, with his back against the wall. Freud, for his part, has turned to the left. He has half sat up, propping himself on forearms and elbows: we see the nape of his neck. He is obviously looking at Martha and Breuer who, sitting side by side with their backs to a window, were waiting for him to wake up — and who have been given a start by the yell. Martha rises abruptly to her feet; she seems very upset.

MARTHA   Sigi!

Freud now appears to us just as Breuer and Martha see him: in his nightshirt, hair rumpled, blacker rings than ever under eyes widened by bewilderment and terror. He takes a few moments to find his bearings. When he has realized that he is in his room and has seen Martha's distress, he relaxes somewhat and gives an apologetic smile.

FREUD   A nightmare . . .

Martha is wearing black. She has been crying a lot, her eyes are swollen. She smiles tenderly at Freud.

MARTHA   Breuer has been waiting an hour for you to wake up.
     He'd like to examine you.
FREUD, *feigned good humour*   Fine! Fine! Approach, torturer!

Breuer has risen: he looks seriously worried. He does not even think of smiling. He holds his instrument-case in one hand, and with the other shifts his chair to Freud's bedside.

MARTHA   I'll leave you. *(To Breuer:)* If you need anything, you can ring: I'm sleeping in Mathilde's room.

As soon as she has turned her back, Freud's smile vanishes. He looks sombre and hunted (as at the end of Part One). But in his face we can read a forceful resolve to peer into himself and decipher his own riddles.

BREUER   Let's have a look at that heart.

Freud answers with a gesture of refusal. And as Breuer, astounded, tries to question him, the gesture of refusal changes into an imperious plea: for Breuer to hold his tongue until Martha has left the room. Breuer understands and holds his tongue. Martha has in any case opened the door. She goes out and closes it behind her.
     As soon as Freud sees the door close, he speaks. In a whisper:

FREUD, *with a rather wild laugh*   I don't have one. I see you understand me.

Breuer looks sadly at him and shakes his head; he wants to speak. Freud, with a gesture, bids him be silent. He is sitting up in bed, his gestures are abrupt and he speaks in a nervous, slightly jerky voice, which he has lowered — out of precaution, not fatigue.

I've just admitted the truth to myself.
BREUER   When?

Initially, Breuer looks at him anxiously. He thinks Freud is delirious.

FREUD   In a dream. It was a clear as day.
BREUER   What truth?
FREUD   Wait! I must remember what was written up: I've half forgotten it.

(He notices Breuer's anxiety and laughs.)

I'm not crazy.

I'm talking about my dream: there were some signs.

At these words, we find ourselves back in Freud's dream (actually, in the memory he retains of it — which he can study from various different angles).

First, the walkers in mourning clothes on the waste land. They still have their eyes shut. But this time Freud is not among them.

FREUD'S VOICE OFF   The cemetery …

Following the movements of Freud's thought, the camera draws near to one of the posts (one of the smallest ones), which bears a sign nailed three quarters of the way up. The (rather vague) impression is of a grave (or of those labels fastened to stakes in 'botanical gardens' and bearing the names of the plants).

There were graves … *(Black humour:)* … Christian ones.

I wonder what they were doing there.

The camera moves in a descending arc round the post (shot at first from behind and above) until it obtains a front view. We then discover, on the front surface of the plain wooden sign, characters and marks traced with a brush (black paint).

I'm trying to read … to read … I shan't manage it. Wait! I'm going to follow an indirect route.

The camera reverts to the men wandering with their eyes shut among the signs, some of which are very tall indeed and nailed far above their heads. It particularly emphasizes their eyelids — closed in every case by a contraction of the muscles that we feel to be violent and deliberate.

There were men … Blind men …

We discover Freud in their midst. His face: the eyelids are screwed up — those of his right eye begin to tremble. One would say he was about to open his eyes.

No. *(Imperiously:)* Opening one's eyelids is absolutely forbidden.

No sooner has Freud's voice off uttered this prohibition (in a solemn, official tone) than Freud's eyes (in his memory of the dream) open wide. He looks at once hunted and malevolent, something which we had not noticed in the dream at all. He is looking at something that is sited opposite and a little below him. He puts his hand in front of his mouth as if he were about to scream (a gesture that should be conventional).

There!

The sign viewed from the front. We see written there: 'You are requested to close the eyes.' The sign remains before us for a moment.

LAUGHTER OFF FROM FREUD   There.
BREUER, *voice off*   What was written there?
FREUD   The Law.

At once we find ourselves back in Freud's bedroom. Breuer, intrigued in spite of himself, is bending forward to listen.

You are requested to close the eyes. I'd opened mine, just enough to learn that I had to close them.

He perceives the sullen astonishment that these supposed revelations have provoked in Breuer, and begins to laugh.

Don't your dreams teach you anything, then?

Breuer shakes his head.

I have the feeling somebody is sending me messages.
BREUER   Who?
FREUD   Myself, I suppose. From myself to myself, about myself. Only, nine times out of ten, when I wake up I've lost the key.
    Words are funny in dreams. They have several meanings at the same time.
    Close whose eyes? My own first of all: out of respect. You are requested to *lower* your eyes in the presence of death.
    My father's too: I had to close his eyes.
BREUER   You did that.

Breuer finds himself slightly more at ease on this terrain: for he has understood in his own way — and outside any symbolic interpretation — what Freud is about to tell him.
Freud lifts his hands and makes a gesture with both his thumbs.

FREUD   Like that!
    That was a gesture. That means nothing. The dream tells me so: I wasn't worthy.

He turns to face Breuer and says, gazing at him with blazing eyes:

I fainted, didn't I.
    Do you know why?

Breuer shrugs his shoulders.

BREUER   Your nerves gave way. I'd been expecting it for the past two days.

FREUD   My nerves are wonderful servants. I fainted to avoid passing the cemetery gates. And to avoid seeing the grave where my father was about to be buried.

The memory of the dream: Freud is in the front row of the gentlemen with closed eyes. He is walking with them. He alone has his eyes open. He falls backwards as in reality. But no one catches him. The men move aside slightly, without stopping their dragging advance, and the procession becomes two: each row divides into two rows, which pass to either side of Freud's rigid body, stretched out on its back, its eyes wide open.

FREUD'S VOICE OFF   I passed judgement on myself, from my innermost being.

We instantly find ourselves back in the bedroom. Freud clutches Breuer's hand and looks at him in anguish.

FREUD   Breuer!

Breuer looks at him: deep, sorrowful friendship.

BREUER   I know what you're going to say. Hold your peace: what's the point?

FREUD, *sombre laugh*   How about our principles, Breuer? Healing through knowledge!

He turns his head and says, looking straight in front of him, with a deep self-disgust that is oddly mingled with sombre pride:

I didn't love my father.
    To be frank, I even think I hated him.

Breuer gives a very faint nod: he does not look astonished. Freud appears surprised by Breuer's attitude.

How did you know?

BREUER   For the past few days, I've known you were thinking that.

FREUD   But Breuer, *I wasn't thinking it.*
    Does one *think* ... such things?
    When he was dying, Mitzi told me so to my face and ... her words slid right past me.

He tries to reflect.

When he was with me, I felt unwell. That's all.
    Very unwell. Asthma. Tachycardia. Migraines.
    And the other day ... when he thanked me, I thought I was sweating blood.
    It's the dream ...

He turns towards Breuer and looks at him attentively.

Am I frightening you?

Breuer lays his free hand on that of Freud, who is still gripping his other hand.

BREUER   Friend!

He looks at him with great fondness. We can sense that he would like to show him his high regard. But Freud tenses from the very first words.

(*With a warm smile:*)

What pride!
    You want to command everything, even your own feelings.
    You didn't love him: very well. That's a great misfortune for you, but it's not a sin.
    He died happy: that's what counts. You honoured him ...
FREUD, *violently*   Playacting! He died the victim of a hoax. I didn't respect him in my heart.
BREUER   Freud, I know some very decent men ...

He is obviously going to say: '... who find themselves in the same situation as you'.

FREUD   They're curs.

(*Very hard, unbending, as if he were teaching the Law:*)

'Thou shalt honour thy father and mother!'

(*A pause.*)

And you, did you love him?
BREUER   My father? Enormously.
FREUD   No: I'm speaking of mine.
BREUER   Yes, I loved him.
FREUD   Why?
BREUER   I've told you: his Jewish gentleness. He was good.
FREUD   So he was nice. But for my own part, I hated him. I'd done so for ten years, twenty perhaps.
    There must be a monster — either him or me. Since it's not him ...

He stops abruptly, his gaze intent. Breuer looks at him in concern.

Wait a moment ... There's a double meaning, I was sure of it ...

In the memory of the dream.
 We find ourselves suddenly back on the waste land.

FREUD'S VOICE OFF   In the dream.

But this time the men in mourning, alone or in little groups, are motionless. Each individual or group stands in front of a sign, heads tilted forward (if it is fastened below them) or raised (if it is on the top of a tall post): in short, they look as if they were reading. They are not in fact reading anything, since their eyes remain closed. But this time, we can read on each sign: 'You are requested to close the eyes.'

FREUD'S VOICE OFF, *as if quoting grammatical examples*   The police abuses its powers and the government closes its eyes. I'm willing to close my eyes to this piece of thoughtlessness ...

The crowd with their closed eyes. Suddenly, Freud is there, with his eyes wide open. He is looking at a sign (on the 1.1. metre post we have described).
 On the sign we read:
 'Close the eyes
 TO' (in block capitals).
 We find ourselves back in Freud's bedroom. Freud, upright, his brow sweating, agitated.

FREUD   To what? Eh?
 Sons close their eyes to their fathers' sins.
 Hide, hide, bury! What pretty work!
 I must have only half done it. Some indigestible memory — it must have remained within me. Not far from my consciousness. Poisoning it.
 Whatever can he have done?
BREUER   Who?
FREUD   My father.
BREUER   He did nothing but good.
FREUD   Then my disgust, my feelings of discomfort, my resentment — it's all causeless. Between him and me, there was ...

With a kind of despair, as if to himself:

But *what?* If my mother's prepared to talk ...
BREUER, *indignantly*   You're not going to ...?
FREUD   Not today. Nor tomorrow. Later on.
 I'll ask her to tell me the story of our life ...
 Did I faint from shame? Did I deem myself unworthy to enter the cemetery?
 Or ... was it a deliberate refusal? A judgement I was pronouncing upon my father: unworthy to be buried?

Very urgently — he is seized by an idea:

Breuer! *(With a faintly humorous smile, but deep conviction:)* Of all my fathers, you're the only one left. Help me.

Whereupon, he at once climbs from the bed and stands up, before Breuer has uttered a word.

[Dream about the card-players. Freud has three fathers. He discovers the meaning of the dream.]

[14]

Half an hour later, in Freud's consulting-room, the shutters are open, dawn is breaking, it is still dark. Freud is sitting at the desk. He is dropping with sleep, but he is furiously writing in his shirt-sleeves on a big white sheet of paper. Under the heading 'transference' in capital letter, we can still read: 'transference is the best proof of the sexual aetiology of the neuroses'. But the handwriting gradually becomes distorted. Beneath the action of sleep, it is becoming more and more incomprehensible. The pen eventually falls from Freud's hands, while a voice (a very natural one, just like a normal rummy player's) emerges from the hubbub.

HUBBUB, *quite simply that of a café filled with customers. It is an undistorted repeat of the sounds of the Aesculapius Coffee House. The strangeness of the dream lies in the fact that these very normal café sounds (chinking saucers, orders, voices summoning the waiter, conversations) should be heard in the consulting-room, without Freud appearing to hear them.*

When the pen drops from Freud's hands, a voice stands out from this background of sound:

VOICE OFF   That's a grand slam! *(These terms may be replaced by jargon appropriate to the* period.)*

Freud raises his head. He sees a café booth (a table, three players) situated at the same distance from his desk that the booth with the three doctors was in relation to the two friends. The setting is not hazy; on the contrary, it is terribly precise. But — as always — details are lacking. In particular, two walls of darkness hide the side partitions (those containing the window and the washbasin). The rest of the scenery is absolutely clear and systematically organized. Freud's desk is still there, cleared of the books and papers tht were piled on it: it is a minister's desk. There remains a glass inkwell and a brand new blotter — unmarked blotting-paper — on an absolutely empty surface. The floor which connects it to the players' booth has nothing to break its continuity. It is the consulting-room floor itself, reduced to a very wide 'carriageway' by the two walls of darkness and reducing the dimensions of the room.

The booth is exactly like those in the doctors' coffee house. It stands against the rear wall; so the coffee-room has disappeared. But on the rear wall, like a symbol of the missing coffee house, a very large painting represents the Aesculapius Coffee House filled with card-players, with orderlies in white coats wearing top-hats.

---

* Freud was a regular player of the popular German card-game Tarock, but Sartre refers to games popular in France (belote) and to terms from other games ('pique, repique and capote' from piquet) in a quite random fashion. [Trans.]

The three players, in morning-dress, are bent over the table. Freud can see only the backs of the necks of the first two, who screen the third from him. When they sit up, he first recognizes Meynert. At that moment, the other two, seen sideways on, have utterly nondescript faces (this must not be taken to mean that they are vague or blurred, simply that actors with unremarkable features will have been cast for the parts). Yet no sooner does he turn towards the second player (the one facing Meynert, seated at the outside end of the bench) than he recognizes him as Jakob. There is no visual transformation. Freud's gaze will travel from Meynert to the hands of the player opposite and will move up from these to his face which, without the substitution being seen, will have become that of Jakob. The face of the third player remains insignificant and unknown. Freud, moreover, does not seem to attach any importance to him.

MEYNERT, *in his own voice*   Last hand?
JAKOB   Oh yes, last one!

The players are bare-headed. The stranger smokes nervously throughout the dream — gold-tipped cigarettes. Jakob seems very animated. His hands tremble, his voice quavers. He looks senile and malevolent. There are no cards on the table. But at once the three men take — from the upper surface of the backrests in the booth — three top-hats and three black books (resembling ordinary vulgates), which now happen to be on this surface (horizontal, of brown polished wood). With a single gesture, they transfer the books to their left hands and with their right hands put on their hats.

They hold their books like packs of cards.

The third player tears out a page from his book and lays it on the table.

MEYNERT   Spades are trumps!
UNKNOWN PLAYER   I've got some.

Meynert and Jakob each tear pages from their respective books and lay them on the sheet torn from the stranger's book.

MEYNERT, *authoritarian*   It doesn't work the way people say, we need a fourth player. We need someone alive.

(Hailing Freud:)

Hey, you there! Come and play with us then.

Freud rises to his feet and goes towards them. He is in Tyrolean dress, a felt hat with a feather on his head. He approaches the players. Meynert shifts up against the wall to make room for him. Jakob and the stranger look at him malevolently.

JAKOB   He hasn't got a top-hat.
MEYNERT   I'll lend him one.

With his free right hand, Meynert gropes for an invisible top-hat (which must be lying on the bench between him and the wall). His hand re-emerges with a top-hat, which he hands to Freud.
The latter changes hats. As soon as he has the hat on his head, the unknown player speaks to him.

UNKNOWN PLAYER, *in Meynert's voice, very disagreeably*   You don't know how to play, of course.

MEYNERT, *in a very indulgent voice, that of Breuer*   We'll teach him!

(Introducing Freud to the two others:) My son!

The two others look at Freud in no friendly manner. He bows, then replaces his hat on his head. They respond with mere nods.

MEYNERT   Sit down.

Freud sits.

JAKOB   I haven't done the introductions. *(Pointing at Freud:)* My son!

Freud rises to his feet and bows. Haughty, disagreeable nod from the stranger. Meynert alone, with a broad smile, raises his hat with a flourish. Freud sits down again.

UNKNOWN PLAYER, *same disagreeable tone of voice*   Wait, you rude child! Stand up, will you!

Freud stands.

UNKNOWN PLAYER   Gentlemen, I present you my son. I'm not proud of him.

Freud bows. Nod from Jakob; Meynert raises his hat with a flourish and a broad smile. Freud sits down again.

UNKNOWN PLAYER   Here are the rules, little idiot. Everyone cheats, no one must draw attention to the fact. Look.

He tears a leaf from his book. This time it is an engraving. An enormous ace of hearts is portrayed in it.
Fresh card: the queen of hearts.

Ace of spades!
King of clubs!
You say nothing. You behave as if you believed what I'm saying.
Understand?

Freud bows.
> *The stranger effects a countercheck. He shows the queen of hearts.*

Very well. What's this card?
FREUD, *childlike but obstinate tone of voice*   Cäcilie!

Freud's voice is that of a child.
> *Freud looks frightened by what he has just said. Jakob and the stranger fly into a rage and point their fingers at him.*

JAKOB AND THE STRANGER   I'm ashamed of you! What a little telltale!
> A little busybody!

Jakob and the stranger together (they are facing one another and bow):

Forgive us, gentlemen!

Freud weeps with violent sobs. Meynert lays a hand on his shoulder. He has Breuer's voice, but it is powerful and funereal:

MEYNERT   Don't listen to us, my friend, we're dead.
FREUD, *normal voice*   Dead?

Freud stops weeping. He looks at his father. In Jakob's place he sees a wax figure representing him. He turns towards Meynert: he is a wax figure. The stranger has fallen forward, face-down on the table. His top-hat has remained on his head. A gold-tipped cigarette is burning away on a saucer.

> *(Freud bursts into Homeric laughter.)*
> > *(The laughter continues.)*

The Aesculapius Coffee House. A huge crowd. Freud, seated alone at a marble table on a raised platform, is triumphantly tearing all the pages from his book and throwing them down on the table. They are engravings representing hearts (seven of hearts, ten of hearts, etc.)

FREUD, *speaking as his laughter continues off*   Hearts!
> Hearts!
> Hearts!
> And hearts again!
> Nobody's cheating.

Throwing down one more card:

The queen of hearts!

It is the queen of spades. Freud's laughter abruptly ceases.

He is at his desk, just as we saw him when sleep overcame him. In his shirt-sleeves. The pen has made a blot on the paper. Freud's head is raised. He takes the pen (obviously in order to write about transference) but sees the scrawls covering the sheet and, with a sharp tug, rips off the page.

On the new page, he writes: 'trans . . .', but then puts down his pen, stands up, paces up and down the room for a moment, returns to his desk, puts out the lamp: it is daytime.

He goes over to the window, cools his brow by laying it against the panes, reflects, then goes back. He is tousle-haired, his face grimed by his sleepless night, dark rings under his eyes; he looks crazy, but crazy with happiness. A joyful exaltation seems to sustain him. He turns away from the window and looks at the rear door. Intently. Following his intent gaze, we shall first see the door.

VOICE OFF   Who is it?

He speaks without his lips moving. Instantly we know who he is referring to: against the door, of which only the upper part can be seen at present, the booth which Freud saw in his dream on the other wall has reappeared, lit by the harsh, clear light of the dream. (But we know that Freud is awake and that this is an image accompanying his thoughts.) The stranger appears to us as he was at the end of the dream. He has fallen face-down on the table. We can see of him only his top-hat, the nape of his neck and part of his back. Meynert and Jakob are temporarily missing from this image, which has retained the schematic character of the dream but also its sharpness.

VOICE OFF, *hesitatingly*   Initially there was Dr Grundgens' head.

The man in the hat slowly lifts his head and we again see his commonplace features, described at the beginning of the dream. No sooner is his face recognizable (view from above) than we see Freud once more — lucid, his gaze penetrating, his back to the window. He speaks without moving his lips.

It wasn't his real head.

We see the booth once more — the player has fallen face-down again. Motionless.

When I see only the nape of his neck, I feel that his *real* head is there, squashed against the table. It was Dr Grundgens, but it was also someone else. He has been dead for ten years and I never think about him.

Why?

Because he was dead.

Meynert and Jakob are in their places, without books, their arms at their sides (memory of the dream simpler than the dream itself). The two players (in profile, motionless) have become the wax figures of the dream.

Three fathers.

Three dead men.

But they told me I was *alive*.

I took the dead Grundgens, in order to persuade myself that the third father was dead too.

The two players have disappeared. The man in the top-hat straightens up very slowly: it is Breuer. He looks in Freud's direction with an air of grievous, desperate reproach.

As we see this living head, Freud's voice off continues:

He makes me uncomfortable.

He paralyses me.

So I wished for his death, without admitting it to myself.

And I offered myself it, without admitting that to myself either.

Slyly.

Cravenly.

In a dream.

We return to Freud, who is still in front of the window and who looks clear-minded and almost gay. His lips do not move.

For a moment this face strikes us as triumphant.

He crosses his consulting-room and goes to sit down at his work-table. He tears off the sheet on which he had written the beginning of the word: transference. He picks up his pen and writes on the blank sheet following:

'On this Friday morning, after thousands of years of mistakes, I, Sigmund Freud, have understood the meaning of dreams.'

As he writes, we hear his voice off:

Sleep is an instinct. Everything starts from there.

*He puts down his pen, and from beneath a pile of notebooks and manuscript sheets takes a fat exercise-book bound in black: '**Dreams**'. This word is written on a label stuck on the spine of the exercise-book. In freeing the exercise-book, he causes the pile to collapse but does not seem concerned. He leafs through the book, which is filled with his handwriting and whose first pages are dog-eared and yellowing. It can at once be seen that it is a kind of inventory of Freud's dreams (and those of other people who have recounted them).*

There is *first of all* the urge to sleep.

A page catches his attention. 'Dream of 22 March 1882 (reconstructed in 1886 in accordance with my memories).'

Together with Freud, we see anew his dream of 22 March.

Freud is lying on a camp bed. His bedroom is narrow and very poor, his clothes are placed carefully on a chair.

He is asleep. He appears much younger than today. Above all, much healthier and fresher. Firm skin, almost plump face, no rings under the eyes. Sleep helps to give him a childlike air. It is morning; the sun is streaming through the shutters. But above all, with all the strength of his slumbers, the sleeper must resist some knocking at the door.

I'd asked to be woken up: I didn't want to miss Meynert's lecture.

Classic scene of the individual who has himself called, but who rebels against his own orders and wants to go on sleeping. A flash is sufficient, provided it gives us the feeling that the sleep's resistance is intense.

Wish to sleep; wish to hear Meynert.

    (At the moment when Freud stands up:)

I found a compromise.
    I went to see Meynert in a dream.

Freud suddenly stands up in his nightshirt, goes to the door and opens it; it leads to the hospital ward we saw in the first scenes of the screenplay. And, indeed, Meynert is just doing his round. Freud (leaving his bedroom in his nightshirt) finds himself immediately at Meynert's side. The latter, of course, is as we saw him on his 'round' (top-hat, cane and gloves). He takes Freud's arm and calmly goes on with his round. Students in white coats or ordinary jackets follow the two men. Meynert stops in front of a bed. This bed is empty (like all the others in the room: schematic character of the dream). But Meynert nonetheless uses it for a demonstration and a clinical inter-pretation, just as if the bed were occupied. He speaks. We do not hear a word of what he says, but we hear the tapping of his cane on the edge of the bed. This is simply the knocking at the door. As the rhythm of the knocking is intensified, the result is that Meynert taps faster and faster with his cane. The cane gets carried away, which gives Meynert (whose face remains that of a teacher giving a lesson) a furious, comical air of great haste.
    Shot of Freud on his camp bed, awoken by the knocking at the door.

Luckily, Mitzi was knocking too loudly.

Freud — the one who is reflecting today about the dream — is still leafing through his exercise-book. A new title catches his attention: 'Dream about little Franz (Martha's cousin, aged four).'
    The text which follows is so dense and closely written that it is indecipherable. For a brief moment, we see only this title and text, while Freud's voice off explains:

He was in Rome. His parents had been with him to see the Tivoli water gardens during the day.
    That night ...

A baroque fountain. Everything spouts water (dolphins, nereids, etc.). On a pedestal, in the middle of the pool, a little faience boy (life-size, aged four) dressed like a young boy of the period emits water through his nostrils, his ears, the tips of all his fingers and the (pierced) toes of his shoes.

BACKGROUND NOISE: *In the pool, a cool, attractive plashing.*

A nanny raising her arms to the heavens in front of a little boy's bed (he is invisible). The covers are thrown back. On the uncovered sheet, a damp patch.

VOICE OFF   He had dreamed that he was a fountain, in order to satisfy his needs without waking up.

Freud has laid down the exercise-book. Under the sentence 'On this Friday, etc.' *he writes:* 'Dream — hallucinatory fulfilment of a wish'.

[Freud with Cäcilie. Associations.]

[16]

At the Körtners' house.

In the hall on the ground floor. Freud and Frau Körtner. The latter, stony, dressed in black, is looking at him without any great liking.
Freud is cold and self-possessed.

FRAU KÖRTNER   Dr Breuer's refusing?
FREUD   He's refusing.
FRAU KÖRTNER   And you want to go on?

Nod from Freud.

I don't know whether my daughter will wish to receive you. Yesterday, she was dead set against you.
FREUD   We shall see.

He prepares to go in to Cäcilie. She checks him.

FRAU KÖRTNER   It's preferable for me to put the matter to her.

She goes in to her daughter and closes the door.
Freud's cold serenity disappears: he is boiling with impatience. To keep himself in counten-ance, he goes over to the piano and looks at Herr Körtner's portrait. Frau Körtner's absence lasts only a moment. He turns round. She looks at him in surprise, then, pointing to the open door:

FRAU KÖRTNER'S VOICE OFF   Dr Freud!
     Please go in.

Freud has recovered his poise. He goes in. Frau Körtner closes the door behind him. From afar we see Cäcilie, propped up on her pillows, as in the preceding scenes. She is in bed; the doll is invisible. Cäcilie looks at Freud with a mischievous smile.
She speaks in a bantering tone as Freud approaches her.

CÄCILIE   And here comes the spirit of seriousness. *Entrée de ballet.*

(She laughs.)

What a dancer! Wherever did you find that 'doctor's step'? It's sheer genius.

Freud (movements still rather formal, but very calm) approaches the bed, nods a greeting, takes a chair and sits down familiarly at the patient's bedside.
   Cäcilie pretends to be abashed.

I'm teasing you, Doctor, forgive me. And as for seriousness, you'd do well to put a few particles of it into this crazy head of mine.

FREUD   You're no judge of faces, Cäcilie: look at me. I'm not serious at all.

Freud is looking very well: the shower and the change of linen have transformed him. Yet he has retained his air of passionate, slightly crazy gaiety. Even in his voice there is something frivolous and wild. He is very sincere (though exploiting his sincerity): he means that an adventurer of science is everything but 'serious'. Cäcilie looks at him, stops smiling, but makes no comment.

   (Smiling:) How are you, this morning?

Cäcilie suddenly recovers her smile.
   A touch of aggressiveness:

CÄCILIE   Very well.
   I wonder if I want to get better.

   (Worldly:)

Do you know that French proverb: 'Pour vivre heureux, vivons couchés'? ['If we want to stay happy, let's stay tucked up.']

She quotes the proverb in French. Freud cannot restrain himself from correcting her. In French:

FREUD   'Cachés'. ['tucked away']

Cäcilie assumes an expression of annoyance:

CÄCILIE   'Cachés!' *(In English:)* Oh yes, I know. You see how serious you are! And watch your French.
   (Pointing to her mouth:) The accent.
   (Like a teacher:) Cachés! Ca-chés!

She repeats the word in French.

FREUD, *without responding to these remarks*   Would you spend your whole life in bed?
CÄCILIE   I'm expecting to.
   I could even earn my living. There are jobs a person can do in bed. *(She continues*

very hurriedly:) We used to know a poor lace-maker, she was paralysed ...

(A pause.)

Freud listens to her attentively. She stops short. In a rather harsh tone of mockery:

Does the great Dr Breuer refuse to treat me?

Freud nods.
   As if it were Freud who were reproaching Breuer for abandoning Cäcilie:

Oh, but you must understand him, Doctor! He treats ministers, generals! Why should he bother with this unhappy little Ophelia?

She points to herself, with a humble air full of coquetry.
   Detachedly, and looking at her left hand which is tracing signs on the sheets:

Even in your own case, my mother had told me you weren't thinking of coming back.

Freud answers with a smile, and in an expressionless voice:

FREUD   I changed my mind.

Cäcilie's left hand continues its movement — whose rhythm intensifies — as the young girl replies with irony and in a very worldly tone of voice.

CÄCILIE   So much the better: I'd have missed you. I adore visits: it distracts me. You'll be a family friend.
FREUD, *without raising his voice*   I'll be your doctor.

Cäcilie stops smiling. She looks at Freud irritably.

CÄCILIE   I tell you I don't want to get better.
FREUD, *indifferently*   That's your affair.
CÄCILIE, *half-angry, half-amused*   Watch out! I'll fight.
FREUD   A duel?
CÄCILIE   Yes. It will be very amusing.

A thought strikes her: her face darkens.

(A pause.)

How about the method?
FREUD   What method?

CÄCILIE   The alternative method: have you found it?

Freud shrugs his shoulders. Evasively:

FREUD   Pooh!

With both hands, Cäcilie absently traces magic signs on the sheet. Freud observes her. She follows his gaze with her eyes, casts a glance at her own hands, instantly checks their movements. Immediately afterwards, her hands placed flat on the sheet, she deems herself calm again, composes her features into a suitable expression, raises her head and turns to Freud with somewhat forced aggressiveness.

CÄCILIE   Well, then? What are we going to do this morning?
FREUD   Play.
CÄCILIE, *frowning*   What game?
FREUD   I say a word and you tell me what it brings to mind.

This whole exchange has the tension of a verbal duel. They lean towards one another, smiling the while, watching each other closely.

CÄCILIE   And then?
FREUD   That's all.
CÄCILIE   And who wins?
FREUD   Me, if I obtain information about your illness; you, if I find nothing.

Shrugging her shoulders:

CÄCILIE   You won't find anything. Just imagine: words!
FREUD   Let's try.
CÄCILIE   What if I lie?
FREUD   I'll know.
CÄCILIE   Let's see.

Cäcilie, frowning, looks at Freud and all of a sudden makes up her mind.
Freud leans back in his chair, pretending to relax, and says carelessly:

FREUD   First word: tree.

Cäcilie looks at him, dumbfounded, then bursts out laughing.
He remains impassive.

CÄCILIE   Tree? That brings to mind a tree. Yes, indeed!
    What would you expect it to make me think of?
    A bitch? A crane?

FREUD   Do you see a tree?
CÄCILIE   In my mind? Yes.
FREUD'S VOICE OFF   What tree?

We see some poplars quite a long way off, by the water's edge; then, suddenly, the trunk of an oak from very close to. At about two metres from the ground. Our gaze slides along the trunk, travelling from the bottom to the top and right up to its leafy crown.

     (Sound of axe-blows off.)

CÄCILIE, *off, with pride*   The most beautiful one. The oak.

The oak tilts. Clearly invisible woodcutters are in the process of chopping it down.

     (The blows off redouble.)

As the oak comes down with a cracking sound:

CÄCILIE, *abruptly*   I hate woodcutters.

     (Cracking sound off.)

Shot of Cäcilie, laughing in Freud's face.

     (On screen:) That's all.
     (Very faintly anxious:) Who won?
FREUD   You. I didn't find anything.
CÄCILIE, *smiling*   I'd warned you.
     (With vague regret:) Nothing at all.
     (Somewhat intrigued — though still aggressive:) I offer you a return match.

He nods.

FREUD   Very well.

He relaxes once more against the back of his chair, half closes his eyes as if he were about to fall asleep, and in a drowsy voice lets slip:

Swan.

Cäcilie suddenly looks at him with a hunted expression:

CÄCILIE   What?
FREUD   I said: swan.

Cäcilie composes her features. She has an air of false calm, but is holding herself in.

CÄCILIE   The bird? I hadn't understood. Very well. That brings to my mind ...
(Voice off — stifled, lying as it goes along:) ... white fur.

The images go by very rapidly, her voice is quick and stifled.
  A man with his back to us: black cloak, black top-hat, entering a building by a carriage-gateway that opens onto pitch darkness.
  The foot of a dark, slimy wall:

(Her voice more and more stifled:) White feathers, wings that fly ...

A rat that scurries at top speed into its hole.
  An old toothless beggar-woman executes an obscene dance — lifting her skirts over her withered thighs — while a dog takes a collection standing on its hind legs with the bowl in its jaws.
  A skater does in fact appear on an ice-rink; but it is the old beggar-woman, who waltzes on her skates, her skirts lifted.

(Painfully:) Majesty. Calm. A girl dancing.

(The word 'dancing' seems to have slipped out.)

No!
  (She corrects herself at once:) A girl skating! A skater gliding across the ice.
FREUD   You're lying!

We find ourselves back in Cäcilie's room. Freud and the young girl are looking aggressively at one another. Freud tries to dominate her but she rebels.

FREUD   You admitted to me that you hated swans.

Cäcilie eludes him: she escapes into wild laughter.

CÄCILIE, *laughing*   Oh yes, Doctor: because they're plucked!
  (With a touch of vulgarity:) If you pluck poultry, what's left? A naked body.
FREUD   Nobody plucks swans.
CÄCILIE   Everybody plucks them all the time.

She swiftly unbuttons her sleeve and slides it up her arm (the arm nearest to Freud, that is, her right arm) to above the elbow.
  She stretches out all four fingers and places the thumb of the same hand against them as if in imitation of a beak.

That animal brings to mind an arm.

Because of its neck, you know.

It's as satin-smooth as my skin. Gliding's voluptuous ...

With her half-bare, raised right arm she imitates the swan gliding over the water (the gliding motion of its head and neck); she passes her bare arm very close to Freud's moustache and beard.

 The arm glides, returns towards Cäcilie; the bend of the elbow finds itself at the level of Cäcilie's mouth. Cäcilie bends her head forward slightly, smiling, voluptuous and full of challenge. She puts the tip of her tongue out and licks the bend of her elbow with roguish sensuality. She stops and pulls her sleeve down again; as she buttons it up, she looks at Freud through half-closed eyes, laughing provocatively to herself.

How serious you are!

 Well? Who won this time?

FREUD I did. I guessed that you lied.

Freud speaks in a light tone and gaily, as if it were a real game. Cäcilie gives herself away somewhat, because she wants to resist.

CÄCILIE All right. But you must find out *why*.

FREUD, *carelessly* Later.

CÄCILIE Then you've only half won.

FREUD So be it.

He rises and takes a few steps, with his back turned to Cäcilie. He looks at some books on the shelves. He picks one up. It is a bible. He opens it. On the fly-leaf, he reads these words printed with a stamp: 'ex libris Dr Josef Breuer'.

 He closes the book again and, replacing it on the shelves, asks without turning towards Cäcilie:

How about the decapitated baby?

 Still hidden in your bed?

There is a silence. He thinks he has disconcerted Cäcilie and turns abruptly round: but he sees a scornful face, not in the least worried, and Cäcilie bursts into laughter.

 She thrusts her hand into the bed and brings out the baby, which she brandishes triumphantly. She holds it out to him.

CÄCILIE Still. *(Spiteful derision:)* There it is! Take it and don't think you can impress me: it's Mama who betrayed me.

 Come on! Take it.

Freud takes it and, as he closes his hand on the baby, seems embarrassed. Cäcilie notices this. To heighten his confusion, she adds in an almost vulgar tone of voice:

Very well. You can feel the warmth of my breast, Doctor.

Freud replaces the baby on Cäcilie's bed, and she at once seizes it, smiling to herself as if in secret complicity.

    Either to prevent her from gaining the upper hand, or because he judges her to be in the proper state, Freud suddenly leans towards Cäcilie, who instinctively shrinks back (she has a strange look in her eyes, exalted, scornful but hunted). He speaks to her in a voice devoid of particular intonation, but quick and quite harsh:

FREUD   Frau Körtner told me something else.

Cäcilie looks suddenly terrified.

CÄCILIE, *hoarsely*   What?
FREUD   She has never suffered from tuberculosis.

    (More gently:)

Why did you lie to me?

Cäcilie makes no reply: her hands clutch the sheet.

CÄCILIE, *sincerely bewildered*   I lied?

She flings herself forward, suddenly beside herself with rage, and thrusts her menacing face into that of Freud, who recoils slightly.
    Sudden explosion of fury:

    (Voice of a prostitute arrested during a police roundup:)

Cop! Filthy cop! Flatfoot! Pig!

She stops as abruptly as she has begun. Freud stares at her dumbfounded.

FREUD   Wherever did you get those words from?
CÄCILIE   From all the poor girls like me who are tortured for nights on end at the police-station by rotten swine like you.

With a violent, crazy look:

Policemen! Judges! Always! Everywhere. Never a word of sympathy.

She starts sobbing.
    In the midst of a flood of tears and hiccoughs:

I'm not a criminal!

I'm not a criminal!
Why am I being treated like a murderess?
I haven't killed anybody!

Freud has sat down again calmly. He looks at her with interest. He says in an objective tone:

FREUD   No, you haven't killed anybody.

Cäcilie looks at him, her eyes shining with anger and some indefinable passion. Her face is blazing; her mouth is twisted into a scornful grimace. There are still tears on her cheeks.

CÄCILIE   What do you know about it?

Freud looks at her without replying, his gaze quite devoid of expression. She calms down gradually, through a very evident effort of will: her breast heaves violently, her breathing is rapid. She dries her tears with a handkerchief she has picked up from the bed; she strives to steady her breathing. She eventually forces herself to smile. Displaying the baby with its broken head:

You can see for yourself: I'm a babykiller.

This explanation (she has killed a pottery baby) has obviously occurred to her because she feared she had gone too far. What is really involved, of course, is her mother's murder; as we shall see, she reproaches herself for it quite consciously. And her resistance to Freud, in this particular case, is entirely conscious. Nevertheless, the explanation of her lie is sincere.

Tuberculosis, that's not a lie, at any rate not one to you. It's a story I told myself — and I ended up believing it.
My poor Papa was kindness itself. But sometimes he was ... thoughtless: he had so much to do!
He gave that dinner, after Mama's accident, when she was still in the clinic.

She speaks in a very normal voice, embarrassed, not looking at Freud, with great charm and a touch of coquetry (but no more than a normal young girl would have allowed herself in those days). Freud listens with an understanding expression, nodding his head.

FREUD   Convalescent?
CÄCILIE   No.
FREUD   In danger?
CÄCILIE   Her life in danger. And I, like a proper little monkey, I took advantage of it to steal her role as lady of the house.

She smiles, seeming to view her self-accusations with the indulgence commonly displayed towards a child's pranks.

That displeased me; especially with regard to my father's memory. So in my daydreams I touched the past up a bit. I imagined that my mother used to be away for long periods — six months every year — in order to have treatment for a lung conditin. So my father was really obliged to return people's invitations — that's unavoidable, particularly in his profession. And as for me, I was really obliged to stand in for my mother.

Freud has assumed an earnest expression. He nods his head; in fact, he is preparing his next question.

She seems at once calmer and somewhat vague.

(Smiling as if to herself:)

That wasn't a crime, was it?

(Amiably:)

FREUD   Certainly not. How long did your mother stay in the clinic?

He questions her very gently — the better to surprise her; one would think he was just asking for administrative details.

CÄCILIE   Two months.
FREUD   And you were?
CÄCILIE   Fourteen.
FREUD   Then I can't understand what you told me the other day.

Cäcilie's face becomes wary and morose.

From the age of five you used to go out alone with your father, and his friends used to treat you like a little lady. Where was Frau Körtner?

Freud imbues the question that concludes his little speech with considerable harshness. But Cäcilie has already grasped what he is getting at. She is on her guard. As soon as she hears the question, she lets her head slump back on her pillow and says, very sulkily:

CÄCILIE   I'm tired.

A silence. Freud continues to observe her.

FREUD   Poor Cäcilie! Do you want me to go away?
CÄCILIE, *rather sly*   No — because I'd be bored.
       But you won't ask me any more questions for today.
FREUD   A truce: agreed. We'll carry on with the duel another time.

CÄCILIE   What are we going to do?

(With a reproach whose bad faith is blatant:)

After all, you are here to treat me.

FREUD   You don't want to be cured.

CÄCILIE   I don't know what I want.

FREUD   Talk to me.

CÄCILIE   What about?

FREUD   Everything that comes into your mind.

CÄCILIE   What if it's only silly things?

FREUD   Silly things will do.

Don't disregard anything.

CÄCILIE   Very well.

You're going to take me for an idiot, my mind's completely empty.

FREUD   One's mind is never empty.

CÄCILIE, *interrogating herself*   What am I thinking at the moment. That you're here, that you've come to see me. That it's morning. Late in the morning.

She closes her eyes.

Wait! I think I was nervy yesterday evening. Oh yes, that's it! I don't know why. I took my sleeping pill and I slept very well and I was very nice to my maid this morning — Marie, you know — because of a dream.

FREUD   A dream?

CÄCILIE   A dream I had during the night. I'm scarcely going to tell you about that.

Freud has reached his goal at last: for an almost imperceptible moment he has the intent, almost pitiless gaze of the hunter. But he controls himself almost immediately. Cäcilie for once is not on her guard: she really believes that her dreams are meaningless. She is taken in by Freud's air of detachment.

FREUD, *with a languid air*   A dream!
Pooh!

(Indifferently:) Why not?

CÄCILIE   Because it's meaningless!

(Unsuspecting:)

Actually, I like remembering my dreams, especially when they're in colour, like this one.

But for you, it'll be so boring ...

FREUD   Yes indeed, that may very well be so.

He settles into his chair as if to hear a story that promises to be tedious.

May I smoke, Cäcilie?
CÄCILIE   That depends. Turkish tobacco?
FREUD   A cigar.
CÄCILIE   A cigar, yes. That's more virile than all those cigarettes …

Freud pulls out his cigar-case, chooses one and lights it while Cäcilie is beginning her account of her dream.

There was a tower.

There would be an advantage in shooting this dream — though only this one — in colour. The colours should be subordinated to the schematic character of dreams. They would exist when Cäcilie mentions them (in the case of the woman, and on the tower). But when they are not explicitly indicated, objects remain in black and white. At the same time, these colours are clearcut and distinct. As far away as possible from being natural. Painter's colours, artificial and very elaborate. With a kind of naïve quality. For example, the red tower is red, almost like in coloured picture-books for children. The tower resembles the lighthouse we showed when Cäcilie was speaking about the seven swans, in the previous session.
    Perfectly round and of considerable height, it is also evocative of a phallic symbol. Behind the tower, a marvellously calm, green sea, with a little white foam on the crests of small waves. But we can never situate the sea and the tower with respect to one another: either the sea is spoken of and that is what we see (the tower has disappeared), or the tower is spoken of and the sea disappears.
    The tower appears at the moment when Cäcilie begins her story. It is in black and white.

CÄCILIE'S VOICE OFF   A round tower.
     In front of the sea.

     (Ecstatic:)

It was a marvellously green sea.

At this momen we see the sea (as if viewed from the top of the tower) but the tower has disappeared.

FREUD'S VOICE OFF   And the tower? What colour?
CÄCILIE'S VOICE OFF, *furious*   Red. But let me talk!

The tower reappears, red. A little, low door at the foot of the building. Above the door, a lantern (like outside brothels) — but its light, red and dazzling, goes on and off regularly like a lighthouse.

CÄCILIE   I wasn't there but I saw everything.
         The woman.

A woman appears at the door of the tower. She remains indistinct, not because of the dream (at least not directly), but because of her position: she is in the shadow of the passageway.

Painted.

The woman emerges from the passageway. She is outside. Stark naked and covered in pictures (resembling tattoos). On her breast and reaching down to her belly, a wild animal fleeing — a hare or a rat — and huntsmen giving chase. On her back and reaching down to her loins, a crowd of gentlemen in top-hats. A loincloth (vaguely reminiscent of the loincloths from Egyptian statuettes or paintings) conceals her genitals. On her sides, laces and buckles have been drawn with a brush, as if the woman were wearing a corset. These networks join the huntsmen to the gentlemen in top-hats.

   Her face is smeared with ochre — as if a white-skinned woman had clumsily tried to give herself the golden skin of an Egyptian. Her gaze is embarrassingly intent, her jet-black hair is pulled tight into sleek coils. On her head, the classic crown of an Egyptian queen (the wife of Amenophis, for example).

CÄCILIE'S VOICE OFF, *she is doubled up with laughter*   A real picture: it was oil paint.

The woman begins to walk, very upright — one would say she was drilling. And at once the surroundings become more distinct (as she walks): she is on a rocky platform (upon which the tower too is built).

   She comes and goes; she moves away from the tower, she draws close to it. When she goes towards the tower, the image is replaced by that of the sea, such as we saw it earlier. When she moves away from it, we see only her — and the rock beneath her feet.

   So we have not been able to see a man whom she suddenly bumps into, as she moves away from the tower.

   This man is very tall, much taller than her, almost a giant. But he is stooped, and tall as he is his clothes are still too big for him: his sleeves come down to the second joints of his fingers. Even his top-hat falls over his ears.

   We see him from the rear, bent over with arms dangling and knees bent (his stance resembling an orang-utan's as much as a man's). But the little we can see of his neck allows us to guess at a fine, well-trimmed, blonde beard.

   The woman draws herself up majestically.

WOMAN   I am the wife of Potiphar.

She takes the right hand of the giant and raises it towards her. She happens to have a gold ring in her left hand. She takes the ring finger of the giant, who does not resist, and puts the ring on his finger. Her gaze remains intent but her mouth smiles.

   She lets go of the hand, which drops down — as if dead. The ring, too large for the finger, rolls across the rock.

(Sound of the gold ring striking against the rock.)

The man runs away. Still bent over like a monkey. He stumbles over a stone and falls forward like a dummy, without even having the reflex of protecting himself with his hands. He remains prostrate on the ground. He is dead or it is just a heap of clothes. The woman looks at him with fierce pride, as if avenged.

VOICE OFF OF THE MAIDSERVANT   It really wasn't worth killing me.

The painted woman disappears. We see the red tower again. Above the door there is an open window; the lantern has disappeared. (The window, by contrast, was not previously visible.)
     A woman is at the window. She has a vulgar, spiteful face (around fifty), which is however very clearly defined (it is obviously somebody who exists in real life). The striking thing about her is simply the fact that her chambermaid's apron barely conceals a very young body dressed in a black dress (about eighteen, apparently) and that her hands are long, slender, very beautiful, with rings. (They are Frau Körtner's hands: we have often seen them. But neither Cäcilie nor Freud will notice this detail and the spectator will only be able to observe it in passing: no allusion will ever be made to it.) The woman repeats in a vulgar, false voice, threatening Potiphar's wife (whom we can no longer see) with her finger.

MAIDSERVANT   Not worth it, not worth it.

She seems to be savouring a hate-filled victory: she is avenged.

SCREAM OFF FROM CÄCILIE, *like the scream of a sleeper having a nightmare.*

At this scream, everything disappears. We rediscover Cäcilie who is talking very animatedly to Freud. The latter listens with a deep attention that contrasts with Cäcilie's amused frivolity.

CÄCILIE   I must admit to you that I screamed. That woke me up.
FREUD   Was it a nightmare?
CÄCILIE   You could call it that. I've had worse.
     How spiteful she looked! I've never seen her like that!
FREUD   Who are you talking about?
CÄCILIE   My maid. Marie.
     It was she who was speaking from the window.
     Oh! I know why.
     It's my fault.
     I disturbed her yesterday afternoon, she was doing the washing, I wanted a glass of milk. At once. And then I didn't drink it.

The glass of milk on the bedside table. Cäcilie is reading. The curtains are drawn. A bedside lamp is burning. The door opens gently.

When she came to tuck me in for the night ...

The housemaid appears. Fifty years old. Her body is worn by labour and devoid of charm. Her face is indeed that of the 'woman at the window', with the difference that it simply expresses fatigue and a discreet surliness. She draws close to Cäcilie, who goes on reading. She is about to tuck in the bed when she notices the glass of milk that Cäcilie has not touched.

MARIE, *offended*   And you haven't even touched it! *(With resentment, though politely:)* It really wasn't worth bothering me.

She picks it up and puts it on a tray to take away.
   She starts tucking in the bed. We see her from behind, old and tired. Cäcilie carries on reading, without making any reply.

CÄCILIE'S VOICE OFF, *addressing Freud*   That came back to me in my dream. How amusing! That proves I felt remorse, doesn't it?

We were looking at Cäcilie reading and could no longer see the maid. Now, all of a sudden, we are looking at her once again: she is a very young girl with a lovely body (in the same clinging black dress — she is wearing the same apron and the same lace cap). She appears the very moment Cäcilie cries out.

CRY OFF, *of amused excitement*   Wait! How funny it is.
   There were two of them.
   The woman on the balcony.
   She was two women rolled into one.
   When I was nine, I had a little maid who was called Lucia. How pretty she was! *(Regretfully, without condemnation:)* She behaved very badly.

We have seen only the young maid. Now we see Cäcilie too. She has grown much younger: she is a little girl of nine. She turns an enraptured, almost doting face towards the young maid.
   At this very moment, we see Frau Körtner, deeply angry. This is no longer the cold woman we know: she is younger, but her face, contorted by a puritanical fury, is intensely disagreeable. In her voice there is an imperceptible vulgarity. We see only her.

FRAU KÖRTNER   Pack your bags!
   I don't want to hear a thing. You're a prostitute, Lucia, and you won't remain a moment longer under the same roof as my daughter: I won't let her innocence be defiled.

FREUD'S VOICE OFF, *repeating the words of the woman at the window*   'It really wasn't worth sacking me.'

CÄCILIE, *in surprise*   Eh?

We find ourselves back in the bedroom. Freud is looking at Cäcilie with an innocent air, Cäcilie appears astonished.

FREUD   There were two maids rolled into one. And you felt guilty towards each of them. That's why you joined them together. The first was saying: 'It wasn't worth bothering me', and the second: 'It wasn't worth sacking me.'

CÄCILIE   Why was she saying that?

He repeats slowly and deliberately:

FREUD   I don't know. *(A pause.)* Your mother had told her that she was sending her away to prevent your innocence from being defiled by the proximity of a prostitute?

No reply. Cäcilie's face appears old and tired. She looks at him, sinks back on her pillows and begins laughing, a soft, knowing, spiteful laugh.

CÄCILIE, *almost under her breath*   Not worth it! It wasn't worth it.

The laugh stops abruptly. She is afraid. She looks at Freud almost imploringly. For the first time, she is asking him for help. For the first time too, Freud seems surprised and rather moved by this imploring fear. He bends towards her.

FREUD   Cäcilie! What is it?

CÄCILIE   There were three of them. *(Rather frantic laugh:)* Three rolled into one!

The woman at the window. She says nothing. She simply makes gestures which emphasize her beautiful hands, with their sparkling rings.

FREUD'S VOICE OFF   Who was the third one?

Threatening movement of one of the beringed hands.

CÄCILIE'S VOICE OFF, *stifled*   I don't know. I *can't* know. *(She repeats, as if she felt her inner resistance as a hostile force:)* I can't.

Freud and Cäcilie facing one another. She looks anxious: what is worrying her is no longer her duel with Freud, it is what is happening in her innermost self. She is confiding something to Freud.
    For the first time, Freud seems less pitiless. He sees Cäcilie make a wretched little grimace and close her eyes. He says in a gentler tone of voice:

FREUD   You're tired.
    Enough for today.

He tries to stand up. She opens her eyes and clutches his sleeve. In sudden annoyance:

CÄCILIE   Certainly not.
   I want to know.
      Don't leave.

   (Smiling:)

What on earth can that accursed dream be?

He sits down again. She grows calmer.

FREUD, *humorous smile*   They're all like that: deep as the ocean.
CÄCILIE   I'm going to tackle it from another direction.

The painted woman outside the door of the tower, back turned to the audience.

FREUD, *voice off*   A painted woman.
CÄCILIE, *voice off*   Don't disturb me! I see the tower.

The painted woman goes back inside the tower and is lost in the darkness.
   The tower. A sheet of red liquid slides across its circular wall: one would think it smeared with blood.

   (Furious:) I haven't shed blood.

FREUD, *voice off*   Who accuses you of that?
CÄCILIE, *voice off*   The depths of the sea.

The tower once again becomes as it was in the first description: painted in bright red.

FREUD, *off*   It's red?
CÄCILIE, *off*   The tower? Yes.
FREUD, *off*   Do you know Red Tower Street?
CÄCILIE, *off*   Of course.

Red Tower Street at four o'clock in the afternoon. A very busy shopping street. Cäcilie, younger (seventeen), goes by with a governess.

FREUD, *off*   What is it?
CÄCILIE, *off*   A Vienna street.
FREUD, *off*   What else?
CÄCILIE, *off*   It's a busy shopping centre. When I could walk, I used to do my shopping there.
FREUD, *off*   Is that all?
CÄCILIE, *off, hesitating*   Yes.

Red Tower Street after dark, as we saw it in the first act: its prostitutes waiting for clients under streetlamps. The shops are shut (the same shops, of course, as in the former evocation).

FREUD, *off*   And at night?
It's the meeting-place for all the prostitutes.
    Didn't you know?

(A silence.)

CÄCILIE, *off*   I did know.

The image of the street at night gradually fades, allowing the red tower of the dream to show through.
    The red tower, with the lantern.

FREUD   In your dream, it was night-time?
CÄCILIE, *once more elated by the quest*   Night! Night! Night! *(Same elation:)* I know what you're going to tell me!

Potiphar's wife emerges slowly from the tower. She approaches the screen, her image grows to inordinate size. Her gaze is still intent, but she gives a coarse wink as if to attract a client's attention.
    The woman moves away; she goes back towards the tower. We see her from behind.

FREUD'S VOICE OFF   The woman who comes out of the tower ...
She was painted in oil as you paint yourself in watercolour each year on 7 January. It was you!

The woman abruptly retraces her steps: when she turns round, we recognize Cäcilie's face, framed by her blonde hair. What from behind seems to be black hair, when viewed from the front, turns out to be a decorative feature of the crown which frames her blonde hair to right and left.
    Cäcilie's face is daubed, as we saw it in the other session, with brush-strokes of watercolour (red on her lips, two scarlet patches on her cheeks, black under her eyes).
    Cäcilie, all dressed up, comes towards us.

CÄCILIE, *off, in a firm tone of voice*   Yes.
FREUD, *off*   You dreamed you were a prostitute, at night, in Red Tower Street.

Cäcilie paces up and down; she eventually enters the tower.

CÄCILIE, *off*   Yes.
FREUD, *off*   Think carefully: what connection is there between prostitution and that watercolour business?
CÄCILIE, *off, hate-filled voice*   She called me a prostitute.

The image dissolves.

Cäcilie as a child, sitting on the ground: five years old. Around her, jars filled with water and watercolours in a black and white metal paintbox. She has installed a little mirror in front of her and is conscientiously daubing her cheeks, her lips (red), her eyelids (black).

FRAU KÖRTNER'S VOICE OFF, *vulgar and spiteful*   What are you doing? What are you doing?

 I'll not let your father take you to the theatre again.

We suddenly see the bottom of Frau Körtner's black skirt near the terrified child. The little girl's eyes look up at Frau Körtner.

 Cäcilie is lifted by her armpits. Frau Körtner lays her over her knee.

 (Howls from Cäcilie.)

FRAU KÖRTNER'S VOICE OFF   You can scream, but you'll get your spanking, little trollop.

 A girl of your age who dreams of making herself up — all the makings of a whore!

A large, fine-looking male hand grasps Frau Körtner's wrist and prevents her from striking Cäcilie.

HERR KÖRTNER, *calm and with authority*   No.

Cäcilie's baby, enormous, with its head, in the window of a toyshop.

CÄCILIE'S VOICE OFF, *today*   He comforted me, he promised me a doll. He was so nice.

Shot of Cäcilie talking to Freud in her room. She is smiling but rather solemn.

CÄCILIE   It was one seventh of January.

 The first time I put lipstick on. The first time my mother called me a whore.

  The first time my father gave me a doll. A real feast-day, wasn't it?

Slightly provocative laugh.

 Freud resumes without paying any attention to the provocation.

FREUD   Watercolour and prostitution: very well. There's the connection. So you imagined you'd become ...

Cäcilie cuts him short with a little laugh.

Thereupon the image of your young maid became mixed up with that of your old housemaid, and the old woman's words expressed the young one's secrets.

The woman at the window. Same costume, same body — young and shapely. But the head has changed: it is that of a very young and very pretty prostitute (her face is still quite fresh-looking — but far too made up).

She leans out of the window and laughs. Following her gaze, we see the Egyptian woman. But if her body which remains naked under the paintings is brown, her face — without the least trace of make-up, but with a few streaks of watercolour — is that of Cäcilie. This time Cäcilie, wife of Potiphar, is very clearly engaged in prostitution. She looks weary and faded. Much older than she appears in reality, and above all than the very young chambermaid who is pointing the finger of scorn at her.

Clamorously:

LUCIA, *vulgar*   Your daughter walks the streets, Madam.
She gets paid less than me. *(Triumphantly:)* Am I the one who has defiled her, poor kid? I haven't set eyes on her for eleven years.

Beside herself with joy at gaining her revenge:

Seems clear she had it in her blood, Madam! And it wasn't worth sacking me.

The image dissolves: Cäcilie and Freud in Cäcilie's bedroom. She is looking at Freud with an expression that is at once quite calm and totally at a loss. She does not seem surprised.

CÄCILIE, *rather provocative, as before*   You must admit, Doctor, it's a strange dream for a young girl?

She laughs. She moistens her dry lips with the tip of her tongue. She looks amused and vaguely dissolute. Freud makes haste to offer a reassuring explanation. He is rather embarrassed by his patient's attitude. This is what leads him to draw wrong conclusions.

FREUD   Does anyone know what young girls dream about?
   In your case, moreover, we know the original traumatism. It's that night in Naples. You've dreamed about prostitution since the time you found your father dead in a brothel.

Cäcilie's face darkens as soon as her father is mentioned. Finally she answers Freud angrily.

CÄCILIE, *furious*   You're not going to mix up that ridiculous dream ...
   (Carried away by her wish to prove that this trail should be abandoned:) To start with, this is the first time I've had it since my poor Papa's death!
FREUD   You'd already had it? *Before* your father's death?

She stops, taken aback. Freud is looking at her in astonishment: he realizes simultaneously that he has made a mistake and that he has just discovered a more important trail. Cäcilie herself appears disconcerted: she knew without the least doubt that she had often had that dream; but it must not be in doubt either that this knowledge has remained (perhaps since her father's death) at the edge of her pre-conscious. She realizes it at the same moment that she expresses it.

CÄCILIE   Yes, certainly!

Thus the doctor and his patient look at one another, equally disconcerted, in mutual astonishment and curiosity. A degree of wavering in their relations: Freud has pushed back his chair slightly, Cäcilie has picked up her baby again and is hugging it to her. But it is Cäcilie who will break the silence: she is enthralled by this new quest — and then she wants to escape the intense anxiety she can feel welling up inside her again.

She makes her confession with a worldly air, at the same time lowering her eyes like a girl taking her first communion.

Freud remains impassive.

For years before that.

When I was fifteen, I used to dream that every night.

(Forcefully:) No! I know what you're thinking! You're totally mistaken. My father *didn't visit* prostitutes. He *never* visited them.

(Passionate defence:) I lied to you: he was sometimes fickle and I think he did make Mama suffer rather: that's the fault for which I can't forgive him. But just think, Doctor! He was so handsome, he was a real Adonis. He *rejected* the most sought-after women. People say the demi-monde is more amusing than our own world: I'm quite willing to believe it. But if he'd wanted a woman of easy virtue, he was wealthy enough to carry off some archduke's mistress. Why should be have needed those wretched creatures I hate so? They are frights, real horrors, the cast-offs of our sex!

The red tower. Cäcilie as Potiphar's wife, but with her blonde head, catches hold of the gentleman in the top-hat by his sleeve and tries to put a ring on his finger.

CÄCILIE, *voice off*   I must have read something unsuitable when I was twelve; with horror I learnt of the existence of such women, and the disgust they inspired in me is so great that I punish myself by dreaming that I'm one of them.

FREUD   What are you punishing yourself for? It must be for some crime, since the punishment is so harsh.

The image dissolves. Freud is standing by Cäcilie's bedside.

She looks at him with anguished eyes.

She tries to laugh.

CÄCILIE   I have a sensitive conscience. And then, in dreams, things are always exaggerated.

Freud smiles and bows to take his leave.

    (Suddenly worried:)

Are you leaving? But we haven't finished.
FREUD   The session is over.

Freud is friendly but reserved. Cäcilie becomes agitated. Her hands flutter over the sheets. She is afraid of remaining alone.

CÄCILIE   But how about the dream? There's a lot left to tell.
FREUD, *calmly*   We'll carry on tomorrow.
CÄCILIE, *sulkily*   But I'll forget everything.
FREUD, *smiling*   Do you like this game all that much?
CÄCILIE   It's not a game, but I like it. *(Imperiously:)* Come back this afternoon.
FREUD   Till tomorrow morning, Cäcilie.

Freud smiles broadly at her. He replies with serene authority: but knows he has just won a round. He offers her his hand; she turns away from him, furious, and does not shake the proffered hand.

APPENDICES

APPENDIX A

'FREUD'
Original Scenario by
Jean-Paul Sartre

First draft
Paris, 15 December 1958

I

Freud at sixty, surrounded by his disciples (the 'Seven'). They are talking about self-analysis. Freud advises against it (other than as complement to a normal analysis). Jones reminds Freud that he began his own many years before (1897). Freud: 'Who'd have analysed me? There was only one analyst in the world and that was me.' Questioned by those present (Freud's self-analysis gave rise to his discovery of the Oedipus complex), he sets about telling them the story of that self-analysis. (The subject of the scenario is really: a man sets about knowing others because he sees this as the only way of getting to know himself; he realizes he must carry out his research upon others and upon himself simultaneously. We know ourselves through others, we know others through ourselves. Freud's voice off will subsequently echo forth each time a brief commentary on events seems necessary.)

or
I bis

The voice off: 'Everything began with my father's death.' The previous scene is discarded and the voice leads in directly to the images of **II**.

II

Autumn 1896. Vienna. A man in mourning, about forty years old — it is Freud — goes into a barber's shop wanting a shave. He is on edge, in a hurry; he discontentedly surveys the large number of customers waiting their turns, all of whom will be served before him. He speaks to the owner: 'What's going on today? Normally at this hour there's no one.' 'At this hour?', the owner replies. 'But it's always full then. You usually come earlier.' This remark seems to upset Freud, who looks at his watch and resigns himself to sitting down beside the other customers.

Meanwhile, the Freud family is growing impatient: it is the day when the father, Jakob Freud, is to be buried and Freud is late. He is also very harshly reproached for having wished 'the funeral to be a quiet one, and very simple'. He arrives, Disagreeable comments. His mother quells the dispute. Departure for the burial.

Night-time. Sigmund is working in his study (ground-floor apartment, 19 Berggasse). On edge and fagged out. Lights a fresh cigar, hesitates, throws it away, stands up and, by way of the common stairway, makes his way to his private apartment on the third floor. His wife is already asleep. He begins to undress. Noiselessly. He is in bed, his eyes open and staring.

A shop (topographically *identical* to the barber's — but it sells round objects wrapped in white paper). No customers. The salesmen pass the objects from hand to hand and the merchandise eventually reaches the woman at the till, who sticks a 'sold' label on each object and throws it on the ground. On all the walls, enormous enamel plaques.

YOU ARE REQUESTED TO CLOSE THE EYES

(The dreams analysed by Freud — of which we shall here utilize a few of the most significant — may seem absurd or preposterous before analysis, *but they are still very commonplace*; only rarely does the fantastic or the mysterious make an appearance in them. Hence, it seems necessary to treat them with *even greater realism* than the scenes of waking life. It is through the absurdity of behaviour in them, and the manifest conflict between this absurdity and the realism of the places and objects, that the particular *surreal* quality and the 'overdetermination' of the dreams recorded by Freud will be rendered.)

Freud sitting up in bed, having woken with a start. His wife is asleep.

Freud's voice: 'The phrase written up had a twofold meaning. It meant: we must close the eyes *of the dead*, we must fulfil our duty towards them. So I was feeling guilty. Why? What had I done?

'For years I have been feeling guilty. What is my crime? *Who am I?*'

He goes back in time, memories appear, incomprehensible and swift: a train passing near some blast-furnaces, a child of three in a compartment on this train looks at the red fires in the night and sobs; a dingy kitchen, two burly men bring in a big wooden tub and receptacles full of warm water; the mother of the family (Frau Freud) tips these into the tub in order to wash the children, who are waiting half undressed (the oldest is three); Jakob Freud picking up his cap from a gutter; Jakob Freud in an armchair (he is an old man) and around him his wife and daughters, thin and ill (the daughters are now grown up). These are almost stills. An engraving recurs three or four times: it represents Hamilcar making his son Hannibal swear an oath, and a voice is heard: 'I swear to take our revenge upon the Romans.' This entire kaleidoscope eventually comes to a halt on one image.

III

31 August 1885. At Vienna. We are in a hospital. A dingy room, for a young doctor. From behind, we see a young man squatting in front of a pottery stove; he is burning heaps of manuscrips with an almost joyful zest. The heat is stifling and smoke fills the room. Now we see him in profile. It is Sigmund Freud; he is twenty-nine. He is sweating and the smoke is making his eyes blink. But he is so absorbed in his labours that he does not even hear the knocking at his door. Eventually he stands up and goes over to the door. Before opening he asks: 'Who's there?' 'Martha' comes the reply from the other side of the door. Only then does he turn the key and let his fiancée in. She — a slender girl (graceful rather than pretty) — surveys this auto-da-fé in astonishment. What is he doing? He is burning his manuscripts, every trace of his past, before leaving for Paris. he has utterly destroyed his Journal covering the past fourteen years. 'Why?', she asks. 'To give my future biographers trouble.' He explains that he cannot leave the hospital before he has relieved himself of the fear that someone might get a look at these papers. We learn that he has in fact won a stipend that will allow him to spend a term in Paris attending the lectures of the renowned Charcot. He speaks while burning the last papers and notebooks. He rises to his feet all black, she brushes him, he washes his face, she drags him off. Hospital corridors. They leave the room.

In the corridor, she asks:

'Why that fear? Why give your biographers so much trouble?'

He does not reply. She — being of lively disposition and quite touchy — is annoyed at his silence and says to him, with a hint of spite:

'In the first place you'll have no biographers. Why should you have?'

He still does not reply. She grows alarmed:

'You've no need to be a great man.'

He replies between his teeth:

'Yes I do.'

The *Ring*, in Vienna. They are walking side by side in the crowd, very proper, not arm in arm. A street vendor is selling broadsheets against the Jews. In verse. He recites a few passages from them. A group has formed round him. Some strollers start to laugh; several of them buy copies of his 'Jewish Tales' or his songs. Freud's face hardens. A man passes in front of him, he has just bought a booklet from the vendor and is laughing to himself as he reads it. Freud seizes the booklet from him, tears it up and scatters the sheets to the four winds. The stroller is astounded and looks at Freud almost in fear. Freud simply says to him: 'Imbecile!' Martha drags Freud away, as the stroller uncomprehendingly surveys the sheets scattered at his feet.

A café on the *Ring*. Freud and Martha seated. Freud silent and tense. Martha waits tranquilly. Freud looks at the customers. They are peacefully playing cards or chess. Abruptly he speaks, without looking at Martha: most of these peaceful people are enemies. They could easily have bought the Songs and the collections of Jewish Stories that the street vendor was selling. Does she understand why he has burned his manuscripts? Nothing must be left behind one: we are living in a hostile country; the 'goys' appropriate everything, distort everything. 'We are Jews, we must be circumspect: everything the goys find out about our lives will be held against us.' We must not yield ourselves up — even to future biographers. She smiles gently at him: let him remain obscure; let him be a good doctor; let him live like everybody else — he'll escape attention. He shakes his head: 'Impossible. We Jews are compelled to *prove* our worth.' He recounts the story of the young Hannibal swearing to his father Hamilcar to take revenge upon the Romans. The Jews are like the Carthaginians: they must impose themselves or be crushed. And everyone has his father to avenge. She asks him if the mild Jakob Freud has made him swear an oath, as the aged Hamilcar did to Hannibal. He twists his mouth, as if the question touched him on the raw, and simply answers: 'No.'

They are interrupted by the arrival of Minna, sister of Martha Bernays, Minna's fiancé Schönberg and 'Cousin Max', a very intimate and dear friend of Martha's. They were about to sit down at another table, but Martha signals to them to come to theirs. Freud, furious, reminds her that it is their last day: 'You must pay attention only to me.' She grows annoyed: it is her sister. Fresh signal: this time the three young people have seen her; they come over. Instantly Freud rises to his feet: he has an appointment with Professor Meynert, a well-known doctor who is his protector, and is obliged to leave. 'But your appointment isn't till five o'clock', says Martha. He does not answer, bows, leaves the café — beside himself with anger. He wanders through the streets, walking with difficulty, breathing painfully; he takes a cigar from a case, lights it and starts to smoke and cough.

IV

At Meynert's. It is five o'clock. Meynert is fifty years old. Great physical elegance; he is a man of the world, he has 'manners'. (Freud appears more forthright and down to earth, but he seems to be afraid of Meynert and, at the same time, to admire him.) Red beard, harrowed face contrasting with a body that has remained young. He expresses his pleasure at having been able, with the help of Freud's former master Brücke, to obtain for his pupil that stipend (incidentally quite inadequate). But he also expresses his surprise that Freud should want to attend Charcot's lectures.

'He's either a simpleton or a quack', he says. 'It seems his students amuse themselves by picking up prostitutes and sending them to him to put on a pretence of suffering from hysteria.' In any case the foundations are not solid. Does Freud no longer believe in the exact sciences? In neurology? Yet he has done some excellent studies, the last of them in March of this very year, on the anatomy of the cerebellum. Freud replies that he is disturbed by the problem of hypnosis, and therapy by means of suggestion. Meynert appears disgusted: it is all mystification. He grows annoyed and succumbs to his favourite mannerism: pulling on his moustache and chewing at it, while tapping his index finger on his left nostril. Freud, mesmerized by this tic, tries to explain himself: it seems to him that neither physiology nor psychology (both of them entirely mechanistic) can account for what there is within each of us. Meynert stares at him in astonishment, rummaging in his beard and tugging at his moustache. Freud stammers: 'In us there are forces ...' 'What forces?' 'I don't know. I can't manage to understand myself. Do you understand yourself completely?' The moustache, the beard, the finger against the nose. Meynert laughs: 'I don't waste my time prying into myself. In any case, I'm clear to my own eyes, as transparent as a mountain pool.' Freud says nothing: the tic fascinates him. A silence. Meynert, all of a sudden, becomes aware of his tic and places both hands flat on his desk: 'It's not myself I want to know, it's the human brain. In any case, if I had the fancy to understand what's going on inside me, I wouldn't go off to study hysterical patients, women who are half neurotic and half playacting.' Freud wonders whether, on the contrary, it is not first necessary to study sick people in order to understand the behaviour of normal men: sickness underlines and intensifies certain characteristics.

Meynert, annoyed, brings the discussion to an end by an offer: 'Go to Paris, since it amuses you. But if you recognize on your return that your great man is merely a charlatan, if you devote yourself to neurology, you can deliver my course of lectures on the anatomy of the brain *in my place*. For I already feel too old to teach the new experimental methods.' A silence. They look at one another. Meynert touches his nostril and chews his moustache.

Freud's voice off:
'I'd loved him like a father. Now he frightened me; perhaps I'd already guessed that this man of genius wasn't well-disposed towards me.'

Breaking the silence, Meynert declares that he is not asking for an immediate answer, but that they can see when Freud returns from Paris. Freud rises to leave.

V

Dusk. Freud in the streets, smoking and coughing. He hears Meynert's voice echoing in his ears: 'I'm as clear as a mountain pool! I'm as clear as a mountain pool!' Max and Schönberg, who have set off in pursuit, now catch sight of him; they rush up and each take him by an arm. Schönberg is very friendly, Max very sharp. 'What got into you? Why did you leave us without a word?, etc.' Freud makes no reply, but he allows himself to be dragged into a little café with a billiard-table. A poor, deserted café. They question him once again. Freud eventually replies. 'You were lacking in tact: you shouldn't have come over.' He adds, looking at Max: 'And especially you, who pay court to her behind my back.' Max is furious: 'I don't pay court to her; I've known her since she was born, and better than you: I'm part of her family.' It is Freud's turn to grow angry: 'Her family! She has only one family now, and that's mine; she'll leave her mother and her sister, and my father will be her father. She belongs to me.' Max, suddenly furious, thumps the table: 'She belongs to you and you're abandoning her in order to go and do Heaven knows what in Paris! If you make her unhappy, I'll kill you.' Freud retorts sharply, in spite of Schönberg: 'What business it it of yours? You're just her cousin, you're not responsible for her happiness and you count for nothing.' Whereupon the other, on his feet in fury: 'Oh! So I count for nothing! Well I could, if I wished, make her give up the marriage.' Schönberg intervenes to condemn Max's attitude; eventually, late at night, after an interminable argument that we are allowed merely to guess at, Max explains that he used to love Martha and starts to weep. Freud, moved and very overwrought, weeps likewise and the two friends are about to become reconciled when Sigmund, realizing that he is weeping, suddenly grows harder, furious at having given signs of emotion and revealed his sensitivity: 'Woe to the person who makes me weep. You're not of my calibre, I can be pitiless if I encounter you in my path.' He goes off, leaving Max dumbfounded and Schönberg indignant at his behaviour. Freud walks through the darkness, rather distraught, Meynert's voice resounding in his ears: 'I'm as clear as a mountain pool.' (The scene of the quarrel, though it reveals Freud's suppressed violence, is still faintly comical, because the participants are so excitable, they change their attitudes so abruptly and, despite their beards, are so young.)

VI

The next day at about eleven. The station. A deserted platform. The track is empty. Freud on the platform, carrying a worn suitcase that is obviously crammed to bursting-point. He asks a railway employee passing by in a great hurry: 'The Paris train?' 'It hasn't even been made up yet; look at the time.' Freud's watch and the station clock both stand at eleven. The employee goes off, adding disdainfully: 'You'll only have to wait for an hour and a half.' Freud sits down on a bench.

Martha Bernays. She crosses the station concourse swiftly. She looks for Freud and eventually finds him. He reproaches her for arriving so late. She reproaches him for arriving so early. Why does he always need to arrive in advance, when he has to travel? He replies that he has a real phobia about journeys. He is afraid of dying on the train — and that is why he burned his papers the evening before. And when the fear of dying disappears, it is replaced by the fear of missing the train.

Martha is not in a good temper. She too reproaches him for going away to Paris. He seems disconcerted and does not reply. She adds some further reproaches: why did he leave them so suddenly, the day before? Moreover, Schönberg has this very morning reported to Minna the quarrel of the evening before; Minna has told her sister everything. Why has he quarrelled with Max? Max is not really in love with her: he imagines he is, taking a childhood friendship for love; she has always kept him at arm's length. Freud knows this very well. Last night, after the quarrel, they could have made up: it is Freud who did not want to. Why? While she is delivering these reproaches, Freud stares into space and still makes no reply. The train is being made up before their eyes. Freud and Martha climb into an empty third-class compartment, where he places his suitcase on a seat to reserve it. They are alone; he turns towards her and kisses her passionately. She returns his kisses with equal passion. Suddenly, he excuses himself: 'There's something unusual in me. Devils under a lid. When the lid is lifted … Where it comes from, I don't know: I wasn't young during my youth; or perhaps there's some other reason. When Max was talking about you yesterday, I lost control of myself entirely and I'd have destroyed the whole universe, you and me included. Everything will change when we're married; when I've got an independent situation.' She smiles at him and relaxes in his arms. He is just kissing her when noon strikes on the station clock. He straightens up suddenly and, as she looks at him in astonishment, he takes her by the hand and forces her to climb down onto the platform. He looks extremely put out. Outside the third-class carriage. He looks irritably towards the concourse. 'I'm expecting Breuer.' She moves away from him in a fury. The passengers gradually arrive and begin to climb into the carriages. It is ten past twelve and the train is leaving at twenty past. At last Breuer appears. He is a man of about forty, with a big black beard. He is tall and cleaves through the groups of new arrivals. He takes Freud by the arms and squeezes them very hard, shaking him slightly. 'I'm late, a patient kept me. Good luck, Freud! Good luck.' Freud seems to relax suddenly; his face is calm and happy. 'I'll be off at once and leave you to your fiancée. No, no: you can introduce me to her when she's your wife.' He hands him a packet. Before he has time to thank his friend, Freud finds himself alone. Freud comes back towards Martha, after he has watched Breuer disappear. He gives her the packet. 'This is why I was expecting him. It's money. 500 guilders. You'll take it to my mother; she doesn't have a penny left.' She looks tenderly at him, she has understood. He adds: 'I love Breuer as if he were my own father; from him, it doesn't bother me. But I'm twenty-nine, I work twelve hours a day and I still pile up debts in order to survive. If you want to understand me, remember that.' They look at one another, he takes her hand and squeezes it with all his strength. Whistle from the guard. 'You belong to me.' And suddenly, imperious: 'Swear to me that you won't see Max again!' She bridles. Whistle from the guard. A railwayman shouts: 'All aboard!' Beneath Freud's gaze, Martha ends by yielding: 'I won't see him again.' Freud takes both her hands and squeezes them passionately. The train moves slowly off and Freud, who has arrived an hour and a half in advance, has to run to catch up with it.

VII

In Paris. The Hospital de la Salpêtrière, one day in November 1886.

A lecture-hall in the hospital. Charcot is giving a lesson on Hysteria, in front of a considerable audience. Freud is among those present.

Charcot studies the case of an old woman suffering from hysteria. He explains in a few words:

1. that hysteria is not a 'simulation' or an 'imagination': it is a real illness, deserving serious study; that it does not affect women only, but men as well;

2. the difference between hysterical disorders (for example, paralysis and numbness) and organic disorders of identical appearance;

3. the possibility of provoking in certain subjects, by means of hypnotism, the disappearance or appearance of hysterical disorders.

Session of hypnotism: the old paralytic patient, under hypnosis, succeeds in walking. When woken, she falls: the paralysis returns.

Charcot's conclusion: Whatever the unknown neurological basis of hysteria, the symptoms can be suppressed by psychological means.

At the end of the lecture, Freud follows Charcot and accosts him as he is washing his hands, in a small room nearby. He says, rather shyly, how much the problem of hysteria interests him and asks whether the revelations obtained by hypnotism might not serve as the basis for constructing a 'depth psychology'. Do not the appearance and disappearance of their symptoms in subjects under hypnosis prove the existence within us of a reality that is intermediary between states of consciousness and purely physiological facts?

But Charcot, a little, bald, affable man, who washes his hands slowly and carefully, confines himself to shaking his head and repeating with a smile: 'Let's not go too fast. Let's not generalize. Steady on.'

This does not prevent Freud from leaving him filled with joy and enthusiasm. And as he walks through the streets, towering over the passers-by, the voice off of Freud in his old age makes itself heard: 'I thought I'd found the way to know others and to know myself. I was convinced *at last* that there was an answer to the questions I'd been asking myself for so long.'

VIII

We see on the screen a Viennese newspaper. And the following advertisement:

'Dr Sigmund Freud, neurology lecturer at the Vienna Faculty, has returned from a six-month stay in Paris and is now living at 7 Nathanstrasse.'

At Breuer's. His wife Mathilde, charming, a very good friend of Freud's. Freud is shown in, wearing uniform. As a reservist, he has been unlucky enough to be called up for training just as he was beginning his career as a practising doctor. He is back in Vienna (after his training) to be demobilized, and is leaving for Wandsbeck (near Hamburg) to get married. For Martha has gone back to Germany with her mother during Freud's stay in Paris.

Mathilde is delighted to see Freud again. But Freud seems very constrained: he would like to speak with Breuer in private. Mathilde multiplies her questions; Freud is on hot coals. Finally Breuer comes in and at once perceives his embarrassment. He winks at

512

Mathilde, who understands and withdraws. Freud, alone with Breuer, admits to him that he does not have a penny: his pay is in fact much lower than he had thought. Breuer must lend him the money for his journey. Breuer at once agrees. But we sense how painful this approach is to Freud. Freud takes the money: he does not say thank you, he puts it furtively into his pocket. He simply says: 'You're far too young to be my father. But if I didn't love mine as I do, it's a father like you I'd wish for.' However, he is far from being downcast: he has told Mathilde how impatient and happy he feels at seeing Martha again and finally being able to marry her; to Breuer he speaks of his hopes and of his enthusiasm for Charcot: in a month's time, after his honeymoon, he will deliver a lecture to the Medical Association. He sees in this lecture (reading of a paper on 'Masculine Hysteria') a contribution of capital importance for psychiatry and the study of the neuroses. At the same time, it will be a brilliant starting-point for his own medical career: from it he will obtain fame and consequently lots of patients. He says to Breuer: 'You at least can understand me: I need to believe in myself. I don't know what I'm really like: I need your support and protection, yet I dream only of achieving total independence.' Breuer reassures him. Freud squeezes his hand in both his own; he hesitates for a moment, flings himself into his arms, then abruptly stiffens and flees.

IX

Dr Freud's consulting-room in October 1886. He waits for patients, who do not arrive. He paces up and down. He sits down. He thinks he has heard a ring at the bell. He goes to the front door himself, opens it: nobody. He sits down again and daydreams: the Doctors' Association, he is speaking, stormy applause; he is back in his consulting-room, an imposing old man — a minister — is thanking him: 'You've saved my life.' Freud smiles, the minister offers him his protection: thanks to this, he will have an outstanding career, he will be a professor at the Faculty of Medicine. The whole of Viennese high society will come to be treated by him: 'Consider me as your father!' Freud — who finds himself abruptly back sitting at his desk — declares forcefully: 'I'm not a man to accept protection like a child!' In fact, the consulting-room is deserted. (Here, what is involved is a reverie, a 'fantasy' which takes place in the real world and retains all the characteristics of reality.)

Martha opens the door at the far end which connects with the 'private' rooms and slips into her husband's consulting-room. He glowers at her but she kisses him and begins to laugh: she will go away as soon as a patient rings. Freud laughs: then she's in danger of spending the rest of her life in his consulting-room. She had come to show him a drawing. It is a cartoon she has come across in a magazine — a lion in the desert is yawning: 'Two hours and no niggers.' The niggers are the patients. Freud explains that the niggers will come: after this evening's session at the Medical Association, when he has read his paper, they'll come.

X

The Medical Association. A great many doctors, Meynert and Breuer are in the audience. Freud finishes reading his manuscript. A final passage on the therapeutic consequences of Charcot's discoveries. The customary practice is to treat neuroses by electro-therapy, baths and massage. Would there not be a case for seeing whether it is possible to cure patients by means of hypnotism and suggestion? He stops speaking, lays down his manuscript, waits. No applause at all. He looks at Breuer, in the front row, whose hands move as if to clap, but then halt in mid air. A neurologist called Rosenthal observes that all this is well known in Vienna. Another that there is nothing new in Freud's paper and it was not necessary to go to Paris just to bring that back. A third: 'It's all false; hysteria is purely feminine. The proof is that it comes from a Greek word meaning uterus!' All these interventions are more dismissive than hostile. Freud listens to them without flinching. A silence: he fastens his gaze upon Meynert, who is chewing his moustache. It is the latter who abruptly explodes. With a violence that at first jars: 'I challenge you to produce a male sufferer from hysteria for us, who presents the symptoms described by Charcot.' He works himself up: 'I find your defence of therapy by means of suggestion all the more singular insofar as you were a real man of science when you left for Paris, and you had a pretty good knowledge of physiology.' And concludes: 'Hypnotism? I pity those colleagues who, perhaps out of altruism, stoop to taking on the role of children's nannies and overwhelming people by suggestion in order to put them to sleep.' He calls Breuer as a witness, 'who enjoys authority in everything concerning neuro-pathology' and who can testify that the symptoms described by Freud for the most part derive from cerebral lesions. Freud waits hopefully for a reply from Breuer. The whole audience turns in his direction. But he says nothing. Freud acknowledges the hit. Meynert, after a brief silence, ends by recalling the value of the proven methods and in particular of electrotherapy. Loud applause. Breuer does not applaud.

Outside the Medical Association, a moment later, exit of a group of irate doctors.

'Meynert put him properly in his place!'

'There you see a young doctor, barely more than a student, who has been the pupil of all these eminent men and yet attempts to teach them lessons.'

'What do you expect, he's a Jew. Oh, I've nothing against Jews, but it takes a yid to go hunting up theories in Paris that everybody knows in Vienna, and that have long been abandoned. These people really have no country.'

Everyone has left the hall now. The street is deserted. A man is waiting for Freud in the shadows. He is the last to leave. The man emerges cautiously from the shadows, and goes up to Freud: it is Breuer. He puts his hand on Freud's shoulder; he encourages him to persevere: 'I resorted to hypnotism myself, a few years ago. And it worked for me in certain cases. It needs study.' Freud looks at him with a mixture of affection and mistrust; without admitting it to himself, he is angry with him for not having intervened during the meeting. He thanks him coolly. Breuer offers him a lift in his carriage, which is waiting close by; Freud refuses: he is going home on foot. He needs to reflect.

XI

A few days later. Freud's consulting-room. He is at his desk, very sombre. The bell rings. His first patient. But he gives no sign of joy. She comes in: her first words are to tell him that she has been sent by Breuer. She outlines her case: as she speaks, we realize that this is one of those typical cases that psychoanalysis later succeeded in treating. Freud listens to her. A moment later — he is still very awkward and shy — he gives his recommendation: electrotherapy, baths, massage.

Martha is waiting for him in the next room, overcome with joy: finally, a patient! He comes in, very sombre. He says: 'Be happy, Martha: I'm going to settle down. No more ambition: I wasn't the man needed.' He'll try to be a good doctor and support his family. He reverts bitterly to Breuer's attitude: 'He was really flabby, the other evening. He sends me patients, but he let me down. This patient — do you know why he's sending her to me? It's certainly to tell me to give up theories and do my job. I shall obey him.' She is in his arms, smiling and tender; we sense that she does not share his disappointment, and is even relieved. He looks at the wall — two images are displayed there: a colour reproduction of a picture depicting Hannibal's Oath, and the famous photo showing Charcot's lecture at the Salpêtrière (as we saw it earlier on) — and adds (thinking obviously about the interpretation he has given of Breuer's behaviour): 'And yet I had a talent for interpreting.' Martha raises her head and looks at him in surprise.

XII

Six years later. In 1892. Breuer has continued to help Freud, to send him patients, to lend him money. He has often taken him with him on his professional trips. It is to him — almost as much as to his own work — that Freud owes his patients (of whom there are still very few). But for six years, Freud has never again written on either the neuroses or their treatment: he supports his wife and three children (Mathilde five, Martin three, Oliver one); he is translating Charcot's *Lectures* into German.

On this evening in March 1892 he is going with Martha to dine at the Breuers'. We see the Freud couple in their brand new setup (two apartments in the same building, one on the ground floor, the other on an upper floor, connected only by the common stairway of the building). Freud plays for a moment with his eldest daughter Mathilde (named after Mathilde Breuer), before dressing to go out to dinner. He seems more sombre and harder than before, except with his children. He speaks less. He retains all his affection and admiration for Breuer; he is still like a small child in his presence. Is he satisfied by this precarious and still very modest situation? Assuredly not. When Mathilde questions him, he will reply: 'We're happy because we've stopped asking for very much: our little Mathilde's smile is enough for us.'

The dinner at the Breuers'. Relations between Mathilde Breuer and her husband seem rather strained, in contrast to the normal state of affairs between them. Mathilde is on edge. Breuer is more and more paternal towards Freud. In the middle of the dinner, he says to him carelessly: 'Are you still interested in hypnotism and hysteria, Freud?' Freud answers that he has never stopped being interested in them. Then Breuer tells him that for almost six months he has been treating a hysterical patient, Anna O., and that this patient – who is not merely very charming, but remarkably intelligent – has herself inspired him to adopt a new therapeutic method, in which hypnosis has its part to play. Why hasn't he spoken of it before? He wasn't sure of himself. Now, the patient is on her way to being cured: 'Do you want to see her? Excellent! I'll come and pick you up then, tomorrow evening at five.' He laughs and adds: 'But take care, Martha; she's formidable.' Martha says that she fears nothing. Freud laughs and says there's nothing about him to attract the attention of women, and that she has nothing to worry about. He adds: 'But when you're the wife of someone like Breuer, Mathilde, it's necessary to be on one's guard: that man is too handsome not to turn the heads of all his female patients.' Everyone laughs. Mathilde more loudly than the others. Martha looks at her: 'Mathilde, what have you done to yourself?' Mathilde looks at her hand, which is bleeding: 'Heavens, I hadn't noticed. I must have cut myself with this knife.' The cut is a deep one, she excuses herself and stands up; Martha stands too, the two women go out. Breuer watches her leave. To Freud: 'A touch of neurasthenia, I think: we'd like to have a child.' At which Freud, as if to himself: 'She gashed her finger and didn't even notice.'

XIII

Breuer and Freud in Breuer's carriage. Here, just as during the meal on the previous evening, the contrast between Breuer's wealth and Freud's straitened circumstances should be visible. In the coupé they speak about Anna O. Illness that dates from her father's death. At the present moment, contracture of both arms. It is a very old symptom, but one that often disappears, gives way to others, but then recurs. 'This time we're on the way to suppressing it completely.' 'But what is this method?' 'You'll see, you'll see.'

Anna O.'s bedroom. A paying room in a hospital. A cheap one: obviously Anna O. is poor. She is in black, very pale, very beautiful, sitting on a chaise longue, both arms glued to her body and her forearms raised, hands slightly clenched, palms outwards, as if she were carrying something heavy. Motionless, her eyes half-closed, it is impossible to tell whether she is dreaming or whether she is waiting. The door opens softly. Breuer comes in, Freud follows him. She does not open her eyes. Breuer looks at her for a moment, then passes his hands very lightly over her forehead. She opens her eyes and turns them towards him. She speaks. Gently, without addressing him: but replying to all his questions. She speaks of her father's death. The contracture appeared immediately afterwards. The next day. She woke up in her bed with her hands and arms in this position. She did not want to go to the funeral, of course. There were too many enemies. Breuer asks gently: 'What enemies?' 'People who knew.' 'Who knew what?' She stands up, her hands remain clenched but slowly her arms extend. She approaches the bed, slowly. She kneels down, scrapes the backs of her hands on the ground as if she were seeking to pick up some very heavy object, her face expresses effort, she makes several attempts. She half falls to one side. Breuer looks at her, with a strange expression: he seems overwhelmed. Freud, cooler but astonished, looks back and forth from the young woman to Breuer. One would say that Breuer surprises him as much as the young woman herself. Anna gets up laboriously, as if she were carrying something too heavy for her; she touches the bed, then suddenly utters a cry and falls backwards. Breuer rushes over, catches her in his arms to prevent her from falling and leads her back to her chaise longue. He helps her to lie down. Her eyes are open wide and she is breathing heavily, but her arms and hands have recovered their formal ankylosis. Breuer looks at her in anguish and says, as if to himself: 'I'm always afraid I've gone too far.' He is leaning over her: she smiles at him, he straightens up quickly. She says, very naturally: 'Good day, Doctor.' Pointing to Freud: 'Who's this?' 'Dr Freud, my best friend.' She bends her head. She would be entirely normal, if it were not for a nervous cough that frequently racks her. She asks what she has done. Breuer reminds her: gradually she remembers having knelt down in front of the bed. She looks frightened. 'What did I say?' He reminds her that she didn't want to attend her father's funeral or meet certain people who had knowledge of a certain fact. She laughs: 'I must tell lies in my dreams: you know quite well that this paralysis began six months later. As for the burial, I was there.' 'And how did the paralysis begin?' 'I don't know.' 'Try to remember, as usual.' 'I don't remember any longer.' She seems frightened and restive. Breuer asks: 'So? No chimney-sweeping of the mind, today.' 'No.' He speaks to her with a gentleness that is quite unwonted for him; he becomes almost pleading: 'I beg of you: we're getting near our goal.' She remains stubborn: 'I want to sleep.' Her pillow slips off, Breuer picks it up and, in order to resettle the patient on her chaise longue, takes her almost tenderly by the shoulders. Freud has lost his hard, sombre expression; looking younger and less strained, he seems on the lookout and contemplates the scene with extraordinary avidity. He seems fascinated by both individuals at once. As Anna refuses yet again to speak, he asks regretfully: 'Is it because I'm here? Would you like me to go away?' Amiably she says no. But Breuer turns to Freud and casts him an imperious glance. Freud goes out. He remains outside the door, nervous and impatient: we sense that he is dying to hear the conversation. He moves discreetly away and starts pacing up and down the corridor. Breuer comes out almost at once, deeply upset: she has refused to say anything. 'I thought I'd gained her trust ... Are you disappointed?' Freud shakes his head: 'No.' Breuer explains: it is a case of dual personality (at times she is capricious and childlike, at times intellectually normal), accompanied by paralysis of both arms, visual and auditive disorders, nervous coughing, etc. When she shifts from one personality to the other, she passes through a state of self-hypnosis during which her ailments are modified — as Freud has just seen. Normally, as soon as she finds herself back in her normal condition, one can remind her of what has just taken place (which she has not really forgotten) and she will recount the circumstances that accompanied the first appearance of the symptoms. And each time that she speaks with absolute trust, the symptom is reduced: after a time her visual disorders, and subsequently those affecting her hearing, ended by disappearing. She is so intelligent that she has understood the importance of these conversations, which she herself terms the 'talking cure' and 'mental chimney-sweeping'. For months she has been speaking freely: only that paralysis of the arms and the cough remain. And the paralysis is about to disappear. But she's afraid: there's something underneath, which she doesn't want to unburden herself of. She has been evading questions for a week now. 'I really thought that today ...' 'I was there', says Freud. 'Yes. I hoped that it was your presence. But after you'd left, she still continued to say nothing. I'll come back tomorow morning and try by hypnosis. She said that you can return whenever you wish.' He adds, with a sort of dreamy satisfaction: 'She said: "Since he's your friend".'

XIV

Next morning. Freud and Breuer in the hall of the hospital. Breuer introduces Freud to a strange man: Dr Fliess, an ear-nose-and-throat specialist from Berlin, who wants to attend the course of lectures on the physiology of the brain that Freud gives as a Privat-dozent at the Faculty, in order to improve his knowledge in this area of the biological sciences. He is a man rather younger than Freud (the latter is thirty-six, Fliess thirty-four), but with blazing eyes (are they the eyes of a madman? or of a genius?), an expression that is at once stubborn and imperious. Freud and Fliess shake hands and arrange to meet at the Faculty. Breuer drags Freud off: 'What do you make of your new pupil?' Freud answers: 'Impressive.'

Anna's room. She is at first capricious and hostile. She mocks Breuer and sticks her tongue out at him. Manifestly, she is in that 'second state' of which Breuer was speaking the day before. But this does not stop Breuer from being visibly hurt by her hostility. However, as soon as he approaches in order to hypnotize her, she seems to relax. Little by little, she lets herself go. A moment later, she is quite calm, her eyes wide open. Breuer speaks to her in a low, insistent, dogged tone of voice. He orders her to trust them, to speak freely about her paralysis, to recommence the scene of the day before and explain it. He stops speaking, they wait in silence. A moment later, her arms extend, she rises and goes over towards the bed, where she kneels down. 'What are you doing?', asks Breuer. 'I'm trying to lift him.' 'Who?' She rakes the ground with her hands, and groans: 'I can't, I'm not strong enough.' She climbs to her feet with difficulty, as if she were carrying a very heavy body. 'What are you doing?' She turns abruptly towards them and looks at them with flashing eyes: 'I was alone and I carried him as if he was my child.' Breuer is right beside her: he leads her gently back to her chaise longue and whispers into her ear. 'Wake up. Speak to us.' She looks at them in astonishment. She says: 'I remember everything.' She had been alone at her dying father's bedside. He started violently at the moment of death and half fell from the bed. We see the scene anew as she describes it. We see her efforts to lift her father back onto the bed: she manages it at last, but he is dead. Freud asks suddenly: 'You spoke of enemies. Who were they?' The question is asked timidly, but Breuer seems shocked that Freud should dare to intervene: he glares at him. But Anna replies serenely: 'Those who knew ...' 'Those who knew what?' asks Breuer, resuming his role as therapeutist, 'That my mother had left us both alone.' 'Where was she?' 'With her family. She didn't love my father.' 'That's why you didn't want to speak yesterday?' 'Yes. I was ashamed for her.' Her arms have resumed their position against her body, her hands are clenched. An interminable wait: is the symptom going to disappear? No. So gently, timidly, Freud asks: 'Have you often relived that scene?' 'For six months, almost every night. It was ... horrible.' 'And then the symptom appeared: you felt paralysed.' 'Yes.' 'Well,' he says, 'that paralysis appeared to prevent you from getting up in the night and beginning the scene over again.' At this moment, without her even seeming to have heard, her arms and hands relax, stretch out and fall limply back beside her body. Freud seems radiant with happiness; Breuer too — but he also seems very annoyed by Freud's fresh intervention. He congratulates Anna, who is looking at her hands in astonishment, but he suggests that she should not nourish any excessive hopes. Perhaps the paralysis will return, perhaps she isn't cured; things are not so simple, time is needed, a great deal of time.

Outside, Breuer lets his annoyance show: 'What did you do?', he asks Freud. 'What does it mean?' Freud explains that for some time he has been wondering whether patients may not *defend themselves* by means of their illnesses against memories and feelings, or against temptations. We have terrible forces within us of attack and defence. She was defending herself. Since Breuer's method is 'cathartic', it was necessary for her also to understand that self-defence. Breuer shrugs his shoulders: she wasn't defending herself; hysteria springs from a special state akin to hypnosis; her paralysis, with her arms *carrying something* or *somebody*, was on the contrary the permanent résumé of the scene she had lived through. He goes off in annoyance. And the voice off of Freud tells us:

'For two or three months, he didn't take me to see Anna again.'

XV

Dr Freud's consulting-room. A woman, young and pretty, stretched out on a couch. Voice off: 'I was trying out the cathartic method on my patients. This one doesn't dare go into shops on her own. Some salesmen laughed at her when she was thirteen.' A small shop. We do not see the little girl of thirteen, but we see the shop as if the camera were the patient's eye (as if the lens were centred by a young girl aged thirteen, of fairly tall, almost adult, stature). Some young fellows are laughing to each other and exchanging winks: 'What a sight! The kid really looks great in those old rags.' Laughter. Freud's voice off: 'I questioned her under hypnosis.' The setting does not alter, but suddenly the counters grow taller, they are seen from below. The camera glides along the counters like a person's gaze and (while the dream becomes that of a single person) discovers, between some jars of candy (whereas previously it was a shop selling hats), a man of about sixty seen from below (as a child might see him) who is laughing — with an innocuous air but terrifying eyes. He comes round the counter and approaches, saying from time to time: 'Are we afraid of the wolf, then? Of the big, bad wolf?' He continues to draw closer and the patient's voice says simply: 'I was eight.'

Shot of Freud and the patient. 'Could you remember that scene?' 'No, I've just remembered it now.' 'And how about the other scene, is that true?' 'Which one?' 'The shop assistants who were laughing at you when you were fifteen?' 'That's true too.' 'And that's the one you remembered?' 'Yes, because the other one is too ... horrible.' 'But it's the other one that counted?' 'I don't know. Probably ...' She sits up on the couch, she says she's feeling better, she thanks Freud with almost doting eyes; she gets up and, all of a sudden, flings her arms round his neck. He remains polite and indifferent, he repulses her with great courtesy. She looks at him in bewilderment, as if she did not recognize him or as if she no longer understood herself. She recoils, stammering some indistinguishable words; he says to her gently: 'It's nothing. A side-effect of hypnosis. Not worth even talking about.'

Fliess, Freud and Breuer in Breuer's study. Fliess has come by chance. Freud thanks Breuer: the cathartic method has exceptional value. A true deliverance for patients: he has applied it in six different cases — hysteria, anxiety neurosis, obsessions — and the results are remarkable. But what surprises him is the importance of sexual problems for his patients. He'd often wondered whether sexuality was not at the root of all neuroses: the method invented by Breuer has brought him fresh confirmation of this. To his great astonishment, these ideas are supremely unwelcome to Breuer. It's quite absurd; where does sexuality enter into the matter? Freud explains that patients defend themselves against sexual desires or sexual memories and that is precisely their malady. Breuer thumps on the table: This is pure fancy. In any case, how is Anna O.'s case to be explained ... in this hypothesis? That girl has never felt sexual desire or arousal, she is utterly cold. He hammers out these last words, staring Freud in the eye. Fliess has said nothing. But when they are on their way down Breuer's stairs, he stops on a landing and says to him: 'Freud, you're right.' Freud looks at him in bewilderment. Fliess goes on: 'Don't let yourself be crushed and browbeaten by Breuer: he's not your father. He's in danger of stopping you at the outset.' Freud, very embarrassed, replies that he is not sure of what he is putting forward: it will take time and many more observations, etc., etc. Fliess makes no reply. They go on down the stairs in silence. In the street, Fliess enjoins him: 'Keep going: you'll succeed.' Freud, overawed, asks him: 'Why do you say that to me? Why me?' Fliess explains: Freud is a visionary, as he is himself. It is visionaries who can be called the salt of the earth: those men who frame a hypothesis before having in their possession the means to verify it. Freud and Fliess are *of the same breed*. There is something within them, a hidden strength. Or perhaps, he adds laughing, they have made a pact with the Devil. Freud seems overawed. But Fliess, with those great, imperious eyes, is more like the Devil himself than like a guardian angel. 'It's your eyes that attracted me', says Fliess. 'They see far.' And displaying his own: 'The visionary can be recognized by his eyes.' Freud asks Fliess if he too has a hypothesis to defend. Fliess replies, with an air at once obstinate and mysterious, that he has several. And he declares that he has discovered a syndrome (migraines, circulatory and digestive disorders, neurasthenia) which can be relieved by an application of cocaine inside the nose, and whose origin is assuredly sexual. He adds: 'I guess at many other mysteries: there's a rhythm in biological phenomena: 23–28, 23–28.' He starts laughing and leaves Freud abruptly, after adding: 'This rhythm is of cosmic origin.' Freud is dazed. Left alone in the street, near a shop equipped with a large mirror, he approaches and cannot prevent himself from studying his eyes in it.

The same evening. Freud's children are in bed. Freud and Martha are undressing. A few words from Freud to Martha indicate his annoyance: Breuer's attitude displeases him, he cannot understand it. Does he perhaps lack courage? He'll never commit himself one way or the other. In contrast with this caution (which he encounters everywhere: Meynert, Breuer and even Charcot), he lauds the intelligence and audacity of Fliess, that fascinating man. Martha does not share this enthusiasm; she likes the calm and moderation of Breuer and Mathilde.

Freud dreams. A dream of resentment against Breuer and passion for freedom: he wants to free himself. At the same time, vague fear of Fliess. (To be chosen from *The Interpretation of Dreams*. Perhaps the dream of the Botanical monograph. Or to be invented.)

Voice off of Freud in his old age: 'My dreams had a meaning: I knew that, from my adolescence onwards.'

Immediately after this, dream about Freud's father. He has a cataract. Freud goes up to him saying: 'When I operate on you, you'll be a visionary.' His father is in bed, at first he has his own head, then that of Fliess, who cries: 'Instead of operating on me, you must save Anna O . . . who's blind.'

XVI

At Breuer's home. Mathilde and Breuer are taking their breakfast. Breuer is getting ready to go off to visit his patients. They are both in rather a bad temper. Mathilde reproaches Breuer for a lack of attention: absorbed in his own thoughts, he has poured himself some coffee without even offering any to his wife; he at once apologizes and pours her some. But this does not appease her: he has just acted as if she were not there; it's not the first time; he'd like to see her at the far ends of the earth, wouldn't he? At these last words, Freud is shown in. He seems very determined; he has lost the timidity he was displaying only the evening before towards Breuer, although he retains at least the outward appearance of a deep respect. He has come to ask a favour: that Breuer should take him along this very morning to visit Anna O. Breuer, embarrassed, answers in an almost disagreeable manner that she has been cured for a fortnight, and that he is no longer seeing her. Freud, very surprised, replies that he has seen his colleague Rosenfeld, who was at the hospital the day before and saw Anna O. in Breuer's company. This is a gaffe. Mathilde rises abruptly: her husband has lied to her! Only the day before he was claiming he hadn't been back to the hospital. What has this woman done to him, then? He can no longer leave her. Breuer, very sheepish, explains. He wasn't lying: it's quite true that

Anna O. is cured; he hadn't seen her the day before, when he spoke of her to Mathilde; but then he got the idea of going back to the hospital, which she was shortly to leave, and making sure that her recovery was definitive. But Mathilde is not in the least calmed by these explanations. The jealousy that she has long dissimulated suddenly explodes, before Breuer's astounded gaze: for six months now, Breuer has done nothing but talk about Anna; Mathilde is obsessed by her, they're never alone, Anna is always between them; only just now, Mathilde is sure, he was dreaming about her. She can no longer endure this life, she'll leave the house if the situation doesn't change. Freud, terrified by the violence he has unleashed, is backing away towards the door when Breuer's voice pins him to the spot: it is a misunderstanding, Freud *must* stay to hear his explanation; if Breuer has been enthralled by the case of Anna O., that is because he has discovered a new psychiatric method. His interest in the girl was exclusively scientific. He is now entirely at his ease, he laughs: he is intending to see Anna O. again this very morning, but that will be only to bid her farewell; that trip to Italy which he has been promising his wife for so long, why shouldn't they make it at once? He has a certain amount of free time available, he needs three or four days to dispatch his current business, Mathilde can take the tickets for next Thursday. And as for this last visit to Anna, he's taking Freud with him to the hospital, in order to relieve his wife of all suspicion. Mathilde seems delighted and astonished: he cajoles her like a child, and when she appears completely relaxed he leaves her, taking Freud with him. On the landing, when he is sure that Mathilde cannot hear him, he says to Freud: 'The devil take me if I'd ever have dreamed … You see, Freud, jealousy is a neurosis.'

In Anna's room: she does indeed seem cured, she is waiting for the arrival of her mother, who lives at Graz and who is coming to fetch her to set up house with her in Vienna. Breuer, rather stiff, very paternal, tells her of his imminent departure for Italy. She hardly seems concerned: she says goodbye to him and thanks him. On the threshold, as they are taking their leave, she coughs several times. They go out; Breuer seems very satisfied, he rubs his hands and says with a detached air: 'Well, Freud, there's a fine case for you; quite conclusive, isn't it?' Freud replies simply: 'She's still coughing.' Breuer shrugs his shoulders and drags him off without another word.

XVII

Outside the Breuers' apartment-building, on the day of their departure for Italy. Suit-cases and trunks are being loaded onto a wagon; the coupé is waiting in front of the door; the Breuers come out with the Freuds, who have come to bid them farewell. Freud will not go to the station: he hates departures and especially those by train. Martha will see them off. Just as Freud is wishing them a safe journey, an ambulance from the hospital stops behind the coupé, an orderly gets out and runs over to Breuer: Anna O. is in a very worrying condition, she's in pain, she's calling for him, he must come as a matter of urgency. Breuer turns pale, Mathilde's face hardens; Breuer turns towards her as if to consult her, she just replies: 'There's another train that leaves for Innsbruck in three hours.' Breuer leaps into the ambulance, Freud follows him; the ambulance goes off with the two men aboard. Mathilde is left sobbing in Martha's arms.

On the stairs of the hospital: we can hear a woman's screams. Tremendous screams that start low and rise to a shriek. Freud asks a passing house-doctor: 'Who's that in labour?' He replies: 'Nobody. It's Anna O. who's screaming. It has been like that since seven this morning.' Breuer, shattered, breaks into a run.

In Anna's room: she is howling. It is a nervous confinement, sequel to a nervous pregnancy. Breuer, almost trembling, says to Freud: 'Calm her, put her into a hypnotic trance: I can't touch her.' Freud goes up to her, he looks intently at her, speaks gently to her, lays a hand on her forehead, she still screams. Breuer comes up in turn, gently and slowly he repeats a phrase, always the same: 'Sleep, Anna, I'm here. Sleep, I'm here.' Gradually she relaxes, eventually she falls asleep. Breuer says to the nurse: 'It's over. She'll be quite calm when she wakes up.' He turns to Freud: 'Let's go.' Freud goes out with him, indignant: 'You're leaving her in this state?' 'I don't want to miss my train. Besides, she's cured.' 'Cured? While you were curing her ailments and her paralysis, she was experiencing a nervous pregnancy; and it's you she thought she was pregnant by — she's sicker than ever. You must stay to look after her.' Breuer digs in his toes: 'I shall never see her again in my life; I've done her too much harm. This method is terrible ... One stirs up the mud.' Freud looks at him with an odd expression: 'Yes, one takes the lid off; the demons come out.' Breuer does not hear him, he repeats wearily: 'I'm guilty towards her, I shouldn't have ... I shouldn't have ...' Freud grows angry: 'You will be guilty if you go away. In the present state of affairs, you're the only one who can cure her!' A cab passes. Breuer stops it and jumps into the carriage, without even asking Freud if he wants to come with him: 'To the station!' The cab moves off and Freud watches it leave in consternation.

XVIII

Freud at home. Martha is very sombre. Mathilde has told her everything. We sense that the young woman identifies with Mathilde. She comes very close to inflicting a jealous scene upon Freud: didn't he tell her that a young woman had flung her arms round his neck. She wouldn't tolerate undergoing Mathilde's fate. Freud explains to her that the young patient in question had just been hypnotized. He is in any case going to give up hypnotism, because patients yield to suggestion in order to please the doctor — and for many other reasons that he does not go into. As for Anna O., Breuer didn't make her fall in love with him: it's a necessary moment in the treatment. 'Do you believe that my patients could fall in love with *me*?' 'And why not?' says Martha. 'Don't I love you?' 'But in their case, it's not *me* that they love. And in Anna O.'s case, it wasn't Breuer.' 'Who, then?' Freud is initially at a loss: 'I don't know ... They shift ... there was a feeling in them ...' And suddenly his face lights up: 'It's a transference.' He understands and explains that they transfer onto the doctor a forbidden or impossible feeling that they were entertaining for someone else. 'For whom?' He doesn't know: what he does know is that he's too aware of not *deserving* the patient's effusions — and too much in love with Martha — to give in to them. It's a matter of a certain kind of relationship between the doctor and the patient; and this relationship is necessary to the treatment, that's all.

He has taken Martha in his arms, she relaxes, she trusts him. She ends up saying: 'In that case, go back to the hospital tomorrow and look after Anna O. You can't leave her all alone.'

At the hospital next day: Freud is about to go into Anna O.'s room, when some orderlies pass ahead of him carrying a patient on a stretcher. They open the door: Anna O.'s bed is empty. Freud asks where Anna is? She seems to be cured: she slept for a long time, exhausted; her mother came to fetch her in the early hours of the morning, and they went off without leaving any address.

XIX

Fliess's departure for Berlin. Two months have gone by: Breuer has still not returned. Freud has just finished his lecture. The students are leaving the hall, Fliess goes over to join Freud. They go for a walk along the Danube. They do not speak much: Freud is very moved. He is very sad that Fliess is leaving. 'I still don't know how I managed to interest you', he says to him very modestly, almost humbly. 'But be that as it may, you've made a deep impression on me.' He'd have liked to work in Berlin, encouraged by Fliess. 'You alone have encouraged me.' He shows Vienna all around them. (They are on a bridge over the Danube and, as they speak, are watching the water flow by.) The city is soft, heedless, vain, unbelieving; it has but one faith: anti-Semitism. A person cannot work seriously there. Fliess proposes that they should hold 'congresses' of just the two of them, in order to keep each other abreast of their discoveries. These 'congresses' will take place several times a year, in Germany or in Austria. Fliess advises Freud to abandon Breuer and pursue his research on his own. Freud seems very perturbed. He replies that Breuer has always behaved admirably towards him; he recalls how, for several years, Breuer lent him money at the end of every month. One last effort must be made. For Breuer's own sake. He has been passing through a very serious crisis recently; he must be helped, whatever the cost … When a boy comes of age and earns his living, it is up to him to help his father. Fliess listens without replying. Freud adds that it is up to Fliess to give him courage: 'You're younger than I am, yet I feel you're far older.' Abruptly he adds: 'We should address one another as intimate friends.' And Fliess replies: 'I agree — but you ought to give up smoking.' Freud is about to obey and throw his cigar into the river. But he thinks better of it: 'That would be too hard: I've too many things to do, to be imposing a fresh constraint upon myself.'

XX

Autumn 1895. Freud's consulting-room. It is night-time. The room, very brightly lit, seems deserted. Smoke fills it. Someone — whom we cannot see — coughs from time to time. At last we discover Freud, engaged in smoking a cigar. Cigar-stubs in an ashtray. Freud is writing: he has finished the page, he stacks it on top of a thick manuscript on his right hand, begins the next page, stops, muses for a moment, pulls over a sheet of writing-paper and starts writing to Wilhelm Fliess. He coughs and discards his cigar. A voice off (Freud's own) recites the letter to us as he writes it.

We learn that Breuer and Freud are jointly writing a book on hysteria. The voice off disappears as we view the scenes it describes. It reappears during transitions, and for commentaries.

Freud and Breuer in Breuer's study, discussing. Breuer thinks that hysterical disorders spring from a state similar to a hypnotic trance, which he terms hypnoid. Freud, annoyed, interprets neuroses quite differently: 'They're defence mechanisms.' He makes the defence of the ego central to neuroses; he explains the case of Anna O. as a defence against an intolerable memory (the night she spent beside her father, her father's death and the need to condemn her mother). The paralysis was a defence against a memory that was striving to resurface. In short, it was a compromise between an intolerable image and the 'defence mechanisms' which repressed that image. Breuer remains unenthusiastic and quite morose. What especially bothers him is that dynamic conception: the psyche resembling an interplay of conflicting forces. But above all he is put out to see his protégé, his 'spiritual son', opposing him with so much conviction. The two men are visibly annoyed, almost hostile. And yet, despite the dreary indifference and the scepticism of Breuer, we see that he is fascinated by Freud's new authority. He objects that, if these conflicting forces exist in ill people, it must be accepted that they also exist in normal people, though to a lesser degree. Freud at once replies that they do necessarily exist. He goes so far as to speak of himself: he knows that within him there are wild forces, and that these are suppressed by powerful inhibitions. How does he know this? "From everything: like everybody, I have slight disorders of a psychological nature. I have nervous coughs, palpitations of the heart and intestinal problems, which regularly precede periods of depression. And then there are my dreams. I've recorded them since the age of sixteen.' 'And what do they mean?' 'I don't know yet: but they're the dreams of a guilty man.' He is perturbed, excited; there is a suppressed violence in him which eventually impresses Breuer. The latter declares that this conception is entirely alien to his own experience: his dreams have no meaning, he does not feel guilty, he does not repress anything. And with no transition he abruptly adds — beneath Freud's attentive and almost mocking gaze: 'I've seen Anna O.'s mother again … They're living in Bahnhofstrasse, at number 12.' 'And Anna, is she cured?' 'No.' He shakes his head: 'It would be better if she were dead.'

Freud looks at him in silence, but the voice off, violent and insulting: 'For whom would it be better? For him! Only for him! And he says he doesn't repress anything!' Against the background of Freud's laughter off, we see a hallway in a bourgeois apartment. The voice off: 'It was him. I'd summoned him for consultation.' There is a ring at the front door; a maidservant admits Breuer (top-hat, pelisse, gloves), who sheds his coat and hat, which the maid hangs on a coat-hanger. The door of one of the adjoining rooms opens gently: it is Freud. He informs Breuer: 'It's a girl. She has been ill for six months.' 'What's the matter?' He answers: 'In my opinion, it's a nervous pregnancy.' Instantly Breuer's face becomes covered in sweat; he recovers his gloves, coat and hat and rushes off, while his voice of the previous evening echoes in Freud's ears: 'As for me, I don't feel guilty and I don't repress anything.' And, when the front door closes again, Freud gives a short, spiteful laugh before going back into the patient's room.

Camera on Freud, writing to Fliess: 'However that may be, I have made progress. In the knowledge of my patients and in my knowledge of myself. Not just of hysteria but of all the neuroses. I now know that they are pathological mechanisms of defence against some intolerable scene that is striving to become conscious. The delirious symptom is designed to mask it. The patient clings to this symptom, he loves his delirium as he loves himself. But if one succeeds in bringing him to discover the scene he is rejecting, he sees it in broad daylight, the repression becomes pointless and the symptom disappears.'

He has just lit a cigar again. He coughs, puts it out and adds: 'The big news here is Meynert's death. As for us, the whole family is well except for me, but I have an inflamed throat. At our next congress, my dear Wilhelm, you'll have to examine me; I entrust myself to you body and soul. Your Sigmund.'

[Scenes to be shot:*
The last contacts between Meynert and Freud. Freud in the presence of the sick man. He looks at this man, whom he so long revered as his father and who finally turned against him. Meynert simply says to him: 'I'm the finest case of male hysteria you could hope to find.'
Views of Meynert's funeral. Freud very sombre.
Freud with Martha after the funeral. She reproaches him for his ill humour. Formerly, he used to say that he'd be quite normal, once he had Martha all to himself: but his depressions have become worse since his marriage. Freud, very sombre, explains that though he no longer loved Meynert, he felt he was burying his father. He doesn't understand himself: he needs friends and enemies simultaneously. Sometimes the same person plays both roles. He is thinking of Breuer.]

XXI

Freud's father is ill. Freud visits him with Martha and the children. Freud meets his mother and kisses her passionately. He remains seated by his sleeping father's bedside.

---

*Sheet found — probably added by Sartre on re-reading the typescript of his synopsis. [Editor's note.]

Martha and the children stay with his mother. Freud looks at his father with a sombre and almost surprised expression. We hear scraps of conversation from the next room — his mother is speaking: 'He's a good patient ... he's so gentle. He never complains.' Freud sees his father at Freiberg, thirty years earlier: a fat man draws alongside him on the sidewalk and knocks his cap into the gutter: 'Get off the sidewalk, Jew, and pick up that cap of yours.' His father looks at the man as he goes off, steps from the sidewalk and collects his cap. We return to the room of the sick man, who groans and turns on his back. Freud looks at his face: it is that of Breuer. He rises abruptly to his feet and goes into the next room, where he apologizes to his mother: he must return to his consulting-room. He leaves Martha and the children. Tramway. Freud gets off outside Breuer's house. (An enamel plaque on the door: Dr Breuer.) He makes as if to go in, then turns on his heel and goes off.

Back in his consulting-room. A maid opens the front door to him: 'No. Nobody has been.' He goes into his consulting-room. Behind his desk, as he sits down, we see the old engraving: Hamilcar is making Hannibal take the oath. Freud sits down, takes his manuscript and begins to write.

The voice off of Freud in his old age: 'There was Fliess in Berlin; but in Vienna I was alone. Quite alone.'

A patient comes in (Letter 60 to Fliess: the dialogue should be taken from there, with a few cuts*). A woman of thirty, very affected. She has been under treatment for a few days. Taking her hat off, she declares: 'I can make myself out as bad as I must; but I must spare other people. You must allow me to name no names.' Then, lying down on the couch: 'Earlier I was unsuspicious. I should have been easier to treat. Now the criminal meaning of some things has become clear to me, etc. etc.' Eventually Freud openly pushes her: 'Let us speak plainly. In my analyses the guilty people are close relatives, a father or a brother ...' She, sharply: 'There is no question of a brother.' And Freud: 'Your father, then.' She bursts into sobs. Freud is no longer listening to her: he sees Breuer lying in a bed (Jakob Freud's bed), saying to a little girl (who looks like Mathilde Freud): 'Come and see your papa, child. Are you frightened of your papa?' The little girl cowering in terror against the door. Breuer's face, laughing, appears between some jars of candy (the shop described by the other patient). Camera on Freud — Breuer's laughter can still be heard — who rises to his feet, puts a hand on his patient's forehead and says: 'Well then? What did that respectable father of yours do?', in a tone that is really nasty and grating. She says, 'I was nine ...'

XXII

A 'congress' at Berchtesgaden. Fliess and Freud have met. They are walking along a mountain path. Fliess is speaking, Freud listens to him in timid admiration. He is once

---

*See *Complete Psychological Works of Sigmund Freud*, Vol. I, London 1966, pp. 246–47. [Trans.]

more as he was in the presence of Breuer ten years earlier. Fliess has the look of a seer; he explains that human life is conditioned by periodical phenomena related to our bisexual constitution; the development of the organism takes place by fits and starts during these periods; the psyche is the result of intermittent intoxications. Every individual is at once male and female: one sex dominates and the other, hidden, constitutes our unconscious. 'Number!', he cries. 'Number! Therein lies everything.' On the basis of these periods, the day of our death is entirely calculable. 'I've worked yours out', he says to Freud, 'you'll die at fifty-one, you've another eleven years to live.' He turns to face Freud: Freud is pale and distraught, he looks very gloomy. Fliess is surprised: is Freud afraid of dying? Freud sits down on a tree trunk, beside the path. It isn't that: it's his quarrel with Breuer. In fact, they've not broken off relations entirely: Freud owes him money; moreover, they haven't finished their book on hysteria. But in any case he no longer respects his former protector. 'To escape my own criticisms, I've always needed to undergo someone's influence. Now … luckily, there's you.' He grows enraged with Breuer, he says that his mere presence is enough to encourage him to leave Vienna. He'd go and live near Fliess in Berlin, if only he thought he could set up a practice. He rises abruptly to his feet: he tells Fliess he's suffering from acute nervous depression. In addition, cardiac problems: arrhythmia, breathlessness, a burning sensation around the heart. All of this in bursts. He exclaims: 'How sad for a psychiatrist, not to know whether he's suffering from neurotic depression or not!' He lights a cigar and coughs. Fliess, who has remained quite indifferent to Freud's confidences, abruptly stiffens: 'Throw away that cigar, wretch! Or you're bringing the date of your death closer.' Freud throws it docilely away. He seems cowed: 'Who'll explain to me why I need a tyrant!' Fliess examines his throat: there, on the spot, in the open air. 'Nasal affection, apparently. Case of nicotine poisoning. The cardiac problems, the depression, it all comes from the nose.' Freud may smoke in moderation.

At the railway-station in Berchtesgaden. Fliess, in a bad temper: the train for Vienna goes through in three quarters of an hour, why arrive so early? All the same, he eventually asks Freud whether he has been successful in pursuing his investigations. Freud replies: 'I'm on the point of discovering everything.' Some children are running around in the station. A child of four near Freud. 'I'm almost sure I've found the key to hysteria and the obsessional neuroses.' He gradually becomes convulsed. 'What's the matter?' 'The train. Anxiety-attack. I've always had a phobia about trains. Don't worry.' He is pale and sweating, his heart is racing. Despite the almost unbearable state he is in, he expounds his discovery to Fliess: neurosis is a sexual shock undergone in childhood, the memory of which is repressed. If the shock has been accompanied by terror, the result is hysteria; if it has been accompanied by pleasure, it becomes transformed later into a feeling of guilt and is replaced by obsessional ideas (obsessional neurosis). Fliess listens without much enthusiasm, and simply declares: 'You should try and find out the period during which the shock occurred.' Freud replies sharply: 'That's not what interests me. I'll get round to it.' 'That's the main thing', says Fliess drily. 'No, it's not the main thing. The main thing is the nature of the shock. I've got my own idea about that. But I'll tell you about that later on.' Fliess looks discontented, he reproaches him for leaving the genuinely physiological domain. Freud says that he's doing no such thing, and that he's counting on Fliess to provide him later with a solid physiological grounding. He adds: 'For the time being, I'm a bit uncertain about the father's role in childhood. While we're on the subject, have you questioned your wife?' 'What about?', Fliess asks. Freud loses patience; his anxiety is redoubled: 'I've asked you at least five times, you always forget, nobody helps me. Your wife calls you: "my little pussycat".' Shot of Fliess, who with his great, fierce eyes looks like anything but a pussycat. Freud goes on: 'Someone used to call her that during her childhood. I've begged you to ask her who the person was.' Fliess does not reply. A slight coolness.

The train finally arrives. Freud climbs in with difficulty, helped by Fliess. They exchange farewells 'until the next congress'. They'll write to one another. The train leaves. Freud gradually calms down. He pulls out his cigar-case, contemplates it for a moment as if wishing to open it, but eventually throws it out of the window.

Shot of Freud, sitting in a corner of the compartment, his eyes intent. The voice off: 'Twelve cases of neurosis, twelve cases of incest in childhood. Some decisive test would be needed.' We see Anna O. again, trying to heave her dying father onto the bed from which he has just fallen. The father has Jakob Freud's features. The voice off: 'She really adored her father. Nothing seemed to have taken place between them. Was that true? I decided to see Anna O. again.'

XXIII

A house in the suburbs of Vienna. A quite poor apartment-building. Freud goes in. He rings at a door on the third floor. A woman comes to open it. It is Anna O.'s mother. She looks austere and hard. What does he want? Freud explains that he is a doctor: Anna knows him. Breuer has given him their address. He knows that Anna is unwell, he is a psychiatrist (he shows his card) and would like to treat her. The mother does not let him enter. 'We've no money left; we can't pay a doctor to make house calls. In any case, there's no more to be done. And above all, no hypnotism.' Freud reassures her: he has given up hypnotism. And if they have no money left, he'll treat Anna free. Her mother looks at him with distrust. Why should he do so? Doctors work for money. Freud replies that Anna's case is very interesting. Especially since she is remarkably intelligent. He almost thrusts the mother back, and enters a rather dingy room that doubles as dining-room and drawing-room. They talk for a moment, and he ventures to remind the mother of the terrible night when Anna, alone at her father's bedside … She interrupts him: 'The night of his death? But I was there!' Freud is thunderstruck. They are both dumbfounded. Freud asks whether she'd been at odds with her husband; the mother swears she hadn't. She has loved only one man in her life, that was her husband, Anna's father — he died in her arms. The child wasn't even there: her father's death was expected from one day to the next, and for two nights Frau O. had sent her daughter to sleep at a neighbour's. Frau O. seems sincerely indignant: 'How could you believe what a mad girl told you? My poor daughter's mad. Stark, staring mad!' Freud declares that he'd precisely never believed it: it was Breuer who'd believed it. In her indignation, Frau O. opens the door of the neighbouring room. Anna is in her bed, curled up and haggard. Her arms move freely, but she now has one leg paralysed. Frau O. asks her if she recognizes Freud. Anna gives a sign of assent. Her mother asks her: 'On the night your father died, where were you?' The patient replies docilely: 'At Frau Rosengarten's.' 'How about me?' 'You were at home, with Papa.' She gives these replies with total innocence. Frau O. says to her: 'What have you been telling these good Doctors?' Anna answers, without seeming to attach much importance to what she is saying: 'Oh, it was a dream.' Frau O. accuses her of not sparing her mother in her dreams. She speaks coldly and harshly. They are on the brink of quarrelling. Freud soothes them. Obviously there is no love lost between the two women. Anna O. looks at her mother with a kind of cold hatred. Freud asks to speak privately with Anna. Her mother answers: 'Do what you can with her!' and goes off slamming the door. Freud alone with Anna. She looks at him mistrustfully: 'You were with the other one, who did me nothing but harm!' He speaks gently to her, promises not to hypnotize her. But he does not look benevolent. We see a strange curiosity burning in his eyes. He sits on a chair, pulled back slightly so that Anna can no longer see him. She moans: 'What are you going to do with me this time? What are you going to ask me?' He replies very gently: 'Just talk. Say whatever comes into your mind. Even the most preposterous ideas. Everything interests me. I ask of you only one thing, which is to tell me sincerely whatever you think.' 'About what?' 'Well, about anything. For example, about your father's death.' She lets herself sink back on the bed, closes her eyes and moans softly; we see that she is getting ready to speak. Freud, behind her, prepares to listen to her; in his eyes he still has that gleam of satanic curiosity.

The voice off: 'The Father! Always the Father! I felt acutely anxious; I don't know why. But I wanted to get to the bottom of it and I knew I'd go on to the very end this time.'

<h1 style="text-align:center">XXIV</h1>

Freud in his apartment. His daughter Mathilde (now nine) is playing with him. He seems to adore her. He is very gentle with her. Martha is watching the scene. Mathilde throws her arms round Freud's neck and starts kissing him. Suddenly he thrusts her away from him. The gesture has been so brutal that the child looks at him in astonishment and begins to cry. Martha seems astounded. 'I've never seen you like that with the children. What's the matter?' 'Nothing's the matter. I'm in a hurry, that's all.' He has a strange expression: a kind of fear. He leaves the room hurriedly.

We find him back at Anna O.'s. The treatment has been going on for a fortnight. He visits her daily. The mother looks at him with distrust and animosity, but she leaves him alone with her daughter. This time, he presses her with questions. He is not the patient, silent analyst listening to the sufferer; on the contrary, he intervenes, he pushes her in a quite specific direction. He is trying to make her say that her father's fall on the day of his death was invented by her as a symbol of another kind of downfall. She tries to resist, but feebly. 'What downfall?', Freud asks. Anna does not know: financial, perhaps? Her father was ruined by the bankruptcy of one of his wife's brothers. 'It's silly!' 'What?' 'Nothing.' 'Tell me. Nothing's silly, everything can be useful to me.' 'I thought I'd fallen when I was little.' 'At what age?' 'When I was ten.' We see the little girl running into a drawing-room, which has a French window leading to a garden. She has hurt herself. She cries out. The father is alone in the room. He stands up, takes her in his arms. 'I always hated that room, after that.' 'Describe it.' She describes it: we see it, as she does so. There is a piece of furniture beside the clock. A piece of furniture that she does not remember. As she utters these words, we see a day-bed in a corner. Freud asks her if it wasn't a day-bed. She says abruptly that it was indeed, that her father used to lie on that bed when taking his siesta. Freud asks her whether her father didn't carry her over to the day-bed, when she fell down. She says he did, and starts to cry. Freud explains to her what a screen memory is. 'There's something there, behind it. What?' She stops crying: she seems frightened. Freud too; their two faces disappear. We see the shopkeeper between the two jars of candy. But this time he has neither Breuer's face nor that of Jakob Freud: he has the face of Sigmund Freud himself.

XXV

In Freud's consulting-room. They are just finishing installing the telephone. He finds it amusing. The whole family is there, as the post-office workmen complete the installation (one of them has unhooked the earpiece and is calling up the operator by telephone, to check that the instrument is working properly). Suddenly there is a ring at the door. The maid announces Herr Breuer. He comes in. He has aged and looks embarrassed. He asks the children very nicely to let him talk to Freud in private. The children go off. Breuer begins by explaining to Freud that he does not want to accept the sum Freud has sent him in partial repayment of his debts. He is not unaware that Freud is still hard up; he does not wish either to consider them as having quarrelled, or to increase the relative poverty in which Martha and Freud's children are living. Freud will have plenty of time to repay him later. Freud becomes angry: he's comfortably off, he has just had the telephone installed, etc. Breuer does not allow himself to be convinced and deposits an envelope on the desk. Freud, still intimidated by Breuer, ends up leaving the envelope on the desk.

Breuer has in any case not come on account of 'this trifle', but on account of two matters of greater importance. In the first place, Anna's mother has been to see him yesterday, to question him about this Freud who is putting such strange ideas into her daughter's head. Naturally, Breuer has vouched for his colleague's competence and serious intentions. But he has not been able to avoid feeling that Freud has shown himself 'professionally incorrect' in concerning himself with a patient treated by Breuer. Freud answers tartly that Breuer has long since abandoned her. In any case — and in his eyes this justifies everything — she is making a rapid recovery. In the past two days she has recovered the use of her paralysed leg. Breuer seems deeply agitated: jealous and worried. He asks Freud if he has taken advantage of the poor patient to verify his new theories. Freud replies that his theories have verified themselves. And Breuer asks, in a toneless voice: 'And it was? . . .' 'The father, of course.'

Breuer has not come just about this. He has come to entreat Freud not to deliver his lecture on 'The Aetiology of the Neuroses'. For Freud, since the success of Anna's treatment, has come to consider that he has proof of his theory: neurosis derives from a sexual traumatism whose memory is repressed; this traumatism is the seduction of the patient, when he was a child, by an adult member of his family, usually the father.

Breuer finds the theory insufficiently grounded. Since the cases of neurosis are so numerous, there would have to be an unbelievable number of adult 'seducers'. No father could be above suspicion. 'Even our own fathers . . .' How lightly Freud accepts this accusation, which makes even his own father suspect. Freud replies that he has thirteen cases. Breuer answers that it's not enough. He reminds Freud of the cocaine business. Freud replies that he is not really a small-time doctor or experimenter: 'I'm an adventurer.' Points raised by Breuer: gossip — and, above all, the mud which Freud is busy stirring up can only harm people. Freud replies: he doesn't care a fig for gossip. As for the mud, he doesn't stir it up just for other people, but in his own case too. He's afraid, he repulses the caresses of his own children, he even suspects his own father. But so much the worse: he *wants to know* the truth and he will know it. Breuer entreats him in any case, in the name of their joint work, not to deliver his lecture. Freud answers him: 'So that's it! you're afraid.' With excessive harshness he reproaches him for his lack of moral courage. Breuer reproaches him for his lightmindedness. This time, the breach has come: Freud accuses Breuer of abandoning him at the very moment when he needs his help, when he's on his way to discovering a new psychology. 'I shall go on alone', he adds. Breuer shows his jealousy by replying: 'Alone? Not at all. You work when you're influenced. You're coming under the influence of Fliess: that's all!' And he goes out, slamming the door. Freud is left alone: he throws the envelope on the floor and stamps on it.

That evening, lying in bed next to Martha: 'I can't even free myself from my debts! I'm condemned to remain under Breuer's domination, crushing me. I'll defy them all: I'll give that lecture, I know that I'll shock them: so much the better. If need be, we'll pack our bags and go abroad.'

A dream: Fliess comes unexpectedly to Vienna. He meets Breuer — and Freud sits down with them at a little table. Fliess is speaking of his sister: 'She died in three quarters of an hour.' Since Breuer does not understand him, Fliess turns towards Freud: 'What did you tell Breuer about me?' At this moment, Meynert appears and says: 'He told everything. Everything! Everything!' Freud replies: 'Non vixit', signifying that he could not have said anything to Breuer since Breuer is dead. Then he looks piercingly at Meynert: the latter grows pale and evanescent, his eyes become a sickly blue — finally he dissolves. Freud exults. He turns towards Fliess and Breuer, but they too have disappeared. Freud declares: 'They can be summoned up at will.'

Wakes with a start. We see Freud get up and dress gropingly, then we find him back at his desk, writing.

Freud's voice off tells us what he is writing as he goes along.

'A dream is the fulfilment of a wish. It seeks to produce an agreeable event or to free us from disagreeable events. It functions exactly like a neurosis. Properly speaking, it is an abbreviated neurosis. By this dream I took advantage of the death of Meynert, who was my protector and my enemy, to imagine that Breuer and even Fliess, my protectors, were dead too and I was finally free — and alone.'

XXVI

The lecture on the 'Aetiology of the Neuroses'. On his way there, Freud passes in front of a medical bookshop. A poster stuck up in the window announces Freud's lecture. Prominently displayed among recently published works, we perceive *Studies of Hysteria*, by Drs Breuer and Freud. Freud proceeds on his way.

The meeting-hall of the Medical Association. It has not changed since 1886. Same audience: doctors. The seats of Meynert and Breuer are empty. Freud comes to the end of his paper. He concludes by a brief summing up, which reminds us that, in his view, neuroses spring from a sexual traumatism in infancy, most often seduction by the father. He compares dream and neurosis, giving a short outline of the full analytical method (free association, especially in relation to dreams). At the moment when he spoke of the seduction of children by adults, there was a real mutter of indignation in the hall. When he spoke of dreams, some of those present began to laugh very loudly. When he stops speaking, silence and a few whistles. Camera on Freud, very pale but resolute and almost satisfied. He leaves the platform while his listeners, rising to leave, confide their shocked indignation to one another: 'It's shameful … Scientific fairy-story. And what fairies! Vague, dirty psychiatry, old maid's fancies', etc., etc.

XXVII

Freud's consulting-room. It is eleven in the evening, he is writing to Fliess. He has begun to smoke again. The voice off reads out the letter as he writes it: 'My Dear Wilhelm, etc., etc.' He begins by expressing his surprise that Fliess is now allowing him to smoke: 'It is the first time that you have contradicted yourself.' Is it because his case is desperate, as when one allows everything to a patient one knows is doomed? Does Fliess think that Freud's heart is really unsound? He'd be able to stand a diagnosis of myocarditis. Death holds no fears for him; he's weary. Let Fliess tell him the truth: Freud will take advantage of it to organize his last years as well as possible.

The telephone rings. Freud lifts the receiver. Someone insults him: he is, says his interlocutor, 'an ass and a swine'. Freud hangs up with a laugh and resumes his letter. His best friends have begun to turn their backs on him since his lecture. The scandal is spreading throughout the city, people ring him up at night to insult him; the minister of public education, to whom the University had proposed the year before that he should award Freud the title of Professor, has announced that he is refusing. He is citing Freud's theories as a pretext — but in fact everyone knows he's an anti-Semite. Freud is withstanding the storm. What affects him most is that his patients, once they've confessed the attacks they suffered during their childhood, don't come back. Numerous treatments have been interrupted. New patients are few and far between.

The voice off is interrupted by the ringing of the telephone. This time, Freud contents himself with smiling and goes on with his letter. But the ringing becomes so insistent that he eventually picks up the receiver. It is Anna O.'s mother. For several days, she says, her daughter has been giving signs of acute over-excitement: she was claiming to be a prostitute. This very evening, she was saying she wanted to resume her former profession and earn some money by prostituting herself. About a quarter of an hour ago, the mother has been woken up with a jump by the sound of footsteps and the front door being softly closed. She has got up and found that her daughter is no longer in her room. Anna has dressed herself in black, and left a note on her bed: 'Don't be afraid. I'm going to earn a lot of money.' Freud asks Frau O. if she has the faintest idea where her daughter may have gone. Frau O. thinks it may be somewhere on the *Ring* (the busiest avenue in Vienna: numerous cafés, theatres, etc.), since Anna had said two days previously: 'If I go back to prostituting myself, I'll always find customers on the *Ring*.'

Freud makes haste to replace his stiff collar and tie, which he has taken off in order to be more comfortable; he rushes out to some stables which rent him out an old barouche for making house-calls on his patients. He then has to rouse the coachman who usually drives him, by hammering on the door with his fist. The driver dresses hurriedly. Freud gives him the order to set off at a smart trot and drive round the *Ring*. Amazement on the part of the driver when Freud orders him to stop outside a café on the *Ring* — the first he comes across — and especially when the doctor climbs down from the cab and goes over to peer into the faces of the prostitutes waiting for customers. In fact, Freud starts systematically going into all the cafés on the *Ring*. In one of them, he eventually finds Anna. It is indeed a café full of prostitutes. Anna, in black, with neither powder nor lipstick, very pale, is making such blatant advances to the customers that the other women are beginning to take offence: Where does she come from, this girl? She has no business here, etc. But she looks so tragic that the men are alarmed by her advances: they move away from her. She is alone at her table, bestowing winks on the customers, but in vain: a space has opened up around her.

Freud approaches. She ogles him, without recognizing him; he sits down at her table as if he were a customer. He says to her in an undertone: 'Come with me.' 'Where to?' 'To your mother's.' She now recognizes him, but she resists: 'You know very well I'm a whore. It's my mother who has sent me to walk the streets.' He eventually persuades her to get into the cab with him: he'll be her customer, they'll go to a hotel. Astonishment on the part of the driver: Freud is bringing back a prostitute, whom he's clasping round the waist and whom he forces to get into the cab. 'Where are we going?' 'I don't know', says Freud. 'Go wherever you like.' Freud, in the carriage, tries to persuade Anna to return home. She refuses: Freud knows quite well she's a prostitute. He eventually makes her admit that she wants to prostitute herself in order to punish herself for having slandered her father; the latter never laid a finger on her, he was the noblest of men, etc. Freud, in order to get her to go back to her mother's, tells her that she never *intended* to utter the slander in question, and that it is he himself who compelled her to do so by his questions. She calms down somewhat, but only agrees to go home after he has told her that he was acting in that way because of certain hypotheses in which he no longer believes.

Freud goes home in the barouche. His gaze is intent, his eyes hard. The driver vainly seeks to engage him in conversation. Suddenly, Freud exclaims: 'I wasn't mistaken. I *can't* have been mistaken.'

In Freud's apartment — which he enters cautiously and on tiptoe — he finds all the rooms lit. His wife is up and fully dressed: she informs him that Jakob Freud has just died.

XXVIII*

We see once again the dream from the beginning (the shop and the inscriptions: 'You are requested to close the eyes').

Freud's voice off:

'Was it really just the remorse of those who survive? Did I feel some other kind of remorse? Was I really guilty vis-à-vis my father?'

Camera on Freud in his old age talking to the 'Seven': 'That was the morning when I began my self-analysis.'

Free associations on the basis of the dream.

We see fragments of the dream again.

The barber's shop reappears as it was in the dream.

It recalls Jakob Freud's shop in Freiberg. Freud's voice off: 'My father's shop in Freiberg. I was less than three years old.'

The parents' bedroom, the marriage-bed (seen from below by a child of three). His father, Jakob Freud, leaping out of bed in his nightshirt. He shouts: 'Get out of here!' We do not see the child, we just see, from outside, the door closing again and hear a key turning.

The door of the barber's shop closes behind Freud. We see him (aged forty) coming out of the shop. He arrives at the station.

Voice off: 'I was leaving on a journey.' A train: we hear a child of three crying in a compartment. Blast-furnaces outside. Smoke, reddish fires.

'They drove us out because we were Jews.' He sees once again the tub full of water, the naked children, the dingy kitchen: 'It's the Vienna apartment. Poverty awaited us

---

*Words added in Sartre's hand at the top of this page: 'Fliess is there for the funeral.' [Editor's note.]

there.' His feelings for his father are linked to that journey.

Camera on Freud writing to Wilhelm, at his work-table. 'My dear Wilhelm. I no longer know whether I'm coming or going. Is everything lost? Anna O. was lying. Her father didn't touch her. And yet, she seemed so sincere. Is it I who made her lie? Why? Was my father guilty? Or is it I who believe fathers to be guilty, because I hated my own father?' He rises to his feet, he paces up and down his office. The voice off: 'Thirteen cases! Do all patients lie? ... Is it necessary to begin *everything* over again?'

He returns to his desk, he continues writing: 'What if my father had taken advantage of my sisters? If that was the reason why I harboured a grudge against him. To close your eyes also means: deliberately fail to notice. *It is best to close your eyes*, that means: the respect due to the dead obliges me to close my eyes to any misdeeds my father may have committed.' In that case, his hypothesis would be true. He drops his pen, his heart is beating too hard, he is in pain. Does he too have an anxiety-neurosis, then?*

XXIX

The next day. He goes to Anna's. The street. He sees fathers with their children. He has eyes only for them. He contemplates them with a kind of horror. A little girl runs towards her father, who takes her in his arms. Freud is fascinated by this spectacle. He turns abruptly away, while we hear his voice off saying: 'What's true?'

Camera on Anna O. lying in bed. She is waiting for him. He tries to tell her he is giving up treating her: he thought he had found the cause of her trouble, but everything has been thrown into question. He tries to bid her farewell. She asks him to stay a little while longer. She has had a dream which has frightened her, she doesn't want to be left without help. He asks her what the dream is. She speaks of her dream. Free associations. This dream obviously betrays a flagrant hostility towards her mother. Freud says nothing to her, but his face brightens.

XXX

Freud, at his desk, continuing the letter to Fliess. Anna O. has this very day recounted a dream to him which betrayed her hostility towards her mother. Why? Did her mother really behave badly? Or is some very longstanding hostility involved? He tells Fliess that he is dead tired, and that his father's death has shattered him: it's the most important event in a man's life. Yet he's carrying on with his self-analysis — but is making no pro-

---

*Handwritten words added: 'Fliess's inadequacy.' [Editor's note.]

gress. He is so weary that we see he is struggling against sleep: several times his eyelids grow heavy. Shot of the door opening softly: little Mathilde (about ten) appears. She has a strange expression. Suddenly Freud is near her. He looks at her with terrifying eyes and starts laughing (but noiselessly) like the candy store man. The little girl looks simultaneously terrified and fascinated. Freud stretches out his arms. At this instant, a huge burst of laughter rings out. Freud and the child disappear, the door is closed. We perceive that it is Freud himself who is laughing in his armchair, at his desk: it was a dream. He reflects for a moment, then writes: 'Wilhelm, I have just been dreaming. I *need* adults, and especially fathers, to commit sexual attacks upon children. I need it to the point where I saw myself attempting to commit one upon my own daughter. I must entertain strange feelings against my father ... And, precisely, Anna O. a little while ago had such hostility towards her own mother ... I still don't understand anything about all this, but the veil is about to be rent asunder. I am sure I shall know both others and myself. Tell it not in the land of the Philistines, but rather than a defeat I sense a victory.'

XXXI

At Anna's. A dream. And associations in connection with it. She was six or seven. She remembers having bathed in a lake with her father. She sees her father again. Freud asks where her mother was? She was bathing too; she used to swim well, she had gone far away from the bank. Suddenly Anna sobs: 'I wished she'd drown.' She begins to recount the whole of her true history: her love for her father, her jealousy of her mother. She *discovers* these feelings that she was rejecting. The fall of her dying father meant for her that her mother (pretty and flirtatious when Anna was a child) was dragging her father down to ruin. But even that was not true; Anna imagined it out of resentment. And her hands had become clenched, her arms had become paralysed in a position that realized her wish to be the only one to prevent her father from falling into a decline. As for the fantasy of her seduction by her father, if she accepted it so easily that's because it corresponded to daydreams of her childhood and even her adolescence.

She seems shattered. But Freud is equally so. He explains to her that she's not a monster. 'There's nobody like me', she says. 'Yes, there is', he says. 'Everybody.' 'You?' 'Yes. Me.' We once again see the journey from Freiberg to Vienna. The tears, the blast-furnaces. The Freud family had stopped at a hotel, while changing trains. The child, lying on a makeshift bed, sees his mother washing herself (her shoulders bare). Freud explains to Anna what he has all of a sudden discovered: if he has always felt guilty, that is because he has desired his mother and because — though loving and respecting his father — he has always reproached him with being too old, with not having been able to help him in his career as a doctor, with having left him destitute. And these reproaches hid his jealousy and his secret wish to see him die.

Anna looks at him, half reassured. He explains to her that she must not be afraid: what is going on in the unconscious must overcome all repressions and appear in the light of day. Then it will be possible to judge in accordance with true morality and all phantoms will dissolve.

He summons her mother — who has likewise had many faults and who was jealous of her daughter. The two women do not dare say anything, but Anna timidly takes her mother's forearm just above the wrist and squeezes it. Her mother relaxes somewhat. They end by smiling at one another. Freud leaves.

XXXII

Freud with Fliess, by the edge of a lake, near Achensee. Freud is briefly setting out the progress he has made: analytic method, interpretation of dreams, and above all Oedipus complex. Fliess is stubborn. He barely listens — in any case, shows scant interest. He is entirely preoccupied by his problem of periods, in which it seems Freud no longer really believes. And he levels the same reproach at him as Meynert used to do in former times: Freud should beware of abandoning the sure ground of physiology for psychological speculations. Truth lies in numbers, in the periods of human life. Freud remains evasive and Fliess ends by confronting him with an ultimatum: is he, yes or no, determined to carry on his research within the framework of the periods established by Fliess? Freud replies evasively: psychological treatments have merely a provisional character; remedies of a physiological nature will be found one day, when more progress has been made in our knowledge of the chemistry of cells. For the time being, it is necessary to eschew a physiological language that is inadequately grounded: it is necessary to act on the psyche and to utilize a psychological language. Fliess grows angry: does Freud no longer believe in periods, then? Freud does not answer directly: he explains the results of his self-analysis. Dissatisfied with his father, who was unable to repair his fortunes in Vienna, he transferred his filial affection first to Meynert, then to Breuer. Ambivalence of his feelings. After his quarrel with Breuer, he still needed a paternal figure: although Fliess was younger than he was, he unconsciously gave him that role. Without him, he'd never have undertaken his self-analysis; Fliess has given him the courage to go down to the 'hidden depths'. Now, he still loves Fliess but in a different way. Freud is finally free, absolutely free; he no longer needs a guardian, he'll work alone. At the age of forty-two, he's beginning to live. In fact, he has altered profoundly: his eyes are still hard, piercing and rather suspicious, but he holds himself more upright and seems much calmer.

Fliess is deeply wounded. He accuses Freud of attributing his own feelings to his patients. Freud smiles without answering. Meanwhile Fliess quickens his pace. Freud: 'Why are you rushing?' Fliess replies ironically: 'Because of your train. You'll have an anxiety-attack if you don't get there in advance.' But Freud, moderating their speed, replies that he has plenty of time. He is cured of his phobia about trains. He even stops to explain. In his self-analysis, he has understood: the first train he ever took, the one that passed in front of the blast-furnaces, was the train of exile and rupture; it was taking the little child Sigmund from Freiberg, where he was living in easy circumstances, to

Vienna, where poverty awaited him. Subsequently trains signified death and misfortune, but this simply meant: passage from prosperity to poverty. His fear of death later became transformed into a fear of missing trains. While he is speaking, a whistle: in the distance we see the train arriving. Fliess says: 'Let's run! You're going to miss it.' But Freud replies: 'Too bad, I'll take the next one.'

At the station: night is falling. It is Fliess who is taking the train. The one that will take him to Berchtesgaden, and from there to Munich and Berlin. The Vienna train will go through twenty-five minutes later. Fliess takes his leave, quite coldly. He climbs in, the train starts to move, Freud waits for him to appear at the corridor window, but the train disappears without Fliess having shown himself. Freud walks along the platform, with a certain melancholy but without real sadness. Freud's voice off: 'I knew very well it was finished: I was alone.'

At this instant, a young doctor approaches. Freud knows him by sight: he attends Freud's lectures, he has read the *Studies on Hysteria* and all his articles, he admires Freud intensely and sees him as his master; the young disciple glimpses the direction which the Master's work is going to take, and the extraordinary benefit that knowledge of mankind will be able to derive from it. The train for Vienna arrives in the station. Can the disciple get in with his Master: he has so many questions to ask? Freud accepts, without any enthusiasm, very courteously but with an ironical curl to his lips. And, as the young man steps aside to let him climb into a compartment, Freud's voice off adds:

'I was forty-one. It was my turn to play the role of father.'

APPENDIX B

COMPARATIVE TABLE OF THE
TWO VERSIONS

For Version I, the page numbers are those of the present book.
For Version II, the page numbers are those of the manuscript.
Scenes marked with an asterisk are included in the Extracts translated above.

I = Version I   II = Version II

PART ONE

Version I

[1] pp. 5-8. At the Vienna hospital, stretcher-bearers, a paralytic woman; Freud appears at the end.

[2] pp. 9-16. Meynert visits his patients, with some students and assistants, among them Freud. Examination of two hysterical patients.

[3] pp. 17-22. Conversation Freud-Meynert on hypnosis. Award of a scholarship.

[4] pp. 23-33. Freud and his fiancée Martha at the Vienna hospital. Freud is burning some folders of notes. The scene shifts to the hospital courtyard, to the street (anti-Semitic street-vendor), to the front of a skating-rink on the *Ring*.

[5] pp. 34-38. Freud at his parents' home, with Martha. Should he leave for Paris or stay in Vienna? (Missing in II.)

[6] pp. 39-41. Quarrel with Martha. (Missing in II.)

[7] p. 42. Martha rings the Breuers' doorbell. (Missing in II.)

[8] p. 43. A dream of Freud's about Franz-Josef and Hannibal. (Missing in II.)

[9] pp. 44-49. Departure for Paris. Freud, Martha, then Breuer on the platform of Vienna railway-station.

[10] pp. 50-53. Before Charcot's lecture at the Salpêtrière, the student Wilkie, Freud-Charcot meeting.

[11] pp. 54-65. Charcot's lecture, examination of some hysterical patients, hypnotism. Wilkie hypnotized.

[12] pp. 66-68. After the lecture, at the Salpêtrière, Freud with Wilkie, then with Charcot. Freud's interest in the latter's experiments.

[13] pp. 69-73. Freud and Martha as newly-weds, in their apartment, they are poor.

[14] pp. 74-75. Freud goes with Breuer to the Medical Association. (Missing in II.)

[15] pp. 76–79. Freud's paper before the Medical Association. Scandal, Meynert's intervention.

[16] pp. 80–82. After the meeting, Freud in the street with Breuer; he is thrown into despair by his failure.

[17] pp. 83–88. Break with Meynert.

[18] pp. 89–90. Freud at the home of old General von Schroeh.

[19] pp. 91–101. Freud with Karl, the old general's son.

[20] p. 102. Freud with the general. His diagnosis.

[21] pp. 103–105. That night, with Martha: Freud, discouraged, quits; he will be a local doctor.

Version II

[1] pp. 1–14. Same scene as [1] I, more developed. Identical text at the beginning.

[2] pp. 15–31. Same scene as [2] I, partly identical text.

[3] pp. 31–47. Same situation, same subject as [3] I, but the scene is more developed.

[4] pp. 47–59. Same scene as [4] I, but different text.

[5] pp. 60–63. Freud at Breuer's with Mathilde and Martha. (Missing in I.)

[6] pp. 64–74. Freud with Breuer in his barouche. They are going to visit Breuer's patients. (Missing in I.)

[7] pp. 74–78. Freud, Breuer and Frau Körtner at the latter's home. (Missing in I.)

[8] pp. 79–91. Freud alone with Frau Körtner, then the latter's daughter Cäcilie. Mutual provocation. (Missing in I.)

[9]* pp. 92–103. Freud, Breuer, Frau Körtner, then Freud with Breuer alone in the latter's barouche. They discuss Cäcilie's illness. Anti-Semitism. (Missing in I.)

[10] pp. 104–117. Freud and Martha at the Vienna hospital. Freud packs his bags. (Missing in I.)

[11] pp. 118–125. Freud, at the hospital, has two dreams which he records, then burns some private writings. (This last episode can be found in [4] I, the rest is missing in I.)

[12] pp. 126–145. Departure for Paris, on the platform of Vienna railway-station. Freud, Martha (without Breuer), then Freud's father, mother and sister. (Same situation as in [9] I, but the scene is much longer.)

[13] pp. 146–148. Before Charcot's lecture at the Salpêtrière, Wilkie. (Corresponds to [10] I, but different text.)

[14] pp. 148–155. Charcot's lecture (beginning): examination of some hysterical patients, hypnotism. (Corresponds to [11] I.)

[15] pp. 156–160. After Charcot's lecture, in the street. Meeting with prostitutes, Wilkie. (Corresponds partly to [12] I.)

[16] pp. 161–172. Freud with Wilkie, on the belfry of Notre-Dame de Paris. Minor parts. (Missing in I.)

[17] pp. 173–189. Charcot's lecture (end), Wilkie hypnotized. (Repeats certain elements of [11] I.)

[18] pp. 190–195. Breuer comes to welcome Freud back at the Vienna railway-station.

He goes home; plans. (Missing in I.)

[19] p. 196. Freud's marriage to Martha. (Missing in I.)

[20] pp. 197–206. Freud's paper before the Medical Association. Scandal, Meynert. (Same situation as in [15] I.)

[21] pp. 207–210. After the meeting, Freud in the street with Breuer; he is thrown into despair by his failure. (Same situation as [16] I.)

[22] pp. 211–212. Freud is excluded from his laboratory. (Missing in I.)

[23] pp. 213–218. Break with Meynert. (Same situation as in [17] I.)

[24]* pp. 219–226. Freud in his family circle with Breuer, he is worried about his future. Transfer of paternity: Jakob gives him Breuer as a father. (Missing in I.)

[25] pp. 227–229. Freud, Breuer and Martha in a Vienna café. 'We're explorers', Breuer declares. (Missing in I.)

[26] pp. 230–236. Freud and Breuer at the Körtners'; the mother and her daughter Cäcilie. (Missing in I.)

[27] pp. 237–241. Freud and Breuer discuss the case of Cäcilie. (Missing in I.)

[28] pp. 241–244. Freud at the home of old General Peter Schwartz. (Corresponds to [18] I.)

[29]* pp. 245–258. Freud with Karl, the old general's son. (Corresponds to [19] I, but the scene is treated very differently.)

[30]* pp. 259–267. A nightmare of Freud's: a mountaineer, he is part of a roped party. (Missing in I.)

[31] pp. 263–264. Freud with the general, his diagnosis. (Corresponds to [20] I.)

[32] pp. 265–270. Freud discusses with Breuer, he is alarmed by what the method of hypnotism reveals to him (ideas of parricide). (Missing in I.)

[33] pp. 271–276. That night, with Martha; Freud, discouraged, quits. (Corresponds to [21] I.)

PART TWO

From Part Two onwards, the differences between the two versions are so considerable that it is no longer possible to make a comparison sequence by sequence. We shall therefore confine ourselves to recording the succession of scenes, first in Version I, then in Version II.

Version I

[1] pp. 109–112. 1892. Freud in his consulting-room with Dora. He is giving her massage and electrotherapy. He learns from her that Breuer is still practising hypnotism.

[2] pp. 113–119. Arrival of Martha. Dora leaves. The Freud couple get ready for a visit to the Breuers; their child Mathilde is six. Freud is in a bad temper.

[3] pp. 120–123. The Freuds visit the Breuers. Fliess, still unknown to Freud, asks the latter the way. Breuer is out. Arrival of the Freuds and of Fliess.

[4] pp. 124–125. Breuer is delayed visiting a young patient, Cäcilie Körtner.

[5] pp. 126–132. Continuation of [3]. At the Breuers': Breuer's wife Mathilde, Martha, Freud, Fliess. Breuer keeps them waiting. Fliess wants to attend the lectures Freud is giving in Vienna; he too believes in the influence of sexuality on the neuroses. Arrival of Breuer. Discussion on the value of hypnotism. A footman comes to summon Freud.

[6] pp. 133–137. Freud at Meynert's deathbed. The latter confesses his neurosis.

[7] pp. 138–141. Continuation of [5]. The same characters, at first with the exception of Freud. Then Freud returns, and expresses the wish to examine Cäcilie too. Mathilde is jealous of this patient of her husband's; at the end of the dinner she wounds herself with a knife.

[8] pp. 142–143. Freud, Breuer and Fliess, in a barouche, go to visit Cäcilie Körtner.

[9] pp. 144–151. At the Körtners' house. Fliess waits. Breuer and Freud question the young Cäcilie, who has just lost her father and has been traumatized by this loss. Breuer hypnotizes her. 'Mental chimney-sweeping'.

[10] pp. 152–155. Flashback. Cäcilie recalls the circumstances of her father's death, but misrepresents them.

[11] pp. 156–165. Freud, Breuer, Cäcilie, continuation of the treatment. Freud in turn questions her. Second flashback. Confession of the truth: Cäcilie's father died in a brothel. The young girl's fury.

[12] pp. 166–169. Freud, Breuer, Fliess, in a barouche, speak about the neuroses and Cäcilie's case.

[13] pp. 170–173. Freud and Fliess, in a barouche. Plans for collaboration. Freud goes to deliver his lecture.

[14] pp. 174–177. Some time later. Freud with Dora in his consulting-room. He proposes to hypnotize her.

[15] p 178. At the same time: Freud's apartment, Fliess is expected. Freud is absent.

[16] pp. 179-181. Continuation of [14]. Freud, in his consulting-room, treats Dora. She remembers, under hypnosis, attempts at sexual seduction of which she was the object as a child.

[17] pp. 182-184. In Freud's drawing-room, with Freud, Martha and Fliess. They are drinking. Discussion about Breuer, who still rejects the hypothesis of the sexual origin of neuroses.

[18] pp. 185-188. Same place, after Fliess's departure. Martha does not like Fliess, does not like hypnotism. Freud's father is unwell.

[19] pp. 189-191. Night of the same day. Freud is writing in his study. Dream in which Breuer and Fliess appear as 'fathers'. The next day, Freud goes out in order to visit Breuer.

[20] pp. 192-197. Same day. Breuer and his wife Mathilde are taking breakfast. Arrival of Freud. Mathilde makes a scene because of Cäcilie. The couple decide to take a trip to Venice.

[21] pp. 198-202. Freud and Breuer at Cäcilie's. She is told of Breuer's imminent departure. Prelude to her nervous pregnancy.

[22] pp. 203-206. A few days later. The Freuds and the Breuers in the street. Preparations for departure. Breuer has forgotten the railway tickets. An ambulance arrives to fetch Breuer.

[23] pp. 207-209. Freud and Breuer visit Cäcilie and her mother. Cäcilie's phantom confinement.

[24] pp. 210-213. Freud and Breuer a little while later, in the street. Breuer is shattered by what he has just seen. He condemns his hypnotic method. He will go away, but will not leave his patients in Freud's care, since he still not like the latter's theories.

The scenes which complete Part Two in Version I are missing in Version II.

[25] pp. 214-217. Freud with Fliess. Freud goes to deliver a lecture at the Faculty of Medicine; Fliess is a member of his audience. Fliess wants Freud to carry on with Cäcilie's treatment, for the sake of his own research and for the sake of Science.

[26] pp. 218-219. Freud and Fliess go to the Körtners' house. Mother and daughter have moved away.

[27] pp. 220-224. Freud in his consulting-room with Dora, who talks under hypnosis and flings her arms round his neck. Meanwhile Martha at the bedside of little Mathilde, suffering from laryngitis. Arrival of Fliess, who treats the child.

[28] pp. 225-231. Still in the child's room. Freud with Martha. Mathilde is saved. Martha does not like her husband's methods, or hypnotism. Freud speaks about transference.

[29] pp. 232-235. A fortnight later, Freud and Fliess on the *Ring*. Fliess is returning to Berlin. From now on Freud will be alone. The pact, the exchange of rings. We learn that Breuer is going back to neurology, giving up psychiatry.

Version II

[1] pp. 277-281. 1888, in Freud's consulting-room. He is with Dora and giving her massage.

[2] pp. 280-290. Arrival of Martha. The Freud couple is getting ready to visit Jakob. Freud's bad mood. Meynert summons him to his bedside. Martha goes alone to see her in-laws. Freud tries to write; eventually he answers his former master's summons.

[3] pp. 291-296. Freud at Meynert's bedside. (Corresponds to [6] I.)

[4] pp. . The same evening, Freud visits the home of Karl; he learns that the young man has died of pneumonia.

[5] pp. 296-299. Freud returns home.

[6] pp. 301-307. A few days later; Freud is treating Dora. She suffers from flatulence, which Freud interprets as an unsatisfied wish for motherhood.

[7] pp. 308-309. Freud cables to Breuer that he is presenting a new theory.

[8]* pp. 310-313. Freud with Dora. She speaks of her husband, who suffers from premature ejaculation.

[9] pp. 314-315. Same evening at the Breuer's house. Mathilde, Martha, Freud. They wait for Breuer; his wife shows herself to be jealous of one of his patients, Cäcilie Körtner.

[10] pp. 316-317. Breuer at Cäcilie's; he hypnotizes her.

[11] pp. 318-330. Continuation of [9]. Arrival of Breuer. Freud speaks of sexuality at the table, shocking the women. Mathilde wounds herself by mistake.

[12]* pp. 331-344. The next day, in Freud's consulting-room: he is treating a spinster of thirty, Magda, in the presence of her father, upon whom she is very dependent. Hypnotism. Freud in difficulties. The patient frees herself. Arrival of Breuer.

[13] pp. 345-367. Freud and Breuer at Cäcilie's. Return of memory under hypnosis. (Corresponds to [9], [10] and [11] of Version I.)

[14]* pp. 368-376. Breuer and Freud discuss Cäcilie's case in a cab, then in a café. Breuer still does not want to hear a word about sexuality. He is in love with Cäcilie, without knowing it.

[15] pp. 377-387. A month later. Freud in his consulting-room with a young woman, then at home with Martha and Mathilde. The latter leaves. Martha informs Freud that Mathilde is jealous and asks Freud to intervene with Breuer. Freud refuses. Breuer arrives. He is going to take a trip with his wife to Venice, and entrusts his patients to Freud.

[16] pp. 387-394. Freud and Breuer at Cäcilie's — her behaviour is strange. Breuer tells her he is going to be away for a few days. (Corresponds to [21] I.)

[17] pp. 394-406. Breuer and Freud discuss Cäcilie's case. Freud doubts whether she is cured, as Breuer asserts. She still has at least one hysterical symptom, her cough.

[18] pp. 407-414. Freud and Martha are present during the Breuers' preparations for their departure. (Corresponds to [22] I.)

[19] pp. 414-420. Breuer and Freud in Cäcilie's room; her phantom confinement. (Corresponds to [23] I.)

PART THREE

Version I

[1] pp. 239-242. Freud in his consulting-room. He is treating Magda, a spinster of thirty-five, who is accompanied by her father. The father, very critical, annoys Freud by intervening. Magda, under hypnosis, remembers having been raped. (Corresponds to [12] of Part Two, Version II.)

[2] pp. 243-245. Freud in his family circle. He is expecting a telegram, for a 'congress' with Fliess.

[3] pp. 246-247. Arrival of Breuer, who brings the introduction for the book he is writing jointly with Freud.

[4] pp. 248-253. Freud in his consulting-room with Doelnitz, whose wife he is treating. Doelnitz is outraged at no longer having the right to have sexual relations with his wife, thanks to Freud.

[5] pp. 254-257. Freud and Breuer; we learn that Magda has just attempted suicide. Breuer becomes alarmed at the results of his method, as used by Freud. The Council of the medical profession might intervene.

[6] p. 258. Freud alone at home. He receives a telegram from Fliess, gets ready to leave.

[7] pp. 259-264. Freud and Fliess at Berchtesgaden, in Tyrolean dress. Fliess asks Freud for precise details, dates.

[8] pp. 265-267. Freud explains to Fliess his theory on the sexual origin of the neuroses. Fliess again asks for dates.

[9] pp. 268-273. Fliess informs Freud of the date at which he will die. He wants Freud to resume treatment of Cäcilie, in order to obtain precise details. Freud realizes that he has a new father in the person of Fliess.

[10] pp. 274-277. Freud and Fliess on the platform of the station. Freud has an attack of phobia.

[11] pp. 278-281. In the train taking him back to Vienna, Freud dreams: he is playing cards with Meynert, Breuer and Fliess, he becomes a child again; appearance of Jakob.

[12] pp. 282-288. Freud at his parents' house, the next day. Flashbacks to childhood scenes: anti-Semitism, humiliations, Hannibal's oath.

[13] pp. 289-293. Freud visits Frau Körtner: he wishes to resume treatment of Cäcilie. Frau Körtner receives him very coldly, besides she is ruined. Freud agrees to treat Cäcilie gratis.

[14] pp. 294-298. Freud in Cäcilie's room — she is paralysed in both legs. Freud is no longer going to hypnotize her; she will say whatever she likes. Cäcilie agrees.

[15] pp. 299-304. Cäcilie's treatment, her dream: she goes out into the street dressed as a prostitute, in search of a customer. She is Potiphar's wife.

[16] pp. 305-306. The telephone installed at Freud's house. He kisses his daughter Mathilde.

[17] pp. 307-311. The next day, Freud at Cäcilie's, resumption of the treatment. Cäcilie

recounts how she had a fall when she was eight. Horror on the part of the young girl when she realizes she has been raped by her father. False memory screening the true one.

[18] p. 312. Freud cables Fliess. (Corresponds to [7] of Part Two, Version II, in which Freud cables Breuer.)

[19] pp. 313–316. They finish installing the telephone at Freud's house. Arrival of Breuer, angry at not knowing about the paper that Freud will deliver that very evening to the Medical Association. Breuer recommends prudence to Freud; the atmosphere becomes more and more heated — they quarrel. Freud reveals that Cäcilie too has been raped by her father.

[20] pp. 317–318. In Freud's apartment, Mathilde and Martha, then Freud and Breuer; breach between the two men.

[21] pp. 319–321. Freud's paper before the Medical Association. Scandal, uproar.

[22] pp. 322–324. Freud writes to Fliess to inform him of his break with Breuer, of the scandal he has just caused, of the loss of all his patients. Telephone call from Frau Körtner: Cäcilie has disappeared.

[23] pp. 325–332. Freud in search of Cäcilie on the *Ring*. He finds her in a bar with some prostitutes.

[24] pp. 333–335. Freud takes Cäcilie home. She confesses that she has slandered her father. She speaks of committing suicide.

[25] p. 336. Same night, Freud returns home. His father has just died.

[26] pp. 337–340. Freud at the barber's. He arrives late at his father's funeral. Fliess and Breuer are there too. A dream of Freud's ('You are requested to close the eyes'). (Corresponds to [5] Part Three, Version II.)

[27] pp. 341–346. Freud and Fliess, the next day. Freud questions himself about the ambivalence of his feelings towards his father. He interprets his dream in the presence of Fliess.

[28] pp. 347–356. A little while later, Freud in Cäcilie's room. He is discouraged, ill himself. Offer of a collaboration: they will proceed by the associative method.

[29] pp. 357–365. Arrival of Frau Körtner; she throws Freud out — he is beginning to know too much. Cäcilie tries to strangle her mother. Flashback to Frau Körtner as a dancer. Körtner only liked prostitutes.

[30] pp. 370–373. Freud in Cäcilie's room, continuation. He sees himself with his daughter Mathilde, questions himself about his feelings as a father, recalls a journey he made with his parents forty years earlier.

[31] pp. 374–377. In Cäcilie's room, continuation. Discovery of the Oedipus complex. Cäcilie wanted to prostitute herself so that her father would love her; she has tried to kill her mother.

[32] pp. 378–379. Freud with Fliess, by the edge of an Austrian lake, six months later. Disagreement, breach.

[33] pp. 380–383. Evening of the same day, Freud at home. Breuer has lost a brother. Freud visits his father's grave at the cemetery.

[34] pp. . Freud meets Breuer at the cemetery. Reconciliation. Liquidation of his adoptive fathers: Meynert, Breuer, Fliess, at the same time as his emancipation from

his real father. 'Now I'm the father.' Loneliness. Martha and Mathilde will be able to see each other again.

Version II

[1] pp. 421–424. Eleven months later. Freud and Martha at the Breuers' house — the latter have just had their first child.

[2] pp. 424–440. Freud brings Breuer some pages intended for their book. He discusses sexuality in them. Breuer still does not want to hear a word about it. Breuer reads the pages. Freud is feeling unwell. We learn that his father is very ill.

[3] pp. 441–444. Freud at the bedside of his father, who says he is proud of him.

[4] pp. 445–448. Freud at his father's funeral. He is taken ill. Breuer takes him home.

[5]* pp. 449–460. Nightmare of Freud's. Breuer examines him. Freud remembers his dream and tries to interpret it ('You are requested to close the eyes'). (Corresponds to [26] Part Three, Version I.)

[6] pp. 461–464. Freud and Breuer return to the scene of the funeral. Breuer entrusts Cäcilie to Freud's care.

[7] pp. 465–498. Freud at the Körtners' with Cäcilie, who receives him very coldly, does not want him as her doctor. Very long scene. Cäcilie is once again paralysed. Hypnotism, but the girl does not fall asleep and jeers at Freud. She is holding a doll that has lost its head. Freud, discouraged, wants to give up.

[8] pp. 499–514. The next day, continuation of the preceding scene. They are beginning to touch on the past of Frau Körtner, Cäcilie's mother.

[9] pp. 514–522. The Freud couple in the nursery, with little Mathilde. Freud wants Breuer to resume treatment of Cäcilie.

[10] pp. 522–536. Freud with Dora. He hypnotizes her. She flings her arms round his neck. Martha witnesses the scene. Dora leaves. (Corresponds to [27] Part Two, Version I.)

[11] pp. 537–539. Freud and Martha at home. Martha, on edge, breaks a glass.

[12] pp. 540–552. In a Vienna café. Long discussion between Freud and Breuer on the subject of transference, which Freud has just discovered.

[13] pp. 552–555. A short while later, Freud at home with Martha. Quarrel. Martha does not approve of her husband's methods — of transference — to which he is leading Dora.

[14]* pp. 555–562. Freud in his study. Dream about the card-players (who are three fathers). Then interpretation, self-analysis. Transference. (Corresponds partly to [19] of Part Two, Version I.)

[15] pp. 562–564. Dora has left. Freud will treat Cäcilie by his new method of transference.

[16]* pp. 565–585. Freud in Cäcilie's room. Return of memory through free association. Dream about the Red Tower. The girl sees herself as a prostitute.

[17] pp. 586–587. Brief encounter between Freud and Breuer; they bury their differences.

[18] pp. 588–596. Freud with Councillor Schlesinger and his daughter Magda, who has
   had a relapse (see [12]* Part Two, version II). Freud hypnotizes his patient, who
   remembers having been raped as a child. Her contractures disappear.
[19] pp. 597–601. Continuation of [16], the next day. Freud in Cäcilie's room, continuation of her return of memory.
[20] pp. 602–610. The next day, in Freud's consulting-room. Freud is discussing their
   book with Breuer.
[21] pp.610–616. Arrival of Doelnitz, husband of one of Freud's patients whom he has
   condemned to sexual continence; the husband complains. (Corresponds to [4] of Part
   Three, version I, text partly repeated.) The man, who has come as an accuser, is made
   to alter his views by Freud.
[22] pp. . Continuation of the Freud-Breuer conversation begun in [20].

The manuscript ends at this point.